# the CRISIS in the
# CHURCHES

# the CRISIS in the
# CHURCHES

## SPIRITUAL MALAISE, FISCAL WOE

## ROBERT WUTHNOW

NEW YORK   OXFORD
OXFORD UNIVERSITY PRESS
1997

Oxford University Press

Oxford   New York
Athens   Auckland   Bangkok   Bogotá   Bombay
Buenos Aires   Calcutta   Cape Town   Dar es Salaam
Delhi   Florence   Hong Kong   Istanbul   Karachi
Kuala Lumpur   Madras   Madrid   Melbourne
Mexico City   Nairobi   Paris   Singapore
Taipei   Tokyo   Toronto

and associated companies in
Berlin   Ibadan

Published by Oxford University Press, Inc.,
198 Madison Avenue, New York, New York 10016

Library of Congress Cataloging-in-Publication Data
Wuthnow, Robert.
The crisis in the churches : spiritual malaise, fiscal woe / Robert Wuthnow.
p. cm.   Includes bibliographical references and index.
ISBN 0-19-511020-X
1. Church finance—United States—History—20th century.
2. United States—History—20th century.   3. Middle class—
United States—History—20th century.   I. Title.
BV772.W87   1997   96-8901   277.3'0829—dc20

1 3 5 7 9 8 6 4 2

Printed in the United States of America
on acid-free paper

# PREFACE

Some topics are ones you'd just as soon not write about. This one was like that for me. I can recall the day I came to realize—reluctantly—that it needed to be aired. I was presenting a paper to a group of religious leaders. The topic was the changing character of churches in the United States. The first part of my talk dealt with the ways in which changing economic conditions were influencing congregations. Generally I am able to relate fairly well to audiences like this, but that morning I sensed I wasn't quite connecting. I thought maybe I was just having a bad day or that the hour was too early. But as I turned to other topics in the second part of my talk, I found the audience's interest returning. I knew the problem was the topic.

Afterward a senior member of the group, whom I have known for many years and who has served prominently among his peers, came up to me. "Did you see their body language?" he asked. I said yes. "They didn't want to hear it, did they?" I admitted they didn't. "But they *need* to," the man said. "Oh, how badly we need to hear this!"

His comment encouraged me to go ahead. Other events have also helped convince me that there are serious problems needing to be addressed. One morning a pastor knocked at my door. He was from another part of the country but wanted to know if I could spare a few minutes for him while he was in town. After some opening comments on general topics of interest, he blurted out, "The real reason I'm here is that I'm thinking of quitting the ministry." He explained the problems in his congregation—the tensions his members were experiencing, the financial burdens he was facing, and his difficulties in knowing what to say. "Is there anything I could read?" he asked. I pointed him to a few things but admitted I wished there were more.

Why is it hard to write about the crisis in America's churches? The main reason is that the crisis is financial—not just in dollars and cents but in the ways in which clergy are addressing the vital relationships between faith and such topics as stewardship, money, work, giving, and economic justice. Many of us may think the churches are already paying too much attention to these issues. But the reality is just the opposite. Clergy are reluctant to talk about finances because they know this topic makes people uncomfortable. So they tiptoe around the issues rather than addressing them directly.

It is also hard to focus our attention on the real problems facing middle-class churches because the mass media have succeeded largely in diverting our attention from these problems. If there is a crisis, journalists want us to believe that it somehow has to do with politics. This is the turf journalists know best. So they report that clergy are stepping out of line and violating the boundary between church and state. Or that clergy are saying ridiculous things about school prayer and creationism. Or that clergy are being threatened by rabid secular humanists for speaking out on abortion or pornography. Journalists love it when the churches are embroiled in controversy. And, sadly, many clergy and parishioners alike have stooped to meet the occasion, focusing all their attention on politics when their own houses are falling into disrepair.

The media are never entirely to blame. Scholars must also bear some of the responsibility for making it hard to talk about the difficulties churches are experiencing. It is odd that this should be the case. Scholarly studies of churches *began* in this country by focusing on where churches were declining, where they were growing, and how they were positioned relative to cities, farms, regions of the country, and racial and ethnic groups (one thinks of H. Paul Douglass, H. Richard Niebuhr, Liston Pope, and others). This legacy continued well into the 1960s when scholars such as Peter Berger, Charles Glock, Gerhard Lenski, and Joseph Fichter examined churches to see why they were declining and why they were failing to address important social issues. A generation later, we are suffering the backlash. Scholars have had it with talk of secularization. They earn their spurs by telling what's good about the churches. The new paradigm now suggests that church vitality is being fueled by competition. As long as the churches try to outdo each other, we need not fear for their survival.

This view may be valid for the long term, but it neglects the fact that churches interact more complexly than that with the resources in their environments. Even when they compete, they need contributions. And getting contributions requires them to meet parishioners' needs and to make hard choices about which needs to address.

To get our houses of worship back in order, many would advocate doing a better job of serving the needy. That seems like the most worthy, selfless way of proceeding. If politics is a diversion, at least we can be safe in focusing on the devastating needs of the homeless, those who are starving in our own country and around the world, and the oppressed and victimized. Seldom does a week go by in most churches when prayers are not offered on behalf of the impoverished and the downtrodden. Middle-class parishioners are challenged to be less selfish, to give more generously, and to think more compassionately about the needs of others. Arguing that the churches need to better understand the needs of the middle class, therefore, is likely to seem hopelessly parochial, if not self-serving as well. It seems to focus attention back on ourselves rather than on others. Yet I believe this is where the problem lies. The churches are in crisis because they have not understood the middle class and have not focused effectively enough on meeting its needs.

Although I have been a lifelong participant in churches and have devoted my professional life to studying and writing about American religion, I have always been somewhat reluctant to write critically about the churches because there were many good things to say and because there was so much else to criticize in the wider culture. But I am convinced now that I can no longer write responsibly about American religion without raising a critical voice.

I do so, however, not by setting up an external standard and judging the churches in relation to it. Instead, my approach is to let those who know the churches best and who are most responsible for them—the clergy—speak for themselves. Many of them, like the pastor who came to see me in my office, are keenly aware of the problems they face. They want to do their jobs better. They want to know that they are not alone. And they want to see how others are handling the problems they are experiencing.

My aim, then, is not to preach to the clergy. If I knew how to solve the problems congregations are now facing, I would probably be a pastor myself. Rather, my goal is to initiate a conversation within the churches and in the wider public about the current crisis in America's churches. As a social scientist, I can muster evidence, weigh it in relation to what we know about the institutional and cultural dynamics shaping American religion, and speak with some degree of detachment about the problems I see. That, at least, is my hope.

This volume builds on and is a follow-up to my previous work *God and Mammon in America*. In that book I examined what working men and women had to say about the relationships between their faith and their work, ethics, money, attitudes toward materialism, charitable giving, and views of the poor and economic justice. I showed that faith commitments make a genuine difference in the ways in which people address these various economic issues but that the difference is often small and sometimes runs counter to what religious leaders might expect. I suggested that much of the problem has to do with the complexities of postindustrial society itself and with the changing rules by which many of us play the game at work or in our families. Implicit in my argument was also the suggestion that churches are not doing their job as well as they might. Thus, it seemed only fair to give the clergy a chance to speak and to examine directly what they were saying on the same issues.

This volume shifts attention from the individual believer to organizations and to the leaders of these organizations. It asks about the health of America's churches and seeks to understand the problems religious leaders are facing as they confront the harsh economic realities of our time.

My perspective, however, is not one that attempts to understand churches simply as organizations or even as communities. I believe that the essence of churches continues to be the word ("the Word," as those in the churches would say)—the teachings, the beliefs, and the discourse and behavior that arise from these teachings and beliefs. I also harbor the view that clergy bear heavy responsibility for shaping these teachings and beliefs. Thus, my focus is less on what they do as administrators and more on what they believe, what they say, and how they attempt to guide their congregations.

This focus is consistent with that of many who have been studying congregations in recent years. They too emphasize that churches swim in shoals of myths and imagery. Stories and storytelling are crucial. However, my view is slightly different. Implicit cues, identities, memories, and myths may be the stuff of which congregations are composed, but most people do not live in congregations as much as congregational researchers suppose. Families may work this way, but congregations do so only for those who are intensely involved. For most people, congregational life is a sporadic and divided experience. Sometimes they listen, and sometimes they don't. But churches do exist for a purpose, and it is up to their leaders to define this purpose and to guide congregations toward fulfilling it. (Otherwise, why do congregational studies at all?) The clergy try to achieve this goal through their preaching and teaching, in their personal counseling, and in their administrative roles. Most of these activities require them to speak. And all of these activities are influenced in some measure by the mental maps that clergy carry with them. This is why we need to know what clergy say and how they think.

For readers who may themselves be clergy, I want to communicate from the outset that I hold the clergy in the highest regard and empathize with the aims they are seeking to fulfill in their ministries. Nothing I say in this volume should be construed as an indictment of the intentions or talents of the clergy. Rather, my goal is to bring to their attention how the churches are being influenced by the cultural milieu in which we live—especially the ways in which this milieu is shaping attitudes about work and money among the American middle class, how the clergy are trying to minister to these areas of life, and what the consequences may be for church finances. I emphasize this goal because I find that among clergy audiences to whom I have spoken about these topics there are some who immediately resonate with these aims, while others conclude, as one man put it, that "it doesn't make much difference what I preach about anyway."

A word is also in order about my use of quotations, stories, and examples from pastors and laypeople. Pastors, especially, seem to find this material amusing when I use it in lectures. This reaction bothers me. I suppose it comes from using stories in sermons as a way of providing comic relief. Some of the stories in this volume are indeed funny, but most are not. I certainly do not present them to show that I have a superior point of view or interpretation. Rather, they are data, in social scientists' jargon. They supply the words that help to substantiate my conclusions. And, in being able to see the exact words that people use, readers can gain their own empathic understanding of what the speakers are saying.

For readers who may be social scientists, I also want to position this volume briefly in relation to other current work in the field. Although I am concerned about the practical implications of what is now happening in the churches, I am also interested in the scholarly study of religion and in advancing the methods and perspectives of such work. I have tried here to bring together two strands of research that previously have largely been separate. One is the work of scholars who have been especially interested in religious organizations, their financing, memberships, and other resources (Mark Chaves, Roger Finke, Kirk Hadaway, Dean Hoge, Larry Iannaccone, James Richardson, Rodney Stark, and Stephen Warner, among others). The other is the work of scholars who have been mainly interested in religious symbolism, meanings, and discourse (Robert Bellah, Peter Berger, Lynn Davidman, Mary Douglas, Clifford Geertz, Evelyn Higginbotham, Albert Raboteau, Wade Clark Roof, and Marsha Witten, among others). The former have sensitized us to the fact that religious organizations need resources in order to survive. The latter have emphasized that religion is deeply concerned with the symbolic expression of sacred meanings.

Although there has always been some interaction between these two perspectives, it seems to me that the opportunity for bringing them together has never been greater. This opportunity has emerged because of wider developments in related fields and disciplines. Studies of formal organizations and of social movements, for instance, are now paying greater attention to the scripts, frames, ideologies, and institutional cultures of these entities rather than focusing on budgets alone. And studies of literature, art, and music are paying more attention to the resources needed to produce these forms of culture rather than looking only at their symbolism. Borrowing is possible from all these sources. In addition, the newer work in economic sociology (represented by scholars such as Paul DiMaggio, Michele Lamont, and Viviana Zelizer) brings in culture in important ways, showing, for instance, how hard currency, status, and markets are actually cultural constructions.

I hope this volume can be read as a contribution to these converging tendencies in the literature. I emphasize that churches are, among other things, organizations that have serious financial needs and that the fulfillment of these needs depends on leaders' ability to make financial appeals and on parishioners' willingness to heed these appeals. But I also show that economic issues—generally or in more specific terms—are subject to cultural construction. I show how clergy—as the professional producers of culture in religious organizations—are influenced by cultural assumptions that derive from their own theological understandings and from the implicit assumptions embedded in middle-class life. I argue that the discourse of clergy, therefore, is shaped in ways that limit its effectiveness, which in turn limits the churches' capacity to reproduce themselves financially. Understanding how contemporary social conditions influence the clergy's discourse about economics, work, stewardship, money, the needs of the poor, and social justice, then, is my immediate aim. Similar studies could, of course, be directed toward a great many other topics as well.

I am indebted to a number of people without whose assistance this book could not have been written. The research on which it is based was conducted at Princeton University as part of a five-year project on religious beliefs and economic behavior. The costs of collecting data were underwritten by a grant from the Lilly Endowment. I wish especially to thank Fred Hofheinz and Craig Dykstra for their interest in supporting this research. Lectures and conversations with faculty and clergy at Princeton Theological Seminary, Southern Baptist Theological Seminary, Christian Theological Seminary, Moravian Theological Seminary, and the Association of Theological Schools helped me to identify and refine some of my arguments. I also want to thank Natalie Searl, Tracy Scott, and Robin Rusciano for their work as research assistants and the many clergy and church members who gave willingly of their time for interviews and for informal conversations.

R.W.

# contents

# the CRISIS in the
# CHURCHES

# INTRODUCTION

Difficult as it may be to believe, America's churches have fallen on hard times. A few years ago, new congregations were being established in record numbers, new facilities were being built in every new suburban development, and more clergy were being trained and hired than at any time in our nation's history. But the economic prosperity that once characterized American religious institutions is now a thing of the past. Financial woes are the order of the day. Many smaller congregations are struggling to avoid having to close their doors. Many of the larger churches have had to scale back programs and put plans for expansion on indefinite hold. Older churches are saddled with historical landmarks—their buildings—which they are having trouble keeping in good repair, while newer churches are discovering the cost of having thrown up buildings too hastily a decade or two ago.

To the casual observer, the signs of crisis may not be evident. Visitors in most cities can find well-groomed religious structures in nearly every neighborhood. Driving by these buildings, we might not suspect that their congregations were having trouble finding the cash to keep going. The telescandals that shook the world of religious television a few years ago left many people with the impression that entrepreneurial clergy are now able to rake in huge sums of money and enjoy lavish lifestyles all too frequently. Having these examples in mind, we might not suspect that clergy salaries have been steadily diminishing in real dollars. In many communities, construction crews are busily putting up the megachurches of tomorrow. Reading about the megafunds required to create these churches, we might overlook the ones that are in bankruptcy or the ones that never get off the ground. From the outside, then, there appear to be ample funds for the churches to run their own programs and—in many instances—to dabble in politics as well. If anything, we might wonder whether the churches have *too many* resources for their own good.

Behind the stained glass, however, a different picture emerges. Mission programs are being canceled. Homeless people are being turned away from soup kitchens because donations of time and money are too small. Pastors' salary increases are being postponed, sometimes for the fifth or sixth year in a row. Youth ministers are being dismissed. Music programs are being scaled back. Second and third calls are made to parishioners begging them to turn in their pledge cards. And at denominational headquarters and in seminaries, church leaders are projecting cutbacks and austerity-level programs well into the next century.

On the whole, contributions to the churches remain generous by the standards of most countries of the world. A tradition of religious voluntarism has encouraged churches to tailor programs to their parishioners' needs and thus to attract financial support from satisfied customers rather than relying on state appropriations. But relative to need—and even as a percentage of disposable family income—religious contributions have declined significantly in recent years. At the same time, cutbacks in government programs have forced growing numbers of the homeless, the elderly, and the chronically ill to turn to the churches for help, and churches have not had the resources to respond. Slow economic growth in the nation at large, periodic recessions in recent years, and massive changes in the character of American industry have also created greater demand within the general population for the economic and emotional support of the churches. Families that have been self-sufficient for decades now find themselves in a sudden cash crunch—and come quietly to the pastor's study seeking help. Working longer and harder, professional men and women are experiencing burnout, facing conflict in their marriages and with their children, and wondering whether the churches might be able to help them with these problems. Even the most well-intentioned clergy are worrying about the extent to which church resources are being stretched by these demands.

Most of the economic problems now facing America's churches have been aggravated in recent years by adverse conditions in the wider economy and by government policies that have restricted funds for social programs. Some churches are slashing budgets and letting pastors go because they are suffering severely from these short-term problems. But the danger of describing the present situation as a crisis is that only the short-term situation may be considered. In reality, the conditions facing the churches are more deeply rooted in long-term economic and demographic changes in American society.

After World War II, the churches experienced two decades of growth and prosperity because the American economy was growing rapidly and because the so-called baby boom was adding significantly to the population of young families who were joining the churches in record numbers. In contrast, the past decade and a half has been characterized mostly by change and uncertainty in the religious realm—including new religious movements, a resurgence of evangelical and fundamentalist involvement in politics, declining memberships in mainline Protestant and Catholic churches, and much experimentation with new forms of spirituality (such as meditation, small groups, and spiritual direction). Shifting political philosophies and different administrations at the national level, as well as the enormous political changes in other countries, have added to this uncertainty.[1]

It is nevertheless evident that longer-term trends are also affecting the churches. The annual growth in disposable family incomes that once characterized the middle class is now slower and less certain. Most churches cannot count on donations to increase just because incomes are rising. The short-term growth in middle-class incomes that came as a result of married women entering the labor force has now stabilized; most middle-class families simply depend on having two incomes and cannot increase earnings—or giving—by working any harder. Smaller families mean that there are fewer children and grandchildren to boost church rolls. Indeed, much of the growth in church membership—as in the population at large—now comes from new immigrants, many of whom are poor and cannot afford to support the churches with large financial contributions. For all these reasons, then, the hard times that the churches are now facing are likely to continue.[2]

Serious as these problems may be, they are nevertheless only the tip of an iceberg. Churches have weathered economic hardship before. During the Great Depression, for example, many churches postponed putting up new buildings and went without permanent, full-time staff for more than a decade, but by the early 1950s most had recovered financially and were expanding their programs to meet the challenges of growing numbers of church members. What makes the present crisis more serious is that it is also a spiritual crisis. Were it only a problem of budgets, careful management would be enough. But the current crisis is much deeper. Fund-raisers cannot fix it.

It is a *spiritual crisis* because it derives from the very soul of the church. The problem lies less in parishioners' pocketbooks than in their hearts and less in churches' budgets than in clergy's understanding of the needs and desires of their members' lives. It lies in a fundamental unwillingness on the part of clergy to confront the teachings within their own confessional heritage. The prevalent theology seldom connects with the ways in which people think about their money or their work, and when it does, the connection is more likely to be one of solace than of prophetic vision.

This crisis pertains most directly to the middle class.[3] For all its interest in the poor, the church in the United States is overwhelmingly a ministry to the middle class. Its buildings are located in middle-class neighborhoods. Its programs are geared toward the interests of middle-class families. It depends on the middle class for its financial existence. This is the reality of the American church. Its members mostly lead comfortable middle-class lives and make up the majority of one of the richest countries in the world. They have the wherewithal to support their churches generously. But they also suffer from the pressures to which middle-class families are increasingly exposed—pressures of working harder to make ends meet, worries about retaining one's job, lack of time for one's self and one's family, marital strains associated with two-career households, and the incessant demands of advertising and the marketplace. These are the daily preoccupations of the middle class, yet clergy have often been reluctant to acknowledge these issues as legitimate concerns or to address them seriously. Instead, it has seemed more "Christian" to provide token assistance to the poor and to pray for the needy who live thousands of miles away. Especially in recent years, it has also seemed more pressing to take up the issues supplied by the media and to become embroiled in culture wars and preach about political issues rather than speaking to the concerns that face parishioners in their everyday lives.

Because they do not find clergy who are concerned about the pressures they face in their families and at work, it is not surprising that many middle-class people are giving less to their churches than they were a decade or two ago. They may still attend services on Sunday mornings, but they receive little guidance about how to be faithful stewards. In fact, most of them have no idea what stewardship is. Those who believe devoutly in the faith of their fathers and mothers are unlikely to consider their work a calling or to approach it any differently than their less devout neighbors. They may consider it as legitimate to give money to the Sierra Club as to the Presbyterian church, and they may turn to Alcoholics Anonymous to find help in coping with the pressures of daily existence because the pastor seems incapable of listening to their problems.

If the churches are to emerge from their present crisis, therefore, they must come to a clearer understanding of their role and ministry in relation to the middle class. It will not be sufficient for them simply to strive harder to meet the needs of the hungry and the homeless or to continue deploring the oppression of peoples in Latin America or decrying injustices to the unborn or to gays and lesbians. Those efforts will, of course, continue. But efforts to assist the downtrodden and the disadvantaged and to speak for greater justice on their behalf can succeed only if the middle class itself is challenged in ways that have seldom been seen in recent decades.

For the churches to regain their spiritual voice in ministering to the middle class, the clergy must play a key role. They must provide leadership and inspiration. They must preserve the sacred teachings of their traditions, making them relevant to the strenuous, pressure-filled lives that most of their middle-class parishioners lead. They must communicate effectively in their preaching and serve as role models in the ways that they lead their own lives. They must understand that middle-class people are much more concerned about how to work responsibly and how to manage their money wisely than they are about the propriety or impropriety of a Robert Mapplethorpe photograph. The clergy must do a better job of relating theology to everyday life, and they must realize that everyday life consists mostly of the work that people do in their ordinary jobs, not the work they do for an hour or two a week in the church basement. Pastors must preach more clearly and imaginatively about stewardship. They must give their members better reasons to contribute to the church. And they must help the middle class understand the relevance of faith in the workplace and in the marketplace.

I do not suggest that clergy can play these roles alone, but clergy must shoulder the lion's share of the responsibility. After all, they are the full-time, salaried professionals who are hired to look after the store. If they fall asleep, it is little wonder that parishioners are unwilling to give generously of their time and money. Indeed, the clergy need to be held accountable for what they say and do, just as other professionals are held responsible for their behavior. When test scores falter among students, the public wants to know what teachers and school administrators are doing wrong. If the churches are now faltering, we must look at what the clergy are doing wrong. We need to ask whether they are preaching boldly and clearly about stewardship, whether they are tiptoeing around the subject of money, and whether they understand the concerns that arise in the ordinary work day of most Americans. If not, or if the clergy's perceptions are far afield of the realities of their members' lives, something is wrong, and the clergy need to be challenged to do a better job.

The clergy must be clear not only about how to minister to the middle class but also about how their own ministries have been shaped by the middle-class assumptions of the culture in which they live. A significant part of the churches' crisis stems from the fact that clergy often remain unclear on both counts. They misperceive the spiritual dilemma of the middle class, failing to realize how pressured middle-class people feel nowadays and how deeply the middle class is afflicted by the complexities of new jobs, new information, and new values. And they fail to recognize the extent to which they have accommodated the wider culture—and thus the extent to which their sermons fall on deaf ears because people are hearing

nothing new, nothing that challenges them to live any differently than their neighbors who have no interest in religion. Like the laity, clergy are earthen vessels,
capable of serving and desiring to serve, yet subject to the same limitations.

The purpose of this book is not to condemn—any more than it is to evoke sympathy for—the clergy but to examine the present crisis in the churches through
their eyes, in their own words, and in relation to what we know about church members and the larger public. I am concerned with the assumptions that clergy take for
granted as they think about their middle-class parishioners; as they preach about
money, giving, and social justice; and as they try to help their congregants deal with
the pressures of their daily lives. My aim is to understand the economic and cultural realities with which the churches are now faced and thus to consider how the
clergy may be able to minister more effectively to the middle class and to better
serve as witnesses to sacred truth and as servants to the needy.

To accomplish that aim, I have gathered information from scores of clergy
throughout the United States and from most of the major U.S. confessional and
denominational traditions. Over a two-year period, visits were made to their
churches, information was obtained about their congregations and about church
finances and budgets and stewardship drives, and each pastor underwent an interview on a wide range of topics that in most cases took nearly three hours to complete. More than 200 of their sermons were also obtained, and all of this information was examined carefully to see how clergy perceive the issues facing them and
their congregants and what they have to say on these issues. We asked clergy to talk
from the perspective of the various roles they play, telling us, for instance, what
they say to people who come to them for counsel, asking them to give us short sermons on various topics, and listening as they described their work as administrators and their views of their congregations. We also contacted most of the clergy we
interviewed a year later to see how things were progressing in their congregations.
In addition, information was gathered on the same topics by interviewing laity,
both in the same congregations as the clergy we talked to and in other congregations, and from a survey that I conducted among a representative national sample
of working men and women as well as from several surveys conducted by other
organizations.[4]

From listening closely to what clergy are saying and from engaging with them
in their search for answers to the present crisis, I am convinced that there is ample
reason to be hopeful about the future of Christianity in the United States. Despite
the current crisis, America's churches have much to offer, and they are doing many
things to meet the needs of their members and to minister to the wider society. But
I am also convinced that the harsh reality of the present situation must be faced
squarely. The time when clergy could speak in vague generalities about biblical
truths is past. They can no longer duck the issues of what it means to be a Christ-

ian in the workplace by saying they are too far removed from the workplace to understand it. And they can no longer avoid preaching about financial giving by framing their stewardship sermons in terms of simply using one's talents wisely or being an appreciative citizen of the planet.

Clergy, especially, need to ponder what those from their own ranks have to say about the present crisis. To that end, I profile some of the churches we visited and report what clergy told us in their own words. Those who are now in seminaries, training to become parish clergy or serving as seminary faculty, also need to consider the presuppositions that clergy are presently bringing to their tasks and the challenges they are facing in ministering to the middle class. Indeed, many of the clergy we interviewed pleaded with us to make this information known in a way that could help the next generation of clergy perform their tasks more effectively. Laity are deeply implicated in the process of rejuvenating the churches as well. They need to know what their pastors have to say and what pastors consider the chief limits to the clergy's role. Knowing what their pastors "really think" may be especially instructive. One of the startling realizations that came from talking to laity, in fact, was that we often knew more about what their pastors thought after a three-hour interview than they did after three years as church members. We had simply spent more time one-on-one with their pastors than they had.

But, in a larger sense, the present crisis in America's churches is a problem that should concern all of us, whether we are churchgoers ourselves, whether we belong to other faiths, or whether we are simply interested in the good of our society. Some of us, having visions of well-fed clergy driving luxury cars and preaching in gilded auditoriums on Sundays, are likely to take quiet joy in the thought that churches are now having to retrench. Some belt-tightening may indeed be in order. Yet to think of the churches as wastrels that need to be brought down to earth is to misunderstand both the present situation and the larger context in which the churches contribute to our society.

Throughout our nation's history, the churches have been a vital part of American society and of the voluntary spirit that has animated American democracy itself. Few organizations have been as pervasive and familiar in local communities and neighborhoods. The churches have ministered to the poor and provided the middle class with places to associate and with vehicles for service. If the churches are now facing hard times, we need to understand the dimensions of this crisis, including its roots in broader social conditions and how it is shaped by changing assumptions within the churches themselves. Rather than assuming that the churches are simply an inevitable feature of the American landscape, we need to recognize the problems they are now facing. Finding ways to revitalize them is in everyone's interest.

# one

# HARD TIMES IN PARADISE

In many ways, the United States has been a paradise for religious organizations.[1] Throughout most of the nineteenth and nearly all of the twentieth century, the United States has enjoyed one of the highest average per capita incomes of any country in the world. Because of this relative affluence, most Americans have had the wherewithal to support the churches at a generous level. Even when people gave only a small proportion of their earnings, they still collectively donated large amounts of money. Unlike most other affluent countries, the United States has supported its churches voluntarily rather than providing them with subsidies from taxes and government grants. In Europe, the churches that were supported in this way often suffered because governments preferred to keep taxes low in order to maintain a competitive business climate rather than allocating more funds to the churches, or because wars or welfare programs created more pressing demands on government coffers. In comparison, voluntary donations in the United States were generous. People gave to the churches not because the government told them to but because they wanted to; sometimes, in fact, they gave money specifically because the churches were an alternative to government—*free* institutions that would not survive unless people supported them.[2]

Separation of church and state in the United States has also produced a favorable religious environment by promoting competition among religious bodies. People who might not have been willing to give money to build a new church became more generous when a rival church down the block put up a better building. Although they professed belief in the same Lord, Protestants and Catholics were jealous competitors, and Lutherans, Baptists, Methodists, and Presbyterians all struggled to keep their respective denominations flourishing.[3]

People gave, too, because the churches were entrusted with many social responsibilities that governments or secular agencies performed in other societies—for instance, hospitals, private schools and colleges, nurseries, and care for the sick and the elderly.[4] For all these reasons, the churches have prospered throughout much of our history: New congregations have been started; buildings have been constructed and maintained; new educational wings have been added; full-time professional clergy have been hired; and droves of church secretaries, choir masters, youth ministers, and Christian education directors have been employed. If the United States has been one of the most "churched" of all industrial nations, these buildings, pastors, and programs have been one of the important reasons.[5] People may have felt a quiet yearning for God in their hearts; they knew it was for God because preachers and priests and church bells and choirs told them so.

But now American churches are experiencing an unparalleled economic crisis. It consists—as all economic crises do—of a gap between revenues and expenditures. Revenues are dropping off, especially when giving is adjusted for inflation or is considered in relation to family incomes. Just as this decrease is happening, the need for resources has never been greater. Increasing numbers of disadvantaged people are looking to the churches for help. The churches are being asked to fill the gaps left by cuts in government welfare programs. Staff salaries are squeezed. Old buildings are in disrepair. New congregants are needed.

It has been difficult to see that a crisis existed because many things are going well, especially in some of the nation's more affluent churches. But there is also growing evidence that the crisis is symptomatic of an even deeper malaise in American religion. People are not drawing connections between spirituality and their daily lives. They are preoccupied with their own economic needs, and they do not feel that the churches are ministering to these needs. Instead, the churches are perceived to be more interested in others' needs. And clergy are caught in the middle, not knowing how to make the best appeals or how to focus their ministries. Indeed, clergy themselves often express concern and uncertainty.

There is growing recognition of the problem, but no effort has been made to gauge its dimensions or to consider what might be done to resolve it. That is the purpose of this book. It brings together a variety of facts and figures, but more importantly, it focuses on the experiences of clergy and of local congregations themselves. I have listened to what they say, examined their sermons, and considered the problem both from their perspectives and from my own as a social scientist.

My conclusions are these: (1) The economic crisis in America's churches is indeed serious, and it needs to be understood in its own right, that is, as an economic matter of grave proportions: (2) The reasons for this crisis are both structural and spiritual, that is, they reflect changes in American society but also in our understandings of faith itself and of its relevance to our work, our money, and our families: (3) Something can be done about this crisis and the churches can retain their vitality, but only if the churches regain their mission to serve the needs of the middle class itself and only if the clergy speak more clearly to the ways in which faith connects with the overall uses of our time and our resources.

The main argument of this book, then, is that the present crisis, while serious and rooted in social conditions that are likely to continue well into the next century, is nevertheless an opportunity for the churches if they can respond actively to the spiritual needs of their congregations. In particular, the churches can save themselves by focusing more attention on the meanings of stewardship, by preaching more actively about stewardship, by helping their members connect their faith to their work, by responding to the pressures and anxieties that grow out of contemporary jobs and careers, and by rediscovering the churches' prophetic voice on matters of money and materialism. If the clergy are able to lead their congregations in these ways, the financial strains presently facing the churches will be alleviated, and—more importantly—the churches will have become more effective in their spiritual ministries as well.

A glance at the following headlines, culled from national newspapers and magazines over the past few years, suggests some of the ways in which economic conditions are adversely affecting the churches:

Churches Caught in Economy's Grip

Expenses Force Cuts in Program

Church Finances in Crisis

Bad Tidings for the Church

Archdiocese Weighs Closing Parishes

Church Faces Empty Treasury

Boston Church Closes Schools

Selling Off Church Artworks

Recession Catches up to Ministries

Church Schools to be Shut

Red Ink at Youth for Christ

Bethlehem on a Budget

Debts Pose Problems for Missions

Financial Worries Darken Church Assembly

Parish Buildings Sold

Collection-plate Blues in Detroit

Earning More, Giving Less

Missions May Go Broke

The list of similar headlines goes on and on.

Many of us—clergy, church members, and interested bystanders—can sit back with relief when we read headlines like this and say, "Whew, it's not happening in my church or in my community." The problems must be happening elsewhere, and they must be linked to the special problems of particular denominations or regions of the country. Journalists actually make it easier for us to dismiss these cases by sensationalizing them. The worst stories get reported, and the worst stories are the ones that describe parochial schools closing because the archdiocese is having to pay millions because of priests who sexually abuse children, or a megachurch going belly up because the head pastor is having an affair with the organist.

We may be vaguely aware that *other* churches are struggling too—because they are in rustbelt sections of the country or burned-over districts where the flame of revival has long since died out. We sit back in our suburban strongholds and our college towns and tell ourselves that the hard times are happening somewhere else. We may even consider these problems examples of the rude hand of justice. If some churches are experiencing hard times, perhaps it is just because they have been preaching heresy or because it is time for old churches to die and new ones to be born.

To think so is to miss the essential feature of what I am describing. The hard times many of our churches are now visibly experiencing are only a symptom of the problem that afflicts virtually all of our churches. Serious financial difficulties face a few—probably more than we realize. Cutbacks and postponed programs are pervasive. Even the churches where smug complacency rules are having to admit that things are not as rosy as they would like. Perhaps their giving *is* up. Perhaps their programs *are* flourishing. But needs have gone up even more, and the churches, individually and collectively, are having a harder time meeting these needs. Their ministries are falling short, even in their own communities, let alone in addressing the needs of the unchurched, the poor, and people in other countries.

But even these needs are not entirely what the current crisis is about. Churches that are faring well are often failing to address the *heart issues* that underlie all giving and all financial programs. Their finances may be adequate, but their grasp of stewardship is not. They have preached tithing—more likely meaning 1 percent than 10 percent—but have forgotten to say anything about the remaining 90 percent of their parishioners' financial burdens. They have asked for an hour on Sundays but neglected the relationship between faith and the forty (or fifty) hours that people spend at work. And they have preached concern for the poor but failed to do much more for their middle-class members than pat them on the back. To say that the problems are heart issues, then, is to suggest that religious teachings—what one writer calls "the murky nave of theological discourse"[6]—is the central matter needing to be understood, not simply church budgets or organization charts.

We need to consider the hard times that have befallen America's churches not as *somebody else's* problem but as our own. The problem is pervasive in the heartland of America's churches—the middle-class congregations that are least in danger of literally having to close their doors because of cash shortages. It starts with the lackluster giving patterns that are already evident in national statistics, and it requires us to think hard about what the churches are really up to these days.

## THE FINANCIAL PICTURE

An initial grasp of the problem can be obtained from crude financial statistics. The grim fact is that contributions to religious organizations have been declining steadily as a proportion of family incomes. According to figures compiled by the Illinois-based research organization Empty Tomb, religious giving as a percentage of family income has been on a downward course for the past two decades, dropping from an average of 3.1 percent in the late 1960s to 2.5 percent in the early 1990s. That decrease amounts to a loss of approximately $2.8 billion annually.[7]

Compounding the problem is the fact that family incomes, adjusted for inflation, are no longer growing either. In the 1960s, for example, they grew at about 3 percent annually, but since the early 1980s they have not grown at all.[8]

Furthermore, there is reason to believe that such figures underestimate the extent of the problem because statistics on giving are generally based on church *members*. Yet a substantial amount of the money churches take in comes from non-members—and, as emphasis on membership has been decreasing in some denominations, this constituency is growing. These contributions are, of course, included in denominational figures, but *average per capita* giving is probably less than the 2.5 percent estimate reported because the number of people contributing has been underestimated. Indeed, when other data on giving—such as self-reports in surveys—are examined, religious contributions appear to be closer to 2 percent of family income if only those who contribute are considered, and closer to 1 percent if everyone is considered.[9]

Figures like these are subject to different interpretations. Sociologist Andrew Greeley, for instance, finds such figures disturbing, noting, "You could build a lot of new schools, help a lot of missionaries and house a lot of the homeless with the missing money."[10] Yet within the churches themselves, there is an overwhelming predisposition to put a good face on things. Believers are taught to put their trust in God, to be thankful for God's blessings, and not to complain. When things are bad, the proper response is to have faith and say that the Lord will provide. It is easy then, in retrospect, to single out the cases in which some unexpected blessing occurred and to neglect other, less favorable outcomes. If a fund-raising drive targeted at $350,000 raises only $200,000, then the pastor looks at the amount and decides it is really quite sufficient after all. Or if plate offerings in the past month have risen, the deacons assume that the financial decline over the past year must indeed be over. Pastors are also reluctant to criticize their parishioners. Despite the fact that average contributions hover around 2 percent of gross personal income, many pastors compliment their members, saying that they "give pretty well," "are really quite faithful," "do their best to tithe," and so on. They are confident that people are giving as generously as they can.

Given this penchant for optimism, it is all the more notable that every pastor we talked to was concerned about the level of giving at his or her church, and every pastor told us this concern was common among other pastors he or she knew in the same community or in the same denomination. Of course, few pastors know exactly what their parishioners' incomes are, and most have not tried to determine if contributions are keeping up with inflation rates. So their evidence is of a different sort than that obtained in surveys or compiled by denominational researchers. Yet it is revealing—perhaps even more so because it comes with the perspective of personal experience.

One pastor calculated that the typical adult in his congregation put in about $13 a week when the offering plate came around. This amount was high, he said. Other churches in his denomination averaged about $10. In these churches the weekly offering constituted most of the money that came in. It was, he remarked, amazing that people put in less each week than it took to buy a full tank of gas. A priest in another part of the country reported that weekly giving in his parish over the past five years had averaged between $19 and $25 per family. He felt that his homilies on tithing—"encouraging people to give 10 percent off the top to God"—helped to keep giving at this level but was disturbed by the fact that giving had fallen off by about 15 percent over the past two years. He seemed not to notice the disparity between his admonitions about tithing and the fact that his members were giving less than 2 percent of their income.

In cold financial terms, the amount of money people give to their churches is indeed quite sparse. Not only is it much smaller than the prescribed "10 percent off the top," but it is also far less than the average family spends on vacations each year. Most people could double their giving by foregoing the purchase of a new camcorder, stereo unit, or television set. Clergy recognize that people could be giving more and feel frustrated by their own inability to solicit larger contributions.

But clergy see the needs of their parishioners as well. It may be that one or two families in their congregations clearly could give more. Others, however, may be asking for prayer because they are about to lose their jobs or their homes. "It's blood money at this point," said one pastor. "I don't feel like I can ask for any more." Clergy are also reluctant to criticize their parishioners or to seem overly concerned about finances. Many of the ones we spoke to complimented their congregations with comments such as, "They're quite faithful," or "The Lord's people generally come through."

Part of the financial crunch, therefore, is that clergy are having to deal with economic realities that they feel ill equipped to handle. It is on their shoulders to be better managers of the scarce funds at their disposal. They preach about stewardship to their congregants, but they know it is they who must learn to be even better stewards than before. They also know—or believe—that the financial management of their congregations can be a frustrating task and one for which they are not well prepared. One national survey of clergy, for instance, found that eight out of ten were very satisfied with their *pastoral* duties but that only three out of ten were similarly satisfied with their *financial* duties. The same study showed that upward of three-quarters regarded their seminary training in theological and liturgical issues as satisfactory, but only 7 percent said the same about their preparation for financial duties.[11] Daniel Conway, author of the study, observed, "Although their hearts are in the right place, pastors, by their own admission, frequently lack the knowledge and experience that is required to oversee the development and management of resources (people, buildings and money) that are needed to support the mission of the church."[12]

The present crunch in giving has also hit some churches harder than others. National studies of trends in congregational finances have not been conducted, but anecdotal evidence suggests that churches in economically stagnant regions of the country and in denominations with declining memberships have been particularly hard hit.[13] Other churches have actually fared well, despite overall setbacks in the economy. Indeed, of the churches we studied, only 25 percent had experienced actual declines in giving during the past three years.[14] The remaining three-quarters had been able to maintain giving at a steady rate, and in fact, in most cases giving had increased at least at the same rate as inflation. To say that *only* a quarter had experienced decreased giving is, of course, to cast the financial picture of American religion in overly optimistic terms. If a quarter of American households were taking pay cuts, we would hear much about the plight of the economy. If one church in four is having to retrench, many of the ministries and programs that the public has grown used to are clearly in danger of being scaled back.

The financial state of the churches cannot be discerned from giving patterns alone. Before moving to other considerations, however, it is nevertheless worth noting that even congregations with favorable giving trends are not always in as good shape as the trends themselves may suggest. In at least a quarter of these congregations, giving is up—but for reasons that do not suggest long-term health or an ability to expand programs. One reason giving has increased in some churches is that serious cutbacks occurred a few years ago. The trend has been up since then but still has not risen to previous levels. Another reason is that clergy—by their own admission—have put out special emergency appeals. Finding themselves in financial jeopardy in midyear, they have begged harder for parishioners to give. How long such special appeals can be sustained is a matter of question. Still another reason that giving is up in some churches is because of new members. Per capita giving may thus be down, but the church is able to run the same programs by virtue of having more contributors. This change means, of course, that the programs may be stretched to meet the needs of more people. It also means that other churches, where these members no longer attend, are probably suffering shortfalls. And it is unclear how long such trends may continue.

## THE INVISIBLE CRISIS

There is a serious dimension to the problem that financial statistics alone do not register. This part of the problem can only be measured in terms of what the churches need and want to be doing but are having to forego or postpone because the resources are not there. Even where giving has not declined, many churches are having to cut back because of rising fixed costs and are faced with increasing needs in their communities that they are unable to meet.

The pastor of a small Baptist church said that giving has held steady in the past few years, but he always "walks a tightrope" in balancing needs and revenue. He said the children's program has been seriously limited by a lack of finances in recent years. Every winter the heating bill for the church is more than $2,000 a month. Much of the problem is an inefficient, twenty-year old heating system. But for the third year in a row the church is postponing plans to upgrade the system. He figures it would cost $50,000, which is an enormous amount compared with an annual operating budget of $78,000. His salary has not increased in the past three years. Plans to remodel the auditorium are also on hold. He thinks the church is going to rely more on unpaid volunteers in the future. But he has not reckoned with the fact that fewer people have the time to do volunteer work.

A priest whose parish budget is nearly ten times that of the Baptist congregation just mentioned also talked about cutbacks and plans foregone. He has frozen the salaries of his staff and is allocating less money this year than last to a fund for the poor. Asked about plans for expansion, he explained, "We *had* plans for expansion, but the economy has slammed the brakes on the whole thing. The demographics that we did several years ago showed growth in the numbers of people in the parish. However, the recession kept that growth from happening, which therefore kept us from really doing anything about expanding." He too is relying more on volunteers—"We're saving thousands by not hiring a youth director"—but he also worries about that trend continuing. The head of his Parish Life Committee also reported that the church has cut back significantly on its giving for overseas development projects and that the music ministry position has been eliminated.

Even in denominations that have experienced numerical growth in recent years, some churches are in deep financial trouble. A Pentecostal church in Oregon with an annual budget of $2.5 million is so deeply in debt that it is planning to sell its building and move to more modest quarters. In the early 1980s, church planners advised the pastor that a larger building would draw more than enough new people to cover the costs. The reality has been quite different. Visitors come, the pastor said, find out how huge the mortgage is, and decide to go elsewhere. "People like to give to ministries," he observed, "not to pay off mortgages." To help keep expenses down, he has let both his secretary and a part-time youth director go and has not taken a cost-of-living increase in his own salary in the past three years.

These examples illustrate the kinds of financial problems churches are facing. Many of the problems have been exacerbated in recent years by the long-term recession of the late 1980s and early 1990s. Particular sources of difficulty vary from congregation to congregation, but the most commonly mentioned include problems associated with overbuilding, such as interest and repayment on mortgages; necessary repairs (such as new roofs, furnaces, and air-conditioning systems), maintenance, and utilities work on buildings, especially older churches; declining memberships; and large increases in the cost of fixed items, such as health insurance and electricity bills.

Even without extenuating circumstances, the pressures of many of these items have been steadily increasing. With salaries making up about half of typical church budgets, increases in payments for Social Security, pensions, and health insurance have pushed up costs by as much as 10 percent annually in recent years. On average, the churches we studied were also having to devote at least 10 percent of their budgets to routine repairs and maintenance of buildings.

Cost-saving measures that have been put into place in recent years also suggest the numerous ways in which churches are attempting to adjust to hard financial times. Nearly all of the churches we studied had instituted one or more of these measures in the past few years: freezes on staff salary increases (in many cases, including cost-of-living increases); firing or not replacing auxiliary staff, such as assistant and associate pastors, youth ministers, music directors, chaplains, and secretaries; putting plans to hire staff to fill vital needs, such as counseling or youth ministries, on indefinite hold; postponing plans for renovation or the construction of new buildings; delaying repairs (of problems such as cracked foundations, rotten windows, and leaky roofs); cutting health and retirement benefits or reducing subsidies for staff housing and transportation; reducing apportionment payments to denominational bureaus; and reducing or eliminating support for programs and special ministries such as homeless shelters, soup kitchens, deacon's funds, and overseas missions.

Most churches are taking these cost-cutting measures in stride, but there is also a human dimension that should not be ignored. Each story is different: the janitor at a Methodist church who confides that she is struggling to pay her bills because she has not received a pay increase in several years, the Episcopal rector who is putting in eighty-hour weeks because he cannot afford to hire an assistant, the Presbyterian parishioners who lament the loss of the historical steeple on their church because tearing it down was cheaper than repairing it, the Latino immigrants who ask why their parish cannot hire a Spanish-speaking priest, or the Baptist deacon who turns the homeless away on Thanksgiving because the fund is empty.

In addition to the dollars-and-cents factors involved, psychological and social considerations are also contributing to the present problems. For instance, church people are no different than other Americans: They value success and want to be part of something that is exciting and growing. Thus, they may give to the new megachurch in town that is throwing up bigger buildings, but meanwhile many of the other churches struggle to make ends meet. Or, as many pastors observed, it is possible to solicit donations for a new program, such as a crisis ministry or a counseling center, but money to fix the roof or to repair the foundation is much harder to raise.

We underestimate the extent of the problem, too, if we think of needs only in static terms. Other institutions have been experiencing cutbacks as well. After government funds for mental health and veterans' programs were cut in the 1970s, homelessness rose dramatically. Insurance companies have been clamping down on reimbursements for counseling and family therapy. Urban-renewal, low-income-housing, and job-training budgets have been slashed. Even the declining quality of public schooling is having adverse effects on many families and communities. As all these needs are increasing, "the challenge is coming back," as the pastor in one African American community put it, to the churches. The opportunities are there for the churches to minister; the resources may not be.

Another factor that fails to receive attention in most published statistics is that giving may remain constant as a percentage of family income and yet register declines because of the changing demographic characteristics of the population. Walk into many established churches these days and see an expanse of gray heads. These are the people who have perhaps given generously to the churches over the past two decades. But an aging church population means more retired people, more people living on fixed incomes, and fewer people giving at the same levels they did when their earnings were at their peak.

Some of the difference may be made up for by the so-called baby boom generation coming into the peak of its earning capacity. Yet many baby boomers have spent periods of their lives outside the churches and may not be as loyal as the older generation when times are tight. A growing number of baby boomers are also part of the "sandwich" generation, having to care for aging parents and children alike. One pastor put it this way: "I know this for a fact, that the Achilles heel of the church is going to be money. And the reason, very simply, is that the baby boomer generation are not givers naturally. The older generation in their fifties and older, who naturally are givers, will give very readily and faithfully and steadily. Those people are getting older and they're dying. And when you lose that generation twenty years from now, the church is going to be in serious trouble. I think there's a solution to the problem. I just don't know that the churches are addressing it."

While many churches are now experiencing difficulties making ends meet, the extent of the problem is nevertheless largely invisible to the outside world and even to many within the churches. The problem is invisible, partly, because the average parishioner knows very little about church finances and because the clergy are reluctant to talk about how bad things really are. "How can I put this tactfully?" one pastor ventured. "Most of the clergy I know are on ego trips. They want to be seen as successful program managers. So they don't talk about the problems. 'Everything's great,' they'll say. They paint a rosier picture than things really are."

Observed another minister, "It's a sore point in our denomination, I guess. People don't like to talk about money." A laywoman added emphatically, "Christians are so polite! It's so hard for them to be confrontational and just lay it out on the table, especially about money. Money's not an easy topic for them to talk about."

Though the crisis is largely invisible, it is nonetheless scary to those on the front lines of America's churches. One bank failure makes other bankers nervous. The same is true of churches. Clergy get together at denominational conferences, just as other professionals do. They hear stories, and they worry. In one case, it was a pastor's best friend who had taken a church with 200 members but with a building that was too expensive for the congregants to maintain. The church was forced to file for bankruptcy. "It was just horrible, a nightmare," exclaimed his friend.

The pastor of a large Presbyterian church in a wealthy suburb said his church has been weathering tight economic conditions better than many other churches, but they have reduced the size of the professional staff and cut back on outreach and mission programs. Like most of the pastors we talked to, he said that take-home pay has not risen for staff in the past several years but mentioned that fringe benefits are eating up more of the church's budget, especially because of rising health insurance costs. The rector of an Episcopal church told us that his diocese—which holds the health insurance policy for all its clergy—recently found that its premiums were going to rise from $380,000 annually to $600,000, so a vote was taken to triple the deductibles that had to be met before reimbursements were made. In another Episcopal diocese we discovered that *half* the churches were struggling to make ends meet, to pay their clergy adequately, and to cover the costs of existing programs.

Another significant area in which financial cutbacks have been made is in denominational-level programs such as support for denominational administrators, publishing, seminaries, missions, and evangelism. A Presbyterian pastor who has served on a number of denominational committees summarized his experience this way: "Our denomination has really had to cut back. My sense is that it's not that money is not being given on the local level; it's that more money is being kept at the local level, far more than what used to be, and it's not getting to the national church, not getting to the national bureaucracy and the program." While such cutbacks have kept money at the local level in the short term, the long-term implications are not positive. Denominations will have fewer resources to start new congregations to meet shifts in population, and local congregations in declining areas will have fewer chances of receiving help from their denominations. In one of the Episcopal dioceses we studied, for example, most of the churches were small, had only a part-time staff member, and relied on diocesan contributions to cover their expenses. As large congregations in the diocese have declined, the diocese has had less money to spend on these smaller congregations.

Liberal mainline denominations, such as the Presbyterian and Episcopal churches, are not the only ones suffering cuts at the denominational level. The pastor of a Nazarene church observed the same thing happening in his denomination. "Our headquarters is in a state of panic. They're talking about cutting back. That's where I think it's most noticeable. People say, look, I want to help the person on the street. Forget home office. So they're talking about something they've never done, and that's paring back significantly in terms of personnel. There's a lot of anxiety over that."

Recruitment and retention of qualified staff is another hidden cost in the present crisis. Some estimates suggest that clergy, counselors, secretaries, janitors, and other staff employed in churches receive at least 20 percent less than their counterparts in secular organizations for comparable work. If present freezes in church salaries continue, this gap will widen considerably over the next decade, making church positions less attractive to the most qualified job applicants. In the short term, the problem may not be significant, especially if churches are currently overstaffed or if employment opportunities are not available in secular organizations either. Over the long term, however, the ability of churches to provide high-quality programs is likely to be impaired if congregations are unable to recruit and retain the best people.

The problem of recruitment and retention, it should be noted, is aggravated by the fact that churches have already begun to suffer in the face of competition from secular employment. At one time, deep religious commitment and a sense of special "calling" could be counted on to channel young people in sufficient numbers into the priesthood and related professions. Increasingly, however, the clergy has been redefined as a profession itself rather than as a calling, and other professions, such as counseling, social work, and nonprofit administration, have begun to provide alternative modes of employment. Therefore, rather than being able to rely on "slave wages and religious zeal," as one priest put it, to keep budgets low, churches are under pressure to raise staff salaries just at a time when the resources to do so are increasingly scarce.

As yet, the crisis has not forced many churches to close their doors entirely. But in some areas the mood has become quite pessimistic. Mainline Protestant churches with aging and declining memberships are among those hardest hit. Especially in sections of the country where the economy has also been languishing, the prospects are dim. In one of the counties we studied, for example, five of the current fifteen Episcopal churches were in danger of having to shut their doors within the next two or three years. In another town, located in a relatively prosperous area of the country, four churches are nestled around a single intersection—and three are in danger of closing.

## ISSUES OF THE HEART

While the financial problems are serious in their own right, it is increasingly evident that these problems are only the visible tip of a much deeper dilemma now facing the churches. That dilemma is how to regain the churches' capacity to speak to the full range of economic concerns facing their middle-class memberships. Indeed, a small but growing number of the clergy and other church leaders are beginning to look at the economic problems currently facing the churches, and, uniformly, their analyses suggest that these problems will not be fixed simply by exhorting people to give more generously or by having better-orchestrated pledge drives and fund-raising programs. Instead, the churches must recognize that giving is always part of a broader set of assumptions that govern our views about economic matters and that relate these views to our beliefs and assumptions about religious faith itself.

"Money will be the downfall of the churches," said the pastor of a Baptist congregation. What he meant is that churches are largely blind to the importance of money, often regarding it as a necessary evil or as something largely outside their ken of expertise. People like him believe that the churches must address assumptions about money head on. People are not likely to give if they feel they are already too far in debt to have disposable cash. Nor are they likely to give on Sundays when they have been bombarded all week with glitzy advertisements that play on their emotions and that encourage them to want more for themselves.

Curiously, the Christian faith has always claimed to be relevant to all aspects of life. Yet when it comes to church finances, these issues are often treated simply as bottom-line concerns rather than as matters rooted in deeper discussions of faith. The way to solve a budget problem, therefore, is to bring in an expert on church finances, hire a professional fund-raiser, put up a chart, or hold a business meeting. "Sometimes I think we trust our bank account more than we do God," mused one pastor.

If the churches are to survive their present and future economic problems, say some pastors, they must take their own teachings more seriously, recognizing that "God as Lord of all" means ministering to parishioners' work lives and pocketbooks as well as to their souls. With growing numbers of middle-class families in debt, churches need to offer programs that teach sound financial management practices. And churches need to combat the allure of Madison Avenue not just by avoiding the issue but by preaching and teaching more pointedly about greed and materialism. "You can't just arbitrarily say 'please give,'" noted one pastor. "You've got to deal with the heart issues."

Issues of the heart are always the most difficult to address. They are not as easy to define as, say, a special appeal to make up a $10,000 shortfall in the annual budget. They concern values, priorities, understandings of how faith pertains to the rest of life, and the use of time and energy. It is not clear that church members themselves are eager to hear these issues being discussed. Church services provide them with a few moments to escape from work. It would be unsettling to have the preacher talking about how to be *more faithful* in the workplace. Or church members feel that as long as the pastor preaches on stewardship once a year, nothing more should be said about money. That Sunday may, in fact, be a good one to sleep late.

Or consider ministering to members' work lives. Where do most church members get the money they give to their churches? From working. A full understanding of giving would thus need to include the relationship between faith and work. Yet, for many church members, giving and work are in completely separate mental cabinets. Consequently, they are quite content with the way the church ministers to their work lives *because* it doesn't challenge them to think about anything. The lay chair of one congregation provided a fairly typical response when we asked him how his church ministers to his work life. "It's a place of refuge," he said, "a place to get away from the day-to-day struggles."

It is also hard to discuss issues of the heart when clergy assume that they and their parishioners are already doing the best they can. Many clergy, it appears, have implicitly accepted the norm that people will give only about 2 percent of their income. To ask for more would be unthinkable. Yet, with rising fixed costs, the churches are not going to be able to do as much as they have in the past unless they do ask for more.

If it is true that many church members are happy with things the way they are and are doing the best they can, it is also true that laity too are becoming more aware that the churches need to be addressing a wide range of concerns about work, money, and personal finances rather than worrying only about boosting plate offerings.

Church people are generally quite loyal to their congregations and to their pastors, not wanting to appear critical or unhappy. At first they give the impression that everything is rosy—that the church is meeting their needs and that they are fully satisfied with its programs. Once they talk for a few minutes, however, their unrealized desires start pouring out, and these comments often stand in sharp contrast to what the clergy understand to be happening in their congregations.

At a suburban parish in New Jersey, for example, the priest we spoke to told us that the parish has no trouble providing all the programs its members want. He thought the parish was in relatively good financial shape; though reluctant to disclose any of the details of its budget, he assured us that everyone was happy with the way things were going. We then spoke to a woman who had been a member of the parish for fifteen years and who was the lay director of one of the church's main ministries to the community. The priest, in fact, recommended that we talk to her. She told us she was generally happy with the church. However, she also said the church did nothing to minister to her in her work life. Asked to explain, she said, "I have more need for Bible study, for prayer groups, and it's not available to me." She also said the parish had provided her with no homilies, classes, workshops, or other settings in which to think more carefully about the relationship between her faith and her money. This woman was particularly interested in what the church could do to help the poor, and she was convinced that the church was playing a useful role in the community. But when asked if the current programs were adequate, she contradicted the priest and said they were not. She also pointed to several educational programs that had been canceled for lack of funds, inadequate facilities for the church's youth program, the need for an associate pastor, and problems in keeping contributions equal to levels of inflation.

At a Methodist church in another state, a woman complained that her church "talks the talk but does not walk the walk." She said there has been a huge emphasis in recent years on putting up a new building, but the church does nothing to minister to the working experiences of its members. "You have to go do a song and dance" to get the clergy to do anything, she observed. And does the church help her understand money in a more godly way? "No, they just want some of it!" She could be dismissed as an isolated malcontent. She is, however, a twenty-three-year member of her congregation and presently serves on two conference-wide committees.

Other lay leaders who were reluctant to express dissatisfaction nevertheless pointed out that their churches do little to help them understand work, money, and personal finances from a Christian perspective. "It would be nice if it did," said one man. "Naw, not really," said another, "it just sorta helps me worry less." Another mused that it had been several years since he'd heard any preaching about finances. Still another said it would help young families in his church a lot if some workshops dealing with problems of work and money could be started.

When I say *issues of the heart*, it is easy of course to misunderstand what the term means. Clergy often talk about the need to give money "from the heart" or make the assumption that if a person's "heart is right," then that person will give generously. In this interpretation, issues of the heart are equivalent to the core of Christian faith itself and are assumed to be linked automatically with giving. The problem is that the issues that really concern people—the "issues of *their* hearts"—are still ignored. Only by identifying these issues can their implications for church giving be considered. I can illustrate this point with two examples.

First, take the issue of unemployment. If a church's focus is only on giving, then the unemployed become irrelevant to most giving campaigns. They have no income, so—even if their heart is right with God—they can be of no help in balancing the budget. At a time when a growing number of middle-class church members are unemployed, the church must recognize that losing one's job is very much an "issue of the heart." The church can minister to this issue by providing support groups for the unemployed, initiating a job referral network, or sponsoring a résumé writing workshop. In doing so, it relates faith to an important issue of the heart rather than letting this issue be defined strictly as a secular or workplace concern. A by-product of such support efforts, moreover, may be that the church's own budget benefits insofar as these people are able to retrain and find new employment.

The second example concerns soliciting volunteers for church programs. This issue surfaced in a number of the congregations we studied. In the typical scenario, a church has a paid staff member to run, say, a youth program, but finances force this position to be cut (or, alternatively, the need is there but cannot be filled). The pastor appeals to the congregation to take up the slack by volunteering to run the youth program. Nobody has time, so the program is canceled. The church survives but with one less program. The issue of the heart, however, is not addressed: Why were there no volunteers? Probably because parishioners (especially women) are already working longer hours at their jobs and have no energy left to volunteer. Were the church to address this issue, it would probably find considerable enthusiasm for a discussion group on how to juggle careers and family. Perhaps the youth group was less urgent than this new area of ministry.

I am not suggesting that addressing the broad range of middle-class concerns more effectively will necessarily solve the churches' present financial problems. Religious leaders will still have to be prudent managers of limited resources. They will have to make fewer dollars go further. But it is abundantly clear that priorities—and reasons for giving—will also need to be examined carefully. If a growing share of church budgets goes to staff salaries, fringe benefits, and maintenance costs, is this what parishioners are willing to support? If a declining share of church budgets is available to help the poor, is this compatible with church teachings? And if middle-class church members are going to add more than a few dollars a year to their annual giving, what rethinking of their values is going to be needed?

## "GOD SPOKE TO MY HEART"

I can perhaps illustrate the kinds of issues that churches need to be addressing more effectively by considering one person whose church has been challenging him to think hard about the full range of issues concerning his faith's relationship to his work, his money, his charitable giving, and his involvement in the church. Jareé Johnson, thirty, has been a member of an independent African American church for the past eight years. He is an electrical engineer and holds an elected office on the administrative board of the church. In addition to volunteering his time, Jareé donates money to the church regularly. Doing so is part of his understanding of stewardship. But stewardship is a meaningful concept for him because it guides his thinking about money in a much broader way. Stewardship, he says, means "setting priorities; not blowing your money." Indeed, his understanding of stewardship has turned his life around. "When I first got out of school," he recalls, "I went out and bought a sports car and bought a bunch of suits and charged my credit cards up and did all those things you're not supposed to be doing." But now he lives differently. "I'm out of debt now. The church teaches priorities. God's word teaches about priorities. It also tells me to put myself in a different perspective."

Jareé talks about giving, therefore, within a more encompassing perspective. "I believe very strongly in faith in God and trust in God for my needs. I trust him for my job. I've trusted him for promotions. I've trusted him to meet my needs and so I believe very strongly that God will do that, that he promised it. And I also believe that God wants us to give. In America, we don't appreciate just how blessed we are. My girlfriend works a lot in China and in India doing missionary work. You go over there and what suffices as prosperity is abject poverty here. And that's how most of the world lives. I think the church has done a lot to bring that sort of a worldwide perspective back into my consciousness. It's helped me to be grateful for what I have, instead of complaining about what I don't have."

When Jareé gives money to the church, he is able to withstand the messages that tell him to keep it all for himself. In fact, one of his friends constantly gives him these other messages. "Tell all these parasites to get off you, man, just keep your money and take care of yourself." When that happens, Jareé says his first reaction is to feel stupid. But then: "I really feel like God spoke to my heart. It wasn't like an audible voice, but in my conscience it came up, what about all the people who've been helped? What about the marriages that have been restored? What about trying to help kids in the inner city? And some of that stuff just takes money. I had to think about it. What price do you put on that? What's it worth to be able to pick up the phone at two in the morning and call somebody and say, hey, I'm really having a tough night, can I talk to you about something? I mean, how do you put a value on that? I really began to have peace about it."

Jareé gives his church a lot of credit for teaching him to think more wisely about his financial responsibilities. "By teaching on finances," he says, "the church helps me to handle money responsibly. It's intelligent to put money in the bank for long-term savings. It's important to share and to be thankful and to be responsible for what we have. And I think my character was enhanced too. Because the church taught about having a more Godlike character, I think my finances are a lot better today than they were."

He also sees an integral relationship between his involvement in the church and his work. Like many people, he describes the church as a refuge from the turmoil of the workplace, but he views the church in a more active role as well; its teachings help him to be a better employee by giving him emotional stability, and he is able to talk freely about his work with other people in his church. Talking about his work helps him deal with the stress but also prevents him from becoming side-tracked by petty issues that are not central to his values. He says the preaching, teaching, and interaction he receives at church help especially in dealing with difficult ethical issues at work. "The continual preaching," he explains, "keeps correct behavior before our eyes." For instance, "you get the expense voucher in and you may have spent more money than you're supposed to, and you can fudge the form if you want to get your money back. But I think being in the church brings it to your conscience that lying is wrong. Even if it may cost you a buck or two on your expense, you don't fudge the forms."

Jareé admits the church could do more; for instance, he would like to have a fellowship group that met for prayer once a week at work, and he says the church would like to start a shelter for battered women and become more active in drug counseling if the money were available. The church has, however, actively worked to address a wide range of economic concerns. The singles group has sponsored a series of studies and brought in some outside speakers to talk about faith and personal finances. Every week the church provides food for children who live in low-income housing nearby. It sponsors a basketball camp for the children as well. Most of the church members are middle class, but these members are ministered to by having low-income and homeless people in the church as well.

Dealing with finances, work, and charitable giving in the fullest possible way has not put Jareé's church on easy street. If anything, the financial pressures have been all the more severe. Last winter, the roof started leaking and the church did everything it could—from praying to selling trash bags—to raise the $22,000 needed for repairs. Sunday-school rooms are overcrowded, and there is a real need for a youth director. But Jareé insists that building "Godlike character," not buildings, is the important priority. He's seen religious leaders using "gimmicks" to manipulate people into giving. That worries him. He hopes God allows his church to have a larger building some day, but in the meantime, he is thankful that the church is doing what it does to keep its members' priorities straight.

If this is what it means to address issues of the heart, then surely all churches must be doing this. Many of them are. But churches always work within the constraints of the culture that envelops them. Pressed with financial burdens, it is all too easy for clergy to deal with these burdens strictly as business matters, just as if

their organizations were selling life insurance or potato chips—"easier to be pragmatic than spiritual," as one pastor put it. Knowing that money is a sensitive issue,
clergy are often reluctant to talk about it at all or do so only in terms of raising
funds for specific needs. Stewardship is easiest to address by asking people to fill
out pledge cards—or by preaching vaguely about God's creation—rather than by
talking about family budgets, financial responsibility, advertising, and consumerism. And the relationship between faith and work is more comfortably handled by offering people a time on Sunday mornings to escape their work than by
challenging them to think harder about their priorities.

The churches' shortcomings in dealing with these difficult issues are clearly evident when comments are solicited from people in the pews. Nationally, only 13
percent of working Americans say they have thought a great deal about the relationship between their religious values and their personal finances in the past year,
and among church members this figure rises only to 20 percent. Preaching about
stewardship is one of the standard ways in which clergy attempt to stimulate such
thinking. Yet only 40 percent of church members have heard even one sermon on
stewardship in the past year.[15]

The comments of individual members are also revealing. A Latina woman who
has served for two years as president of her parish, for example, said flatly that her
church "doesn't help" her in figuring out how to use her money wisely. She said she
would welcome financial advice and instructions on financial planning. At another
church, a parishioner described a number of "gimmicks" that had been used in
recent years to increase giving—selling family photos to members of the congregation, putting on festivals, even selling alcoholic beverages. She thought these
approaches were inappropriate, ineffective, and did more to hurt the church's image
than to help its finances. She thought the clergy needed to rethink their whole
approach to stewardship.

Getting people to think harder about the implications of their faith for their
finances and their work is something churches should be doing, most clergy would
probably say, even if they were not pressed by financial burdens themselves. But in
a time of deepening economic crisis, the churches could also serve themselves by
fostering more serious attention to these matters. At least, the evidence we have
from surveys suggests that serious reflection on economic matters goes hand in
hand with higher levels of giving. For instance, church members who have thought
a great deal within the past year about the relationship between religious values and
their personal finances gave $1,526 on average to religious organizations, compared
with only $625 among those who had thought a little about this relationship. And
by a substantial margin ($1,353 to $547), those who had heard a sermon in the past
year about stewardship gave more than those who had not heard a sermon on this
topic.[16] The fact that a majority of church members do not think about the impli-

cations of their faith for their finances and do not hear sermons about stewardship is, therefore, a significant part of the churches' present financial woes.

## THE ROLE OF THE CLERGY

These problems are not entirely the clergy's to solve, of course. But clergy are there to lead. They have more information about the church's needs as an organization than anyone else. They are likely to have access to a great deal of information about their parishioners that comes to them in confidence. And they, of all people, should have a vision of what the church could be doing to minister to its members and the wider community.

This point was driven home to me as I considered the comments of one pastor and then those of one of his deacons. The pastor could recite budget figures and cost estimates in detail, and he spoke about the various ways in which the church was trying to minister to people and his desires for expanding these ministries. The deacon, in contrast, said there were problems but generally wanted us to know that he was happy, however things came out. Asked how the church ministered to him, he said it helped him to pray and to think harder about his decisions. When asked what else the church could be doing to minister to his work or his finances, he responded, "That's a great question. I can't think of anything right now!"

Parishioners of course know what their *own* needs are. Generally they understand these needs much better than the clergy do. But parishioners are for the most part unskilled in thinking about how the church might make more effective appeals. They are much more likely to see the problems of the church as unsolvable. One man, when asked what should be done, said he guessed people just needed to give more. But then he chuckled and said, "With the economy the way it is and a lot of people out of work, that would be tough."

Parishioners are at an even greater disadvantage in churches where the clergy refuse to divulge financial details. These situations are rare but not nonexistent. Several of the clergy we spoke to were reluctant to give us copies of their budgets, and a few were willing to speak only in general terms about church finances. Some of the laity we contacted also expressed dissatisfaction with the way clergy kept things to themselves. The lay chair of one congregation, for example, complained that she had asked repeatedly for an annual accounting of where the money went, but the pastor "always gave his summations in verbal form." She added, "When you start bringing in $8,000 every Sunday, that's $32,000 a month, or more than $300,000 a year. I wanted to see where that money went, but reports never materialized."

Curiously, the clergy have probably been doing a better job as financial leaders than they have as spiritual leaders. Although stories of fraud and mismanagement occasionally make headlines, these cases are actually quite rare. Most clergy have an excellent grasp of their churches' budgets, know where the money goes, and understand clearly what financial needs they are facing in the next two or three years. They are realistic, able to tighten their belts to make ends meet, and generally able to draw on expertise among the laity in their congregations. By trial and error, they have picked up useful skills in raising funds. For example, studies show that parishioners would give more generously if they knew what the churches do with their money; accordingly, many clergy have started special fund-raising campaigns targeted toward clear, specific needs such as a new roof or a new furnace. In all these ways, clergy defy popular stereotypes that make them out to be dreamers who are too idealistic to balance their budgets. Yet they show less aptitude in relating finances to faith itself.

The problem is not that clergy are unable to talk about tithing or stewardship or the temptations associated with greed and overwork. As I show in later chapters, clergy can talk with considerable sophistication on all these issues. The problem is that clergy seldom have a clear understanding of the way in which their parishioners actually think about money, work, and other economic issues. Clergy can make an appeal for money, therefore, but are less able to minister to the pain and confusion that really concern their parishioners. As a result, the churches use their middle-class members largely as a money source, siphoning off token contributions that remain largely unrelated to the daily lives of these members.

Collecting money in this way has been sufficient to run many churches for many years. The present crisis can be weathered, perhaps, by doing more of the same. But it also presents an opportunity for the churches to do something more. If they need to look earnestly at giving patterns, then they can also challenge parishioners to think harder about what their money means to them, how to manage the other 98 percent of their money more effectively, how to cope with the demands of the workplace, and how to minister more effectively in the workplace.

What should the clergy be doing? A prominent view is that the clergy should focus mainly on initiating programs. The logic here is that people will give more if there are programs that appeal to them. An effective pastor is thus a person who can sense rising needs and start programs to meet those needs. This strategy works well when resources are already plentiful because there is room to experiment. But when resources are scarce, congregations are likely to find themselves in a cycle of diminishing expectations. People give less, so programs are cut, which further reduces members' interest in giving, and so on. The pastor of an Assemblies of God church on the West Coast said this was precisely what happened when his church was forced to cut its staff a year ago: "It's kind of a catch-22; when you cut staff, then you don't have as much service available to people, which is kind of a spiral down if you don't stop it."

Given the emphasis that has been placed on pastors as program leaders, the view I want to suggest is likely to seem unlikely. Nevertheless, it is consistent with the longer-term mission of the church. That is, I aim to reexamine the ways in which faith and economic issues are *understood* and, on that basis, to reconceive how these topics are dealt with in preaching, teaching, pastoral counseling, and discussion sessions. The solution is *not*, as many of the people we interviewed suggested, simply to talk more about the financial needs of the church—"becoming more vocal about it," "keeping it on people's minds," "preaching about it more often." In fact, that solution is likely to have mixed results. In my survey of American working men and women, 30 percent said they would actually give less money if the churches talked more about finances than they do now.

Again, then, the answer is not to increase the quantity of appeals for money but to reconsider the quality of these appeals, that is, to talk about the broader relationships between faith, work, money, giving, the poor, and economic justice. To do so is not necessarily an easy task. It is nevertheless one that most clergy can warm to. They recognize that their ministries should focus on these deeper issues of the heart. To focus narrowly on church finances, in contrast, is something most of them would rather avoid. "I'd rather not think about church finances," an Episcopal priest told us. "They're the least favorite part of my job," lamented another.

## LOOKING TO THE FUTURE

Unless things change, the present crisis will only deepen in the future because the programs, remodeling, and maintenance that are being foregone today will only make it harder for the churches to compete successfully for adherents and donors in the years ahead. In the words aptly spoken by one pastor, churches "will start dropping like flies" over the next two decades unless serious action is taken now to deal with the economic problems that are already apparent and to educate clergy and laity to address the more drastic problems that will appear in the years ahead.

If the present crisis were attributable to a short-term downturn in the economy, the churches might weather the storm simply by battening down the hatches for a couple of years until the sun comes out. Clergy, however, are reluctant to say their problems are rooted in a short-term recession. Their experience demonstrates—as have some statistical studies—that giving is not that closely linked to monthly income: people drop $20 in the plate whether they are earning $5,000 a month or

$6,000.[17] Where the problems are clearly aggravated by the larger economy, they are also of longer duration, for example, layoffs in the lumber industry or in pharmaceuticals from which those industries might never recover. And other problems, such as declining memberships, rising costs, or a need for new buildings, are not going to be solved by short-term upswings in the economy.

The most farsighted religious leaders believe the present crisis may never be fully resolved but that it will necessitate a long-term shift in the way that churches conceive themselves. Rather than paying for expensive auditoriums that seat thousands of people for a few hours a week, churches may be forced to downscale, existing largely as fictional collectivities and doing their work mostly in small fellowship groups that can meet in living rooms and basements. Electronic networks may be another way of curbing costs. Instead of meeting at all, people can pray with each other by telephone or hold Bible studies by conference calls. Hotlines can be used to screen parishioners' requests, saving professional counselors' time by siphoning off all but the most urgent messages.

These cost-cutting tactics, however, do not satisfy the continuing need to address the issues of the heart. Hard times have always been thought by prophets and sages to produce deeper faith. Thus, there is an opportunity in the present crisis to think more deeply about the needs and desires of parishioners and about ways to challenge them not only to give more generously but to live in a more godly manner.

# two

# ANATOMY OF THE CRISIS

Viewed from a distance, the crisis facing America's churches is one that concerns them collectively and generally. It is a problem that in one way or another touches the ministry of every church. Some may survive longer—and prosper—by siphoning off donations that might have gone to other churches in their community or by temporarily enlisting the enthusiastic support of the previously unchurched. But the churches have always been strongest when there has been strength across the board: when Catholics and Protestants alike were strong and when small churches and large ones, or liberal congregations and fundamentalist ones, were all contributing something to the overall mix.

Still, painting with a broad brush severely limits our capacity to understand what is going on in *particular* churches and thus to grasp fully how the various segments of American religion are being affected by the present crisis. Many of the problems remain invisible to the view one gains from a distance. They can only be seen up close because different churches are experiencing the crisis differently and because pastors are approaching the problems from their own points of view, often without benefit of support and counsel from others.

What we must do, then, is to gain a clearer sense of the anatomy of the present crisis by examining how it is evident in several specific congregations. Such an examination will disabuse us of the idea that only some churches are suffering while others—perhaps those with the best leadership or the most gifted fund-raisers—are doing quite well. The problems are simply different, never absent. Once we have taken the pulse of several particular churches, we can turn to an analysis of the problem from the standpoint of the various people involved and the particular issues that most concern them, looking at what we know about church members themselves, at the ways clergy perceive the problem, and then at the specific ways in which churches are attempting to minister to the economic lives of their parishioners. This analysis will help to identify the nature of the present crisis more clearly and thereby to offer some suggestions about what may be done to address it.

Of the churches we studied, I have chosen five to describe in some detail. They represent much of the variety evident in American Christianity today—variety in size, confessional heritage, denomination, ethnicity, and region. A close look at these congregations shows not only that congregations are economic communities but also that their programs and finances depend heavily on pastoral leadership and on the ways in which clergy understand the relationships between faith and the economic circumstances of their parishioners' lives.

## CORNERSTONE BIBLE CHURCH

Founded in 1951, Cornerstone Bible Church has been in existence long enough to be well established in its community, a middle-class suburb on the edge of a small city near the Atlantic coast. In many ways, however, it is almost new and still struggling for its life. Like many small churches, its fortunes have waxed and waned considerably, depending largely on the energy of its pastor and whether two or three new families could be recruited to replace ones who had moved away. During its first two decades, the membership gradually increased to the point that the congregation was able to construct a large, contemporary A-frame sanctuary a mile from its original building and to hope for further growth. That hope, however, was not realized. For more than a decade the church suffered from what, in retrospect, appears to have been inadequate leadership. Some of the members realized the problem at the time, and many left rather than try to go against the pastor. Then, four years ago, there was a serious fight in the congregation over an action of the pastor that some people describe as immoral and others as simply bad judgment.

From more than 100, the membership dwindled to sixteen. Faced with a $2,500-a-month mortgage on a building capable of seating 400, the people had no idea what to do. When the pastor left, they called on another pastor in the area to supply preaching free of charge. Then they hired a part-time pastor, who soon left, then another one, who also left. Two years ago they felt financially secure enough to call their present pastor, Rev. John Higgins, and since that time he has built the membership back up to around 100. He has done so mainly by canvassing the neighborhood to find young couples with children who are currently without a church but want one. Cornerstone offers them conservative evangelical preaching, classes, and home fellowship groups but makes few other demands on their time and tries hard to shed stereotypical images of what "church" should be about. Pastor Higgins says his attitude is to follow the Bible, but if the Bible is silent, then feel free to do things differently.

He considers the church to be breaking even now. But it does so only because half its land is supplied free of charge by the utility company that owns it, and because the associate pastor works for nothing, earning a living through a second job. Moreover, Higgins himself has no college or seminary training, so his own salary is substantially lower than those of other clergy in the area. Even so, Higgins says there are many times when he simply doesn't know where the resources are going to come from. As an independent church, Cornerstone has no denomination on which to call for financial assistance. His main hope is to draw in new members through aggressive evangelism in the neighborhood, "maxing out" with 500 members. But with a full schedule of his own, relying solely on volunteers for music and Christian education, and faced with competition from several megachurches[1] in the community, he feels he may be fortunate to see any growth at all. Meanwhile, a large empty space at the rear of the sanctuary from which the pews have been removed symbolizes some of what the church is experiencing. Higgins says he sometimes thinks the building has become a "noose" around the congregation's neck, killing it financially and keeping it from doing anything else in the community.

The church is also facing serious needs among its members. Most of the men are college graduates (some have graduate degrees) in middle-management positions at large chemical, aircraft, and engineering firms in the area, and three-quarters of the women work, many as secretaries and office assistants. But average family incomes are below the state median, and layoffs are all too common. The members who left four years ago were in their forties and fifties, so they could contribute financially at a higher level. Most of the new families who have started attending in the past two years are in their thirties. With small children and less established in their jobs, they contribute less. Most of them live from one paycheck to the next, saving nothing and having to struggle to pay their bills. Many come to the church deeply worried about their jobs. Some come after their jobs have been terminated. Every once in a while Pastor Higgins finds out about some serious need. For example, one couple with a small baby were down to their last ten dollars and had no money to buy food, so the church gave them $75 dollars from its deacon's fund.

Fortunately, that sort of need doesn't arise very often. If it did, the church would be unable to respond. Mostly what it tries to provide is reassurance that God will somehow provide. Higgins says he doesn't understand money very well but just assumes God will take care of his needs. Occasionally someone in the congregation will get a better job or an unexpected check will come in the mail, which affirms his belief that things will work out. He also tries to teach his congregants the doctrine of Christian stewardship, explaining to them that they are not the owners of God's wealth but God's managers while they are here on earth. As managers themselves, they understand what that means. They know it is wrong to go gambling or to do crazy things with their money. But for Pastor Higgins the important teaching is not so much to manage prudently but to detach, that is, worry less because God is ultimately in charge. It frustrates him to think that his congregants are racking up huge bills on their credit cards instead of being more careful with their money. At some point in the future, he hopes to think more about finances and try to counsel his members on this topic. At this point, though, he focuses more on getting them to feel better about having, or not having, money. He treats his appeals for the church the same way, trying to deemphasize money itself and argue for a broader view of stewardship. Thus, he tells people they should give only if God moves their heart. He dislikes fund-raising and tries to let the church's needs be known obliquely, for example, by mentioning them in a prayer. Anyway, he says, it's the treasurer's job to worry about finances, not his.

There are serious needs in the community surrounding the church. Especially in the winter, outsiders call Pastor Higgins and beg for food or financial help. Usually he tries to respond, but he doesn't offer them money unless people come directly to him. Some of the other churches in town have been trying to organize programs to help the homeless. Cornerstone does well to take care of its own. Its philosophy of separation from nonbelievers helps legitimate focusing on its own needs first. But Higgins would like to do more. He knows God wants the church to help the needy, but right now he feels he's doing all he can.

Cornerstone is typical of many small congregations. Its members are quite loyal to the church because they feel a sense of personal responsibility for it and they know the pastor and count other members among their friends. There are reasons in many of these congregations to be optimistic. People take heart in the fact that attendance is substantially up compared with a few years ago, and they can point to ways in which the church has made a difference in the lives of some of its members. Yet churches like Cornerstone are facing difficult economic needs. They often struggle to meet stiff mortgage payments or to respond when major repairs to their buildings are needed. Their pastors work long hours at extremely low wages. And the church may have little sense of how to increase levels of giving or how to minister more effectively to the financial concerns, work problems, and associated family pressures that its members are experiencing.

## SAINT ANDREW'S EPISCOPAL CHURCH

Saint Andrew's Episcopal Church sits magnificently on the corner of two tree-lined avenues about five blocks from the center of a small city on the West Coast. Its red-brick exterior is highlighted by a large wooden cross above the front entrance. The sanctuary is to the left; an office and educational wing spans the corner to the right. The building, erected in 1938 and modernized in the 1960s, exudes elegance and stability but also blends nicely with the informality of its surroundings. Stained glass and gothic arches are nowhere in evidence. The roofline is contemporary. Yellow, red, and green banners brighten the interior. Dark walnut pews and wood paneling add an atmosphere of dignity and restraint.

By most standards, Saint Andrew's is flourishing. Founded in 1851, the church is one of the oldest in the state. It has enjoyed the patronage of some of the city's wealthiest families. Some made fortunes in the logging and lumber industry; others have been prominent in banking and medicine. Currently the church roster consists mainly of professionals such as lawyers and teachers, managers still associated with lumber or with some of the newer electronics firms, owners of small businesses, environmentalists, and a few students. There are about 800 in all. Like many Episcopal churches, the membership declined during the 1970s.[2] But for the past ten years or so, that trend has been reversed. Currently about 250 adults and nearly 100 children attend services on an average Sunday, up about 50 percent from a decade ago. Each week there are three services, an early eucharist following the traditional rite and attended mainly by older parishioners, a family service with special events for children, and a later service attended mostly by young-to-middle-aged adults. The congregation prides itself on its diversity, reflected not only in the variety of its services but also in the fact that it was the first Episcopal congregation in the state to employ a woman priest, in the fact that members would not be likely to make an issue of homosexuality if the topic arose, and in the fact that it embraces a wide variety of political views. With an annual budget of $200,000, it has been able to pay its rector a good salary and support a number of other programs.

But appearances can be deceiving. During the past ten years, demands on the church's resources have risen dramatically. Part of this rise stems from increasing membership itself. Numbers have grown, but with more young families and a stag-nant economy, giving has not risen apace. Staff time is stretched to the limit as a result. The rector, supported only by his wife (who earns a part-time salary from the church) and an intern (who works unpaid), finds it difficult to minister ade-quately to the hundreds of families who attend faithfully, let alone the larger num-ber whom he would like to draw back into the congregation. Another problem is that the physical plant needs to be renovated and expanded. More than twenty years have passed since any major work was done, and the congregation fears its present growth will be interrupted unless it can provide more adequate seating and classroom space.

The most serious demand on the church's resources, however, has come from the changing economic circumstances of the city itself. Things are not as bad as in many "rustbelt" cities in the upper Midwest or on the East Coast, but the logging industry has been in a long-term slump as a result of Japanese competition,[3] avia-tion and electronics firms have experienced serious fluctuations, and unemploy-ment has been above the national average. The downtown area has shifted from an economy based on shops, small businesses, and corporate headquarters to one com-posed mainly of government offices. Jobs in this sector grew during the 1970s but have experienced major cutbacks during the past decade. Most who have retained their jobs commute in from the suburbs and care little about the economic climate of the downtown area except for the impact of rising crime rates on their personal security. Those who continue to live in the center city work mainly at low-paying service and clerical jobs. Homelessness abounds, as do other problems such as chronic unemployment, inadequate funding for schools and community services, and a growing need for day-care and latchkey programs. With fewer resources available from public agencies, a growing share of these services has been placed on the downtown churches.

Rector Stuart Morgan believes deeply that the church should be actively involved in trying to meet these needs. The Episcopal church, he observes, has a long history of involvement with social concerns. Yet when he came to Saint Andrew's eleven years ago, virtually nothing was being done to help the needy other than making some token donations to secular agencies and encouraging members to volunteer through programs sponsored by other churches. His own conscience has been pricked by needy families coming to him for assistance and by reading newspaper stories about the homeless in his community. He remembers a working-class church he attended while he was in seminary: There, people would pray openly about being out of a job or homeless people would join the service and ask for help, and people would respond right there ("You can stay at my place tonight"). His goal is to get people at Saint Andrew's to relate their faith that directly to economic needs in their community.

He has had some success getting his parishioners involved. Recently, for example, the church has joined a coalition of other churches and agencies in the area to help feed and house the homeless. Saint Andrew's takes responsibility for the project twice a year for a week at a time. In its first week, it housed forty homeless people in the ten classrooms in its basement and provided them with food. Rector Morgan and a lay committee divided the work into 175 tasks and were able to involve approximately 100 people from the congregation in performing these tasks. There is also a Social Aid and Awareness Committee that congregants support as part of their regular giving to the church and with some special offerings for the needy.

The prevailing mood of the congregation, however, is one of concern about the economic well-being of its middle-class members themselves. When people talk about economic issues, they focus less on the plight of the poor than on whether their own standard of living is adequate or not. People worry, for example, about being stuck geographically because they know it would cost them more to live elsewhere. The older ones wonder whether their savings will last as long as they do. Middle-aged parents worry about adult children who are struggling to establish themselves financially. They also worry about meeting their mortgage payments and how to afford a new car. Several families have been hurt by cutbacks in the wood-products business. One man was laid off by a local television station and still does not have work seven months later. Another man recently finished a Ph.D. only to discover that managing an apartment complex was the best job he could find.

What aggravates the situation is that middle-class Episcopalians have been conditioned to keep their fears mostly to themselves. At parties, Morgan observes, a dozen people will be standing around in the kitchen ("always the kitchen, never the living room"), and once in a while he will hear a comment about having enough money for retirement, or perhaps a discussion of how much it costs to send kids to college. But for the most part, he says, "Episcopalians tend not to express their financial concerns very openly." Even when they pray during the Sunday services, they are much more likely to pray for the dead than they are for some aspect of their work. It's not "dignified" to pray about money, work, or even unemployment. Thus, serious financial difficulties are often kept secret from friends in the church. Morgan finds out about them only when people are faced with such acute distress that they come to him for counseling. Otherwise, he knows far more about the health, addictions, and domestic squabbles of his parishioners than he does about their finances.

Morgan also admits that few of his congregants seem interested in genuinely relating their economic concerns to their faith. Instead, parishioners seem to divide their lives into two compartments, separated chronologically as much as psychologically. During the first half of their lives they focus on material success, assuming that spirituality is something to be taken seriously only in old age. Then in their later years, they may indeed become more interested in spirituality but are comfortable enough economically that faith does not truly influence their thinking about financial issues. The Episcopal church, Morgan says, reinforces this separation when it makes faith "ethereal and eternal" rather than something of practical relevance in everyday life.[4]

In Morgan's view, the solution to the problem is simple—deceptively simple. If people would get involved in caring for the needy, they would realize how privileged they are and worry less about themselves. Getting people to back off from the "selfish, greedy, consumer thing that we live out in this country," he says, should be the top priority. And that is where helping the poor can make a difference: "When you sit down with someone who hasn't had a real meal in five days, you suddenly don't feel so sorry for yourself because cable TV went up and now you have to drop it and just go with the regular channels from your antenna; and it doesn't seem so bad driving your new car home."

He muses nostalgically about a time when he and his wife lived abroad in an underdeveloped part of the world in near poverty themselves. He says it was a liberating experience to have so little that it didn't much matter if someone broke in and stole it or not. "We would ask departing Americans for their half-empty boxes of food and flour and sugar," he recalls. "I had never been in that situation in my life, and what it showed me was we're incredibly well off. It was a glorious time of no material things." He thinks people would worry less about their own needs, and perhaps even feel less financially insecure, if they saw how poor people live.

The church would also benefit, he believes. Morgan wishes his congregants would tithe instead of giving 1 or 2 percent of their income as they do now. He knows people would have less money for themselves if they did. In fact, he strongly disagrees with preachers who see *financial gain* as a reward for tithing. But he does believe tithing is associated with worrying less about one's finances, and vice versa. Thus, seeing that poor people can get along with a lot less than middle-class people would help, he feels, in freeing up his congregants to give more generously to the church.

Somehow, though, that strategy hasn't worked. Morgan's preaching about letting go of material things sounds nice but idealistic and somehow out of touch with the way his congregants live. The few who become genuinely involved with helping the poor find their lives blessed, but make few visible changes in their own lifestyles as a result. In fact, seeing people who were once employed and successful now among the homeless does more to stir up middle-class insecurities than it does to calm them. For the majority, life is tough enough already without having to worry about the poor as well. Their marriages are at the breaking point because both spouses are working too hard to think about anything else, and they are try-ing hard just to be responsible to their families and their employers.

The church—like many mainline Protestant congregations—is thus at an impasse. While its rector emphasizes the needs of the poor, his middle-class parishioners seem to focus on themselves. Meanwhile, token help is given, but the needs of the poor become all the more serious. Less than 5 percent of the church budget goes to help the needy, and even that much generates concern because it represents a trade-off with salaries and the development program. Morgan himself is optimistic that things will improve, and he points to individual cases of needy people being helped as evidence. Yet his own comments reveal how little is being done relative to the enormous needs in the community. For example, a wealthy man who was not a member of the church recently decided to give a share of his estate to the city's poor, and in less than two months nearly $100,000 was given away. Even this much hardly made a dent in the problem, and it was ten times as much as the church donates in an entire year. For their own part, his middle-class members remain stoical, but more and more of them seem to be victims of stress and burnout.

## SAN XAVIER'S ROMAN CATHOLIC CHURCH

"It's a mixture of blacks, Poles, Vietnamese, and Hispanics, but the Hispanic pop-ulation is by far the largest." This is how Father Juan Martinez describes San Xavier's. The parish is located in a large city in the Southwest not far from the Mexican border. It is a lower-middle-class neighborhood, consisting mostly of one- and two-story apartment buildings, some modest single-family houses, and small businesses displaying Polish, Vietnamese, and Spanish names. The church itself reflects its environment. The sanctuary and bell tower are built in mission style with Romanesque arches and red tile roof. Nearby is a school for elementary students (85 percent of whom are Hispanic) and a plain brick two-story parish house. Mesquite and mulberry trees outline the property, as they do most of the neighborhood streets.

San Xavier's was started seventy years ago. The present buildings were con-structed in the 1940s. It currently ministers to about 2,500 members, judging from the number who give at least something to the church each year. On any given Sunday, about 1,700 attend services. Of this number, about 1,000 attend the Span-ish mass. There are five other masses in English and one in Vietnamese each week-end, and during the week two masses daily in English and one on Wednesday evenings in Spanish. Father Martinez regrets that most of the masses are in English because the Spanish mass on Sundays fills the entire auditorium and requires 200 folding chairs in addition. But, he explains, he is the only Mexican American on staff. The head priest is bilingual but does not preach in Spanish. Neither of the other two priests in residence speaks Spanish at all. And of the other eleven administrators and secretaries, only one of the deacons and one of the secretaries are bilingual. Nor is this parish unique. In the same diocese, Father Martinez says, there are about 700,000 Catholics, 70 percent of whom are Hispanic, and only two of the diocesan priests are Hispanic.

In the past twenty years, San Xavier's has undergone a major transition. Like the city in which it is located, where new immigrants have increased by 170 percent in the past decade, the parish has become increasingly diverse.[5] What was once a predominantly Anglo community of middle- to upper-middle-class families has now become overwhelmingly Hispanic. Though the membership count of the parish has remained constant, the composition has thus changed dramatically. The Anglos who still attend are mostly elderly women of Czech, Polish, or Yugoslavian ancestry. The Hispanics include a number of young families who are bilingual and who either grew up in the parish or moved in from a neighboring parish. The largest influx into the community, however, has been about 2,000 families from Mexico and Central America who speak no English at all. Members of these families now make up nearly a majority of those who attend services. But at least three-quarters seldom attend or never attend. Father Martinez says they do not trust the church because its leaders are predominantly Anglo and have been slow in adapting to the needs of the community.

One of the biggest irritants for Father Martinez has been the church's insistence on families registering in the parish in order to be considered members. Many of the Mexicans in the community, he explains, came to the United States illegally and are fearful of registering for this reason. It was also customary in Mexico that they would be considered a member if they simply lived in the vicinity of the church. Now, living in the shadow of San Xavier's, they see no need to register, but if they have not done so, they are rebuffed when they come to have their children baptised or to ask the priest to visit a member of their family who is ill. It has, therefore, been frustrating for Father Martinez to draw this wider population into the church.

Those who do come, though, are for the most part devout. Personal confession is still commonly practiced, nearly all coming at least once a year but many coming more often. Many come to the church daily for personal devotions, and there is overwhelming support for the church's teachings on controversial issues such as abortion and clerical celibacy.

Besides adapting to the changing ethnic composition of the community, San Xavier's is now faced with a serious financial crisis of its own. Many of the Anglos who attended the church twenty years ago were professionals, managers, and ranchers who were able to give large sums of money to the church. The current membership is composed of lower-middle-class and working-class families with total incomes of around $25,000 to $30,000 a year. They earn decent wages in construction, restaurants, landscape work, their own small businesses, or offices. Among second-generation Mexican Americans, many of the women work as nurses, paralegals, secretaries, or clerks. But few of the first-generation women feel comfortable working outside the home, and family incomes often must support two or three, or as many as four or five, children and in some cases relatives still living in Mexico. Even the most devout, therefore, are unable to support the church very well financially.

Father Martinez says his parishioners take pride in being self-sufficient and in caring for the needs within their own extended families, so they never ask the church for money. But there is a long list of families that, for one reason or another, have had to depend on the church for food. In the typical case, a woman with two or three children in tow comes to the church office while her husband is at work and asks for assistance. Someone from the church then makes a visit to their home with a bag of groceries. In many cases, these visits reveal that the family is also living in substandard housing and without electricity or water. Many more go without adequate medical care in order to make ends meet. Father Martinez would like to do more to help them. Especially for undocumented residents who cannot rely on public services, the church is the only place that can help. His resources, however, are never sufficient. Not only are finances limited but his own time, he says, could be taken up completely ministering to the poor rather than performing the other duties expected of him as a priest and teacher. In addition, many of the parish's other programs are suffering from financial problems. The school, for example, is inadequately staffed, and the buildings are beginning to fall into disrepair after nearly two decades of neglect.

The problem at San Xavier's is not entirely a function of shrinking family incomes. Father Martinez believes it also reflects the church's inability to communicate effectively and to minister to the needs of its established members. He cites the example of a woman who gave recently with heartwarming generosity and yet for a reason that he finds troubling. She had come to him after the service six months earlier, saying, "Father, give me a blessing. I want you to touch my head because I have such misfortune. I came here and I don't have a job. I have nothing. I'm suffering. I just feel like I can't make it." Then, just the week before we spoke to Father Martinez, she came again, and this time she handed him a check for $100. She had found a job and was grateful. He tried to give the money back, but she said, "No, no, no, because if I give it to God, I know he is going to give me prosperity and help me even more."

This view, he says, is quite common in his parish. People give expecting financial blessings in return. But when financial blessings do not come, they become disgruntled. They also dislike it when the church asks for special offerings. For example, there is typically a second collection, a sacrificial offering, for the nuns or the clergy or some missionary activity. People tell Father Martinez that it seems like the church does little besides ask for their money. One woman, he recalls, said, "Father, you should write on that billboard in front of the church 'All denominations welcome—especially fives, tens, and twenties!'"

For Father Martinez, then, the crisis at San Xavier's—like that at many Catholic churches—is not fundamentally economic but spiritual. The parish's economic problems are severe but symptomatic of a deeper issue. The church has desperate financial needs. It must encourage its members to give generously, even sacrificially from their meager incomes. But it must avoid making them feel that money has become the center of parish life. It must minister to their spiritual needs, giving them hope and encouragement, helping them to keep their families together and retain their jobs, and bringing them to a clearer understanding of what it means to be God's stewards. It must minister financially to the hungry and the jobless. But it also needs to focus on the struggles of its ordinary members, reminding them of the relevance of God's grace in their everyday lives.

## REDEEMER BAPTIST CHURCH

Not far from the state capitol building—in an Eastern metropolis of 300,000 people—stands a two-story, red-brick edifice that looks as if it really should be two buildings instead of one. The reason is that one half used to house the Salvation Army and the other half a Presbyterian church. Currently it is the home of Redeemer Baptist Church. Begun seventy-five years ago, it is one of the oldest black churches in the city. The pastor before the present one served the congregation for fifty-one years. During that time, the mortgage on the church building and parsonage that had been constructed in the 1920s was paid off, and then in the 1950s, when the city decided it needed the area, the present property was purchased and eventually the partition between the two buildings was removed in order to provide seating for some 800 people. The church is within view of a monument erected to commemorate the Revolutionary War and, beyond that, several high-rise office buildings that have gone up in recent years as part of the city's redevelopment plan. Adjacent to the church is a large parking lot surrounded by a seven-foot chain-link fence topped with barbed wire. In the other direction is a row of aluminum-sided duplexes built in the 1920s and, across the street, three-story apartment buildings a century old, some with shops on the ground floor. Redeemer is by no means in the worst part of town, but it is on what its pastor calls "the crusty edge."

Like many other downtown areas, the neighborhoods and businesses in the vicinity of Redeemer have been in a long-term slump. Until the 1960s, the city was relatively prosperous, but then businesses began relocating along interstate highways in the "exurban" areas. The better-paying jobs left with them. Suburban shopping malls replaced downtown department stores. Most of those who still worked in state office buildings or for the county court, the Internal Revenue Service, or several banks and insurance companies commuted into the city from seven to fifteen miles away. On the books is a twenty-year plan to revitalize the city. But little investment capital, scarce parking, few incentives for people to come into the downtown area, and high crime rates have impeded serious progress.

The clientele at Redeemer mirror some of the changes that have been taking place in the city. About 70 percent of its members are in white-collar occupations, mostly in management positions and in the professions. They hold jobs in several large brokerage firms that have national headquarters in the area, in the offices of pharmaceutical and petrochemical firms, as vice-presidents of banks, in state government, and as school administrators and teachers. The salaries are good, allowing people to live comfortably unless they lose their jobs or experience some emergency. Most of these jobs are located in suburban and exurban areas. The people generally live in single-family housing developments or condominium complexes located in the same communities as their jobs or, in the case of two-career families, located within commuting distance of both jobs or in neighborhoods selected because of schools with good reputations. Most of the women do, in fact, work outside the home, generally in service and support jobs such as computer operations, nursing, and office administration. The middle-class members, therefore, live some distance away from the church itself but commute to services because they like the pastor and the programs or, in some cases, because most of the churches located in the suburbs are composed overwhelmingly of white members. The other 30 percent are employed in blue-collar occupations, ranging from low-paying jobs in fast-food restaurants to higher-paying (but scarce) jobs as auto workers, mechanics, garbage collectors, or in construction, or are currently unemployed or retired.

Redeemer Church has been thriving in recent years. Most of the members who had drifted away during the last years of the previous pastor's tenure (when weekly attendance fell to a low of 200) have returned. About 1,500 are now on the rolls, 1,200 of whom are considered active and about 800 of whom attend regularly. Just having new leadership has helped enormously. Pastor Tom Hill, a man in his early forties, exudes energy and self-confidence. His preaching and leadership skills have won him national recognition within his denomination. The church is also a bustle of activity for special interests such as a program for youth, home Bible study groups, prayer fellowships for young mothers, missionary meetings, choir, and a new program for addicts and substance abusers modeled after Alcoholics Anonymous. On the church calendar, virtually every day of the month has at least three or four activities listed. The church is also a vibrant center of theological, social, and political discussion. Its members are perhaps best described as theological moderates, attracted by some of the newer and more liberal interpretations they hear about or read but reluctant to abandon the more conservative beliefs of their heritage. On social issues such as abortion and homosexuality they are quite conservative, but on political issues, such as banning nuclear weapons or working for economic and racial justice they would for the most part take a liberal stand.

The key to the church's success, Pastor Hill believes, is its efforts to cultivate a deep and abiding sense of trust in God. That means having faith in God and in God's purposes rather than becoming too dependent on one's own talents, career, family, or lifestyle. But it also means that the church must provide for its own. It must function like a mutual aid society, much as guilds did in the Middle Ages or as mutual-benefit insurance cooperatives did in the nineteenth century. The logic is simple: People pay to the church while they are able, and then if they ever need it, the church is there to help them. Pastor Hill explains, "We have a very large benelovent fund and the concept is if you give now while you don't need it, there will be something there when you do." He says people give liberally, believing that those who have resources should help those who don't and that they themselves may be recipients at some point in their lives. In one instance, for example, a family was about to lose its home because it couldn't meet the monthly mortgage payments. Because they were active members, the church gave them money to tide them over. In another instance, an older woman who had given faithfully to the church for fifty years was able to secure financial assistance for a daughter who was in danger of becoming homeless. She was told she had "banked" the money by giving it to the church all those years.

In recent years, despite hard times for some of its members, the church has accumulated a considerable surplus in its benevolent fund. The problem the church faces is thus not an economic shortfall, as is the case in many churches, but a crisis in deciding how to distribute its funds in a manner that is both consistent with its philosophy and agreeable to its members. Older members and those with lower incomes want to see the benevolent fund remain strong. They have contributed the most to it and have heard it defended over a longer period of time or, in the case of the lower-income members, are most likely to benefit from it. Blue-collar workers at the auto assembly plant, for example, are constantly worried that the plant will close, leaving them with few resources besides the church. Middle-class members, in contrast, are expected to pay more into the fund because they can afford to, but they are also least likely to benefit from it. Their jobs are more secure. They are also more likely to be transferred to another part of the country, meaning the end of the church's obligation to them. What has been described as a growing gap between the black middle class and the black working class (or poverty class) is thus played out within the church itself.[6] On the one hand, black churches find themselves ministering to a new middle class that, as C. Eric Lincoln has argued, may be part of the larger "conservative, consumer-oriented body of Americans who have made it by struggle and effort and hold to a spectrum of values which sets them apart from the masses and makes them candidates for even a higher rung of social and economic status."[7] On the other hand, the church also finds itself dealing with what Harold Dean Trulear has described as an "underclass" that is increasingly depicted as an "other" in American society.[8] The church's teachings about helping those less fortunate than oneself, of course, help to temper the potential for conflict between the two groups. But church leaders are often placed in an awkward position.

Pastor Hill, for example, wants to retain the logic of a benevolent association because it encourages giving as well as loyalty to the church and because it is indeed a way to provide for the needy. Because he is the person with authority for deciding how such funds are to be used, its presence reinforces his power in the congregation. Yet he also recognizes that the economic health of the church depends heavily on the contributions of its middle-class members, and their interests include youth programs, music, better Sunday school classes, and improvements to the physical facilities. Even ideas about helping the needy sometimes shift away from helping poor families within the congregation to doing more to minister to families outside the congregation and to participate more actively in wider community efforts. Pastor Hill—like the pastors of many black churches—is thus faced with a constant dilemma about how best to administer the benevolent fund and, in the process, how to keep peace among the various factions in the church.[9]

## GRACE CHURCH

From a distance it looks like a shopping mall, a sports complex, or the campus of a community college. There is an auditorium large enough to seat 2,000 comfortably, an office building that includes a small chapel and learning center, and six two-story educational buildings. All have been built within the past ten years, their contemporary lines giving them the appearance of still being virtually new. Only the name, spelled out in two-foot letters above the front entrance, indicates that this is a church.

Grace Church is one of a growing number of "megachurches" in the United States. Like others in the Midwest, South, and Southwest, it has grown rapidly in recent years. Its membership now stands at 7,000 and its average weekend attendance at around 5,000. It started from scratch in the late 1960s when an Assemblies of God minister came to town and started holding revival services. The community was ready. A small city in the Midwest, it was populated by semiretired farmers who still owned their land and drove out from town to oversee the work; a growing cadre of agribusiness managers; petroleum executives and oil workers; the faculty and administrators of a large state university; and the doctors, lawyers, teachers, hairdressers, and fast-food operators who provided services to the rest. They were part of the Bible belt. Most believed in God, just as their parents and their grandparents had. They were Baptists and Methodists with a few Presbyterians, Disciples of Christ, and Roman Catholics mixed in, all members of established churches. They were political conservatives who supported Lyndon Johnson's war in Vietnam, sent their boys off to fight, and disapproved of the campus protests they read about in the newspapers. With hippies and drugs coming into their own community, they hungered for something solid to believe in. Rev. Paul Fisher provided it. He preached not only repentance but a close personal walk with God. The charismatic gifts of speaking in tongues, prophesy, and the ability to interpret divine revelation were offered as evidence of God's love. People quietly slipped away from their churches to join the new revival. Others who hadn't been to church since they were children came as well.

The church has experienced steady growth. Early on, its leaders decided that their affiliation with the Assemblies of God was more a disadvantage than an advantage. The clergy wanted freedom to develop their own plans without having denominational officials looking over their shoulders. Congregants were from so many different backgrounds that many did not feel comfortable with this denomination's official views. So the church disaffiliated itself and became "nondenominational." Its leaders and publications make a point of stressing this word. They also dance around other labels, preferring a mixture of terms, including ones they have invented themselves. For example, they use phrases such as "evangelical-charismatic," "spirit-filled," "new wave," "third wave," and "radically sold out." Recently the staff did a self-study to find out what labels were most apt and decided that the church is genuinely ecumenical, nondenominational, and new wave. As one staff member explained, "It's a new movement that is making the lines really blurry among mainliners, nondenominational, evangelical, and charismatic churches, and that's really beyond the labels of the 1970s and 1980s."

Its aim is to be an all-purpose, full-service church, an organization that provides something for everyone. A glossy booklet, complete with color photos, that the church makes available to newcomers and sends out to the community provides brief descriptions of the various programs. In addition to the four weekly worship services (which are offered in sign language for the hearing impaired and on cassette tape), the church offers children's classes for each grade level, junior and senior high youth groups, ministries for singles and young adults, Bible classes, and home fellowship groups. The church's size allows for much variety in many of these programs. For example, married couples between the ages of thirty-five and forty-five can choose from seven different home fellowship groups in various locations, or they can join any of ten other fellowship groups that also include singles. The church also operates a fully accredited elementary school and a high school, a Christian counseling center, and a jail ministry. The learning center includes more than 15,000 books and a rapidly growing library of Bible films, classic movies, and educational videos. There are also recovery groups for alcoholism and divorce, a program of visitation in local nursing homes, a Bible Institute for continuing education, career counseling, support for foreign missionaries, and an intramural sports program.

To direct and administer these programs requires a sizable staff. There's a senior pastor and four executive pastors. Each of the executive pastors oversees a department, or an area of ministry in the church. One is in charge of all education and discipleship from junior high through adults. Another is executive pastor for church ministries, overseeing areas such as men's ministry, women's ministry, the pastoral care ministries of the church, equipping lay ministers for the church, and home group ministries. There is an executive pastor of outreach, who oversees foreign mission work, home mission work, the congregation, the counseling center, the evangelism ministry, the outreach ministry, and any national works to which the church contributes. Then there's an executive pastor of administration, who oversees all the administrative functions of the church and the school as well. Below the executive pastors are the pastoral-level clergy: a minister of singles and prayer, a pastor of music, a pastor of visitation, a pastor of children's ministry, and a pastor of counseling. Finally, there is a level of directors: a director of campus ministry, a director of junior high ministry, a director of senior high ministry, a director of evangelism, a director of administration under the pastor of administration, a director of children's ministry, and a director of jail ministry.

It is not cheap to support this many staff and to operate so many programs. The church's annual budget is approximately $4.5 million, which covers everything from buying music for the children's choir to paying the salary of the senior pastor. Staff salaries and costs associated with operating the school make up the two largest categories of expenditure. So as not to become stagnant or ingrown, the church has a policy of allocating 30 percent of its operating budget each year to "outreach." Over the past decade, it has also had to raise millions to pay off the loan on its buildings.

By most indications, Grace Church is in solid financial condition. Its budget is on the rise, and it has a $3 million building program under way that it expects to pay for within three years. But even here the outward signs of prosperity hide some troublesome conditions. Although its members are encouraged to tithe their incomes to the church, the figures suggest that few do. Per capita giving amounts to no more here than it does in national surveys and is even below that of many other churches at the evangelical or conservative end of the theological spectrum. The church thus has to rely mainly on its huge size in order to support its programs, and it depends on drawing in new members whenever it wants to expand these programs. It has also inadvertently cultivated a fee-for-service mentality rather than a spirit of sacrificial giving. Indeed, more than a quarter of its annual income is directly tied to fees paid for specific services such as schooling, counseling, babysitting, book sales, and video rentals. Much of the remainder is linked informally with services as well. For example, parents contribute because of the church's ministry to children, young single career people give because the church has a special ministry for them, and so on.

A church of this kind functions well for people who can indeed pay for the services they receive. What it provides for the poor and needy in the wider community is less clear. This is not because the clergy fail to recognize the importance of meeting these wider needs but because the priority attached to these needs is greatly overshadowed by the church's other programs and ministries. The result is token support that in fact amounts to far less than appearances might indicate. One of the pastors, for example, explains that "benevolence" is a central teaching of the church. "The people," he says, "are very involved in giving to others." He cites as an example the fact that a special offering for benevolent purposes is collected each month. "It's a very sizable amount. And from that all kinds of things are done in the ministry of the church: utility bills are paid, rents are paid, food is provided for families out of work, counseling services, just innumerable ministries are provided through the benevolence ministry."

Yet church records indicate that the amount given for benevolence is actually less than 1 percent of the church's total budget—less than the church spends each year on printing supplies and postage. Grace Church is thus an example of what many religious leaders—like the pastors at Grace Church itself—describe as the "new wave" in American religion. It is truly the church of tomorrow, the church of the new middle class at the end of the twentieth century. To operate churches like this requires as much money as it does to operate fifty churches of average size. To raise the necessary cash, these churches hire professional fund-raisers who mount high-publicity campaigns. Sometimes the return is in the tens of millions of dollars. But churches of this size are particularly vulnerable to the harsh economic realities that face the American middle class at the end of the twentieth century. Like corporate giants, they fly high and pay their staff good salaries when business is good. When business falters, they are forced to lay off staff and to cut programs severely. And business does falter—when local industry experiences cutbacks, when the senior pastor falls from grace, or when a more attractive competitor moves in a few miles down the road.

## CONGREGATIONS AS ECONOMIC COMMUNITIES

As these brief descriptions indicate, each of these churches is quite distinct, differing from the others in size, location, theology, ethnicity, and social class. Each, nevertheless, illustrates the financial pressures that are now facing America's churches. Cornerstone Bible Church is so small that it is scarcely able to pay its pastor's salary and meet the payments on its mortgage. Its members are mostly in middle-class jobs, including the professions and clerical positions, and they are working harder than ever to please their employers and to keep their jobs. They are faithful Christians, but they are also busy enough that it is hard for them to support the church any more than they already do. Saint Andrew's Episcopal Church enjoys an upper-middle-class clientele and has sufficient numbers to keep afloat, but it is experiencing new demands because of the desperate situation of the poor in the wider community, and it is having to adjust to the tensions brought about by the suburbanization of its membership. San Xavier's Roman Catholic Church struggles to meet the economic and cultural challenges presented by its expanding Hispanic community. Redeemer Baptist Church is caught between ministering to a needy working class and finding new ways to appeal to its growing constituency in the black middle class. And Grace Church raises millions for its expanding program of ministries and services but does little for the truly needy.

While the financial crisis can sometimes be measured in dollars and cents, these examples also point to the fact that the crisis in America's churches cannot be gauged solely in financial terms. None of these churches is in any imminent danger of having the bank foreclose on its mortgage. In fact, none has had to scale back significantly in its programs. Each is clearly pressed to stretch its finances as far as possible. And there are major questions about priorities and allocations. Finances are thus at issue. Yet the crisis itself is more spiritual than economic. It arises less from the fact that these churches, in varying degrees, are trying to minister to the poor, although that is a relevant issue. Its source lies neither in the overall health of the American economy nor in the special hardships faced by those at the bottom but in the fact that each of these churches is ministering primarily to the middle class. Their financial condition depends on the support they receive from their middle-class members. And that support, in turn, depends on the preoccupations of the middle class, its needs, its priorities, and the ways in which the churches are ministering to these needs and challenging these priorities.

The financial concerns that have arisen in the nation's churches are thus merely a symptom of a deeper and longer-term problem. Raising the cash to operate church programs—whether those programs are static or expanding—depends on motivating middle-class parishioners to give generously of their time and money. And motivation requires people to have more than a superficial understanding of giving and to do more than simply show up at a church meeting. Motivation to support the church depends on having a solid understanding of why the church should exist and of knowing that the church—and one's faith—is relevant to all aspects of one's life. As these examples indicate, pastors generally realize that faith must be relevant if their members are going to give generously. Pastors also know that their middle-class members do not lead lives of quiet, affluent serenity but are troubled with fears about their jobs, concerns about their own economic security, and anxieties about their money and their possessions. Yet pastors are also aware that these issues are changing and that it is difficult to understand fully what their members are experiencing and what their needs may be. The deeper crisis, then, lies in the churches' failure to grasp or to deal adequately with the spiritual dilemma of the middle class. It is to that dilemma that we must turn next.

# three

# THE SPIRITUAL DILEMMA
# OF THE MIDDLE CLASS

Betsy Swedborg, forty-six, is a single mother who works as a community education specialist. She lives in a small house with her teenaged son in a Midwestern city that prides itself on good schools, ample social services, low taxes, and full employment. Her income is slightly above average for this part of the country, and she definitely considers herself part of the middle class. Yet life is a constant struggle. Her son was only four when she and her husband filed for divorce. With only a year of college, she began working as a secretary and gradually moved up the ranks of the community services hierarchy to her present position. Taking night classes, she spent a decade finishing her college degree, and she is now taking master's-degree-level courses that are required for a certificate she must have if she is to keep her job. She works at least fifty hours each week, including four evening meetings and some Saturday meetings.

The hardest part of Betsy's life is just finding enough time to do everything. Her work is physically and emotionally exhausting. She says emphatically that she comes home feeling drained much of the time. Asked what she does to take care of herself, she responds, "Unfortunately, I don't have a lot of time to do things for myself. I'm afraid I don't have very good habits." Even maintaining close friendships has been hard. She'll plan to have lunch with someone and then have to reschedule because of a meeting. "I feel like I'm in a catch-22 situation," she says, "trying to work on a relationship with a friend and also trying to meet the needs of my position."

Finances are not easy for Betsy either. She isn't exactly worried about putting food on the table, but she feels it necessary to work hard in order to buy the things she wants for her son, such as living in a neighborhood that is relatively safe and has a decent school system, buying him the things he wants for Christmas, and saving money so he can go to college. "I need to earn as much income as I possibly can to continue the lifestyle that my son and I are used to—which is probably middle income," she explains. Feeling this way, she says she has "no other options" but to keep her job and to work as hard at it as she can. There have been a lot of times, she says, when her finances have made her feel "very sad, frustrated, insecure, and just really scared."

What kind of support does Betsy receive from the church? None. She decided a long time ago that she was just too busy to be involved in the church. For her, the basis of Christianity is summarized in Jesus' commandment to love others as yourself. She feels she has plenty of opportunity to do that in her work and by caring for her son and her aging parents. She doesn't need the church telling her to be kind. That has been one of her values for as long as she can remember. She also knows the church is not there to help her. She shoulders her work responsibilities and her financial burdens by herself. When she comes home drained, the last thing she needs is a church meeting. Working with people all week long, she just wants some time to be by herself, to relax, and to get a good night's sleep.

Frank Malloy, sixty-two, says the church and its teachings are central to his life. He is an attorney, widowed, who lives in Chicago and attends services regularly at Blessed Mother Roman Catholic Church. His mother was also a Catholic and his father was an agnostic who never went to church but who experienced a deathbed conversion. Frank thinks his father would have joined the church much earlier but that there had been "some controversy about tithing." In any case, when Frank was a child, his father never allowed him to attend church with his mother and two sisters. That piqued Frank's curiosity. When he left home to join the navy, he started attending and took his first communion. After his time in the navy, Frank studied for four years at the University of Notre Dame, where he especially enjoyed the required religion courses. He has been attending church regularly ever since.

He works in the probate division of a large bank handling estates and trusts. Two years ago, the bank found itself short by about $1.7 billion because of some dubious loans it had made and decided to cut back drastically on its work force. Frank was cut from full to part time. He likes the free time and has been doing some traveling. He has always enjoyed his work because it gives him an opportunity to help people. He handles trusts for widows, orphans, and a great variety of other clients. He dislikes office politics and hates the stress and the competitive pressure that are part of his job. Over the years, he has made some difficult choices about how far up the corporate ladder to climb and how much pressure to put on himself.

At this point in his life, Frank is not particularly troubled about money. He has had to trim his expenditures since shifting to part time, but he has plenty of money and is looking forward to a long retirement. He gives some money away too. But lately he feels like a man besieged. Too many organizations have been asking him for donations. "Throw the Catholic church in there," he says. "It's always scream-ing for money. It has an insatiable desire for money." And, if that isn't enough, he receives letters from priests, ex-priests, and missionaries—all running orphanages and saving rainforests and doing good works. "It all cuts into your Catholic contri-butions," he explains.

"The church has its faults," Frank says, "because, well, because it's just a bunch of people and we all make mistakes." Because it is "the original church," though, he feels loyal to it, mistakes and all. He sort of "steps into the myth of it all," and that makes it okay. Mostly, he believes in the importance of leading "a good moral life." "I don't go around spouting religious sayings," he boasts, "and I don't go overboard on religious ceremonies."

Frank says the church has never influenced the way he works or the way he han-dles his money. In fact, he is suspicious of people who try to link these things to their "religious feelings" or to specific religious teachings. His view is more that religion supplies a kind of moral foundation that nearly everyone in our society shares subconsciously. Thus, in handling his money, he says he doesn't pilfer and he doesn't cheat. If he stops to analyze the reason why, he says it's just that, well, "this is the way you do it." You have a "foundation," and if you don't, maybe you go around mugging people.

His view, then, is that people are on their own when it comes to making deci-sions about their work, their money, and how to spend their time. They should try to be moral and good. If they are, they will be rewarded by feeling good about themselves. The church—and spirituality—are separate from these aspects of his life. He understands stewardship as "the current program they're promoting here in the Archdiocese of Chicago." Although he gives some money to the church, he says he hasn't "entered into the spirit" of the church's campaign. "I've been concen-trating on yours truly for a while," he acknowledges.

Sherlynda Hodge, thirty-three, lives just down the street from the African Methodist Episcopal church that she attends every Sunday morning and evening. A college graduate who works as an inventory planner for a computer firm, she lives in the left half of a remodeled twin house with her husband, teenaged daughter, and three-year-old son. When Sherlynda finished college, the only job she could find was clerking in a liquor store. After she had done that for several months, she and her boyfriend decided to move to another state. Two months later, Sherlynda was back. Her boyfriend had abandoned her, and she was pregnant. For the next three years, Sherlynda lived with an aunt, looked after the baby, and got odd jobs cleaning houses and doing babysitting. Toward the end of that period, she got a job at the company she is with now and met the man who would become her husband.

For the past three years, Sherlynda and her husband have worked different shifts in order to share the work of caring for their son. Her husband generally works nights, so days go by when she seldom sees him. She says the main reason she stays at her present job is the benefits. "It's a very boring job," she admits. She enjoys the people she works with, but the work itself consists entirely of scanning purchase orders and figuring out what materials need to be replenished in the warehouse. She complains, "I really don't like my work at all."

The only tangible connection between Sherlynda's life from Monday to Saturday and her life on Sundays is that she takes her son to the day-care center at the church in the mornings before work and picks him up on her way home. She also makes sure her daughter goes to choir practice on Thursday evenings. Otherwise, the church could be two galaxies—rather than two doors—away. Sherlynda has been active in the church most of her life. Choir, Sunday school, youth group, potluck dinners. She says she goes because she believes in God. She tries hard to do what God wants her to do, and she says the Lord is her "only hope" because "the world is so mixed up." She thinks more people should get involved in the church. But, as far as she can recall, she has never heard any religious teachings about money. Her faith does not influence her attitudes about work or how hard she works. She says she doesn't know what stewardship is. She does think a person should "pray and do what is right." She also says it is important to "try and help other people" rather than "only care what you can get out of every situation."

## MIDDLE-CLASS RELIGION

By almost any criteria, the majority of American church members belong to the middle class. Only one church member in six, for instance, lives on less than $20,000 a year—the level at which families with children are considered to be living in poverty. At the opposite extreme, only 4 percent of church members have family incomes in excess of $100,000. The median family income for church members is about $45,000, slightly above the national average for working Americans. By occupations, most church members also belong to the middle class. About three-quarters, for instance, work at professional, managerial, clerical, sales, and service jobs or operate their own businesses. Among married church members, about three-quarters of spouses are also employed in these occupations. Even in terms of education—with 61 percent having some education beyond high school— the majority of church members fall into the middle class.[1]

When church members are asked to describe their own financial situation, it is also clear that most fall broadly within the middle class, having to watch their expenditures, of course, but having enough to satisfy their families' needs. In one survey, for instance, people were asked about their economic circumstances, and among church members only 19 percent described their current economic situation as being sufficient to cover only the basic necessities; the remainder were about evenly divided between those who said they have a small amount of money left over after covering basic necessities and those who said they have a moderate amount left over; only 3 percent said they have a lot left over.[2]

Although there are vast differences in incomes, education levels, and types of occupation, most Americans also *perceive* themselves to be part of the middle class. In his book *Speaking American*, David Kusnet described this perception well. "Americans who aren't millionaires or mendicants appreciate being called 'middle class,'" he wrote. "It doesn't matter where they work, talk about 'the middle class,' and most people think you mean them."[3]

It is appropriate, therefore, to say that most churches in the United States are middle-class churches. They may include some families who are impoverished, homeless, or employed as unskilled laborers, but the majority of their members are likely to be drawn from the middle class. It is also fair to say that most of the churches' financial support and volunteer time comes from the middle class and that the assistance churches are able to give to the needy and disadvantaged depends on middle-class donations of money and time.

The middle class has the potential to support the churches generously. Most parishioners are part of what John Kenneth Galbraith has called "the contented majority."[4] They have flexibility in their budgets that allows them to donate to charitable causes of their choice. But the middle class is also experiencing greater demands on its time and money. Employers are asking employees to work longer hours, and advertisers and retailers are searching constantly for ways to draw families—including children—more completely into the consumer market. Since the 1970s, the housing market has shifted, making it impossible for many younger families to afford their own homes and forcing many others to settle for life in crowded apartment complexes—condominiums with euphemistic names such as Society Hill—rather than living in single-family houses. Most middle-class families now depend on two incomes, rather than one, to pay the bills. Dual careers make commuting time longer in most cases and add expenses for child care. Middle-class families are finding it harder to save money to send their children to college or to finance their own retirements. Compared with their parents and neighbors, many middle-class families are, indeed, suffering from what Barbara Ehrenreich termed the "fear of falling," either from literally losing their jobs or from shattered hopes for a more comfortable lifestyle.[5] And this fear is about much more than simply paying the mortgage. As another writer observed, the fear is about losing one's "place in society."[6]

Charitable agencies, having grown in number and functions as a result of cutbacks in government programs, are also vying for scarce donations of volunteer time and dollars. These demands mean two things for the churches: first, that the churches may have to work harder in order to maintain the loyalties of middle-class members and thus to attract their donations of time and money, and second, that the churches need to minister effectively to the needs of the middle class, focusing on problems experienced in careers, in the workplace, and at the bank.

The point that churches' programs and financial health depend on garnering commitment from the middle class is fairly easy to substantiate. Of every $1,000 received by the churches, $680 will have been given by people with more than a high school education, $900 will have been given by people who work in middle-class occupations, and $920 will have been given by people who earn more than $20,000 a year. In short, the bulk of churches' financial support comes from the middle class. And it comes from those who, for whatever reasons, have become sufficiently motivated to attend services regularly and to take their faith seriously. Indeed, $760 out of every $1,000 will come from those who attend services every week on average, and $770 will be donated by those who say their religious commitment is "very important." Anything churches do to meet the needs of middle-class members and to motivate them to become more involved, therefore, strengthens the churches' financial well-being; conversely, failing to spark the commitment of middle-class members contributes to the problems that many churches are now experiencing.

How well the churches are ministering to the needs of the middle class requires somewhat more detailed consideration. We must look at several specific areas of concern, examining how widespread these concerns are among middle-class people, and then consider how people are relating their faith to these concerns and how active churchgoers differ from those who are less involved.

## PRESSURES IN THE WORKPLACE

The most notable source of pressure in the workplace is simply the increasing number of hours that people are having to work. According to one study, the average American now puts in a total of about *one full month* more on the job per year than was true a generation ago.[7] Not counted in this estimate is the fact that more and more people are employed in professional occupations in which evening and weekend work is common and that most women are now gainfully employed outside the home, whereas this was not the case a generation ago. At present, two-thirds of all church members who are employed at all work more than forty hours a week and one church member in six works more than fifty hours a week.[8] And 65 percent say they are working harder now than they were five years ago.

The vast majority of church members are glad to be working, of course. They take pride in their jobs and derive much of their self-esteem from performing well at their work. Indeed, 82 percent say that their work is a very important source of their self-identity. Yet a large number of church members is concerned about how much they have to work and is faced with serious pressures, work-related stress, and too little time to do the things they really want to do. Seventy percent, for instance, say they have little or no energy left over for other things when they come home from work. The same high proportion complains about not having enough time for themselves. Fifty percent wish they could work fewer hours than they do. And an equal number say they should be getting more sleep than they do.[9]

Betsy Swedborg basically likes her work in community education services. She says she especially enjoys the diversity, working with different kinds of people, the chance to be creative ("when I have time"), and the chance to "strive for excellence." It gives her pleasure to meet people's needs, such as senior citizens' needs for health education or new immigrants' needs for English-language training. But Betsy also finds her work extremely frustrating. Working for a public agency means that there are never enough funds to do what she would like. She has to cut corners rather than achieve excellence. She also says that the bureaucracy is "something I dislike immensely." There is constant pressure too. Some of it comes from having to work too many hours and do too many different things because the staff is too small. And she always feels pressure from residents who want more than she can deliver. There is also routine conflict occasioned by dissatisfied clients.

Apart from the hours, middle-class work is a source of special emotional stress, conflict, and dissatisfaction for many people. Among church members with jobs, nearly a third (29 percent) say they are dissatisfied with their current jobs. A third (32 percent) say their work drains them emotionally. More than a third (40 percent) say their work is physically exhausting. About one person in two complains of other problems—high pressure (56 percent), extreme competition (47 percent), and a lack of opportunities for advancement (48 percent). In all, 53 percent of church members who are working full or part time say they experience significant amounts of stress at their jobs at least once a week.

Frank Malloy is working fewer hours now than he ever has before, but he says the emotional pressures are still taking their toll on him. Working hard has never been difficult for him. His father was an accountant, and his mother paid close attention to how well the children were raised. Both parents were sticklers for rules, obedience, and earning high marks. If Frank came home from a date five minutes past curfew, his father was there to punish him. His mother would drill him on his homework every night. Those values helped him make it through law school. They sometimes conflict with his daily schedule, however. He has to work with an enormous variety of people, and most of his work consists of "gray areas" in the law where he has to make tough decisions. Part of him enjoys the challenge. But another part wants to buckle under the stress that arises from the incessant ambiguity. "It takes a lot out of you because you jump from one situation to another," he observes, "and emotionally you get drained. Physically it isn't that demanding, but emotionally you get drained."

Sherlynda Hodge also finds her work emotionally exhausting—not because it is too diverse but because it is endlessly the same. It makes no use of her college training, and it offers no opportunity to learn new skills that might help her get a better job. The other problem is that Sherlynda feels there is "a lot of game-playing with upper management." There is a lot of pressure on everyone at her workplace. She complains that "there's a lot of bad things going on that we just have no control over." She feels she is being treated unfairly and that the new managers at the headquarters location are making bad decisions. Most of all, she fears that her job is going to be eliminated or moved to another city.

These examples, moreover, do not include the more extreme problems that a substantial minority of church members experience. For instance, approximately one church member in ten—who is now working—has been laid off within the past year. At least one in eight has taken a pay cut in the past year. Nine percent have experienced discrimination in the past year, and 4 percent have been victims of sexual harassment.

Faced with making choices about their work, many middle-class men and women also worry about burnout, whether or not they are in the right job, and whether they need to be considering something else. Nearly half the work force (45 percent)—among church members—say they have experienced burnout at work during the past year. A third (32 percent) say they have been wondering if they were in the right line of work. And a quarter (27 percent) say they have been feeling *seriously* burned out. Many church members do, in fact, change jobs. Not counting work they did prior to adulthood, 79 percent have been involved in more than one line of work and 52 percent have been involved in more than two lines of work.

Betsy Swedborg illustrates some of the complexity of these concerns. When asked about burnout, she says she *thinks* maybe she has experienced it but isn't sure. When she is overworked and feeling overwhelmed, she thinks maybe she is in the wrong line of work. But she also feels that burnout is a matter of one's attitude. She doesn't blame the situation as much as she does herself for letting it get to her. Frank Malloy also feels burned out, spent. He says the trouble began when the bank introduced computers. He didn't mind the new technology. But there was now a whole new level of middle managers—people who had power because they controlled the computers. Frank says he wouldn't go into the same line of work if he had it to do over again. For him, though, it was too late to get into something else.

Added to these concerns are the growing problems associated with balancing work commitments and family commitments. These problems are especially significant among parents, including the growing number of working women and single mothers, who work long hours to support their families and then have little time to spend with them. A substantial minority of church members say they have experienced trouble arranging for child care, getting household tasks done, or juggling schedules with busy spouses. A majority (56 percent) also admit that bad days at work make them cranky with their families.

Sherlynda Hodge says there is constant conflict between her work and her family. When it snows, she has trouble getting the children to school without being late for work. When one of the children is sick, she calls in sick herself rather than take a vacation day. On the rare occasions when she has a chance to work overtime, she does it because she needs the money, but then she often has trouble finding a babysitter. She also finds it hard to make time for herself. "I don't have much of a personal life," she says. "Once I go to work and I come home with the kids, I don't do anything for me. It's all for them. So I don't even have a personal life."

How well do the churches minister to these needs? Judging from what people report, not very well. One indication is what people do to relieve the stress that develops at work. Only about a quarter of church members (28 percent) say they routinely pray or meditate. Scarcely anyone (4 percent) talks to their pastor. The most common strategies for dealing with stress are to watch television, get some physical exercise, or go shopping. Another indication of how well the churches are ministering to work-related needs comes from members' ways of resolving major ethical dilemmas at work. More than half (54 percent) say they would discuss the problem with their boss. More than a third (36 percent) would talk it over with coworkers. One in five (20 percent) would find something helpful to read. Only one in eight (13 percent) would talk about it with their pastor.

Betsy Swedborg says she doesn't need the church to tell her to be responsible, to work hard, and to be frugal. Those values have been part of her makeup since childhood. Betsy's father died when she was three, and her mother worked very hard to make a living and to raise Betsy and her two sisters. When Betsy was six, her mother took her to the bank and opened a savings account. Betsy took her birthday money each year, invested it, and watched it grow. She says it was a good way to learn the value of a dollar. She says her mother was always quite open with her about how hard she worked and how important it was to work hard in order to achieve success. If Betsy still went to church, she would feel that these values were being reinforced. That would make her feel good. But she has no time right now for such luxuries.

Frank Malloy compartmentalizes his work completely from his churchgoing and his spirituality. At work, he simply tries to do what is right. He does not seek advice from anyone else, and he finds no inspiration when he goes to church that helps him to work harder or be more creative or make better-informed ethical decisions. His way of dealing with stress is to get out into nature. That refreshes his spirit much more than going to church.

Sherlynda Hodge mostly compartmentalizes her life as well. She is thankful that God has given her children, a husband, and a place to live, and she tries to lead a good life. If pressed, she would probably say that her faith helps her make it through the day when the pressures build up. She certainly does not consider her faith irrelevant. Yet it seems odd to her to think that her church might be more relevant to the rest of her life than it currently is.

Doubt about how the churches are ministering to these needs is also raised by looking at the differences between active churchgoers and those who are less active. For instance, those who attend religious services every week are almost as likely as those who attend less often to say they are dissatisfied with their work and to complain of burnout. They are also just as likely to report that one of their favorite ways of dealing with job-related stress is to go shopping.[10] In addition, the two groups are virtually indistinguishable in terms of motives for working hard and doing their work well. Both are about equally likely to say they work hard in order to fulfill their own potential, to help others, to make more money, and to win praise.[11]

## FINANCIAL PRESSURES

Work and money are closely related, of course, but financial pressures take on a life of their own, creating anxieties that are often only partly attributable to what kind of job one has. The bottom line for most middle-class families is that they feel severely pressured financially. In fact, 70 percent of employed church members say they have been worried in the past year about how to pay their bills. And nearly this many (59 percent) say they think a lot about money and their personal finances. These proportions are high, considering the fact that most church members (69 percent) also say they are making more money than ever before.

Betsy Swedborg feels she is constantly having to make hard choices about how to spend or invest scarce resources. As a single parent living in a middle-class neighborhood, she recognizes that she has less "earning power" than most families. She knows she has to cut corners in order to get the things she really values. For instance, she takes pride in not allowing her son to wear expensive clothes, using the money instead to buy a home computer that both she and he have used for doing homework. Betsy feels especially pressured now because her son will be starting college in a few years. She says it has always been a matter of living from one paycheck to the next. Her ex-husband is not going to help with the college expenses, and Betsy feels it isn't practical for her son to work his own way through college. She is working as hard as she can to make sure she keeps her job and possibly receives a raise. Meanwhile, she says she worries a lot, and this too bothers her. She thinks it isn't appropriate for people to worry. She feels she should be more confident that everything will turn out well.

Many people also experience anxiety from having to make hard decisions about how to use their money. Specifically, 72 percent of church members with jobs say they have been bothered during the past year by anxiety about purchases or other decisions involving money, and a majority (52 percent) say they have felt guilty about the way they spent their money.

Betsy Swedborg says she learned as a child to associate having money with a feeling of security. The purpose of money wasn't to buy lots of things but to have a backup for times of necessity and emergency. That attitude has helped her through tight financial times but has also made it hard for her to be generous in spending her money on herself, her family, or others. For instance, she had to do some redecorating of her house recently, and she says it made her feel "materialistic" to be spending the money. A lot of times, she says, she plans hard, does her best to make the right purchase, and feels "excited" about the opportunity to get something, but then things never seem to work out just right, leaving her disappointed. "It's just something I have," she muses. "You have it, but it's anticlimactic."

Middle-class expectations—encouraging people to want more and to make more money—also contribute to the anxieties of many Americans. Virtually all church members (82 percent) admit to wishing they had more money. A substantial minority (43 percent) actually say that making a lot of money is a very important source of their personal identity. And nearly three-fourths (71 percent) say this about living a comfortable life.

Sherlynda Hodge says she has always "loved money" and tried to get as much of it as she could. When she was growing up, she would shovel walks to earn money. She also stole things from the neighbors and made bets. She was always glad when her grandmother invited friends over to play poker. Usually there was some extra money the next day for candy or going to the movies. Right now, she and her husband are doing some repairs to the house. They know it will cost $300 more than they planned. Making up the difference is one of the reasons Sherlynda is thinking a lot about money these days. But what she really wants is about $500,000. "If I could get $500,000, I'd be content," she muses. "I figure, first of all, I could pay my house off. My husband and I could both get a brand-new car, and then we could put money away for the kids' schooling."

Most middle-class people compare themselves with their parents financially. They often have little understanding of how their parents made or spent their money or what they thought about it, but they could see that their parents had or did not have money for certain things. And many middle-class people now feel frustrated because money seems to be tighter for them than it was for their parents. Betsy Swedborg, for example, says her mother managed to do pretty well for herself, despite having only an eighth-grade education, by purchasing some real estate that grew considerably in value during the 1950s and 1960s. In comparison, Betsy has far more education, holds a more prestigious job, and works more hours per week but has been able to accumulate virtually nothing. She says it would take another $40,000 a year for her to feel comfortable. Despite the fact that she enjoys her work, she says she fantasizes about having enough money to quit—just for a while, but long enough to go home and get a really good rest.

As with work, the churches could be doing a lot more to bring faith to bear on financial concerns, judging from what people say. Fewer than one church member in five says he or she has thought a lot during the past year about the Bible's teachings concerning money or how to relate their faith more directly to their personal finances. Most are like Frank Malloy. It amuses him to think that God cares anything about his money or what he buys.

Comparing more active and less active members also suggests that the churches are not making a strong difference in the financial aspects of most people's lives. Those who attend religious services every week are only slightly less likely than those who attend less often to say they would like to have a lot more money and to admit that they worry a lot about their finances.[12] The two groups are also nearly the same in saying that they value having a beautiful home, a new car, and other nice things.[13]

## ISSUES AND VALUES

Beyond work and money, a number of larger issues and questions about values characterize the middle class, raising concerns that are also connected with how they spend their time and money. Most people feel they need to be thinking about their values and yet fear they do not have sufficient time to do so. Among church members with jobs, 71 percent say they want more out of life than just a good job and a comfortable lifestyle. More than a third (35 percent) feel they need more time to think about the really basic issues of life. And more than half (53 percent) say they would like to spend more time exploring spiritual issues.

Betsy Swedborg feels that her mother "had a better balance in her life" than she does. She wishes she did not have to work so hard and that she was not so driven. It is hard for her to relax and have fun. Frank Malloy feels he has pretty much lived his life. He has few regrets, but he does worry about his friends, his children, and his nieces and nephews. "You can be very prosperous," he muses, "and get so carried away with it that you lose your other values. You become a workaholic, and you forget your friends and family." He isn't sure how people are going to maintain balance in their lives with all the pressures they are now confronting.

Many Americans are facing ethical decisions that confuse them. Betsy Swedborg says her previous boss often used to ask her to do things that she wondered about. Generally, she tried to probe for an explanation, and if she felt comfortable would go ahead and do the things he asked. She did not seek advice from anyone else at work or in her circle of acquaintances. Sherlynda Hodge says she tries to do what is right at work, but she also admits that doing something shady or unethical depends entirely on who is asking her to do it. She says she mostly wants to avoid getting into trouble. "I'm very chicken that way," she confesses. When she is faced with really serious decisions, she has a friend or two she can turn to for advice. She does not put her pastor in this category. She also says it is hard to know how she would bring her own values to bear on difficult situations. The underlying problem is that she has detached her basic identity almost totally from her work. She just goes through the motions.

Most of us are deeply concerned about the character of our society. We say that American culture is too much dominated by materialism, consumerism, advertising, and the influences of big business—as well we might when studies show that shopping has become the number one pastime of American teenagers and that college students aspire to be "financially well off" more than anything else in life.[14] We also express concern about the poor, the environment, crime, and our nation's schools. Among employed church members, for instance, 90 percent say that our society is too materialistic, 93 percent think children nowadays want too many material things, and 78 percent believe that advertising is corrupting our basic values.

Middle-class church members are, by and large, loyal Americans who have faith in one another and who try hard to do what is right. Yet they are also deeply concerned about the problems that seem to threaten the very fabric of American society. Overwhelming proportions, at least, say that each of the following is a serious or extremely serious problem in our society: the condition of the poor (93 percent), the breakdown of families (93 percent), problems in the schools (92 percent), moral corruption (90 percent), political corruption (90 percent), corruption in business (87 percent), selfishness (84 percent), and the breakdown of communities (78 percent).

Betsy Swedborg thinks racism and sexism are two of the biggest problems in America: "People of color not having the same opportunities that you and I have. There is still a vast difference in pay between men and women." She thinks education needs to focus more on giving opportunities to the disadvantaged and on teaching those with advantages to be less biased and more compassionate. She does not have much time to think about these issues. But she does feel she is part of the solution, working as she does to provide education to the community. She seldom makes cash donations to help the poor, explaining that most charitable organizations cannot be trusted, but she has found ways to work harder on behalf of poor families and to get them special opportunities through her job.

Frank Malloy looks back over the changes that have taken place during the past half-century and decries what he sees. He thinks that advertising and big business have gained too much influence and that the American public is too interested in material things. "Take sporting, for instance," he suggests. "It used to be that you could enjoy yourself canoeing. Well, then came the speedboats, and after the speedboats you had waterskiing. Okay. Now the latest craze is you got all these scooters where you stand on it. It has to be a motor of some kind, and who benefits by that? The Japanese. They recognize the weakness in the American people having to have gadgets, and they manufacture them and they sell 'em to us, and you got your problems here."

These issues, importantly, come full circle at times. The middle class lives in smug complacency much of the time. But it also reflects on itself and is sometimes troubled by what it sees. Betsy Swedborg recently took a class in human relations as part of her master's work. She said it opened her eyes to some of the problems of the middle class. "I think people tend to be relatively self-serving and self-centered," she says. She thinks we are this way mostly because of the culture in which we live. "When people work as much as they need to, they have limited time for themselves and for their own families. They almost appear self-centered. I don't know that they necessarily are, but it's maybe a matter of survival." She sees herself in this way. "I may appear very self-serving and very self-centered, but I don't have a lot of time. And I need to take care of my son, and I need to take care of myself before I can do a whole lot with other people."

Saying that "economics" makes us behave like this can be a convenient way of excusing ourselves for our shortcomings. Yet the feeling of wanting to do better and of being trapped by our circumstances is very real. "In today's society it costs so much to be able to live and exist that people have to work hard to be able to do it," Betsy Swedborg laments. "They don't have a lot of time for everybody else." She thinks this situation is regrettable but that it is also just "reality."

Yet it is unclear that the churches are helping people to think through these issues. In their opinions on most of these matters, active churchgoers do not differ significantly from the less active. And in many instances, the two groups do not seem to hold substantially different views about what needs to be done.

For instance, those who attend religious services every week are virtually no different from those who attend less often in saying that the condition of the poor, problems in the schools, and political corruption are serious problems in our society.[15]

The concerns that Frank Malloy expresses about the church he attends are not atypical. He fears that commercialism is corrupting the church as well as the wider society. Pointing to the use of marketing firms and fund-raisers by the church, he worries that this method of appealing for money will simply create a backlash. "They're gonna call you up and say why don't you increase your contribution and someday, you know, the telephone gets slammed so damn hard that it'd be put out of commission." Because he does not feel that he gets very much from the church himself and does not hear any convincing arguments about how he should live his life when he does attend church, it seems mostly like a duty—an unwelcome obligation—when he is asked to support the church. If he supports it at all, he does so at the minimum possible level.

## THE SPIRITUAL DILEMMA

The middle class, then, is caught in a spiritual dilemma. On the one hand, it enjoys enormous resources—education, job training, places to live, food on the table, longevity, relative freedom from fear and violence. It feels that there is much to be improved about the society and the world, and it feels itself responsible for how it behaves individually and collectively. On the other hand, it feels overburdened with too much work and too many bills; it suffers from stress and anxiety; it wonders what its values should be and wishes it could cut back and get its life more under control; it even recognizes the need to think about spiritual concerns. Faced with this dilemma, the middle class turns in large numbers to the churches to find help and as a means of helping others. Yet the churches don't seem to be making much of a difference in middle-class lives.

Part of the dilemma hinges simply on the question of how to find enough time to seek out the answers that the churches might have. Someone like Sherlynda Hodge has never really had time to sit and read books about faith and work or to attend seminars and classes at the church on this topic. And she is not atypical. Middle-class churches are built on the premise that their members have enormous  quantities of unfilled time. They can use this time to read religious pamphlets, listen to tapes, attend Bible study groups, serve on church committees, and ponder the Sunday sermon over large plates of roast beef. Middle-class parishioners may, of course, have such time, but it is also being eaten up by worthy activities that are part of the expected course of everyday life—commuting, remodeling the basement, chauffeuring children to piano lessons and scout meetings, entertaining one's coworkers. Churches are thus finding it harder to get their members' attention—even when there is something important to be said.

The dilemma also consists of feeling motivated to support the churches financially at a level sufficient for the churches to actually run their programs effectively—and thereby convince contributors that their offerings were not in vain. People like Frank Malloy are not atypical. They would like the churches to be doing good. Helping the poor, protecting the environment, communicating the gospel more effectively, and helping immigrants learn English and become productive citizens—these are some of the challenges. But Frank Malloy is unwilling to give money for the archbishop to use to hire fund-raisers to solicit more money. So the church ends up doing little and expecting little.

Perhaps the problems are insuperable. Nothing can be done. Everything is up to the economists and the government. But economists and government officials are not likely to address the spiritual needs of the middle class, nor are they capable of bringing the resources of religious faith to bear on these needs and on the broader concerns of the middle class. The churches are the most likely organizations for doing so. But the fact that churches seem not to have a large effect on members' lives, together with the problems that churches themselves are facing, raises difficult questions about the future of the churches.

Betsy Swedborg has not stopped attending church just because she is busy. She gradually lost interest because the church was doing little to challenge people and to encourage them to lead better lives. Until she was an adult, she attended church every Sunday. She tried to listen to the sermons, but she noticed that most of the congregation was glassy eyed and that some people were sound asleep. She observed church people to see if they were living their lives any differently than those she knew who did not attend church. She couldn't see any difference. In both groups, some people were rude and disrespectful and many were good. She still believes in God but has come to the view that "it doesn't necessarily take going to church to be a good person." What really matters, she believes, is being kind and caring. "Even though I don't go to church regularly, I at least try to treat people with respect and be kind and caring," she explains.

We need to look at the people who are minding the store, the clergy, to see if they perceive the problems of the middle class the same way that members do. We need to consider what clergy are trying to do for and with their middle-class members. And we need to understand the frustrations that the plight of the middle class are causing the clergy to experience.

# four

# WHAT THE CLERGY ARE SAYING

Pastors are astute social observers. They watch and listen, trying to discern what is uppermost in their congregants' minds. Their effectiveness as pastors depends on it. So does the financial condition of their churches. To gauge the crisis in the churches, it is thus necessary to examine the mental maps of the clergy, both to see how their views compare with the concerns of middle-class church members and to understand what clergy perceive as the important connections between religious commitment and middle-class life. Particularly, how do they think about the economic realm? What do they say its relation to faith should be? And why is it such a troublesome topic?

If there is a problem in the churches, it is not because pastors fail to recognize the importance of economic matters both for the financial health of their ministries and as concerns in the lives of their parishioners. Their theological training convinces clergy that faith in God should have implications for all of life, including the work people do and the ways in which they spend their money. Pastors emphasize that people of faith should be especially responsible in the decisions they make, work harder and longer than other people, spend their money wisely, and be diligent in supporting the church. This emphasis resonates strongly with the norms of economic responsibility that already pervade the American middle class. Clergy are also at least partly attuned to the spiritual dilemma that arises from the pressures under which middle America exists. Many pastors are aware of how little free time their members have. Pastors understand that parishioners may not have energy to attend church meetings or do volunteer work. Pastors are also keenly aware of the pressures that encourage church members to spend money on material pleasures, even to the point of going heavily into debt, rather than living more simply or having more money to give away. Pastors can scarcely be faulted in their perceptions of the middle class; most are themselves residents of middle-class neighborhoods, have working spouses, and are raising children amidst the present culture of over-consumption. But pastors are also overwhelmed by these issues. Faced with the task of providing leadership, they instead admit to feeling frustrated, feeling guilty for doing too little, and feeling uncertain about how to be more effective. In order to understand the problems that are facing middle-class churches, therefore, we need to consider closely the assumptions that clergy are making about economic issues, the difficulties they perceive, and their own sense of frustration.

The clergy with whom we spoke uniformly regarded the economic realm as an important area of ministry. Unlike the laypeople we considered in the preceding chapter, pastors believe firmly that work and money should not be placed in a separate compartment from spirituality. None of them takes the economists' view that money is simply a value-neutral medium of exchange. Instead, they argue that economic behavior should be decisively influenced by a person's faith. In their mental maps, economic behavior is like a country, faith like the globe. The one is subsumed by the other. The pastor of a Methodist church put it this way: "Faith is totally inclusive. It involves every aspect of your life, from the way you participate in sports to the way you work, to the way you live at home, to the way you relate, to the way you give." At Cornerstone Church, Pastor Higgins remarked, "We believe that God is the source and resource of everything that we have. We don't have anything because we were ingenious enough or intelligent enough to get it. We believe that it came from the hand of God." A Roman Catholic priest asserted, "God is Lord of everything, including our financial needs and our financial perspectives." The pastor of an inner-city Presbyterian church put it even more strongly: "There's no such thing as faith that's not connected to all of life, particularly the economic life."

Among all the realms of life that are subsumed by faith, economic behavior is regarded by pastors as one of the most important because it symbolizes an individual's priorities. If a person purchases an expensive new car, that purchase is presumed to reflect on his or her priorities. If that person gives money to the church, the pastor also makes assumptions about how this gift is connected with a person's values. For many pastors, the church budget is thus a barometer of the spiritual health of the congregation. As one minister explained, "It's a process of prioritizing. If your giving level goes up, then you know what people are doing. If it goes down, then you also know how it's looked upon."

Besides symbolizing priorities, the economic realm is considered particularly important because it is a special area in which trust, or faith, may be necessary. One of the priests we interviewed emphasized this point, asserting that giving is a clear way of connecting faith with our physical existence. It requires faith to trust that God will supply our physical needs, but in an affluent society this trust may seldom be tested. By giving away 5 or 10 percent of one's income, one is forced to a greater realization of faith. With family budgets squeezed, it becomes necessary to trust God that one's bills can still be paid. The part given away, the priest observed, may also necessitate an act of faith in today's world. One has to have faith that the church will use the money wisely. The pastor of an independent Bible church made a similar point, arguing that trusting God, rather than material possessions, is the main point to be understood. Paraphrasing Jesus, he said, "Don't lay up for yourselves treasures on earth, which are depreciable, and stealable. They're ephemeral. But rather lay up treasures in heaven."[1]

Then, too, most pastors are candid in admitting that economic issues are especially important to them because the financial welfare of their congregations depends on it. The pastor of a suburban Baptist church, for example, noted that he is constantly encouraging his members to think about their lifestyles, their finances, and their contributions because the church needs over $300,000 each year to operate and is now facing an additional $100,000 need for repairs to its building. Another pastor said he has to reeducate his members on economic issues about once a year because the turnover in his congregation makes it hard to keep giving at a constant level. When asked what sorts of relationship they would like to see their members making between faith and economic matters, in fact, many pastors jumped immediately to a discussion of religious giving.

Among pastors with a more conservative theological orientation, economic issues are also regarded with emphasis simply because so much attention is paid to them in the Bible itself. The pastor of an Evangelical Free church, for example, estimated that about 70 percent of Jesus' parables dealt with the idea of stewardship in one way or another. Many of Jesus' teachings focus on people's work, what they did with their time, their wages, and their employees. A significant portion of the proverbs also have to do with work and the use of time. The majority of the issues raised in the prophetic texts, the issues for which the prophets were condemning their cultures, were concerned with work and the fair treatment of employees and the poor. In this pastor's view, the entire Mosaic law could in fact be interpreted in a way that has implications for the economic relations among individuals. The important thing, he said, is that economic relations be viewed in moral terms and that morality be understood in terms of those relations' humane purposes. "It wasn't some god in heaven looking for ways to make rules that would make life difficult. He's a god who is very, very concerned about the very subtle damages that people do to one another. And it's very important that we help people to understand that."

## EMPHASIZING RESPONSIBILITY

If economic behavior cannot be divorced from faith, pastors argue that individuals should take greater responsibility for understanding this connection and for putting its implications into practice. In the first place, they assert, people should take responsibility simply for establishing an appropriate perspective on work, talents, and money—seeing them as divine gifts rather than individual accomplishments. The pastor of a conservative Baptist church said that above all, he wants his congregants to realize that they are God's stewards, which means "being responsible for everything, not just what they give to God." Another explained that stewardship means seeking God's purposes in everything, honoring God with our lives, and living with a sense of gratitude.

In contemporary parlance, a divine gift is not simply something to be appreciated but something to be used wisely. Indeed, the proper way to show appreciation is to invest, work diligently, and put the gifts one has received to good use. The pastor of a mainline church located in an upper-middle-class suburb chose especially to emphasize this positive connection between diligence, having money, and its attendant privileges. "Money," he said, "is the direct result of using the talents that God has given us—to cash them into exchangeable coin. And then that exchangeable coin becomes power. It's the power to purchase the necessities of life. It's the power to protect oneself from unexpected catastrophes through insurance and savings. It's the power to provide security, monetary security, for the future through investments."

A responsible individual should, therefore, draw a large number of connections between the spiritual and the economic aspects of his or her life. The pastor of a liberal Protestant church on the East Coast argued, for example, that people should be asking about how they use their abilities, and for what, and what they are doing vocationally. "I would hope that people who are working for a firm would ask not only if the specific thing they're doing is honorable, but is what the firm is doing honorable and worthwhile and contributing to society. I would hope they would think about consumption in terms of faith issues. I would hope they would think about ecological issues. And I would hope that they would think about economic issues as they relate to the entire society, not just to their own personal welfare but to the kind of society we are building. For example, does it carry the biblical ideas of justice and fairness and peace for all?"

Pastors also insist that parishioners should take economic responsibility for their own families; care for individuals in their immediate circle of acquaintances who may be in need; and by extension, play a responsible role in supporting the church to which they belong. "We do have a responsibility to take care of our own," asserted a Presbyterian pastor. "As the Apostle Paul said, anybody who doesn't provide for his own is worse than an infidel. And so we do have a responsibility to use the power, called money, to support people." A Catholic priest emphasized that the sense of responsibility a person feels toward his or her family should also extend to the church. He says the perspective he tries to convey is that "my church is my family. I buy into this family. Out of love I want to give to what it's doing. I believe in this. I believe in the gospel that's being preached, the evangelization of the people, the person on staff who works with the poor, our social services director. I believe in the adult education program. I believe in my priest and in what he's preaching. I believe in his presence at death and at birth. I believe that this is my family. I'm proud of it. Of course I'll give to it."

Economic responsibility, in this view, starts at home. But it also extends to a wider circle. Believers have a responsibility to support other charities besides their own church and to help the needy as well. Said one pastor, "Money is the power to reach out and help others through charitable giving." Said another, "The point is that money is not just to be used for your own benefit. It is to give." He said he wants people in his church to become more involved in giving of both their money and their time, especially to help disadvantaged people in the inner city get a new start, finish high school, learn skills, and become productive members of their community.

Middle-class pastors are thus inclined to place extraordinary emphasis on the *individual's* responsibility to God. To be sure, the doctrine of stewardship acknowledges that all things come from God. It is, however, the believer's responsibility to *recognize* this fact. The individual is also charged with making wise economic investments, using God's gifts responsibly, providing for the needs of his or her family, supporting the church, and giving generously to the needy. The economic realm, in short, is no picnic for the middle-class parishioner. As the clergy see it, people should be hard at work in the Lord's vineyard.[2]

That this emphasis is indeed a middle-class trait becomes evident when comparisons are made to the remarks of clergy who have ministered to working-class congregations. Although some of them also stress the importance of being obedient and responsible, there is a much clearer sense of God, rather than the individual, being in control. Consider, for example, how Pastor Marvin Douglas explained the issue. He is currently the pastor of a middle-class African Methodist Episcopal (A.M.E.) church in the Northeast. Before that, he spent seven years in an A.M.E. church in an industrial city in the Midwest serving members who were mostly unemployed and in abject poverty. The difference between the two churches, he said, is immense. In his present congregation, families tend to be self-sufficient, and there are community programs for those who are not. In the previous congregation, the community had been deteriorating for twenty years. When the carpet mills closed down, people were left stranded with no skills and nowhere to go. Blacks and whites were at odds with each other. Families broke up. His congregation included teenaged mothers, families receiving public assistance, drug addicts, and alcoholics. Many of them had little reason to get up in the morning.

What Pastor Douglas tried to communicate to these people about economics was simply that God is in control. "God is still in control of the world. And God will take care of his people in some manner. If you're a Christian and you trust in God and you have faith in God, you will not go hungry, you will not starve, you will not be homeless if you put your faith in God. And God will open up doors, he'll make a way for you to survive. You have to believe that." His message was far different from the message heard in most middle-class churches. The pastors of middle-class churches also acknowledge that God is ultimately in control, of course, but they place practical emphasis on *us*—each one of us individually must do our part to work hard, to invest wisely, and to give generously. Wesley's dictum—make all you can, save all you can, give all you can—remains very much in evidence.[3]

## THE TROUBLESOME WORLD

If the economic realm is a world in which the middle-class Christian must be responsible, it is, nevertheless, a world that most clergy consider troublesome. Many of them see it as an expansive, imperialistic world that seduces people, drawing them into it, tempting them to want more, work more, and spend more.[4] "I think the biggest problem is that our wants usually exceed our capacity to get them," one pastor explained. "People tend to spend money on bigger cars and bigger homes and more elaborate vacations, and they don't relate their Christian responsibility to the way they handle money." Another pastor saw a fundamental contradiction between the "theory of ownership" that characterizes the American economy and the "ideal of giving" found in Christianity. According to the theory of ownership, "You work for stuff and then you purchase it and then you own it."

But in Christianity "Jesus' teaching is that that's really not our function. Instead, everything is owned by the one who created it. It's here for our pleasure certainly, but it's also here for the purpose of extending God's kingdom. That implies taking particular care with God's creation."[5]

The word that comes up most often when pastors talk about economic issues is *selfishness*. The material world is, in their view, the main arena in which self-seeking, greedy behavior prevails. In theory, it is also a realm of creativity, of productive coauthorship with God in exploring the mysteries of nature, and even a realm in which the necessities of life are attained. In practice, however, clergy look mainly at consumer behavior and worry that people are spending too much on themselves and not giving enough to the needy. A Southern Baptist pastor put it this way: "We live in a selfish society, a self-centered society. The biggest difficulty we have in becoming what God wants us to be is that we want to satisfy ourselves. We spend most of our energies and most of our income on ourselves rather than trying to meet people's needs, or in witnessing to them about Christ."

Concern about inequality comes up less often than remarks about selfishness. But pastors often refer to the needs of the poor as evidence that their middle-class congregants are living selfishly. One pastor, for example, pointed out that there were people within walking distance of his church who could not pay their utility bills, while there were church members taking three-week vacations to Hawaii. "They know there is a need," he said, "and yet they want to give themselves something." Many times, not only in his church but in all churches, he said, "our own desires take precedence over the needs of people in our communities."

The material world is especially troublesome, many pastors told us, because it is so alluring. To be sure, they themselves feel alienated from it. But they perceive most of their parishioners to be less capable of experiencing such detachment. The reason is that money—and even the pursuit of money—provides security; so much so that people depend on it rather than God. For example, Rector Morgan at Saint Andrew's recounted a conversation with a banker in his church who had recently come to the realization that he would have a great deal of trouble walking away from his work and his possessions. "I would like to feel that I had the freedom to be able to do that if the circumstances were right," the man told him. But, he said, "I fear I'm living totally in an illusion. I've made so many commitments—family commitments, financial commitments, real estate commitments, investment commitments—that I'm in bondage." The man said he was afraid that when "push came to shove" he wouldn't be able to let go. In fact, what scared him even more was that he really didn't want to find out. The problem, Morgan concluded, is that most people (unlike the banker, whose schedule was not terribly demanding) don't even have time to think about such issues. Consequently, people live in bondage without even understanding their situation.

Some of the pastors with whom we talked have also become keenly aware of the struggles their parishioners face. They talked about the time pressures people are under, especially when both spouses hold full-time jobs and try to raise children at the same time. They mentioned families in their congregations who have taken pay cuts or who have suffered emergencies and are therefore having to take on extra work or pare back their expenditures. At Redeemer Baptist, for instance, Pastor Hill talked about the members of his congregation who have lost their jobs because of cutbacks at a local automobile assembly plant. He also said his members are quite concerned about the lack of jobs for young people because they want their children to stay nearby when they grow up. Some pastors are also aware that job-related stress can be a major challenge to congregants' faith. For example, an Episcopal priest in the Midwest described how one member, the foreman of a construction crew, was under exceptional pressure because of seasonal deadlines. For this man, an important lesson to be learned is that "he can't be free simply to displace that pressure on others." According to his priest, "he's also learning how to verbalize that and to talk about it in a fairly overt way."[6]

Pastors are generally sympathetic to the struggles of their parishioners, often finding themselves in the same boat. But they are also reluctant to consider these struggles strictly as the result of economic forces beyond anyone's control. Starting with the assumption that economic commitments reflect priorities, they worry more about the underlying values than about the economic pressures themselves. They fear that something has gone awry with their congregants' values. Or, in a more sympathetic vein, they recognize that just the task of thinking about priorities is a struggle for many people. One pastor, for example, said his Sunday school superintendant arouses his sympathies because the man travels a lot, works overtime, and yet frets about whether his priorities are right and worries if he is giving as much time to the Lord as he should.

Many pastors would be happy to see their congregants struggling in this way. In their congregations, they say, such cases are rare. The majority, they feel, are all too willing to compartmentalize their faith from the economic part of their lives. "Sunday is here; Monday is there" was the way one pastor described it. Another said his congregants saw the two as "quite disparate things." He lamented that "the one doesn't have much to do with the other."

Tokenism is another idea that clergy mentioned frequently in explaining how the economic realm is troublesome. They worry that people may find symbolic ways to relate their faith to their work or finances but that they will not truly be influenced by the connection. One pastor, for example, complained about the proverbial parishioner who drives his Mercedes to his beach house every Saturday and then gives only $10 to the church on Sundays. Such behavior is problematic in pastors' minds because it violates their sense of economic responsibility. They invoke an implicit principle of proportionality. The $10 donation helps just as much if it comes from a millionaire as if it comes from a poor mother of five, but it does not show the same personal priorities. Other forms of tokenism that pastors mentioned included helping the poor and even supporting the church's outreach programs. Said one, "I don't want to confuse our social ministries with having a dynamic relationship with the living God."

## SOURCES OF FRUSTRATION

The economic realm is sufficiently alien—sufficiently troublesome—that it is a source of special frustration for many members of the clergy. They feel it is difficult to make a difference because they are up against an entire economic and cultural system. Advertising is often a symbol of the forces that they feel are overwhelmingly against them. The pastor of a Lutheran church, for example, said it was an uphill battle to get people in his congregation to think differently about economic issues because of "all of the appeals that go to people through advertising, and being drawn into that, and even young children being affected by that." He sensed that his parishioners were caught trying to keep up with the Joneses and yet struggling to pay their bills. He figures people in his congregation look to him for guidance in some general way but is not sure that he has given them much.

Another source of frustration is that they feel their parishioners are genuinely too busy with life to listen to their admonitions, let alone take them seriously. The pastor of a mainline Protestant church in a Midwestern city, for example, said he would like to have people come to the church on Wednesday evenings to study the Book of Luke. But when he stops to reflect on their schedules, he realizes that "they get home at 7:15 and they haven't eaten dinner and seen their kids; they don't want to be here at 7:30 to study Luke. In fact, *I* don't want them to be here studying Luke. I want them to be at home with their children." With that realization, he has shifted his attention to Sunday mornings because at least people are already at the church. But then he finds that many of them are out of town, either for short vacations or on business. "I mean, there's no consistency. So I struggle with that, and we haven't figured out how to do that very well." He realizes that things are different in his congregation than they were in more homogeneous neighborhoods where the church was in the same location in which people lived and worked. In fact, he finds people are even too busy to listen very well if they do come to the church. "I mean, what's the point of getting fifteen people, men and women, in here in the evening and have them literally fall asleep in the middle of the class? I'm a pretty good teacher. It's not that it's boring; it's that they can't even stand up!"

Another reason clergy feel frustrated in addressing economic matters is their sense that people don't want the pastor to meddle in their financial affairs. As one pastor lamented, "It's like asking how much they weigh!" Or, as another observed, "Anytime you start talking about money, people get nervous." Consequently, many pastors feel they have no sense of how much their congregants earn or where their money goes. Some of the ones who did feel they knew also seemed to be operating in the dark. For example, several argued strenuously that their members gave 10 percent of their incomes to the church and yet reported figures indicating that family incomes were about one-fifth as high as actual figures for the community. Others gave estimates of congregants' family incomes that seemed questionable in terms of their parishioners' occupations.

It is not, however, just that pastors feel their parishioners don't want them meddling. Many pastors are aware at some level that people in their congregations are worried about losing their jobs or having trouble paying their bills. Even in more affluent congregations, parishioners may be suffering from anxiety about being in the wrong kind of work, having to make tough ethical decisions, or feeling that their jobs are not personally fulfilling. Some of them come to their pastor for counseling. But pastors also feel frustrated because there is a norm of self-sufficiency that often prevents parishioners from turning to each other for help. The pastor of one church, for example, said he has tried to develop small groups where people can come and talk about their problems at work. He finds, however, that people in his congregation are extremely reluctant to share their deepest feelings. They put up a facade of being invulnerable. He thinks this is partly attributable to religious tradition itself. "You are taught to be independent, autonomous, and self-sufficient," he said, "and if you work hard and manage right, you will be okay." So people feel guilty if things are not going well. As another pastor exclaimed, "It would be much more embarrassing for someone's business to fail than for his marriage to fail!"

The sense that one is waging a losing battle is also a source of frustration to many clergy. They feel the value system of Christianity is fundamentally at odds with the secular culture, especially the latter's emphasis on materialism and economic self-interest. A man who ministers to an affluent congregation in Chicago, for example, said he constantly feels that he is butting against the "culture of accumulation." He tries to speak on behalf of different values. Yet he feels doubly frustrated because any time he criticizes television or advertising, the people in his congregation who work in these fields say, "Hey, don't pick on us." Some pastors candidly admitted that they monitor their messages for fear that people won't listen or, worse, quit attending and contributing. Others believe their members come to church mainly to receive reassurance and to go away feeling better about themselves. Being challenged to spend their money differently is the last thing they want to hear. As the pastor of a Baptist church in Texas explained, "God is a giving God, and our goal should be to conform our lives to his image. We can't do that without becoming givers ourselves." But doing that, he admitted, is hard. "Most of us come on Sunday mornings wanting to have a wonderful time and feel good about ourselves." Or, as another pastor put it, "What they're looking for is self-affirmation on Sunday morning. They've had a tough week, and they want to get a little peace. They want to feel good about themselves so that they can go out again on Monday morning and do the same thing that they did the week before."

Some of the clergy felt they were bucking not only the secular culture but misperceptions in their religious heritage as well. This was especially true of the Catholic clergy with whom we spoke. They felt the church had done a poor job of educating parishioners in the past about how to think about giving. People had been told simply that it was their responsibility to support the church financially. They had not been given a spiritual basis for doing so. Thus, it was possible for people to look at buildings and programs, or to think about the church's property and investments, and assume the church could get along without their contributions. "It's almost like the NIMBYs ['not in my backyard']," said one. "Let someone else do it. There's been no good education on giving. When you were little, your parents put money in the collection and that's how it got there and it wasn't up to you." To this day, he said, people come up to him and say, "The churches always have their hand out, don't they?" He wishes people could see the church as "we" rather than "they."

An Episcopal priest in an affluent section of Chicago, troubled especially by the failure of his parishioners to draw connections between their work and their faith, also placed some of the blame on church traditions. In his view, the church had perpetuated this situation by being focused too much on the family. "The paradigm of the family church," he said, "is for nice little people to come on Sunday mornings to do their church stuff." That paradigm, he said, must change. "The church has be in the places where people actually spend most of their time during the week. Their lives are really centered in the arena of business. So for the church to sit back here in the suburbs and say, 'Here we are and we're open on Sunday mornings. Come on in' is naive. In fact, it's irresponsible."

None of these difficulties is so powerful that pastors simply throw up their hands and do nothing to minister to the economic values of their congregants. Indeed, many of the ones we talked with mentioned some kind of program or activity that was intended to help congregants draw closer connections between faith and economic behavior. For example, at the very moment the pastor of an upper-middle-class, mainline Protestant church in Dallas was being interviewed, there were ninety-one people in the fellowship hall downstairs attending an eight-hour seminar called "Your Work Matters to God." Developed by a businessman in the congregation, its purpose was to encourage thinking about how to apply standards of honesty and integrity in the workplace.

In some of the more prosperous middle-class churches, pastors pointed to growth in their budgets as evidence that parishioners were truly interested in relating their faith to economic issues. For example, the pastor of a Korean church with approximately 700 members pointed out that his congregation was giving generously to the support of a variety of missionary works, colleges, orphanages, and community programs. Similarly, the priest at a Roman Catholic parish in New Jersey mentioned a new tithing program he had initiated to demonstrate that his congregation was interested in faith-finance connections.

Quite often, pastors were inspired too by particular acts of generosity within their congregations. One, for example, recalled how a wealthy woman had recently marched into a meeting, plopped down $1,000, and challenged each of the others to do the same. Other pastors were inspired just by the fact that a few of their parishioners seemed to be listening to what they said. An Episcopal priest in suburban Philadelphia, for example, admitted that most of his congregants didn't have a clue about the meaning of stewardship, but it was "exciting" to him that he could name several who did.

Some of them also pinned their hopes on new programs they could initiate at some point in the future. The Chicago priest, for example, said he dreamed of a day when the Episcopal church would operate from a new paradigm. Sometime in the next twenty years, he hopes, it will become mandatory for suburban churches to hire an ordained staff member with an office in downtown Chicago. People, then, could come to see him or have lunch with him there. He could also run Bible studies and prayer groups in the workplace. "If there was any connection to be made, it would be that he came here on Sunday morning. But the church would be represented by that person. That's where the body of Christ would come together."

## FEELING OVERWHELMED

Occasional programs and glimmers of hope notwithstanding, most of the pastors we spoke with felt overwhelmed by the economic realm. Many of them admitted as much, pointing out that they had done little to motivate their congregants to relate their faith to this area. The pastor of a small Presbyterian church, for example, said she preaches about stewardship believing people are paying attention, but she has little indication from them that they have in fact listened. The Lutheran pastor who was concerned about the effects of advertising, caught short by the thought that people may be looking to him for guidance, mused that he should probably try to run an adult Sunday school class on the topic sometime. Others said they had done a little but felt they didn't understand the issues well enough or have the time to do more. In several cases, clergy were genuinely intimidated by the subject. A man with a doctorate who was widely respected for his preaching and who had held offices in his denomination, for example, said he wanted to preach on the topic of bankruptcy and Christian responsibility but felt he just didn't understand the nuances of the subject well enough to do so.

While most pastors acknowledge the importance of relating faith to economic behavior in a wide variety of ways, some of them whittle down the issue to more manageable proportions by focusing the bulk of their attention on giving and church finances. Asked what they are doing to encourage parishioners to relate the two realms, they turn immediately to their favorite fund-raising techniques. One pastor, for example, said he was working out a better system of contacting members during the annual pledge drive.

Other pastors take a much wider view of what must be done to apply Christian principles to economic issues but do so in a way that makes the task truly intimidating. Discussions of economic justice, in particular, seem to follow this path. A Presbyterian pastor, for example, went to some length to talk about the problems of capitalism, exploitation, and the need for better relations between workers and managers. He told how he had played a role in labor negotiations in a previous congregation. But the thrust of his remarks was to indicate that such involvement was very difficult to generate. He was doubtful that any of his present parishioners were likely to become very active in such issues.

Not feeling confident about how to help their parishioners relate work and money to their faith, some pastors also deflect attention elsewhere. In giving lip service to the idea that faith embraces all of life, they nevertheless undermine the importance of economic issues by pointing out that a "social gospel" is not the same thing as the real gospel or by asserting that people simply need to straighten out their priorities in their own unique ways. They also emphasize symbolism, arguing that the church can be nothing more than a beacon of light in a dark world rather than making an actual difference to the majority of its members.

On the whole, pastors' sense of efficacy in addressing economic issues is quite low. As moral leaders, they betray doubt and uncertainty. Their language itself reveals that they feel little authority to speak about concrete issues other than church finances. The image they present is of a weak voice surrounded by a vast sea of obstacles. They cling to an occasional testimony about good deeds or good thoughts, but even those positive examples are sometimes diminished by their concern about tokenism.

## THE CRISIS IN MINISTRY

*Crisis* is not a word pastors are fond of using. They prefer to be optimistic about their ministries. But listening to them discuss their frustrations and observing how gingerly they treat the relationship between faith and economic concerns, one gains the impression that there truly is a crisis of significant proportions in America's churches. The clergy recognize that economic issues must be dealt with if faith is to be relevant in all parts of life. They want their parishioners to be responsible stewards, understanding their possessions and talents as God's gifts and using these gifts wisely in their work, for the support of their families, in helping the needy, and in maintaining the churches themselves. Most pastors can point to some successes in getting this message across. But most of them readily admit that the successes are few.

In theory, the problem is finding ways to challenge middle-class church members to be more responsible in the use of their time and money. In practice, the problem is one of ministering to the needs and hurts of these members themselves. Their struggles must be attended to enough that they can understand what it means to have faith and to give generously as a response to that faith. Most pastors realize this at some level, and yet their language suggests that they are often failing to connect with the issues that are on their members' minds.

The failure to connect is evidenced by the fact that economic behavior for most Americans, men and women alike, consists above all of their time at work. Yet when asked without prompting of any kind to talk about the relationships between faith and economic behavior, most pastors did not mention their parishioners' work at all. They talked instead about church finances, pledge drives, and the responsible use of money. At Grace Church, for instance, Rev. Fisher emphasized the following when asked what connections he wants people in his church to make between their faith and their economic concerns: "We'd hope very much for them to look at biblical principles of giving and sharing. We're very much involved with tithing and offerings. One example, the last Sunday of each month we have a benevolence offering, and it's a very sizable amount each month. And from that all kinds of things are done in the ministry of the church: Utility bills are paid, rents are paid, food is provided for families out of work, counseling services, just innumerable ministries are provided through the benevolence ministry. They are very actively involved in their faith, and their economics are intertwined, they're not something separate." Those pastors who did talk about work did so primarily in the context of lamenting that people had too little time and energy left over for meetings at the church. Very few mentioned the attendant strains on marriages and children or the gender issues that arise in the contemporary workplace.

What pastors sometimes did recognize was that members are extremely reluctant to discuss economic issues with them. This reluctance was especially true of
money. As the pastor of a Mennonite church remarked, "I don't know if it's just
Mennonites or everyone, but they'd rather talk about their sex lives than their
finances. Finances are extremely private." As a result, pastors draw their inferences
from pledge cards (which are sometimes shielded from their view as well) or from
the occasional member who decides to seek financial counseling from the clergy.

Thus, it was evident in many of our interviews that clergy themselves sensed a
gap between their own views and those of the laity. While they could generally
point to one or two faithful members who saw things as they did, they were convinced that the majority did not. In most of the churches, pastors doubted that
their parishioners shared their concern about the financial well-being of the
church. They perceived laity to be unwilling to make genuine economic sacrifices,
sometimes conveying the impression that laity did not appreciate the kind of sacrifice that they themselves had made in choosing to enter the ministry. In a more
positive vein, some clergy also indicated a gap between the kinds of economic pressures experienced by laity and those experienced by themselves.

Pastors' sense of a gap between their own orientations and those of the laity is
understandable. Judging from what they say, there is indeed a considerable gap.
Compared with what laity themselves report, clergy are much more likely to think
about faith and economic issues in terms of church finances than laity are. Clergy
take the doctrine of stewardship as a given. Laity quite often say they have no idea
what the doctrine is at all, or have trouble expressing it in concrete terms. Pastors
also emphasize individual responsibility, charging laity with the duties of controlling their expenditures, thinking properly, taking responsibility for the financial
health of the church, and giving generously to the needy. Laity are likely to be worried already about their finances and their jobs. They want comfort, perhaps the
teaching that God is in control, rather than sermons telling them to shoulder even
more responsibility.

Some pastors recognize that they are operating from a *church culture* that perpetuates its own traditions and practices but often has little to do with the daily lives
of church members. A poignant example was given by a pastor who had recently
taken a leave of absence because his wife was in the final stages of a terminal ill-
ness. During these months he attended services at a wide variety of other churches
in surrounding communities (finding he could not attend his own church without
having to assume pastoral responsibilities). What he discovered, he said, was "the
irrelevance of the pulpit." Pastors were preaching familiar sermons about familiar
topics, but in his view they were failing to connect with the real struggles of their
middle-class congregants.

If there is a gap between clergy and laity, the two nevertheless do share common
ground, and this ground may well be the necessary starting place for working

together. Clergy and laity alike sense that something is wrong in American culture and that the problem somehow is centered in the economic realm. They worry that materialism is a major social problem and that advertising is corrupting their children. Church members are indeed reluctant to talk about money, not only with clergy but even with their closest friends. Thus, they feel alone when problems arise at work or with their finances. They also feel inadequate to deal with these issues, having been trained by their teachers and by the mass media to think that only economists can understand such problems. Not surprisingly, laity feel just as confused as clergy do about giving to the church itself.

It is also evident from what we have considered in this chapter that work, the consequences of work for family life, money, church finances, and giving to the needy are all specific areas in which connections need to be made between faith and economics. Clergy want their members to make these connections, and if such connections are to be made, specific teaching, preaching, and instruction must take place. Work, in particular, appears to be an issue sorely in need of greater understanding. We turn to this issue in the next chapter.

# five

# MEETING NEEDS
# IN THE WORKPLACE

Christianity has always recognized that its followers must earn their daily bread. Yet it has also maintained that the human spirit is not nurtured by bread alone. There is thus an inherent tension in how the churches minister to the work lives of their adherents. In American culture, however, this tension has been greatly diminished. The clergy have adopted a view of work that is thoroughly secular. They minister to the emotional needs of the American work force but inadvertently contribute to these needs in the first place. The clergy are thus playing a valuable role in the lives of their parishioners, but this role also characterizes a vicious cycle in which the churches are caught. It consists of preaching about work in a way that demands high levels of commitment, both to the job and to the church, but that fails to consider the ways in which work has changed for most Americans. Not finding what the clergy have to say about work very relevant to the real demands of their lives, parishioners are thus likely to compartmentalize spirituality and work— or to give less generously and attend less often because the churches are failing to minister to this central area of their lives.[1]

As they preach and provide counseling about work, clergy of course are interested in saying things that are both consistent with their own theological convictions and sensible to their listeners. Thus, the problem is neither that they say nothing about work nor that they make arguments that seem ridiculous or utterly idealistic. The problem is that clergy are caught in cultural conditions that make it hard for them to speak with special authority or to say anything distinctive about work. They tell people, for instance, to choose work that will make them happy, choose responsibly, pay attention to their feelings, and cultivate a good attitude no matter what they do. Who would disagree? That, precisely, is the rub. Nobody will disagree, but it is also easy for people to say that the church has little effect on their work. Even active churchgoers, like the ones we considered in chapter 3, will say that religious teachings had little influence on their choice of work and that their religious convictions do not shape the way they work on a daily basis.

My point in raising this criticism is not to suggest that clergy should stand up next Sunday morning and tell people to choose jobs that will make them *unhappy* or to be *irresponsible* about their work. Rather, my argument is that we have come to the point in our society that we can scarcely imagine *how* clergy might be able to guide us more effectively in our work.[2] We may seek their advice if we already happen to be loyal members of a church. If so, we may trust the pastor to give us good advice because he is a person of faith. But the pastor's counsel may be so similar to what we would hear at school or from our friends that we could just as well get it elsewhere. Moreover, the most explicit counsel we may receive is to pray for a good attitude about our work. But attitudes are only one dimension of our existence. How we actually behave, the decisions we make, whom we interact with, and what we say are equally important. If religion now influences only our attitudes, then its power has surely been weakened. And if the main criterion of faith-informed attitudes is that we are happy, then we have become the measure of faith and the end of faith, displacing God and the glorification of God. Our very orientation to faith encourages us to pursue a self-interested orientation that puts ourselves ahead of the church and its needs. The place to begin trying to understand this vicious cycle is the way in which the calling is portrayed in America's churches.[3]

## THE CALLING

The calling of God to one's vocation or line of work remains an important teaching in the eyes of most clergy. They regard this concept as a vital component of Christian doctrine, and they want people to understand it. Indeed, all of the pastors we interviewed said the calling was a teaching that the churches should emphasize. Not one diminished its importance relative to other doctrines. Nearly all spoke eloquently about it, and none claimed to have difficulty understanding how to discuss it. The pastor of a Presbyterian church in Chicago put it well when he asserted, "It's one of the dynamic, cutting edges of Christianity. We are all called to be faithful children of God, and our occupation becomes the way to work out our Christian vocation." He said the church should be in the business of articulating what that vocation means. Other clergy expressed similar sentiments about the calling. For instance, an Episcopal priest explained that "it answers one of the great questions for us, the great fundamental question of 'Who am I?' and 'Why am I here?' 'What is my purpose?' It helps to arrive at those answers." A Lutheran pastor in Oregon drew an immediate connection to Martin Luther's emphasis on the calling, saying that Luther was right in arguing that "our callings are not simply secular means of making money or a living but are God's means of utilizing our gifts and interests to his glory." Catholic clergy, emphasizing that *vocation* is more commonly used than *calling*, also stressed its importance. As one priest explained, "It shows a personal concern on the part of God for each person. It's like knowing that the hairs on our heads are numbered, as the scriptures say. It's an intimate thing to know that God is personally calling me to do his work. You have a role, and things would not be the same here without you."[4]

But most of the clergy with whom we talked felt the idea of a calling is lost in American culture. A Methodist pastor in Missouri, for example, said she doesn't think the people in her church feel any sense of calling at all. A Presbyterian pastor in Virginia framed his response in broader terms. "Obviously," he asserted, "the whole notion of vocation is tremendously lost today. The only people who have a calling, who have a vocation, are those who are paid poorly, and so we make up for it by exalting their professional life by calling it a calling. For example, a nurse has a calling, a minister has a calling, we pay them not what they're worth and so we exalt it by giving them a calling." The pastor of a Methodist church in New Jersey was only slightly more optimistic. He thought some of the people in his congregation who worked in the professions probably thought of their work in idealistic terms similar to that of a calling. He noted, however, that people would not use the term in actually talking about their work. It would seem impolite to them, like speaking too openly about fears of death.

In these views, clergy appear to be largely correct. Among the American labor force as a whole, only 30 percent say they mostly agree with the statement "I feel God has called me to the particular line of work I am in." Church members are only slightly more likely to agree (40 percent) than the rest of the labor force. Only 31 percent of churchgoers, moreover, say their religious values influenced their decision to pursue a certain line of work.[5] When people are asked to describe their reasons for choosing their line of work, and to discuss what they like or dislike about their work (allowing them to use whatever language they wish), even fewer opt to talk about a calling. A man who works in the banking business in Chicago, for example, gave a typical reply when he said he did not feel that God had called him to his line of work. The only way that religious values had influenced him was that he decided he did not want to work for a religious organization. On a day-to-day basis, he said his religious values also did not influence his work because his policy was simply to be honest, which he would try to be anyway. Yet this man was the son of missionaries, had attended a Christian college, and described himself as an evangelical Christian.

Believing that the idea of a calling is valuable but little understood, clergy consider it an important aspect of their ministries to encourage parishioners to view their work as a calling. Their teaching on this subject is clearly one of the ways in which they try to draw connections between faith and the economic lives of their middle-class members. Indeed, nearly all of the clergy with whom we talked said they had preached on the topic, mentioned it in sermons, or tried to counsel people in their congregations by discussing it with them. How clergy understand the calling is thus a key to grasping how they attempt to minister to the work lives of their parishioners.

## THE GOSPEL OF HAPPINESS

The theme that emerges most often in clergy's remarks about the calling is that people should pursue personal happiness in their work. Pastors do not always put the theme this bluntly, but they clearly emphasize contentment, satisfaction, doing work that one enjoys, and gaining psychological gratification from that activity. They deny that God would ever expect a person to pursue work that made him or her unhappy. They also assume, some more explicitly than others, that God positively wants people to be happy. Thus, the right work, the career to which an individual could feel called, is work that makes him or her feel good about what he or she is doing. A Presbyterian pastor, for example, expressed the common view when he observed that people sometimes do not have a choice of jobs, but if they do, they should think about their interests and talents and then ask themselves, "What will be most fulfilling for me?" A Lutheran pastor said the important thing is for people to reflect on all aspects of a prospective job, considering whether they will be satisfied with it and "experience joy." He recognizes that happiness "sometimes will not materialize," but he figures a person is in the wrong line of work if there is "a sense of drudgery." A Methodist pastor likened work to one's hobbies, using this analogy to make a similar point to that of the Lutheran minister. He said he loves to play baseball and is reasonably good at it. If he were to choose another occupation, he would try to get into something that he could love as much as baseball.

The theme of happiness is clearly in evidence in the sermons clergy preach about work. Virtually every one of the sermons we examined, in fact, stressed that God wants people to be happy and that something is probably wrong if one's work is not a source of personal happiness. The pastor of a nondenominational church in California, for example, drew from the New Testament example of believers "exhorting" other believers to make the following point about happiness in general: "What they were saying was not life is a drag and be miserable now and someday you'll get to go to heaven and be happy. But they were saying that there are dimensions of victory, of triumph, of confidence, of abundance that are available to every believer now." The pastor of a Mennonite church in Pennsylvania took as his text the following passage from Ecclesiastes: "A person can do nothing better than to eat and drink and find satisfaction in his work." He argued that happiness on the job is one of God's true gifts. (He did not discuss the writer's lament in the same passage: "All is vanity under the sun.")

One of the more detailed expositions of happiness in work was given by the pastor of a large Baptist church in Texas. His theme was the "attitude" that God wants people to have toward their work. Drawing his audience in, he began by suggesting that some of them probably loved their work and couldn't wait to get up each morning, while others probably hated their work. Without passing judgment on the latter, he posed the example of a man he knew who had been a coach for eighteen years. The man told him that it never seemed as if he was working at all because he loved what he did so much. How, then, could other people learn to have such happiness? "You know," he observed, "I think if we're going to be happy in our work, we need to be enthusiastic about our work. The word *enthusiasm* comes from the Latin word *enthus*, meaning 'engodded' or 'god within.' And people who really are excited about their work are people who are enthusiastic about their work. And I believe if you're going to be enthusiastic about your work, you need to love what you do. A lot of us don't love what we do. We need to learn to love what we do."

Learning to be happy in our jobs, he argued, depends on realizing that God loves us and cares about what we do. He had in mind something similar to the idea of a calling, but it was not so much a theological concept as an ongoing attitude. "So many times," he lamented, "we just leave God at home. We leave God in a box, or we just leave God in the church. That's for Sundays. And we don't take the great power source with us. We don't take that great avenue of peace and contentment with us into the workplace. That's why we're miserable." His inference was clear: Being close to God makes one happy at work; being unhappy at work is a sign of not being close to God. Thus, the believer not only has a formula for happiness but a duty to be happy. Not only will he or she benefit, but God will benefit as well. "If you work with a song in your heart and a smile on your face and a spring in your step," he concluded, "then God is going to be pleased." Whistle while you work, we might say, is the Christian way.

Some of the pastors we talked to felt it especially important to focus on happiness because, in their view, the church had too often associated work with unhappiness. One pastor, who said he tries to preach an upbeat sermon about work every Labor Day, characterized the older view this way: "One interpretation is that work is a curse and that God wanted us to occupy leisure land. He put us in a fairy-tale garden where we were to just sit back and enjoy the fruit of the land and everything was going to be wonderful. Then we messed up and because we messed up, we had to go to work. Work is our punishment for sinning." He said people find it refreshing when he tells them God is a worker and that they can find pleasure in their work. At Cornerstone Bible Church, Pastor Higgins was also intent on combating negative images of God. "He's not this cosmic killjoy that wants to ruin our fun and rain on our parade and take away all of our joy," he explained. In his view, God creates each person with an intrinsic capacity to enjoy life; all we have to do is find out how to maximize our enjoyment.

Sermons are one of the most important ways in which clergy communicate their ideas to their congregations. When the subject is work, clergy also try to guide their flocks by providing individual counseling. Asking clergy what they would tell someone who came to them seeking career advice is thus another way of determining how clergy understand the subject. Their responses again reveal how much emphasis they put on personal happiness. At San Xavier's parish, for example, Father Martinez explained that when people come to him for advice about their jobs, he always asks, "Are you happy where you are now?" Then he tells them, "You have to be happy in what you do. If you are not happy, then you're not going to enjoy anything." Sometimes, he observed, people say to him, "Father, I'm not happy." Then he counsels them to change jobs until they are happier. "There'll be a risk, but you can change things, you can find a place where you will be happy. If you're miserable at work, then you're going to produce misery for those people that come to you. So you have to find a place where you are comfortable with yourself."

Pastors who deal with quite different kinds of people also stressed the central pursuit of personal happiness. A Methodist pastor who routinely counsels young people, for example, said she always begins by asking about what they most enjoy doing. "Do they like to be with people, do they like to be more by themselves? Do they like to work with their hands, or do they like to do more abstract things? Maybe they like to write, or maybe they like math." She said she "just tries to help them find some things that they like." Another pastor, an older man who deals mainly with professionals and managers his own age, said his main concern is to keep people from becoming bored or dissatisfied with their work. He doesn't want them to feel frustrated. A Lutheran pastor in suburban Chicago made a similar point. He said most of his parishioners enjoy their work, so he doesn't feel he needs to say much. He is concerned, however, when he watches people getting off the commuter trains at night and sees how worried they look.

The advice clergy say they would give people does not seem to differ measurably from the advice their parishioners would receive anywhere else. If happiness is the main consideration, the way to identify the right career is through such standard activities as taking preference tests, checking out employment options, thinking seriously about one's talents and goals, paying close attention to one's feelings, and talking with trusted friends. The pastor of a Baptist church, for example, said he encourages people to ask themselves whether a prospective job is reasonable for them and whether the hours are right and the pay suitable. He knows jobs in his community are difficult to locate, so he tells people to take seriously anything they can find. "I think," he observed, "that common sense enters into it a lot. You have to decide by what's out there and by what you feel comfortable doing." The pastor of a large Methodist church said he tells people to ask themselves the following questions: "What do you want to accomplish? Do you feel qualified and capable of doing this particular job, and if not, what would be your plan to get qualified? Do you have other options? And what are the motivating factors that make you think you want to do this?"

Such advice pays special attention to rational thought. A wise, responsible person is someone who carefully gathers information, weighs his or her options, and makes a decision based on all the relevant facts. Asked what sort of advice he gives, a United Church of Christ pastor in Connecticut, for example, said he begins by taking a personal history, finding out about the person's educational background, work experience, aptitudes, and abilities. He said, "We're dealing with reality here. I don't think God works devoid of reality. I'd have to find out where the person is in their life. We've got some work to do. We can't pull it out of a hat." Another man, an Assemblies of God pastor, was even more emphatic about the role of reason. "God gives us the great ability to think," he observed, "the ability to reason. I'm overwhelmed when I think of the privilege I have to read and reason and make decisions. I think we're responsible to God for that."

However, this process is less rational than it may appear on the surface. Clergy end up placing a great deal more emphasis on feelings than they do on rational processes themselves. They do not, for example, suggest answering a series of test questions about interests and talents, running the results through a computer, and following whatever the computer—or, for that matter, a trained guidance counselor—suggests. Instead, they encourage people to let their feelings be the ultimate source of guidance. After considering the various pieces of information, they should simply ask themselves which option "feels right." To the extent that God has a hand in these matters, then, it is evident most clearly in a subjective sense of peace, assurance, or feeling comfortable.

An example of how feelings are emphasized comes from a pastor in Kansas who recounted what he had said recently to a man in his congregation who came to him for advice. The man said, "I have a job offer that's going to be a substantial increase in money." The pastor replied, "Talk to me about it. What will you be doing?" And the man said, "Well, it will require travel." The pastor knew the man has a six-year-old daughter, so he probed until the man acknowledged that he might be gone four or five days at a time. Then the pastor asked directly, "How do you feel about that?" The man realized he felt a bit uncomfortable, so instead of taking the job, he sold his house and bought a less expensive one.

The role of faith is easy to overlook in these accounts. Clergy appear to present themselves as advisers, not because they have any special wisdom to offer but simply because they are available. Their parishioners trust them and come to them as a sounding board. Their role is to encourage reflection and paying attention to how one feels rather than being swayed too much by salary offers. As one pastor put it, his task is simply to ask, "Does this feel right to you?" God plays much the same role. Prayer is a way of quieting one's thinking, not worrying so much about the outcome, and trusting that good will come from whatever decision one makes. "The Lord expects us to have faith," said the Baptist pastor, "but he doesn't expect us to be stupid and just take flying leaps."

In emphasizing happiness, clergy generally deny that God prefers individuals to choose one particular line of work rather than another. That idea sounds too deterministic to most of them. They prefer to think that God gives people a wide range of options and expects them to be responsible enough to choose a line of work that they enjoy. A United Church of Christ pastor said it seemed crass to him to think that "God has to be somehow running around making people do this or that." Others acknowledged there were undoubtedly certain occupations that were better for some people than for others. But they saw this more as a matter of personality styles, talents, and interests than anything else.

Clergy trained in Calvinist traditions were somewhat more likely than other clergy to retain a sense that God's will involved specific occupations. But they also interpreted Calvinism as providing a general principle for living rather than as a way of understanding particular jobs. One Presbyterian pastor, for example, explained that God's will is the same for all of us: simply to live faithfully. Thus, a faithful person should weigh his or her abilities and interests and "make a faithful choice as to how to live that out." He or she would, in this sense, have to decide on a particular occupation. But any number of occupations might be suitable.

A few clergy from theologically conservative denominations insisted that God probably targeted people for specific jobs. But generally, evangelical clergy were somewhat more likely than liberal clergy to give an additional reason why God does not care which particular job a person chooses. In their view, it is important to find God's will for everything one does. Thus, one's work matters to God and should be pleasing to God. What is even more pleasing to God, though, is the devotional aspect of one's life. A believer should pray, read the Bible, and live according to God's moral law. If those tasks are done, the believer is likely to be happy no matter what kind of work he or she is doing. As one pastor explained, it's like choosing a wife. Within limits (that is, not marrying a non-Christian), it is less important which person one marries than how faithful one is in marriage. By the same token, the Christian at work should, as one pastor put it, simply do "the things that God expects every Christian to do: study the Scriptures, be ashamed before the Lord, pray that you don't faint, and assemble together."

The most vivid description of what God expects came from a Baptist pastor who likened God's calling to the dreams of a parent. He said he had often gone into his children's bedrooms to comfort one of them who had awakened in the night. After rocking them to sleep, he would sit there for a while with the child on his lap and dream about their future. He said he didn't dream that one would become a doctor and another a lawyer and another an executive. He dreamed that they would grow up healthy, whole, and happy. He figured that was the sort of hope God had for his children as well. God wanted them to be happy no matter what their occupation was. For God to insist that they be one thing or another, he felt, would be too constraining.

Happiness, then, consists only to a small degree of the contentment derived from feeling that one made the right choice in entering a career in the first place. It is in larger measure a matter of day-to-day feelings and perceptions. It depends on having the right *attitude* toward one's work. Many of the remarks already considered indicate this conclusion. The pastor of a Japanese church in California also gave it particular emphasis. Noting the rise of a phenomenon in Japan known as "death by overwork," he argued that people in his congregation too will experience burnout and stress unless they remember each day that God cares about their work and wants them to enjoy what they are doing. Another pastor explained to his congregation in a sermon on working that what they must experience is a change in attitude. Each day, he said, their attitude must be that they are really working for the Lord, not just their employer. Still another pastor warned his parishioners that work would inevitably become "repetitive, meaningless, and just plain unpleasant" unless they remembered to pray each day and thank God for their jobs.

This emphasis on day-to-day happiness, it is worth observing, bears significantly on the much-considered question of whether the clergy are still emphasizing the proverbial "work ethic" or whether their teachings have turned in other directions.[6] The work ethic is still evident. For example, some clergy still empha-size that people should strive for excellence in their work as a way of glorifying God. There is, however, a shift of emphasis. The assumption is not that people will strive more for excellence if they work to glorify God. It is rather that people will strive for excellence anyway, so the important thing is to get their motives straight. Thus, the believer may not work any differently from anyone else (other than not working for a bad company) but understands his or her work differently. Pastors also argue that people should exercise responsibility. Yet taking responsibility for one's work is much more likely to mean taking responsibility for one's feelings than simply working hard or doing the job well. It is, therefore, not surprising that reg-ular churchgoers do not work longer hours than the unchurched. However, they are somewhat more likely to express satisfaction with their jobs.

The work ethic is perhaps indirectly reinforced in this way. At least clergy some-times mention that people will probably do their jobs better if they are happy with their work. They also encourage what has been called an "intrinsic motive" for working, as opposed to extrinsic motives such as working merely to earn money. Clergy often explain what they mean by happiness, for example, by contrasting people who work because they love their jobs with people who work in order to obtain money. The latter case is assumed to be more common but is considered less legitimate than the former. For example, a Nazarene pastor in the Midwest asserted that he sensed people in his community were not interested in thinking about the calling, preferring to associate the idea with pastors rather than their own work. He said their logic was probably as follows: "I want to live in such-and-such neighborhood where the houses cost such-and-such. What kind of jobs pay the sort of money I will need to live there? I'll pursue the sort of job that will get me the money to get me the house." The pastor of a Southern Baptist church in Texas expressed a similar view. He thinks most people's understandings of work are "dol-lar-driven," but he tries to get his church members to consider what they would really enjoy doing. The typical response, he said, runs something like the following: "I really do enjoy teaching, but they're just not paying anything and I just can't see myself going to four years of college or five or six to get a master's and make this. I'd much rather go to ITT or some technical school and become a plumber. At least I can make $40 an hour." He said he encourages people to think about the meaning of work rather than the economics of working. But when he finishes, the person usually says, "That was a great speech, pastor, but I think I'd better do what will make me a good living." The Methodist clergywoman quoted earlier illustrates that such views are not restricted to conservative churches. She said she wants peo-ple to love their work and to feel fulfilled by it. That, in her view, is the true mean-ing of the calling. But most people, she said, have a "calling to money" rather than a calling to their work. She recalled the years she spent as a campus minister. Students would come to her feeling unhappy, and she would realize that they were majoring in a field they didn't like but pursuing it because it would pave the way for a lucrative career.

Reflected in these remarks is the assumption that American society has become so materialistic that people do not think about their jobs except as a way to make money. The churches can play a role, therefore, simply by prompting people to think in broader ways. The Methodist clergywoman also provided a good illustration of this argument. She said the students she talks to are so absorbed with the idea of making a lot of money that she tries to "deprogram" them. She tries to get them to be true to themselves. She does this not so much by giving them answers as by asking pointed questions: "Is money the most important thing in your life?" "How can you become a whole person?" "How can you be true to your dreams of what you would like to do and who you would like to be?"

The trade-off between happiness and money is an idea that many clergy gravitate to intuitively. They have made this decision themselves. They know they are being paid less than their colleagues in other professions. But they also insist they are happier. One pastor, for example, observed that he had majored in prelaw but had decided as a senior to go to seminary instead. After serving as a pastor for several years, he earned his doctorate and became a college professor. His first love, however, was still the pastorate, so he decided to return to a congregation. His church is small and financially struggling, but he feels he is happier than he would have been in law or teaching.

Some clergy extend this idea by encouraging their parishioners to take their cues from the congregation rather than the secular world. In this view, the congregation is a kind of enclave. It helps people be happy by giving them the right messages about their work. Right messages include striking a balance between work and family, or working for the fun of it, rather than taking on a higher-pressure job that may pay better but requires moving to another community. The former message was especially evident in the Hispanic churches we visited. Hispanic men and women often experience tension between the supportive extended families to which they are loyal and the demands of the workplace. One priest told us that his parishioners come to him asking if they are going to have to push and shove and stab each other in order to get a good position. He tries to tell them that it is okay to be competitive but that they should not neglect their families and church. The pastor of an independent charismatic fellowship composed of Anglos made much the same point. She said she discourages people from thinking too much about their jobs, promotions, and money. She tries to help them be true to their families and to others in their congregation. People, she feels, can be happier if they balance work with warm Christian fellowship.

Personal happiness is, of course, not the only goal that clergy stress in their teachings about work. A few emphasize service in their discussions of the calling as well. But these remarks are infrequent and are generally couched within a larger discussion that attaches even more importance to personal happiness. A Presbyterian pastor, for example, said it is important to consider the needs of the world in deciding on a career. But when asked what he says to young people who come to him for career advice, he said the main questions he poses are: "Would you have fun doing it? Is it challenging? What would you be doing that you would feel proud to tell your children and grandchildren about? What sort of contribution are you making to the common good in this job?"

The deemphasis on service means, incidentally, that clergy are much more likely to view the church itself as a way for parishioners to serve others than to consider that service may also be accomplished in the workplace. The pastors who saw church and family competing with careers and money were especially likely to define the former, rather than the latter, as the main arena of service. Others assumed that people were working because they had to; because they were eager to have more money than they needed; or, in the best scenario, because they derived personal satisfaction from their work. But they seldom talked about secular work in terms of its value to the wider community.

The most full-blown language for talking about the calling as personal happiness is the language of therapy. In this language, the starting place is an assumption that people are generally screwed up. They are trying to be somebody else, or they are struggling with addictions or dysfunctional backgrounds. Instead of being screwed up, God wants them to experience wholeness, that is, to have peace and joy in their lives. The way to achieve this wholeness is to realize that one is unique, is called, not so much to perform a particular task as to be a distinct individual. Once one realizes this uniqueness, it becomes possible to focus on one's personal fulfillment. This realization itself will give one more energy. The result may not be wealth or success, but it will be happiness. And what differentiates this understanding from a purely secular therapeutic orientation is the view that God also works within the individual, whether that person knows it or not. Thus, there is a kind of divine force that helps the individual in attaining true happiness in life.

## MIRRORING THE CULTURE

In many ways, it is not surprising to find clergy emphasizing happiness in their discussions of work. The pursuit of happiness is a prominent theme in American culture. Addressing this pursuit is a way for the churches to be relevant. However, the question remains whether clergy are saying anything distinctive or are merely reinforcing the culture in which they live.

The answer to this question will, of course, vary from church to church and from pastor to pastor. Nevertheless, some general tendencies must be considered. The extent to which churches' emphasis on happiness mirrors the prevailing culture can be assessed by considering more closely what the clergy were trying to communicate as they talked about work and happiness.

One clear conclusion to be drawn from the foregoing remarks is that language itself is part of the problem. Many of the clergy we talked to were trying to express thoughts about deeper meanings in life. Yet the words they used are either sufficiently vague or sufficiently popular in the secular culture that it is difficult to know precisely what is being said. Terms such as *happiness, satisfaction, fulfillment, contentment,* and *enjoyment,* or phrases such as *doing what you like,* are often used interchangeably. Some of these terms are meant to suggest transcendence, a life-encompassing commitment that may involve struggle and pain as well as good feelings, and a deeper contribution to the development of the whole person. Yet, if presented to audiences who hear the same words repeated in beer commercials, it is perhaps doubtful whether these deeper meanings register. To communicate more precisely, the churches may need a richer language in which to talk about happiness, fulfillment, and related ideas. Meanwhile, it is all too easy for such ideas to become formulaic slogans used to shut down conversation ("Yes, sure, I just like what I do") rather than to promote deeper reflection. As one pastor admitted in talking about fulfillment, "I guess that's the word, isn't it? It's kind of new to me."

Imprecision of language, however, reflects another problem. The clergy's authority to speak about work at all has significantly eroded in modern culture. The fact that clergy resort to words drawn from the worlds of advertising, therapy, and vocational counseling is symptomatic of the declining influence of theology. Seldom do they speak from a rich tradition of theological debate (as they might if discussing the Eucharist). Except for an occasional reference to Luther or Calvin, they speak only in broad terms about the calling. They are quicker to affirm its importance than to say what exactly it means. They revert to personal examples in trying to explain it. They admit reluctance to guide people too strongly in thinking about their work, preferring to say instead that individuals must decide these questions on their own. Their role is more that of a sounding board than anything else.

Most of the pastors we talked with did not, of course, believe that they were merely mirroring the wider culture. Indeed, they saw themselves as opposing something dangerous in contemporary society. That danger, as we have observed, is materialism. Pastors were often clearest in conveying what they meant by happiness when they contrasted it with the pursuit of money. They assumed that most people work simply to make a better living than they need and that a better reason to work is to do something that provides personal enjoyment. But, in making these arguments, clergy are not presenting as distinct a message as they may imagine. Although Americans are indeed quite materialistic, most people already claim to be working because they enjoy what they do rather than doing it simply for the money. And they are already quite willing to express concern about materialism, whether they are church members or not. Whether people really perceive the trade-off between happiness and money the way pastors portray it, therefore, seems doubtful.

The churches may perform a useful function in reminding people that working for money may, in fact, not bring them happiness. But it may also be that defining happiness in this way rings less true for most people than it does for the clergy. The reason can be understood by considering what people themselves say and what is distinctive about the role of pastors. The average middle-class American does not, in the first place, believe that he or she is working simply to earn money. Thus, when clergy talk about people who do so, the likely reaction will be to think the message applies to someone else. It is also easy for someone listening to such a message to conclude that clergy are really talking about themselves. Many of them quite consciously gave up a more lucrative career to enter the ministry. For them, then, the trade-off between happiness and money may be more of an issue than it is for their parishioners.

Clergy clearly do try to make their arguments about work relevant to the lives of individual parishioners. They personalize the subject, preaching about daily satisfaction and advising about career choices. But this very choice of framework is also a reflection of the individualistic culture in which we live. Seldom do clergy invoke the kingdom of God as a way of discussing how individual callings may contribute to something larger than the sum of its parts. Seldom do they speak about work as a way of contributing to the understanding of God's handiwork or helping the poor or alleviating suffering. Instead, they adopt a counseling mode, focusing on how an individual can maximize his or her own happiness. This approach, of course, is to be expected when clergy are asked to advise individuals about career decisions. But it also provides the framework in which many of their sermons are cast.

The emphasis on individuals taking responsibility for their career choices and for their day-to-day happiness, it should be noted, is quite compatible with middle-class culture. Several clergy, in fact, observed that in most times and places people would have had little choice in such matters. In contemporary America, though, clergy assume that choice is prevalent. What they do not reckon with fully, however, is the fact that choice is not quite as abundant as advice books might lead one to think. Judging from what working Americans themselves say, they are often guided by circumstances in choosing careers. They are also enormously influenced by the advantages or disadvantages of their parents' income and social status, family obligations, the fortunes or misfortunes of particular companies, and economic cycles. In emphasizing responsibility, therefore, clergy have perhaps unwittingly shifted attention increasingly to that which the individual presumably can control: his or her feelings about work.

One final observation is that the churches' emphasis on personal happiness resonates well with utilitarian understandings of the market system itself but also suffers from the same weaknesses. Utilitarianism, too, stresses the importance of personal happiness and often assumes that the marketplace is an arena in which to seek happiness. In turn, all benefit as individuals do whatever maximizes their happiness. But the pursuit of individual happiness does not contribute to the general good unless some conception of good is built into understandings of happiness in the first place. A theology that emphasizes individual happiness in the marketplace but that does not take account of inequalities in the ability to pursue such happiness would be deficient in this respect.

## COPING WITH WORKPLACE PROBLEMS

The main implication for parishioners of this emphasis on personal happiness is that something is wrong if people are not happy in their work. For some pastors, the implication is simply that a person has chosen the wrong vocation. For others, dissatisfaction with work is a sign of spiritual malaise. A Methodist pastor, for example, explained that people who were unhappy with their jobs were probably not fully in tune with God's will and might even be on the path toward rebelling against God. A Baptist pastor, talking about the youth in his congregation, worried that they were not taking their career choices seriously enough. He recognized that work was a major commitment and thus a potential source of deep satisfaction. So if people were, as he said, "floundering," they were in need of spiritual guidance.

But the fact is that people simply do not experience the kind of happiness the clergy are propounding. They are generally satisfied with their jobs, but they do experience stress, frustration, and even burnout. They gain intrinsic meaning from their work but also recognize that financial obligations are part of the reason they work. Clergy themselves are aware of such feelings. Yet they want people to be happy, and they tell them they should be happy. So they wind up devoting energy to counseling people, encouraging them in their pursuit of happiness.

The standard way of looking at this situation is to say that people are in need because of the pressures of their jobs and that clergy are simply helping take care of this need. It must also be recognized, however, that clergy are contributing to the problem in the first place. By telling people God wants them to be happy, they are setting up an unrealistic view of life. They are denying biblical traditions that associate work with toil, strain, and sweat or that recognize pain and suffering as universal elements of life.

The churches are thus caught up in a vicious cycle. They tell people they should be happy all the time. This message may be something people like to hear, but at another level it does not ring true. It does not square with their experiences on the job. Thus the churches must expend energy helping people feel better about themselves. This vicious cycle is not necessarily bad for the churches. It gives them a role to fill, but it also redefines their role, diverting their energies from many other functions toward ministering to the feelings of the middle class.

The church has thus adapted well to the market economy in which most of its members function from Monday through Friday. It sets up few standards that might conflict with the functioning of the labor market. It does not tell people consistently to work harder than their peers or to work less hard. It tells them mainly to be happy, to have a good attitude at work, to find fulfillment on the job. When these goals are not achieved, the church then has something to do. It does not tell people to seek a different career. It merely tells them to adjust their thinking. They come to the church for counseling. If they gain comfort and inspiration there, they are likely to return. But they are not likely to go away with a more profound sense of how their work should be considered in the building of God's kingdom.

# six

# PICKING UP THE PIECES

Most middle-class church members have steady jobs, earn decent salaries, and pay their bills on time. They live in comfortable homes, provide for their children, and pursue careers they find interesting and fulfilling. But their lives are also filled with pressure. They experience job-related stress; suffer from periodic burnout; face ethical dilemmas at work; and have trouble juggling the demands of jobs, families, and personal interests. Sometimes the pressures become too great. They lose their jobs, run into serious difficulties with coworkers, succumb to addictions, or find their families falling apart. On such occasions, they turn to their churches. With increasing frequency, the churches are being called on to help parishioners cope with these issues.

How churches respond to the work-related needs of their members is, however, not simply a matter of supplying services, but a function of the ways in which pastors perceive the workplace and their own role in relation to it. Pastors are products of their own backgrounds, training, vocational choices, and the particular ways in which they come into contact with parishioners. Many are trying to address the needs that grow out of parishioners' work. But, by most indications, the churches are doing less than parishioners would like. Pastors may be inadvertently limiting the effectiveness of their own ministries as well. Indeed, an important dimension of the current crisis in middle-class churches is their failure to minister more effectively to the spiritual needs of working men and women. To understand this problem, it is necessary to consider pastors' contact with parishioners, their perceptions of parishioners' needs, what they are doing to minister to these needs, and what challenges are implied.

## LIMITED CONTACT

The contact clergy have with parishioners is, of course, limited. They see them on Sundays or at church meetings but seldom at work. Clergy are interested in what their members do for a living and claim to understand their problems and interests. They can recite the occupations of their more prominent members and repeat conversations with some of these members. Pastors' comments, however, betray their lack of familiarity with what actually goes on in the workplace. Most of them have never worked in secular careers themselves. They may, in fact, have entered the ministry as a clear alternative to such careers. They think of the church as a special place, a haven, somewhat protected from the pressures of the marketplace. The secular workplace is thus different in their minds, known from afar, like a land populated by foreigners.

The head pastor of a large Presbyterian church said he knew the careers of most of his members. It was, he said, only natural for him to know because he cared about his members. But when asked what kinds of problems or concerns people brought up in discussing their work, he immediately backtracked. He said he did no counseling, so all he knew was that people sometimes mentioned their work in casual conversations. A Baptist pastor has driven their routes with a couple of salesmen in his congregation. He said these excursions gave him a better idea of the pressures they face and allowed him to discuss issues that would not have come up otherwise. He would like to be a fly on the wall where some of his other parishioners work, but he knows this is not possible. He admitted he has little sense of the work most of his members do. A Catholic priest thought it was a novel idea to ride shotgun with a parishioner but said he would have little understanding of what his congregants did even if he spent time with them at work. The reason was simply that they worked in professional and technical occupations that he did not comprehend.

Other pastors said they have a good sense of the work their parishioners do. They could list the occupations of the leading families in their churches, tell stories about the people they are counseling, and mention conversations they have had at dinner parties. They know people are interested in their jobs, so they initiate conversations after church, such as "How'd it go at the office this week?" And people will say, "Oh, okay," or "It was really busy," or "I was in Cincinnati this week." But when pressed, these pastors also acknowledged that the workplace is largely shielded from their view.

This shielding is especially the case in communities where newer, larger churches are being established. The pastors we talked to in rural areas and in small towns had a reasonable sense of what their members did. They knew them personally, had been in their homes, had walked their land with them, or had been customers in their stores. Pastors of urban and suburban churches, in contrast, ministered to people who generally worked outside the neighborhood of the church and performed specialized tasks that clergy could not grasp as easily.

It is thus the special problems—the emotional crises and family strains—that clergy know something about. Parishioners are distraught enough that they bring these special problems to the church. They come to the pastor's study suffering from acute depression as a result of losing their job. Or the pastor knows they are experiencing difficulty because their spouse comes in on the verge of filing for divorce.[1] Or parishioners may bring their grievances against coworkers to the pastor because he is a neutral party who will listen. In other cases, they may comment on their work by sighing and saying how busy they are, hoping to derail the pastor from inviting them to serve on yet another church committee.

## THE BURDENS OF THE MIDDLE CLASS

Middle-class church members are seldom in danger of having nothing to eat, being evicted from their homes, or having no access to medical care. But they do carry the American economy on their backs. They are faced with constant time pressures, heavy decision-making responsibilities, and job-related stress. More than a few struggle to pay their bills, find themselves shackled with credit-card debt and huge mortgage payments, and face periodic bouts of unemployment or painful transitions to new jobs and new communities. These are the burdens they bring to their prayer fellowships, Sunday school classes, or pastor's study.

From what pastors say, one of the most common work-related problems is that parishioners have trouble handling everything they are expected to do at work and still having time for their families, their church, or themselves. The pastor of a suburban church near Philadelphia said one of the most frequent comments he hears is people worrying about the travel their jobs require, or the evenings away from their families, and yet feeling the need to spend this time in order to make enough money to buy their children things and send them to good schools. A priest bemoaned the fact that many of his parishioners seemed too busy with their work even to sit down for a family meal. One couple, he remarked, had sold their dining room table because nobody used it. Another priest noted that women in his parish were especially troubled by trade-offs between their families and their jobs. Some of them had lost jobs because of pregnancies or needing to care for sick children. Others worried about finding child care and found male coworkers unsympathetic to their situations. The pastor of a rural church in the Midwest put it best: "They just have too much hay on the fork!"

In virtually all of the churches we studied, married couples with children were, in fact, maintaining dual-career households. At the lower end of the middle class, both partners were working in order to meet rental or mortgage payments and to buy household necessities. At the upper end, both spouses were working because they had devoted years of their lives training for careers, saw these careers as worthwhile endeavors, and enjoyed the extra cash. Pastors nevertheless worried about the ill effects of such work schedules on family life. A number emphasized that latchkey children were being neglected in their congregations and wished there were resources for supplying better day-care and after-school programs. Some noted that their members were hiring housesitters but were probably breaking the law by hiring illegal immigrants and not complying with tax regulations. A few mentioned that extramarital affairs had occurred between employers and house-sitters.

Another problem mentioned by many of the pastors we talked with is the emotional strain of having to do too much or too many different things at work. Pastors seldom blame their members for simply being too ambitious or taking on more than they can handle. Instead, they blame the economy. They sense that workers are caught up in a system that makes unreasonable demands on them. This image resonates well with their sense that the workplace is not exactly friendly territory.

The pastor of a church whose members mostly hold middle-management jobs said it had become common in his city for companies to pare down their employee rosters as a way of maintaining profit margins in a more competitive economic climate. As a result, those who were left had to do twice as much as before. The consequences, he said, were "pressures that don't seem human." Another pastor remarked on the same problem. Observing how the labor force has been cut back in his community, he said that people are having to do more with less. "They're taking on more work of the people who once helped them. They're now doing the helpers' jobs plus their own, so there are longer hours." The result, he said, is that "they're away from their families, they're very stressed when they come home and not really able to enjoy quality time with their family." He thought many of his parishioners were worried about someone else taking their jobs. "It's ruthless and dog-eat-dog. I have seen things come into the parish life, and I've said to people that I'm close to, 'My God, is that what goes on out there every day?' and they say yes."[2]

These economic pressures are aggravated by the fact that many middle-class Americans have no community structures to protect them. They live as autonomous individuals, exposed directly to the marketplace. A Baptist pastor explained the connection: "It used to be you grew up in a community, your family was within that community. And maybe there was a sense of too much control, even oppression, but at least there were some structures in place, you had generations of people to deal with. Most of our people here don't have their families. They've relocated here. They are involved in an upward process that's requiring more and more demands of them. They've not developed good relational skills. They don't have support structures. So their inner resources are caving in on them."

Christians are taught to be peacemakers or at least to get along with those in their daily circle of contacts. Yet conflict in the workplace is another source of stress from which church members are scarcely exempt. Many pastors are faced with counseling parishioners who are at their wits' end as a result of conflict with their bosses or coworkers. One of the pastors we talked to had just been counseling a woman who had been having trouble with a coworker for several months. At first she had been jealous of her coworker because the boss always seemed to be asking about the other employee. The woman had come to her pastor at that point trying to overcome her jealousy. Then, just recently, the other employee had been terminated, and it turned out that the firing of that person had been the boss's reason for asking questions. The woman now felt sympathy and was wondering what she could do to help. Another pastor estimated that 98 percent of his congregants' concerns about work focused on interpersonal conflicts. "Fighting, quarreling, backbiting, lack of appreciation or recognition of their abilities, all of the different politics that are involved in the employment situation," he observed. "Those are the types of problems that are brought to my attention."

A striking number of pastors also said that unemployment had become an issue of concern in their congregations. Sometimes a member of a pastor's own congregation would come for counseling as a result of having been laid off. The pastor of a Presbyterian church in Chicago mentioned a man whose job at a large manufacturing firm was suddenly terminated. At age fifty-two, the man found himself having to rethink his life. He had no idea what to do next, so he started coming to see the pastor each week for advice. Another pastor said he had recently invited the men and women in his congregation who were unemployed to come to his house for dinner and a chance to discuss their problems. He and his wife were surprised when eighteen people arrived.

At least one congregation had also experienced the little-known trauma employ-ers may face in having to terminate the jobs of trusted friends and associates. One couple owned a small computer company and, when the bottom fell out of their market, had to let most of its staff go. Both the husband and wife felt guilty and ashamed, especially because some of their employees belonged to the same congre-gation. Had the pastor not stepped in, the couple might have left the church entirely rather than reconcile themselves to the situation.

In other cases, pastors were faced with the side of unemployment that govern-ment statistics seldom reveal—the disruptions of family relationships. Divorce, alcoholism, battered spouses, and child abuse were all mentioned.[3] Pastors fre-quently blamed the workplace for these problems. They talked about men who were too busy climbing the corporate ladder to spend quality time with their wives and children. They also talked about career women who were not staying home with children. By implication, they suggested that families would be stronger were it not for the demands of the workplace.

Some of the strains mentioned went beyond the nuclear family. Like many lower-class families, the middle class survives by taking care of its own through extended family networks. These networks reach out widely in congregations, linking middle-class members to less fortunate relatives. As a result, pastors are sometimes called on to counsel not only those directly affected by economic hard-ship but those indirectly affected as well. A Methodist pastor in Texas talked about a mother and daughter in his congregation who had come to him within the past week seeking counsel about a married son and brother who was unemployed. Neither he nor his wife had been able to find steady work, so they were financially dependent on the mother, whose retirement savings were rapidly being depleted as a result. The mother wanted to help her son but realized the situation was causing friction between her son and daughter. So she turned to the pastor for advice.

Another issue that pastors brought up repeatedly was ethics. Parishioners came to them with troubling questions about activities they feared were morally ques-tionable. One man was close to being caught up in an insider-trading scandal on the futures market. Another, an attorney, was worried because one of his clients had been convicted of fraud in the savings and loan industry. He wondered if he too might be morally culpable. Still another, a physician, was constantly having to make decisions about terminating the life-support systems of dying patients. And another, a human resources manager, was trying to decide whether it was ethical to break company rules in order to give terminated employees a better chance of find-ing a new job. In each case, pastors found themselves having to think hard about what advice to give.

A few pastors, especially ones in theologically conservative churches, also talked about problems their members had at work as a result of being Christians. They mentioned members being offended by their coworkers' language or, in some cases, being ridiculed by coworkers for their faith. A conservative Baptist pastor said one of his parishioners had recently come to him complaining about her boss. He said the man "had a foul mouth and was really offending her by using the Lord's name in vain." The pastor of a Korean church told a similar story about a man in his congregation who had recently confronted his business partner about the use of offensive language. Another pastor observed that a newly converted Christian in his congregation was trying hard to reform his language and his drinking habits but was having trouble because fellows at the garage where he worked kept tempting him to go drinking with them. He said the man was under a lot of pressure because of this situation.

But it was not only conservative churches where such comments surfaced. Pastors in liberal settings also worried that the workplace was increasingly an alien world for the committed Christian. As pastors, it seemed distant, mysterious, even hostile to them personally. And, often with the help of one or two telling examples, they argued that it must be this way for their parishioners as well. They assumed that people had to hide their faith or be more aggressive and competitive than their faith would encourage them to be. As the pastor of a liberal Presbyterian church explained, "There is a yearning to be overt about who they are as Christian people and their own relationship with Christ, but they live in a setting and work in a setting which discourages all kinds of religious expression."

## THE PASTORAL ROLE

How well are the churches meeting these needs? Believing that people should, above all, be happy, pastors feel a responsibility to help their members cope with the strains generated by their jobs. They preach, provide counseling, and initiate special programs. Indeed, they expend a great deal of time and energy helping their members pick up the pieces when economic pressures shatter their lives.

One of the most common ways in which pastors try to minister to the needs of their middle-class members is of course through preaching. Pastors are ambivalent about the amount of commitment parishioners exhibit toward the workplace and other material interests. They worry that people are too caught up with their work and with making money. So, in their preaching, pastors try to instruct people to stand back, smell the roses, and at least think hard about their priorities. They draw a distinction between material values and spiritual values, encouraging their members to seek the latter. A Baptist pastor cautioned his listeners that more and more people were working longer hours and spending more time away from home, all in the interest of being successful. But, he warned, their only reward would be the "three As"—aloneness, adventure-seeking, and adultery.

A significant element of pastoral ministry to the American middle class is thus defined simply by the sense that economic demands are constantly expanding and therefore need to be squeezed back into their place. What they are crowding out, according to many pastors, is the time people need to spend with their families. Indeed, it is striking how often pastors draw a distinction between the spiritual and the material and then associate families with the former, arguing that it would be godly for people to spend more time with their families and devote less energy to their work. The pastor of an affluent Presbyterian church recalled that he had recently preached a sermon in which he had encouraged people to think about their priorities. Distinguishing spiritual values from material values, he had spoken about how the people in Jeremiah's day had lost their sense of spiritual values. "Jeremiah says they were all greedy," he summarized, "that they're all given to material gain. And one of the problems of our day is that we're very prone to forget the spiritual values, which, of course, involves the spiritual values of relationships in the home."

Another pastor drew heavily from a book he had read recently in explaining why the family held natural priority over the workplace. He said the typical person wakes up in the morning snug in bed, comfortable, secure, and probably with a loved one close by. This moment is the primordial reality, that which is most real, most meaningful, the deepest truth, the most fully understood. But then the person gets up, shifts gears, puts on a public face suitable for presenting to a world of strangers, and leaves the safe haven of home for the workplace. "The dawning of the day," he concluded, "is a time of pain." For him, then, going to work signified struggle, whereas the family provided a place of centeredness.[4]

Pastors do not speak with a single voice about the proper place of work among personal priorities, however. While they sometimes encourage members to spend more time with their families, they also believe it is their role to inspire members to work harder. They seldom say directly that people should spend more time at the office. But they encourage them to put in a full schedule of hours, take pride in their work, put in extra effort, derive a sense of dignity from what they do, exert themselves to the fullest, and produce at the highest level of quality. A Methodist pastor had recently preached a series of sermons on the Ten Commandments in which he tried to draw implications for the workplace. Knowing that his middle-class parishioners would never contemplate armed robbery, he warned them instead against "time theft." He said it was wrong for an employee to arrive late or leave early. He said they should always give a "full effort." He also reminded his listeners that people would be watching them, knowing that they were Christians, so they should always do their best in order to witness to their faith.

Other clergy stressed the same point in their own ways. The pastor of a Presbyterian church in the Midwest said he wants his congregants to know that they are "representatives of the colony of heaven on earth," whether they are performing surgery or working as secretaries. "Their work ethic," he explained, "bears witness to the love and grace of God."

Besides preaching, many churches provide counseling for families faced with economic or job-related pressures. Some of the larger churches have specialized counseling programs or ministries, but in most of the cases we observed the pastor served individually as the front-line source of such assistance. Indeed, nearly all the pastors we talked to mentioned spending a regular portion of their time each week meeting with parishioners who were suffering from an acute work-related issue of one kind or another. One pastor had been meeting regularly for several years with a man who had lost his business and gone through a divorce about the same time. The man was devastated and simply needed a trusted friend he could turn to for support. Another pastor mentioned a man in his congregation whose business had recently gone into bankruptcy. He said he spent time every day with this man, either talking with him in person, praying with him, or giving him encouragement over the phone.

Counseling frequently focuses on the side effects for busy two-career households of financial and job-related stress. Pastors could nearly always name at least one couple in their congregation who fell into this category. An Espicopal priest provided the following illustration (one he estimated could be repeated 500 times in his community): "I had two people come in. They've been married for ten or fifteen years. The only time they have together is jogging at five o'clock in the morning. That's their time together. In the dark. They schedule it. I think she works, but he's the one who's sort of the major worker. But they come home and they fight. They start fighting about little things, and they start fighting about daily issues and stuff. Well, they come in to see me, and they talk about how they're starting to get pretty violent in their fighting, and they're beginning to use language like separation. They're reaching out for help, and they have some experience with me, so they think they ought to come in and see me."

Usually pastors said the main part of their counseling ministry is simply to listen. They give people a chance to vent whatever is bothering them. They try to be sympathetic and understanding. Sometimes they use special counseling techniques as well. For example, one pastor was dealing with a man filled with anger because the rules of his job prevented him from really helping the disadvantaged children his program had been set up to serve. The pastor taught him role-playing techniques that helped him get in touch with his rage. The counseling process also involves prayer in most cases. By praying, the pastor is able to say supportive words that might be awkward to say directly to the person being counseled. The pastor also prays for divine guidance and comfort.

Some churches have also created special programs to help parishioners with work-related needs. At a large Methodist church with a staff of seven pastors, the "outreach minister" has been given the task of helping unemployed members find jobs. He maintains a bulletin board on which members or employers in the community can post announcements about job openings. He also uses the many personal contacts he has, as well as the various fellowship groups that meet at the church, to develop informal networks that may generate information about jobs. At a suburban Presbyterian church the board of deacons has been given the task of developing such information and providing physical and emotional support for unemployed members. Another church has initiated a day-care program to help working parents.

## THE CHALLENGE TO THE CHURCHES

These examples reveal that churches are indeed involved in ministering to the economic needs of their middle-class parishioners. The needs are great, and at least some efforts are being made to alleviate these needs. In fact, this level of need is probably one of the reasons why the churches have remained strong in American society. They are responding to the side effects of the American economy. They are not simply concerned with the discards of that system—the elderly, the mentally disadvantaged, and the homeless. They are ministering to the disrupted lives of the middle class as well.

But it is also clear that the churches could be doing more than they are. The limited contact pastors have with the work experiences of their members is a significant part of the problem. Many pastors seem to be unaware of how little they understand the work lives of their parishioners. They assume that they have a good understanding, but their information is biased in the same way as the views of other service workers. It is easy, for example, for therapists to believe that the mental health of the entire American public is in jeopardy[5] because they see one segment of the population and draw inferences from that segment. By the same token, clergy draw inferences about work from the congregants who come to them with special problems. It is easy for clergy, based on this evidence, to conclude that people are overwhelmingly dissatisfied with their work.[6] Indeed, this conclusion may be one of the reasons why clergy emphasize the pursuit of happiness as much as they do. They do not take sufficient account of the fact that most people actually like their work, find it a source of personal meaning, and regard it as an avenue of service. As one astute pastor observed, "It energizes them, it excites them, it takes the best they have." Parishioners may find it puzzling, therefore, to hear clergy bemoaning how awful things are in the secular workplace. Since this is where parishioners spend many of their waking hours, they may long to hear deeper messages about the theology of work, its significance, its trials, and its rewards rather than jeremiads about how bad work is or palliatives emphasizing individual happiness.

The pressures, disappointments, and struggles of those who do come to pastors with work-related problems are, nevertheless, real, and the churches must learn how to minister to these needs. Their leaders must realize that many people still feel uncomfortable even admitting that they need the church's help. Some of the pastors we talked to, for example, figured people in their congregations were struggling financially as a result of layoffs or low-paying jobs. But they said they really didn't have specific examples because parishioners seldom confided in them about such problems. Others said they knew about specific families who were having trouble but felt uncomfortable approaching them with help or sympathy. They felt people would be embarrassed if the pastor knew they were not as successful or self-sufficient as they appeared.

The priest at a Catholic parish in New Jersey said he had an idea that something was wrong when he stopped at the home of one of his parishioners one afternoon and the man, a high-level executive of a large corporation, came to the door. A few days later, the man started coming to mass on weekday mornings. Then there were rumors that the man had, in fact, lost his job. The priest wanted to say something but decided the matter was too private. Some time later, after the man had found another job, the issue finally surfaced. The man said he had been overcome with guilt and shame. He was afraid even to take a walk during the day for fear the neighbors would start talking. He felt as if he were letting his wife and children down. It seemed that his manhood was at stake. He needed encouragement but did not know how to ask for it.[7]

Most of the pastors we talked to seemed eager to show that their churches were involved in work-related ministries. But, to a critical observer, many of the ministries mentioned seemed incidental to the fact that people worked. Bible study groups were often mentioned as ministries for working people but could be considered so only because they met at times when people were not working. They did not focus on issues that arose particularly from work experience. Other pastors, struggling to think of something they were doing, mentioned seminars on marriage and family that, they argued, included some consideration of working, or they talked about counseling programs for stress and depression, some of which, they figured, could be attributed to working. A few of the churches actually sponsored Bible study groups that met where people worked. Upon closer consideration, though, these programs turned out to be the initiative of individual members and had little to do with any plan of the church to minister in the workplace. They existed despite the church rather than because of it. And, as one pastor recognized, they depended so much on particular individuals that a transfer or layoff could suddenly end the operation completely. Other programs were specifically designed for people in the workplace but more, it seemed, to distract them from their work than to enhance its meaning.

It is also clear that some churches have had difficulty dealing with the changing status of women in the workplace. Several pastors talked about counseling couples who were having trouble reconciling their careers. They said it was difficult for a wife who might be earning a lot more than her husband to be truly "submissive." Others had breakfasts for businessmen but "ladies' aid societies" for women. The pastors who noted a need for day care often admitted that their church provided none. One pointed to a "mother's day out" program but conceded that it was designed for women who were not working. Another admitted that the church's philosophy was to encourage women to stay at home with their children. He said providing day care would encourage the opposite. Thus, the church offered nothing, despite the fact that 70 percent of its female members held jobs outside the home.

Judging from what pastors say, the churches are also having trouble spreading the gospel to nonmembers with whom their members come in contact in the workplace. They feel they spend time ministering to the needs of their own members but fail to motivate these members to minister to others. Parishioners compartmentalize their Sundays from their Mondays. As one pastor noted, he sometimes meets people in his community who work with members of his church, and they don't even know that these members are Christians. They will say something like "Oh, I didn't realize they were religious." Other pastors lamented that members lived within their own social circles instead of making inroads into the community. The pastors themselves feel frustrated because they do not have contacts in the workplace, and they fear their members are reluctant to talk with others about their faith.

This problem is aggravated by the fact that few churches sponsor Bible studies, prayer fellowships, or support groups that actually meet in the workplace. Often they recognize that the workplace is where people spend most of their waking hours, yet they assume the workplace is off limits to religious groups. They in effect allow corporations to operate as secular entities, hoping only that the individual lives of church members will make a difference. They assume that the support working men and women receive on Sundays will be sufficient.

Another problem is that pastors frequently express frustration with the results of their sermons. They feel they are saying the right things but wonder if anyone is listening. Sometimes they take solace in the biblical metaphor that they are sowing seeds, telling themselves that God will bless their efforts with fruit, even though it may take many years for any fruit to be evident.[8] Especially in large churches, pastors express this concern. They do not know their parishioners well enough to have any sense of whether people are paying heed to their words. They also spend their time administering programs rather than talking with people individually. Thus, they realize that sermons may quickly be forgotten rather than being reinforced by personal relationships.

Still another problem, however, is that parishioners do heed what the churches are saying but hear only part of the message. In a society that encourages the work ethic, it is easier for people to hear that God loves them more if they work hard than to understand that God loves them anyway, no matter how much or how little they work. This is especially the case when pastors emphasize that the way for Christians to show their faith is by doing their work just a little better than everyone else, or when they say, as several pastors did, that the Christian should never sacrifice excellence but should also add an extra dose of caring, commitment, and the "human touch." It is not surprising, therefore, that regular churchgoers frequently say they have heard sermons about working harder and overwhelmingly agree that people who work hard are more pleasing to God than people who are lazy.[9] But they are also more likely to say that feeling comforted and thinking about something besides their work is more important when they go to church than hearing sermons encouraging them to work hard.[10]

Sermons extolling the virtue of hard work can be inspiring, motivating dedicated parishioners to expend even more energy on their jobs than they otherwise would. But such a message can also have tragic consequences. A poignant example came from Father Martinez at San Xavier's. When asked what he tries to communicate about work, he said he encourages his parishioners to work hard, take their work seriously no matter how menial it may be, and regard their work as a source of personal worth and dignity. But a few moments later he acknowledged that four men in his parish had committed suicide within the past year because they had lost their jobs.

Another pastor said he had quit preaching sermons about working harder and had entirely abandoned Sunday school programs about ethics, careers, and jobs. He said he had done all these things in the early years of his ministry. But one day a prominent member of his congregation remarked, "That's what I do all day long, every day. And you fill me with anxiety. You fill me with guilt." He said, "I just want to come here and pray and relax and be quiet."

Our conversations with pastors also revealed that church work is suffering as a result of members being too busy pursuing their careers. Although pastors are generally sympathetic with parishioners who are having to work harder and longer just to keep their jobs, they nevertheless lament the fact that it is difficult to schedule meetings or to secure volunteers for important lay leadership positions. Some said they were having to rely more on paid professionals, which, in turn, was forcing them to raise more money. Others were simply scaling back.

In addition to the fact of work crowding out church activities, pastors also complained that the mentality of the workplace seems harder and harder to exclude from their parishes. Sometimes they look enviously at the management skills of their members and wish they themselves were better trained to run their churches as complex organizations. They inadvertently slip into business jargon, talking about management by objectives or reveling in well-crafted organization charts. But they also worry that something is being lost as churches become businesses. A Catholic priest told of a recent meeting, the aim of which was to revise the schedule for weekend masses. Before long, he said, the meeting devolved into "fault-finding, arguments, and people knocking what was rather than trying to understand what's happening." It seemed to him that they were "seeing a church board as a board of directors of General Motors rather than a pastoral board that's helping the pastor to plan on how to shepherd the people." Church, he asserted, should be "more of a spiritual thing." Or, as an Episcopal rector observed, "We were trying to provide all sorts of programs and activities. But then people started complaining that church was no different from their work. They want it to be different."

Pastors who devote time to counseling their members about work-related problems also reveal the frustrations associated with this role. They generally feel the time is well spent, saying it makes people feel better when they pray with them. However, they sometimes wonder if they are really being ministers or just standing in for the sympathetic friends and family that people do not have. One pastor said members come to him and talk about their problems but do not seem to be interested in finding answers. They feel better because they have unburdened themselves but leave without really working on solutions to their problems. Another pastor said candidly, "I'm no expert. The world out there is too complex." He did not mean he was untrained or felt unable to counsel people about personal problems. But he was gun-shy because he had never worked in the kind of environments in which his members were employed. They had technical expertise and were faced with issues that he did not understand, so he felt intimidated.

In other cases, pastors expressed satisfaction with their role as counselors but betrayed the individualism and relativism that have become widespread in American culture. They argued, as the literature on problem solving does, that people must come up with their own solutions. But they went a step further, asserting that there were no right or wrong answers, not even on ethical issues. Their view was that individuals simply have to pay attention to their feelings and do whatever they decide is most comfortable. The role of pastor was not to supply guidelines but to encourage and support the individual in whatever decision he or she made.

One pastor had been confronted recently by a member who was worried that raising tobacco was not in keeping with his faith. Another parishioner asked his pastor if it was wrong for him to own a large block of stock in a beer company. Another situation involved a church member who worked for a company that sold weapons to South Africa and Iraq. In all three cases, the pastors refused to offer advice, saying it was more important to support their members in whatever decisions they made.

It is difficult, of course, to fault pastors for playing this role. Theological conceptions of evil have largely given way to understandings that emphasize the good in human nature. Pastors have learned that honey catches flies better than vinegar. Perceiving the workplace as a world of struggle, they feel a special burden to provide love and acceptance when people come to church. One pastor put it this way: "Working in today's world is hard. These are not bad people. These are good, real, genuine, loving people. They don't need to be criticized. They don't need to be talked down to by the preacher who has a captive audience. That's not what they need." So pastors try hard to make people feel better about themselves.

As a result, some pastors worried that they were only helping people solve their immediate problems rather than encouraging them to focus on deeper spiritual dimensions of life. As one pastor observed, "People come in wanting to figure out how to get Johnny to the dentist or worrying about who will put the garbage out. But they don't take time out to get back to the root questions: Who are we? What do we believe in? What's important to us? When we're sixty-five and look back, what are we going to say we did with our lives? What is this business of the soul anyway?"

Picking up the pieces when people's lives have been shattered by the pressures, strains, and disappointments of the workplace is thus one of the significant ways in which the churches can minister to the middle class. Church members would like to see their pastors doing even more of this work, and some pastors are responding. It is clear, however, that the churches are shouldering responsibilities in this area that sometimes strap their resources and that many pastors are ill equipped to handle.

These challenges are serious. Pastors are already overwhelmed with the duties of their offices. Asking them to minister to the special needs that arise in the workplace may be expecting too much. Yet the key issue is not so much time as greater understanding. Pastors need to understand clearly that secular work is itself a meaningful, satisfying activity and that it is important not simply as a means of feeding one's family but as a form of ministry and service. They need to understand that classes for people who happen to work are not an effective substitute for classes that actually deal with the spiritual dimensions of work. They need to recognize that an absence of day-care programs will not keep women from working but will only make their work more difficult.

The churches that have developed special ministries for working people prove that the problems are not insolvable. At one church, a thriving support network for unemployed men and women emerged under the leadership of a lay personnel manager in the congregation. The pastor had been instrumental only in getting the group started. Other pastors in the area may not have had the same resources but could have channeled unemployed people to the same group if they had known about it. At another church, a woman in the congregation organized a women's resource center to deal with a wide range of issues confronting working women. The church underwrites its expenses but otherwise lets it operate on its own energy. Several pastors had been challenged to do more by reading books detailing the lack of support that some businesspeople feel in their churches. A few had taken time to study the issues themselves. Rather than preaching through a book of the Bible, they developed a series of sermons on the theme of work itself. Perhaps the best single suggestion was from a pastor who said he had simply rethought the idea of ministry. "Lay ministry," he said, "usually means the pastor trying to get laity involved in programs at the church." Instead, he suggested, "it should be about our commitments in everyday life—including our work."

# seven

# THE DEMISE OF STEWARDSHIP

Roy Steuben, thirty, attended Sunday school every week at the Lutheran church near his home while he was growing up. After high school, he switched to the Mennonite church because the girl he was dating (and would eventually marry) was from that denomination. He is a thoughtful, articulate, hard-working man who earns a decent living as a pastry chef. With his wife and three boys (ages eleven, seven, and four), he lives in a modest house in a semirural Pennsylvania town near the restaurant where he works. The church is an important part of his life. He attends services faithfully with his family except on the occasional Sundays when he has to work. Most of his friends belong to the same church. He enjoys greeting them on Sunday mornings and talking with them at church dinners. His religious beliefs, he says, rank at the top of his commitments. He wants his sons to "know the Lord" and to "base their lives on good religious and moral beliefs." Most everything, he asserts, "revolves around what is said in the Bible."

Since joining the Mennonite church, Roy has come to a deeper understanding of what it means for Jesus to be his personal savior. The pastor's sermons have helped him apply his faith to his everyday life. He says he tries to regard his body as God's temple, considers it pleasing to God when he works hard, and believes in the importance of caring for others. When asked if the Christian doctrine of stew-

119

ardship is meaningful to him, he says yes. But when asked to explain his understanding of it, he says, "I'm at a loss."

This is not an isolated case. In talking with church members, we found many committed Christians who had difficulty explaining their understanding of stewardship. A math teacher in her early thirties who had attended the Catholic church since childhood, for example, said that stewardship was meaningful to her, but when asked what it meant, she retreated: "Well, I guess it is. Does that mean when you help someone?" A Baptist man who was deeply interested in religion and who talked at length on the subject said, when asked about stewardship, "I'm sure it's meaningful, but right now I'm blocking on it."

Other people expressed greater confidence about their understanding of stewardship but also faltered when asked to explain more precisely what they meant. An active member of an Episcopal church, for example, brought up the idea of stewardship herself and mentioned that she served on the stewardship committee at her church. But when asked to say what stewardship meant, she could assert only that "I have a responsibility to use whatever I've been given wisely, not foolishly."

As these examples suggest, people can *think* the idea of stewardship is meaningful and still not have a very clear sense of its meaning. There are also a substantial number who do not even regard it as very meaningful. In the American labor force as a whole, in fact, only 22 percent say the idea of stewardship is "very meaningful." Forty percent say it is "fairly meaningful." But 20 percent say it is "not very" or "not at all" meaningful, and 18 percent are unsure whether it has meaning to them or not.

Why is this? One reason, of course, is that the public at large is simply not exposed to teachings about stewardship. One person in three does not belong to any religious organization, and about the same number never attend religious services or do so only once or twice a year. Church members have a much greater chance of hearing about stewardship than nonmembers do. But a second reason is that church members themselves may not be exposed to the idea. In fact, only 40 percent said they had heard a sermon on stewardship in the past year. Moreover (a third reason), even this group does not always come to a full appreciation of the concept. Indeed, only 42 percent of those who had heard a sermon on stewardship in the past year said the idea was very meaningful to them.

To understand what is going on, therefore, it is necessary to examine how the clergy themselves understand stewardship. Clearly, this concept is *potentially* one of the ways of drawing stronger connections between Christian faith and such matters as work, money, and charitable giving and in this way to help the churches withstand the troubles they are presently facing. But what do clergy have to say about stewardship? How well do they understand it? What difficulties do they perceive as they try to communicate its meaning to parishioners?

## CENTRALITY OF THE IDEA

The problem is not that clergy have abandoned stewardship as part of their own theological understandings. Most of those we talked to spoke eloquently about it. Indeed, there was substantial agreement about its centrality to the Christian faith. They argued that stewardship captured the essential relationship between the believer and God, on the one hand, and between the believer and material possessions, on the other hand. Stewardship taught the believer to acknowledge God's ownership of all things and encouraged the person of faith to exercise responsibility in managing these things. It was, they said, a doctrine that the churches should be emphasizing. Only one raised any objections to the teaching at all, and he did so on grounds that believers sometimes exercise stewardship as a matter of duty rather than realizing its attendant joys.[1]

God's ownership of everything—the entire created order—and the individual's responsibility to acknowledge that ownership and to behave responsibly toward it are the essential points of the doctrine of stewardship. Clergy express these ideas in different ways, depending somewhat on the language of their confessional traditions, but there is little underlying disagreement about the basic doctrines. "Stewardship deals with the offering plate on Sunday morning, for one thing, but that's relatively minor," a Presbyterian pastor explained. "I think stewardship deals with ecology, caring for our air and our water and the soil and the produce of the land. Protection of animals, things of this kind. This is good stewardship. 'This is my father's world, let me ne'er forget,' the hymn goes. Are you familiar with that hymn? Okay. God has said, 'Here is the world, care for it, keep it, make it productive,' and I think stewardship impels us to take good care of the world that God has given to us. We are his stewards. A steward is a person who is in charge of a master's assets. These are God's assets."[2] At Saint Andrew's Episcopal Church, Rector Morgan summarized the same idea: "The three T's, time, talent, and treasure; stewardship is the use of all of it."

There is substantial agreement among clergy that good stewards should not be governed by their own self-interest. Stewardship means using resources for higher ends rather than devoting them entirely to achieving personal goals. A Nazarene pastor, who equated stewardship with the individual's response to God's grace, captured the essential unselfishness of the idea nicely. "Because of what God has done in Christ," he explained, "I am a steward of everything that I have, including my time and my money and my abilities. So stewardship is a matter of me saying that I choose *not* to be lord of my own existence, but to say what does it mean to be informed by Christ in terms of how I do life." In his view, stewardship forces us to examine our lives. It does not tell us exactly how to spend our money or our time but sends us warning messages if we are thinking only about ourselves.

Detachment is a popular way of describing this non-self-interested orientation. Stewards are limited partners. It is their job to do the best they can with what has been given them, but they also know that everything does not rest on their shoulders alone. At a large Baptist church in Houston, the pastor explained this idea by drawing an analogy with the way he relates to his children. "They don't belong to me. They are a gift from God. I have a trustee responsibility to do what I can and really then let them go and, in a sense, give them back to God." Letting them go is the key phrase. He said the same idea applies to our bodies. We do not let our bodies go in the sense of not taking care of ourselves. But we also know that we must detach from our bodies at death and even on a daily basis keep from becoming obsessed with how we look.

The most specific way to apply detachment and non-self-interest to the use of personal resources, pastors agree, is to devote our talents generously to the benefit of others. "Any talent that one has," explained a Presbyterian pastor, "is not simply for one's own selfish use. One ought to ask the question, What do I do with this and how do I use it so others may benefit from it?" Exactly what it means to benefit others is, of course, subject to interpretation, but pastors speak—as do secular observers—of the value of promoting the happiness of others, working for the greater good, and making the world a better place.

The pastor of a Reformed church in New Jersey told us that stewardship covers just about everything, from "plate offerings" on Sunday mornings to our view of animals, but the underlying principle, he said, was to use our talents to make other people happy and the world a better place. He offered several examples: "If somebody is good at painting, they can make the world a better place by the arrangement of colors and oils on a canvas and making the world beautiful and making somebody happy or bringing a smile to somebody's face. Somebody else can teach children how to sing or to dance or to play football. Whatever it is, whether you have a skill or a talent, to share that with other people. Because—there's always a because—we do this because we are committed to the Lord Jesus Christ, who has called us to be his witnesses in the world. And you see, whether it's football or painting or playing the piano or whatever, we're trying to make the world a better place than it now is and people in it happier than they now are. That's stewardship."

There is also substantial agreement among clergy that stewardship necessitates a holistic view of life. Good stewardship implies an orientation that excludes nothing. It pertains especially to one's resources. A better understanding of stewardship is thus an important way in which people of faith can begin to make specific connections between their faith and their work, their money, their material possessions, and their attitudes about economic issues.

Although stewardship is often interpreted narrowly (for example, as giving money to the church), most clergy insist that the idea must be understood in more encompassing terms. Stewardship means "being conscious of the sovereignty of God," and that means "being aware that all we are, all that we have, all that we ever will have or be belongs to God," the pastor of a Korean church explained. Another pastor, who had just been studying the origins of the word, observed that *stewardship* is associated with the old English word *sty*, as in "pigsty." A ward of the pigs or the ward of the sty, he said, was very important because you traded pigs in order to survive. *Stewardship* is thus "a very holistic term." In this pastor's view, the concept includes our abilities, talents, and resources but also our visions and our relationships. "I really think we need to talk about being good stewards of our visions and our ideas as well as our money and resources," he said. "We need to think about it more holistically."

"The Lord does not do what we are always prone to do," observed the pastor at an Episcopal church in New York. "And that is to try to make a dichotomy between spiritual and material things. It's all of a lump. We are total people. The way I spend my calendar time, the way I spend my checkbook money, the way I think about my spiritual life, it's all a part of this business we call stewardship, and you can't chop it up."

Thinking about stewardship in this way means that faith has implications for all of life. People should think and behave differently not just on Sunday mornings but in their work, at the bank, and at the shopping mall. Arguing that stewardship implies "accountability" with one's time, money, and talents, a Presbyterian pastor in Virginia asserted the need to draw out these implications in specific ways. "I am anxious to tear down the barriers between so-called spiritual and so-called secular things," he said. "I want to get people to think, Am I being a good steward of the gifts God has given me, the talents he's given me, the opportunities he's set before me, the money he's given me? Am I being a good steward of those in the whole of my life? In the workplace? In my family? In my church? In my community?" Noting that there is a "narrower definition" that focuses only on church giving, he added, "That's okay, but I think we need to see the larger picture of stewardship too."

If stewardship includes everything, it also includes institutions. Clergy mostly speak about it as an individual activity; but some also emphasize the fact that individuals—as stewards—often function as leaders, managers, and representatives responsible for whole organizations and for the disposition of collective goods. At a church in Chicago that has been quite active in urban politics, the pastor stressed that stewardship "is the responsible living out of one's citizenship in the world as a disciple of Christ." Claiming that stewardship is "the most relevant theological term around today," he insisted that it pertains to how people vote and how they

124 THE CRISIS IN THE CHURCHES

exercise responsibility for their families, communities, nations, and world. "I don't think it's a responsible Christian position to vote on the basis of my self-interest alone and to lower tax rates. I think that is an immoral position. A steward will say, 'How can I be responsible for the life of my community?'"

With varying emphasis, clergy also register substantial agreement that steward-ship has significant implications for understanding the natural environment. The same pastor in Chicago was outspoken in his arguments about the environmental implications of stewardship. "My sense of stewardship is that you don't buy ecolog-ically damaging stuff," he observed. "We can't, any one of us, redeem the environ-ment, but we can, in fact, begin to behave differently. We can recycle paper. We can quit blowing our hydrocarbons into the air. We can buy cars that use less gas. We can write letters."

At a small evangelical church in Kansas, the pastor also made a strong plea for thinking about stewardship in connection with the natural environment. "Don't say, 'I'll let the earth people worry about that,'" he cautioned. "The great sin of our culture is what we've done to the earth. Stewardship means avoiding aerosols, pariticipating in recycling, and not hiding your paint cans in the bottom of your garbage. All that has to be an expression of your faith." At a Baptist church in Atlanta, the pastor also spoke with passion about the environment. "I'm a lot more excited about it than I am about abortion," he remarked. He said he wasn't going to become involved on either side of the abortion controversy because he doesn't have strong feelings about it. But he thinks every Christian should be concerned about the environment, including recycling, protecting the forests and streams, and being politically involved because "if we don't, we're all going to die from it."

If clergy sound like they have simply jumped on the bandwagon with other environmentalists, some at least state clearly that the churches have a special mis-sion to speak on environmental issues. They feel that people with genuine religious convictions should have a broader understanding of the environment than people who view it strictly in naturalistic terms. If God is the creator, they argue, then people who believe this must take a balanced view of the created order rather than siding with extremist interest groups. "It is clearly impossible to have no smoke-stacks at all," observed one pastor. But, he said, purity of the environment must be weighed very heavily against the benefits of industry and technology.[3]

In all these ways—its opposition to untrammeled self-interest, its holistic orien-tation, and its concern with the natural environment—stewardship remains a cen-tral and potentially powerful teaching in American churches. Clergy have not aban-doned it, but they have modified it to their contemporary audience. In doing so, they have perhaps enhanced the likelihood of middle-class church members being able to grasp the importance of stewardship. As we will consider in a moment, how-ever, adaptation also weakens the message and introduces ambiguities.

The most obvious way that clergy have adapted teachings about stewardship to middle America is by recognizing that most Americans have ample resources at their disposal. Arguments about protecting the environment often refer implicitly to Americans' capacity to live less extravagantly and to the political and technological resources they have for curbing ecological problems. More commonly, clergy stress the fact that Americans have been blessed with affluence as an argument for being generous in giving their time and money to the churches and to the needy. "Freely you have received, now freely give" is delivered like an introit at many Sunday services. "We just need to be faithful in giving back a portion of what God has so richly blessed us with," argued one pastor. "Many of us have been blessed with the ability to make money," said another, "so we shouldn't hoard it. We should give generously."

Another way in which clergy adapt the idea of stewardship to contemporary society is by bringing in examples from middle-class life. We have already considered examples such as playing the piano, working as an artist, or teaching children to play football. Clergy also talk about the jobs at which people work—and do so by significantly altering the connotations of biblical metaphors. The idea that stewardship is like being a slave (expressed in Pauline epistles) is one example. Slaves are owned by someone else, so stewards should think of themselves as God's property. "I don't have any right to myself; I am simply a slave of the Lord," explained a pastor in Michigan. "What he wants me to do, I do because I've turned my life over to him. That's called the lordship of Christ. It's a very keen theological term that is used all over the church." The steward is thus someone who is "in the world but not of this world"—a person set apart from other people who behaves differently. If this notion seems impractical, the pastor nevertheless makes it more attractive to middle-class life. He said that people can pretty much trust their feelings to know "what's right *for you* and what's wrong *for you*." As a concrete example, he said, "If I'm a good CPA, I should be using part of that for him." He also said, "A dedicated Christian who really desires to serve the Lord and who wants to make as much money as he can is doing the work of the Lord." In fact, he mentioned several members of his church as examples. "They have been given tremendous financial awards. They are wealthy. They have set up foundations to use to give missionaries and ministers help. And they're out there still making money, and I encourage them, I say hey, make all you can, but give all you can."

Much the same argument was made by the pastor of a large evangelical church in Pennsylvania. He too said that good stewards should be like slaves who own nothing and are totally subservient to God. "You belong to Christ, your life belongs to him, he wants you to live for him. He's a jealous and passionate God, and he wants us to live for him." All of one's time and money belong to God, he explained. But then, as if sensing that such a scenario might not be very attractive to the professionals and managers who make up his congregation, he added, "It's for our benefit." He noted that stewardship is consistent with being creative in business. He also cited some of the wealthy people in his congregation as important contributors who have helped to "build the kingdom."

Management is, in fact, one of the most frequently used metaphors for making stewardship relevant to today's world. The connotation is that stewardship is like working for someone who expects a lot, perhaps pays you too little, and has little tolerance for play, but whom you can probably escape once in a while by taking a day off or going on vacation. At Cornerstone Bible Church, Pastor Higgins explained that being a good steward is pretty much like being a manager at McDonald's. If the manager acted like he owned the place, the owner would fire him. The good manager knows he is accountable. He has to account for every penny that comes in, and he has to provide quality food and service. He has to do the best he can. "I believe that the mark is excellence," said Pastor Higgins, "doing our very, very best."[4]

## DIFFICULTIES WITH THE MESSAGE

Although clergy agree that stewardship is an important teaching, many of them say it is a difficult idea to communicate. Clergy with whom I have discussed the survey findings mentioned earlier are generally not surprised. Some of them insist that their own members understand what stewardship means, but many fear that their members have only a shallow grasp of the concept. The pastor of a suburban Presbyterian church in New Jersey said her parishioners seem not to understand the idea of stewardship at all. "They still think everything they have is *theirs*, not God's," she asserted. She blamed herself, saying she received no training in seminary about how to educate people to understand stewardship. Down the road a few miles, the pastor of a Reformed church made a similar comment. "They don't think about it very much," he said, explaining why he feels his members do not understand stewardship. "They're spending all their time with their nose to the grindstone, their shoulder to the wheel, and they don't stop and think, 'Hey, how am I doing as a steward?' It's not a high-priority item in their catalog of thoughts."

Even in churches where pastors place a great deal of emphasis on stewardship, it is difficult to communicate the idea effectively because *self-interest* is such a prevalent way of thinking. A Lutheran pastor who defined stewardship as "the care of and the use of all that we've been given to the glory of God and to the service of others" admitted it is "tough" to get people to apply this idea to their lives "because of people tending to be so individualistic." He thinks "the me generation and just think about ourselves" makes it hard to understand any kind of "corporateness," which he regards as part of the Christian faith.

Another Lutheran pastor said he has trouble convincing people that their successes are not "just because they're so darned good" themselves. True to his theological tradition, he feels that self-interest prevents us from seeing life, as we should, in terms of God's grace. We're "very grabby and very clutchy," he said. "I think of people who have just self-aggrandized themselves, their position, their power, their little pile of things." He mused that a "dramatic failure" once in a while might make us more appreciative of what we have and, therefore, more attuned to the idea of stewardship.

Stewardship is also a difficult concept because self-interest encourages us to think in relativistic, calculating, situational terms, whereas many pastors regard stewardship as an absolute, morally binding obligation. "The hard thing in the world today," observed a Southern Baptist pastor in Texas, "is that we've changed our values and we do not have a collective sense of values. There's no collective sense of moral absolutes, and so everybody has what they would call their own price tag for everything." He said that a true understanding of stewardship requires us to erect a boundary between this sort of pricing and an "appropriate value system" that is "part of God's economy."

Self-interest makes it especially difficult to conceive of stewardship in terms of making real sacrifices to help other people. We are perhaps content to think of ourselves as God's managers—as long as we reap the bonuses of highly paid chief executive officers (CEOs). We may even give lip service to the idea that everything belongs to God—as long as God doesn't interfere with how we use it. Still, Americans are a sufficiently generous people that selfishness alone may not be the primary reason why clergy feel frustrated in communicating the idea of stewardship. The more pervasive problem may be that self-interest encourages us to think more in terms of choice, freedom, options, and lifestyles than in terms of responsibilities. When this happens, stewardship is sometimes redefined to mean little more than choosing the lifestyle that makes us happiest.

In their efforts to combat self-interested thinking, it is also clear that clergy sometimes talk in ways that may actually encourage such thinking. Nobody argues directly for being selfish rather than helping others. But there is a fine line between ideas of self-interest and arguments about developing one's self and cultivating one's talents. Most clergy agree that stewardship involves the wise use of individual talents. Some clergy argue that it is legitimate to devote virtually all of one's energy to developing and expressing these talents and say that the operating norm is not so much using them to help others but to find one's own level of comfort. "If somebody has the talent to make money, money, money," one pastor remarked, "I think that's up to them."

Clergy also permit self-interest to enter their arguments when they try to convince people that stewardship makes sense because they will be better off financially or happier because they have been good stewards. Such arguments are particularly common in appeals to give money to the church (chapter 9), but clergy also bring them up in defending stewardship more generally. One example comes from a Presbyterian pastor in Texas who believed very strongly in the importance of stewardship. Yet, when asked how he would apply the idea of stewardship to today's world, he argued that people are simply better off if they give some of their money away than if they keep it all for themselves. "I believe with all my heart that I can do more on 90 percent with God as a partner than I can do with 100 percent by myself," he asserted. "I think that's been proven out. I mean, those aren't just clichés. It's been proven out in my life, over and over and over again."

The point is not whether he is right or wrong. The point is that audiences hear selectively. Most clergy believe that there are other reasons to practice stewardship besides self-interest. Yet, with self-interest taught in college classrooms, boardrooms, and in the newspapers as the only motive that counts, it is easy for church members to conclude that stewardship isn't a very special doctrine after all. Instead of coming to church and hearing that they should serve God because it is right or because God commands it or because God is God, they find out that the churches are saying pretty much what everyone else is saying.

The difficulties associated with communicating stewardship to a self-interested world can be attributed to the wider culture rather than blaming them squarely on the clergy. A second set of difficulties, though, arises from the fact that pastors inevitably play a dual role. In their so-called *prophetic* role, they are called on to speak critically about prevailing assumptions and lifestyles. In their so-called *priestly* role, they are the wardens of the church, charged with keeping its pews occupied and its coffers full. The inevitable tension between these two roles arises forcefully whenever stewardship is at issue. Prophets want to speak against self-interest, against working too hard, in favor of using one's talents wisely at the office, and on behalf of the environment. Priests know they must focus parishioners' attention on supporting the church. One of the reasons that stewardship in its prophetic sense is not very well understood or applied is simply that clergy emphasize its other meaning.

When we asked pastors to talk to us about stewardship, we encouraged them to tell us how they understood it in the broadest possible terms. Repeatedly, however, we found that the church was their frame of reference. They immediately talked about serving the church, doing church work, and giving money to the church. Others mentioned some of the broader meanings of stewardship but then provided concrete examples that focused entirely on the church.

A Catholic priest in Texas told us that stewardship is "the involvement of people in the church work ministry. Helping out in church work, helping out in feeding the poor, the hungry, the needy, making sure that there is someone available to see them. Okay, that's what stewardship for me is. Someone who is willing to come in and say, 'Father, I want to do this, this, this, and this.'"

In a Polish parish in Chicago, the priest offered a similar definition of stewardship. "It means the manner in which we support our church," he said, "as well as the manner in which the church uses the resources that we have."

Protestant clergy also associate stewardship with doing church work and supporting the church. The rector of an Episcopal church in Illinois defined stewardship broadly as "responding in ways of generosity to the fundamental givingness, grace, and giftedness of life that God has given us." But, when asked how he would apply that understanding in the world of today, he shifted immediately to talking about his budget. "We do not raise money here like other institutions," he explained. "We do not say we have a budget and we have a need and you've got to come up with this amount in order to help us do that." He asks his congregation "to prayerfully respond to the question, 'How has God blessed me?'" If stewardship means generosity, it most specifically means generosity in supporting the church.

The pastor of an evangelical church in Pennsylvania showed how this connection sometimes creeps into discussions and claims more attention than the speaker intends. He wanted us to understand that stewardship means realizing "that you belong to Christ" and that "he wants you to live for him." To make his point more concrete, he added that some people in his church "give their lives entirely to God's service." What he meant was people going into "full-time ministry" and "missions." By implication, people in other professions apparently were not giving their lives entirely to God's service.

Occasional remarks like this—in conversations and in sermons—are reinforced by the fact that most churches have annual *stewardship* campaigns that also focus on giving time and money to the church. These campaigns are essential if churches are going to raise the funds and elicit the person power needed to operate in the coming year. But people who feel they are doing God's bidding in other spheres of life or by supporting other organizations are unlikely to see that stewardship, in its broader sense, still applies to them if the really "good stewards" are the ones who ask to teach Sunday school classes, serve on church committees, and make large financial pledges.

Focusing stewardship on the church is not limited to discussions of donations or pledges, either. Since most clergy agree that stewardship involves the wise use of one's individual talents, we asked them to tell us what that might mean in the case of someone whose talent was music. We chose this example because it was an ambiguous stimulus: One could talk about it in the context of life more generally or within the church. We wanted to see what clergy regarded as an appropriate, godly application of musical talent.

The responses demonstrated that clergy themselves are not unmindful of the broader ways in which musical talent might be put to good use. A few, for instance, said it would be good stewardship just to develop one's talent and to use it for one's enjoyment and for the benefit of others. But clergy know their own churches much better than they do anything else. So most clergy slip into giving examples that focus on the church and, in so doing, imply that this is *really* the way to be a good steward. They mentioned members who sing solos or who play the piano at services. One, who had a fairly broad concept of stewardship, suggested, nevertheless, that the best thing might be for someone with musical talent to "sing spiritual songs." Another imagined someone who was a traveling musician but indicated that stewardship would mean "witnessing" to other people on the road.[5] Still another—Rector Morgan—argued that someone who played for the symphony "might or might not be glorifying God" but that the same person would be glorifying God if they played at the church.

Apart from the difficulties that self-interest and church interest create, clergy also have trouble speaking clearly about stewardship in relation to work and money. Stewardship clearly pertains to the ways in which people use their time and thus has important implications for the activity that most people say they would rather not spend their time doing—work. In the past, stewardship has often been taken to mean a kind of puritanical existence in which work took priority over everything else. Now that leisure has become an activity that most people work hard at, and now that work itself is considered—in some quarters—as an addiction or an obsession or a source of stress and burnout, clergy tie themselves in knots trying to explain how people should be good stewards in their work.

Many clergy still express the traditional view, arguing that good stewards strive for excellence in their work, work longer and harder than everyone else, and demonstrate that they are good Christians by outperforming their heathen neighbors. Pastors may not tell their parishioners to work a certain number of hours each week, but their view of *how* work should be done means having to devote an inordinate amount of time to it. Taking a painting contractor he knew as an example, one pastor spoke glowingly about how carefully this man did his work. "He's up on a scaffolding, painting on top of something, and one of his workers will say, 'Why are you painting that? Nobody will ever see it.' And he says, 'Because I'll know the difference.'" In the stewardship sermons we collected, pastors often spoke favorably of Japanese workers who spend long hours on the job, of business owners who had succeeded by working hard, and of musicians and athletes who excelled by practicing harder than anyone else.

The work ethic is emphasized especially in churches where there is a strong sense that Christians must be exemplary models of godliness. At Cornerstone, for instance, Pastor Higgins explained that it is important to do everything one can to improve oneself and to do one's job to the best of one's ability. "I'm putting God on display in my life," he said. "This church, here, everything that we do, we're saying that this is how we feel about God, this is what we think about God. Well, if it looks like a dump and it's really run shoddy, if it's sloppy, then we don't have a very high opinion of God."

Even if pastors do not equate hard work with good stewardship, this idea becomes part of the subculture of many congregations, especially when so many laity believe it is more godly to work hard than to be lazy. At one of the churches we studied, the pastor reported on a recent meeting with his board of deacons. For some reason, the chair of the board asked each member to say how many hours he worked each week. Every member claimed to be working at least seventy hours a week. It was a matter of pride, the pastor observed.

Rather than encouraging us to work ourselves to death, most clergy recommend *balance* as a principle for good stewards to emulate. "We can say enough is enough, and we have to," explained the pastor of a nondenominational church. Paraphrasing the Apostle Paul, he argued that Christians should "make it your ambition to live a quiet life, make it your ambition to work with your hands and to live a quiet life." He said that "ambition" should be redefined as gaining a "balance between work and leisure." Another pastor said that the work ethic has gotten out of hand, and he credited the church with some of the blame. "People think they have to work fifty or sixty hours a week to be a good person," he observed. But, he said, "a lot of the marital difficulties that I work with, and with other problems, one of the major factors is the time constraints, the job overload, the tremendous amount of hours put in at work by one or the other spouse or both."

How to find the right balance between work and pleasure, though, is a question on which the clergy are divided. Some take a sober view that is still close to nineteenth-century asceticism. They argue that work should cease primarily in order to rest and to fulfill other worthwhile obligations, such as doing church work. They do not believe it is good for people to cease working simply to have fun. The opposing view is also widely in evidence. Clergy argue that God made leisure too, and that if we happen to live in a leisure society, great, enjoy it.

The clearest example of the ascetic view came, perhaps not surprisingly, from a New England clergyman who argued—like his Puritan ancestors—that good stewardship means relaxing just enough to perform at one's maximum level. "It isn't a question of resting in order to have fun or in order to satisfy a desire to have fun," he explained. "It's a question of taking enough of a respite to stay healthy and to keep not only a healthy body but a healthy mind and a healthy attitude."

At one of the rapidly growing megachurches we studied, the pastor spoke enthusiastically about living the good life, including putting our work aside more often just to have fun. Stating that stewardship should involve an efficient use of our time, he hastened to add, "It doesn't mean God wants us to live miserable lives." Citing evidence from the book of Ecclesiastes, this pastor asserted that God "wants us to eat, drink and be merry. He wants us to enjoy life." Sometimes, he said, he encourages his congregation to work fewer hours, to ask themselves if work isn't perhaps "pure addictive behavior," and just to spend more time enjoying the moment. Rector Morgan—musing that perhaps he had been ruined by his Anglicanism—went further, asserting that people should "be relaxed and spend a lot of time skiing and enjoying nature, and life, and God, and friends, and good music, and a glass of wine."

At a Lutheran church in Illinois, the pastor was having a harder time knowing how to instruct his parishioners on the right relationship between hard work and stewardship. He thought his older members worked too hard and his younger members didn't work hard enough. He personally was ambivalent about "that old nervous work ethic," but he couldn't quite understand why parents who worked hard seemed to have children who were lazy.

Quite often, it appears, pastors are genuinely torn by the conflicting images of work in their own traditions and by the confusing messages they perceive in contemporary culture. Some turn confusion into a virtue by preaching about paradox. Yet it seems doubtful that such teaching communicates much about stewardship other than its complexity. One of the best illustrations of this complexity is evident in the comments of a Unitarian pastor. Because of Unitarianism's historical roots in Puritanism, he has thought a lot about the work ethic. He explained, "In many ways we carry a lot of that traditional, intense work ethic in us. And since we emphasize character and say that one is saved by the deeds that he or she does, we tend to be really hard on ourselves. That's where some of the burnout stuff comes from. So I would say, for most of us life is a passionate affair. Yet we also entertain the idea that leisure is important and that one has to have the ability to look at things paradoxically, if not ironically, and don't take the work too seriously. It's almost like, well, it's the most serious thing that we have to do, yet don't take it too seriously." He seemed troubled by his own inability to put it any more clearly.

Just as they do with work, clergy run into ambiguities and contradictions when they apply the idea of stewardship to the pursuit and uses of money. Repeatedly, pastors lauded parishioners who could make a lot of money, arguing that this was a clear example of good stewardship, especially if it meant that these people gave generously to "God's work." "We encourage people to go as far as they can [in earning money] and to max out whenever they can," asserted the pastor of a large Baptist church in Houston. Another pastor explained that he had been raised to think that living simply and not thinking much about money was the right way, but he has been "wrestling" with that understanding. His view now that he is in charge of a relatively affluent congregation is that "people who have the abilities to make money need to be encouraged to do just that." Making money, he said, is just a way of being a faithful steward. "If God has given somebody the abilities, the mind, the know-how, the technique, the timing, whatever, to be able to make millions, then go for it and make it." The pastor at another church said he has several very wealthy members, and he just tries to encourage them: "I say, hey, make all you can!"

Generally, pastors who like people to make lots of money state explicitly that this approach is right because those people can then give lots of money to worthy causes—such as the church. But pastors also register concern about this view. They know that most people are unlikely to be rich, even though they want their rich congregants to feel especially welcome. They know that wealth is not simply a matter of having the talents to make money. Or they believe that talent leads to money but recognize that money has negative consequences as well. One of the Presbyterian pastors we spoke to commented on these consequences among some of the wealthy members of his church. "You have talent, you're not voracious, but because you have talent you end up in one of these big jobs. You never even quite planned it that way. You're moved up, you're transferred. Then suddenly you've got a lot of money, so you buy a house. And you keep moving up, and you have more responsibility, which takes more time, but then you've got a family. And you have these built-in conflicts. You love your job, but you pay a terrible price."

Sometimes clergy also talk about the "arrogance" of the rich and the need for people to take a more "organic" view of their relationships with other people and with the environment. And some clergy who argue that people should make all the money they can also pause to express concern about highly paid CEOs who are laying off their hourly workers and to lament the "kinky" lifestyles of the rich and famous. Congregants, therefore, are likely to come away having heard that stewardship means using whatever money they have wisely but also suspecting that God's servants have a special place in their heart for the rich.

Ironically, another reason why stewardship is a difficult subject to communicate is that much of what it implies seems to be what middle-class people are doing anyway. Pastors may hold the wealthy in high esteem, or they may encourage parishioners to sell everything and devote their lives totally to missionary work, but they rarely express such views. More commonly, middle-class church members hear practical advice that sounds pretty much like what their mothers, teachers, employers, and therapists have told them all their lives. Be responsible. Pay your bills. Think good thoughts. Take care of yourself.

As one example, consider the annual stewardship sermon at a suburban Presbyterian church. It focused on stewardship in the broadest sense but sought to give parishioners concrete illustrations of how they might function as good stewards. Taking its first cue from Jesus driving the money changers from the temple, the sermon suggested that expressing our anger rather than keeping it inside is an example of good stewardship. Then, turning to the tale of the widow giving her last coins, it underscored the importance of being faithful in small things but cautioned against going to ridiculous extremes. It might be wise for the church to save postage by economizing on mailings but not to save left over communion bread from month to month or try to capture the church mouse to send to the poor. Other words of advice suggested scheduling one's time carefully at the start of each day, following the advice of "fitness folks" in taking care of our bodies, guarding our health, renewing our minds through study, not getting too tired out, doing well at our jobs, paying attention to our relationships, and getting out to vote. One might have heard Ben Franklin sitting in the corner muttering, "Waste not, want not."

Stewardship of this kind is basically middle-class virtue. Be dutiful in everything, but don't get too exhausted. Do your best in everything, but don't let anything slide either. The point is to get people to reflect on their lives. Don't keep in your anger. Well, yes, I guess I need to go speak my mind to someone. But the standards are largely internal to the person. Do I feel I am suppressing my anger? Do I feel exhausted? Do I really care about my work? There are no objective standards, nor is there any notion of divine insight or wisdom.[6] In an earlier version of such sermons, God would have been pictured as empowering the individual to try harder or to look more honestly at his or her conscience. That part is now gone.

Which brings us to a final point. Stewardship becomes a weak tool in the hands of many clergy because of the implicit deism that prevails in American culture and that discussions of stewardship specifically convey. In common parlance, deism is not an explicit philosophical orientation rooted in the writings of Voltaire, Thomas Jefferson, or Benjamin Franklin but simply the assumption that God has pretty much left things up to us. Stewardship now implies that we are caretakers, responsible to God, of course, but more or less for a planet that we have on permanent loan. Contemporary caretakers do not check in with the boss very often or receive very explicit instructions on what to do. Rather, they are like good business managers: Not knowing exactly what the owner expects, they simply try to do what's good for the company.

"A steward is a manager of resources entrusted to him or her," explained a Presbyterian pastor in Illinois. "So if it's individual stewardship, you are managing the resources at your disposal in a wide and creative way. Theologically, you are to manage them in a way that would be pleasing to God. And I define what would be pleasing to God as what would be good for human beings because you never know what's going to be pleasing to God. It's a little easier for me to think what would be good for human beings." He's not sure, though, that there is anything special about Christianity that helps people to be good or to do good. Indeed, he fears that stewardship itself causes problems because people try hard to use their talents wisely and then get swept up in responsibilities that overwhelm them.

## LESSONS FROM THE CLERGY

It is little wonder that the concept of stewardship is hard for most church members to grasp clearly. Hearing ideas that are clearly simplistic, or hearing clergy speaking in divided and ambivalent tones, church members are likely to say with Roy Steuben that they are "at a loss" about stewardship. Yet the churches can ill afford to write off stewardship as a lost cause. If they are to minister effectively to their members' concerns about work and money, and if they are to secure generous donations, they must speak *more* about stewardship, not less.

What should they say? Pondering the numerous sermons, remarks, and candid reflections of the clergy we interviewed leads me to argue that there *are* some valuable insights about stewardship—and how best to apply it in the world today—that need to be emphasized. These insights are subject to the same difficulties, ambiguities, and opportunities for misinterpretation that I have just discussed. But these insights also help to correct some of those problems. Clearly, it is impossible for clergy to present all the various ramifications of stewardship as fully as they might like in a single sermon or even in a series of sermons. It is also unlikely, if not impossible, to expect church members to devote precious minutes amidst busy schedules to reading tomes about stewardship or attending long seminars on the topic. So clergy and other religious leaders must be selective in what they emphasize. Certainly they need to continue emphasizing their basic understandings of stewardship and its centrality to the life of faith. The following, I believe, are also points particularly worthy of emphasis.

First, the churches must continue to emphasize stewardship and to do so in a way that features its *theological* significance rather than depicting it simply as commonsense, middle-class virtue. One of the clearest statements we heard about the theological significance of stewardship came from a pastor who serves at a large interdenominational Protestant church in New York. He argued that stewardship is not, in the first instance, about material possessions or how *we* should use *our* time or gifts at all, but about God. "The first thing we've been entrusted with is the grace of the kingdom, the gospel itself. It is the fact that we are stewards of the kingdom—the fact of grace, the fact that we've been called by God's grace into his family. We're stewards of the grace of the kingdom. And our talent is the measure of the gospel's grace entrusted to us." Only by starting with an appreciation of the nature of God, he argued, could we put our own talents in the right perspective.

If clergy are to communicate the theological significance of stewardship to their congregations, seminaries and divinity schools have a special responsibility to prepare clergy for this task. "The heart of 'stewardship education,'" wrote Robert Wood Lynn, "is learning how to develop one's own vision of God's grace and its impact on every aspect of daily life." Lynn argued that clergy must learn to think about stewardship in terms other than fund-raising and money management. "We need new theological insights and a much more creative theological imagination," he asserted, "to really teach stewardship to the next generation of church leaders."[7]

Second, the churches need to emphasize balance. As one reads through sermons and commentaries from other eras, especially before the Industrial Revolution, one finds that balance was emphasized more than anything else. Words such as *temperance* and *moderation*—that now frequently have negative connotations—were prominently featured. The idea was quite different from the kind of stewardship that connotes five evenings a week serving on church committees and eighty hours a week at the office developing and using one's talents to the highest possible degree. With burnout, stress, child abuse, and marital dissolution at record rates, some clergy are beginning to rediscover this language of balance.

Roy Steuben's pastor at the Mennonite church is one example. "Even the good things in life can be used to excess," he cautioned. "A person could be using some gift at the cost of depriving themselves of their family relationships and their personal health and well-being. So there has to be a careful balance. 'Yes, I can contribute to church life, to society, to community, and I first of all have to take care of myself and my family and want to make time for them.' To use the words of Jesus, 'What good is it to gain the whole world and lose your own self, lose your own family, lose the ones near you?'"

Some clergy are finding it possible to use traditional language to argue strongly for a life of balance. The concept of the calling, for example, provided a United Church of Christ pastor with a formula emphasizing balance. "The Lord God, I believe, calls us to four activities," he stated. "God calls us to worship, he calls us to work, he calls us to rest, and he calls us to play. We need to have all four of those activities in our life and in balance. If we have one which is really dominant, we've got a problem. They have to be balanced, the worship, work, play, and rest."

Clergy are also able to draw from the life of Jesus to suggest reasons why people should strive for balance. "Jesus set limits," observed the pastor of an Evangelical Free church. "He knew his boundaries well. When he was exhausted at the end of the day, he withdrew from the crowds and went up into the hills. And he took a boat to the other side to get away from the people. That was keeping his boundaries."

Third, the churches need to expose the secular messages that push middle-class Americans to engage in well-meaning but excessive, self-interested behavior. Responsibility has long been a featured item in sermons on stewardship, and it may be important to emphasize responsibility in certain areas, such as paying greater attention to problems in the community, taking more time to parent one's children, or understanding the implications of misconduct with drugs or sex. But the middle class is already bombarded on all sides with messages about responsibility. The church need not be another source of guilt. As one pastor asserted, "I don't see that we should put people on a guilt trip by telling them how they need to go out and develop their talents."

Exposing secular messages also means formulating arguments about stewardship in ways that explicitly challenge the prevailing ideology of self-interest. One of the pastors we interviewed was working on a sermon about stewardship to be given the next day. He said the point he wanted to make was that people should be generous with their resources, not because they expect to get something in return but just because "God has given you everything." People become incredibly generous, he suggested, because "you're just so thankful, and that knowledge transforms you, and you want to give away a lot of the stuff. Suddenly you don't need to keep as much for yourself as you thought that you needed to keep. And you want to figure out how to share your resources with other people."[8]

Fourth, the churches must present themselves as symbols—as metaphors—for understanding faithful service, rather than depicting themselves as the only places in which legitimate service can take place. This is a scary thought. Churches are richly symbolic, yet clergy have often found it difficult to say that something is symbolic for fear of diminishing its importance (or reality). Yet it is clear that the churches do not have a monopoly on doing God's work. Stewardship must take into account the ways in which people serve from Monday through Saturday, not just on Sundays. As symbol, the church serves as a reminder and puts in more concentrated form what people do at other times. The Nazarene pastor in Kansas put it this way: "Symbolically, every time I put a dollar in the plate, I'm putting me in the plate and saying 'You can use me however you want.'"

Yet it is not enough to say that giving to the church is symbolic—and leave it at that. Whatever donations of time and money go to the church need to support organizations that perform ministries not possible in other walks of life and yet that complement other forms of stewardship. One of the striking gaps in pastors' understandings of stewardship, in this regard, is its relationship with worship. As places of worship, churches can amplify and support parishioners' sense of the God whose ownership of creation they claim to observe. The churches can also tighten the connection between worship and stewardship through a more creative use of ritual.

An example of how churches might use ritual more effectively comes from an

Episcopal church we studied in Virginia. To dramatize the connection between environmental concerns and an understanding of God's created order, the church has instituted a rogation ceremony on the sixth Sunday after Easter each year. Rogation is an old English custom that seeks God's blessing as farmers plant their seeds each spring. Traditionally it included plowing, singing, and a procession through the fields. The pastor described how his congregation has adapted the ceremony to their circumstances. "We go out to a part of our grounds that's a meadow, and we have appropriate readings for the meadow and the streams. And then we go over to the playground and use that as a workplace and think of it in terms of a workplace where we spend time and ask God's blessing. And then we end up over in the graveyard. We sing as we process. And we end in the graveyard, where people are buried and they've joined the saints. It's a teaching thing for children, trying to make it come alive. We do this regularly, and it's a lot of fun." He is convinced that activities like this are needed to make the idea of stewardship more meaningful.

In addition to staging their own rituals, clergy can also encourage parishioners to rediscover the value of rituals in their daily lives. One man told us he lights a candle every day for a few minutes in his office as a reminder that everything is God's and part of the spirit of God. A Methodist pastor told us she likes to dig in the dirt with her daughter and talk about how God is present in her garden. An African American pastor in California encouraged his listeners to have family prayers oriented toward stewardship. "My grandfather and grandmother would have their children bow their heads before every meal," he said. "And old Granddad would thank God for everything that God had given to them. The woodlawns and the horses, the sawmill, and the rich family tradition. It was a ritual of supreme importance. Not only for Grandfather to focus on God, but to get the concept across to the kids that everything that he had was on loan from God, and he was to be a caretaker. Friends, can we get it? What must happen to us to have this truth become a part of our lives?"

Finally, the churches must also be enablers. Exhortation must be accompanied by organization. Stewardship is little more than a subjective attitude unless people are supported in their efforts to live responsibly, to protect the environment, and to use their resources for the benefit of others. Pastoral counseling, training in financial management, and opportunities to serve the needy are among the ways in which churches can turn talk about stewardship into action. Such activities can be performed in cooperation with other churches and with nonreligious agencies in the community and in the workplace. Through such arrangements, the church then becomes a *tangible* expression of stewardship that embraces life most fully.

# eight

# MONEY MATTERS

The parsimonious comedian Jack Benny loved to repeat a joke about being approached by a mugger who demanded, "Your money or your life!" to which Benny, after a long pause, replied, "Don't rush me; I'm thinking, I'm thinking!" Money *is* arguably our most cherished national obsession. We want it desperately; we devote many of our waking hours to working to obtain it and a good deal of our spare time to spending it. Clearly, money matters. When we have it, we feel more free and lighthearted. When we don't have it, we feel like failures. We scheme to get more of it, subscribe to magazines to get pointers about it, read columns in the newspaper and watch programs on television about it, fight with our spouses and children over it, and stand in awe of those who have amassed great quantities of it.

The American middle class, collectively and individually, has more money at its disposal than any other majority group in history has had. The churches of the American middle class can scarcely escape this fact. Their own fortunes depend on the willingness of the middle class to contribute a portion of its money. But middle-class churches also have a responsibility to help their members deal with the concerns that inevitably arise from having money and from wanting it. Middle America is bombarded with messages about money from every side—from employers, advertisers, retailers, investment counselors and brokers, family mem-

139

bers, and the people next door. Much of the time, we blindly follow these messages—scrambling to purchase the same toys and pursue the same lifestyles as
everyone else. We do not do so, however, without misgivings. We worry that advertising is corrupting our values and that materialism is destroying our society. We
want to use our money wisely and wish not to be greedy, shallow materialists.

The churches have an enormous opportunity at their disposal if they can help
parishioners with their concerns about money.[1] The desire for counsel—and for
comfort—is there. Middle-class church members are, in fact, far more interested in
thinking about how better to handle their money than they are in debating the
peripheral political issues that have occupied so much of the churches' attention in
recent years. And the economic retrenchment that many middle-class families have
begun to experience adds to this interest. "Finances is where the rubber meets the
road," said Reverend Higgins at Cornerstone Bible Church. "This is where our
faith is tested."

Quite often, church members are, of course, interested only in finding religious
reasons to feel good about their pursuit of the almighty dollar. As one pastor
lamented, "I think the people in my church consider *shopping* a spiritual gift!" But
church members at least give lip service to the idea that faith should help them to
be less materialistic, less obsessed with making money, and more committed to
higher aims and ideals.

If clergy look to their own traditions, they know that there is much to say about
money and material possessions.[2] Christianity has always been vitally interested in
matters of everyday life, not just with removing its followers to an ethereal plane of
spiritual insight. Throughout its history, Christianity has been concerned with
instructing its followers in setting their priorities and in guiding their moral and
ethical conduct.

Among church members nationally, 65 percent say the Bible contains valuable
teachings about money. Yet only 19 percent say they have thought a great deal in
the past year about these teachings.[3] Or, as one pastor put it, "People really don't
think about money in relation to their faith; they only think about it in November
when it's pledge time." And one of the clearest reasons is that clergy are reluctant
to expound on the biblical teachings that focus on money, or they do so in a way
that does not connect with the concerns of their members. Clergy find it difficult
to preach about money and difficult to challenge parishioners to apply biblical
teachings to their thinking about personal finances.

Why this reluctance? Are clergy convinced that money doesn't matter? Do they
not have opinions on the subject? Or, if they do, what do they think the churches
*should* be doing to help parishioners deal with their concerns about money?

• • •

## SILENT SHEPHERDS

The main reason that clergy are reluctant to speak more often and more forthrightly about money is the prevailing middle-class taboo against *anyone* discussing money—especially in church. In the public at large, fewer than one person in four ever talks about his or her personal finances with close friends. Among church members, only *3 percent* say they ever discuss their finances with fellow church members. And only *4 percent* have ever discussed their finances with a member of the clergy. These are noteworthy figures, given the fact that everyone is concerned about money. In many other societies, different norms prevail; for example, in Israel and China friends and neighbors know what each other's salaries are and openly discuss pay raises and bonuses. In our culture, though, people generally shield even their own children from information about family finances and consider it improper to ask the price of ordinary purchases. "It's considered good to make money," one pastor explained, "but not good to talk about it; it's a very private thing. That's our mindset." With so few people talking with fellow church members or their pastors about personal finances, clergy are shielded from *having* to address concerns about money. Indeed, when we asked clergy what sort of advice they gave people who came to them with questions about money, a majority said they simply had not been faced with such requests.

The taboo against discussing money is heightened in churches because of a prevailing myth that dominates popular religious thinking, namely, that churches are "communities" or "fellowships" in which such petty distinctions as those based on having money or not having money are irrelevant. Ask any pastor to characterize his or her congregation economically or in social-class terms, and the typical response is, "Oh, we have *all* kinds of people here—some have money, I suppose, and others don't, and there is every gradation in between." The subtext is, "We're all God's children; no distinctions here." And if one pushes pastors on the issue, the typical response is, "Sure there are differences, but I can't imagine how those differences matter in *my* church." Here, the subtext is that we are above all such matters; we are not "respecters of persons"; we treat everyone equally.

Equality of treatment may or may not be the case. The effect of *thinking* it is the case is nonetheless real: People shouldn't talk about money because it is in *bad taste,* as several pastors pointed out, to do so. Somehow, the assumption is that money cannot be mentioned without displaying how much of it (or how little) one has. There seems to be no recognition of the possibility that worries about money or principles for handling money might be common to everyone in the congregation.

Of course, it *may* reduce conflict in churches to maintain a sanctimonious silence about money. But not talking about it does not mean that distinctions based on money are as effectively banished from the churches as clergy like to think. If parishioners do not hear about money, they can still see. They can see that the person wearing a $500 suit is more likely to hold an office in the church than the person wearing a ragged sweater. They can see that the pastor is especially grateful for the volunteer time of a woman who happens to be married to a rich businessman and has no need to be employed herself but is less appreciative of the single mother who has no time for church committees because she is working to support her family. As one pastor observed, valuing people with more money "is a real common problem" in the churches. "It's tempting to respond more to middle-class prospects than to the poor single guy who's walking in the door and you know has more loans than he or she has resources," he admitted.

Nor does it make sense to assume that parishioners leave petty distinctions at home just because they cannot give voice to them at church. When sociologist Michèle Lamont interviewed middle-class men about their perceptions of themselves and of others, she found it quite common for her subjects to admit that they felt they were better than other people because they had more money and did not like to associate with people who had less money than they did.[4] Some of these views may be muted in the churches, but surveys show that church members are just as likely as nonmembers to admire people who make a lot of money.[5] And if money doesn't matter in churches, then it is hard to understand why blue bloods still cling together in Episcopal churches, bankers gravitate toward Presbyterian churches, and skilled laborers populate the ranks of Pentecostal churches.

Another reason for pastors' silence about money, quite understandably, is that they feel unqualified to give certain kinds of advice. In all our interviews with laity, we came across no one who had turned to the pastor for advice about purchasing stock or investing in land. Yet some of the pastors we talked to seemed fearful that their parishioners wanted this kind of advice. Rather than say the wrong thing, they felt it was better to say nothing at all. "I'm a general practitioner," the pastor of a suburban Baptist church explained. "I have a lot of different subjects that are thrown at me in the course of a year, and I'm not proficient in a lot of them. When I see a need that I can't handle, I refer people to a specialist, like a doctor. So I send them to a counselor."

A young, highly educated woman who pastors a small Presbyterian church in a suburban community elaborated on her reluctance to speak about money. "I have basically done my teaching in areas that I know *really* well and don't have to do a whole lot of homework on," she explained, "because my schedule here has been so crazy. You know, if I had to do something that I had to spend a lot of time researching, I couldn't do it. I'm the only pastor here, so I really don't have that kind of time. That's why the classes I've taught are either ones I've already taught or already know my material really well." She added, "I guess one of the main reasons why I haven't preached on money is that I just really don't know how receptive people are. I mean, I think I did do one sermon on it, but I just don't know how receptive they would be to it."

There is also a popular impression among pastors that parishioners would rather discuss *church* finances than personal finances or broader religious teachings about the handling of money. On the surface, church finances are of greater interest, pastors believe, because they are the common responsibility of the whole congregation. How much to pay for a new organ arouses more interest than layoffs at a particular plant in the community for this reason. But clergy also suspect that the heat generated by such discussions reflects concern smoldering beneath the surface about personal finances. So clergy play along, encouraging people to talk about the organ in hopes that something will be said inadvertently to address the unspoken concerns as well.

Surprising as it may be, yet another reason that clergy give for keeping tight-lipped about money in church is avoiding the appearance of evil. The argument goes like this: There is nothing inherently wrong with most of the ways in which people make money, but our society is very complex and ethical questions are hard to decide, so you might have ways of making money that you feel are perfectly legitimate, but other people might disagree and think you are doing something wrong; thus, the less said about your dealings, the better! An example of this logic was used recently by the pastor of a large mainline Protestant church in counseling a man who was troubled because he had inherited a brewery. The pastor convinced the man that there was nothing wrong with running a brewery because even Jesus had turned water into wine. "It isn't producing beer that's a problem," the pastor explained, "but whether or not beer drinkers misuse it." Still, he said, some of the man's friends and fellow churchgoers might see it a different way. "Who knows you own it?" the pastor asked. "If they don't know, don't worry about it." The man went away, the pastor said, greatly relieved.

There *is* one place where the silence about money is broken: the pastor's study, when a family whose heat and electricity have been turned off come for help. They come secretly and with shame, asking for a short-term loan, a kind word, or a prayer. And such visits, from what pastors say, are surprisingly rare—not because the middle class is exempt from such difficulties but because people are too proud to admit their problems, even to the clergy. As one of the priests we interviewed pointed out, "There's a certain prestige that goes with having money and success and stability and security. To admit that you have a money problem is to say that those are weak areas." Also, conversations with parishioners about financial emergencies are rare because many clergy, especially in large churches, are so removed from their members and because ministries have become so specialized that pastors have no contact with such problems, unless the pastor happens to be in charge of the church's counseling ministry.

The fact that money becomes an item of discourse only under such circumstances adds to the burden of silence. The shame of financial failure forces parishioners to keep up pretenses—like the man who told us he didn't venture out of his house during the daytime for several weeks after he lost his job because he didn't want anyone to suspect he was out of work. Fearing they may strike a raw nerve, clergy are then reluctant to discuss money even in more public settings. Implicitly, the only message communicated is that nobody at this church has any problems. The silence in the churches about matters of money is not complete, of course, but it is important to acknowledge the forces that make it harder for clergy to discuss these matters frankly.

## AMBIVALENT LEADERS

In addition to the norm of silence, clergy views on money are governed by a deep sense of ambivalence, and this ambivalence sometimes discourages them from talking openly about money as well. Clergy are not isolated from the American culture. Living in it as members of the middle class themselves, they experience the same pressures that many of their parishioners do. They do not want to appear to have all the answers to questions about personal finances because they know they do not. They struggle to make ends meet, make purchases that turn out to be foolish, and find themselves wanting the amenities of middle-class life just like everyone else.

A large share of the clergy's ambivalence toward money stems from the assumption that financial realities are simply the facts of life to which we all must adjust. God cuts no special deals for people of faith. Thus, there is little to be said other than try hard, do your best, and use common sense. "I think people just have to do what they have to do" was the way one pastor put it. "I can speak of the stress and strain myself," he added. "My advice would be try to live within your means." He said he would just have to be honest with people, too, and tell them he was struggling with the same things.

Yet clergy also express the special ambivalence that is common among outsiders and among people in all marginal social positions. Clergy are, by virtue of their occupation, part of the middle class but not "of it." They hold an allegiance to the kingdom of God, a loyalty that transcends and distances them from American culture. Squeezed as many of the clergy currently are by the hard times that have descended on the churches, they also feel unable to participate fully in the material aspirations of the middle class and thus express their alienation by criticizing it. "I, myself, would like to have a Ferrari," joked one pastor. "Just my bad luck that a Ferrari costs so much money." Other pastors were more serious about the financial pressures they feel.

"Tennis shoes in my day cost $6," ventured a clergyman in his early forties, "but now they're $120 because they have the special built-in air things that protect you. I don't know that we need all that." Sounding much like any beleaguered breadwinner, he complained, "All your commercials today are telling you that you're not going to be appealing if you don't have this kind of toothpaste and you don't drive that kind of car. I think the pressures have directed us to gratifying our physical desires too much." Then, speaking more as a pastor, he added, "This world isn't our home. When you look at all the saints, most of them had just what was on their back and they went out and they worked for God and they trusted him to provide the rest." In contrast, we now feel that if we "don't have that IRA in the bank and we don't have our college money there in the bank for our kids by the time they're twelve, then we're failing."

For this pastor, it helps to keep his own perspective on money by interacting with missionaries. They remind him that he too is an outsider to middle-class America. When he sees missionary children excited just to have a dish of frozen yogurt, he feels stronger about resisting the pressures to have a lot of money. He admitted, though, that it is hard for him to communicate this idealism to his congregation. "I'm not sure that I'm having any effect," he said. His ambivalence, then, like that of many clergy we talked to, does not inhibit him from preaching about money at all, but he feels conflict, not knowing whether the pressures he senses are simply inevitable or whether they are ones he should try to encourage his parishioners to resist.

Another source of ambivalence (hinted at by this example) stems from our sense that it is not quite patriotic to be critical of the material advantages of American culture. We may agree that Americans are too materialistic and believe it would be better to live more simply, yet when we compare our standard of living with that of other countries, we are justifiably proud to have the privileges that we take for granted. Thus, we wind up voicing criticisms but mostly taking them back even as we speak. A conversation we had with a priest about the United States in comparison with Third World countries provides an example. He said he had seen a film recently in which a man from a Third World country stood up and said, "We want to have things like the North Americans do." The priest wasn't sure that was a good attitude to have. He said, "I think we get lost when we no longer live a life of simplicity." But, he added, "I love our country for what it provides me, and I do share in its many benefits."

Clergy also experience ambivalence about money for pragmatic reasons. They believe our culture is too much oriented toward money. Yet the culture is so pervasive—so much the world in which we live—that they feel compelled to compromise with it in order to be heard at all. They fear, simply, that people would dismiss them otherwise. The pastor of a Mennonite church provided an interesting example of this kind of ambivalence. As a Mennonite, he felt strongly that people should live simply, and he pointed to the ways in which Mennonites and other "intentional communities" had attempted to do this in the past. But he also asserted that "money reigns and money has power." We may be victims of the culture, he said, but he acknowledged that "you have to make money to stay in business."

In fairness to the clergy, some of their ambivalence about money must also be credited to their knowledge of theology. They are unable to speak definitively on the subject of money because they find themselves torn between competing theological emphases. Take the question of materialism again. Clergy argue that Americans are too materialistic, basing this judgment on the fact that scripture emphasizes spirituality rather than the objects and goods that feed our physical appetites. Yet clergy also emphasize that God created the material world, placed us in the world, and intended us to enjoy it. "It's like a beautiful painting," one pastor observed. He said it would be foolish not to admire the painting's beauty.

The pastor of a liberal church in Philadelphia also emphasized the inherent ambivalence of religious teachings. "The New Testament, as I understand it," he said, "is ambiguous about money. That is to say, there are some passages where it's flatly condemned to be rich, but Jesus also had wealthy friends, and while he was committed to the poor, he didn't hate the rich." The pastor of another church explained that, in his view, there are always going to be competing arguments. "I don't think that many of the choices we have ever get fully resolved in some pure vacuum sort of way," he asserted. "I think we have to live with the tensions."

In their own minds at least, clergy recognize that the way to reconcile these competing theological emphases is to keep them in tension, thinking about them, talking about them, trying to understand them, and then prayerfully making concrete decisions with these orientations in mind. Or, as the pastor I just quoted said, "Keep raising the questions—the questions about what we value." But in practice, the norm of silence often discourages clergy from helping their parishioners think through these issues and from promoting discussions about them. Even when the desire is present, other issues often seem more pressing or more interesting. Curiously, then, issues that are clearly of importance to laity and that are understood by the clergy to be complex and to require careful attention are relegated to that great residual category of relativized individualism in which it is said that "every person must make their own judgment."

## AMBIGUOUS VOICES

Despite their reluctance to mention money and their ambivalence about it, some clergy do try to address the topic. In our survey of working Americans, we found, for instance, that 32 percent of church members said they had heard a sermon on the relationship between faith and personal finances in the past year. But what do people hear?

Both from talking with clergy about what they say and from examining the transcripts of their sermons, we must say that clergy often tiptoe around the topic of money as if they were taking a walk through a minefield. One of the most common ways of doing so is to sneak up on the topic like an adolescent hoping to steal a quick kiss in the dark without getting caught. "Oh yes," said one pastor, "I preach a lot about money." Asked what he preaches about, he said, "Oh, I tell them that God gives us the gift of time, he gives us our energies, he gives us our talents, so therefore we owe him thanks for what we have." By implication, one can pray a kind of blanket prayer—"Thank you, God, for all our blessings"—and not have to say much more about money.

Another way in which clergy speak with ambiguous voices when they talk about money is to focus on it, but only to make other points. One of the most common patterns we found in sermons that deal in some way with money or material possessions is that these sermons are not really about how to deal with finances from a faith perspective at all; instead, their purpose is to invite listeners to pray for personal salvation. Finances enter the discussion only as a negative example—a false hope, a diversion, a temptation that must be put aside for people to turn to Jesus. Consider the following, a sermon that actually did make some important points about money but that ended, like many other sermons, on a very different note. "You think you're comfortable, but that's temporary. It's no sign of God's approval. And one day it'll come to an end, and if you've never trusted in Christ, it'll all be stripped away and you'll end up in that place of conscious agony, conscious separation from God forever and ever, and continual reminders before your mind of what might have been, if only you had not been blinded to the truth of your need and the offer of salvation. Believe on the Lord Jesus Christ and thou shall be saved."

I am not suggesting that preaching should be any less about trusting ultimately in Christ than it is. But when money is dealt with only as a stumbling block along the road to personal salvation, I doubt that listeners receive much instruction about either money or salvation. They are probably willing to concede that money will not buy their way into heaven. But they still know that they have bills to pay, jobs to do, and decisions to make about their money. If salvation has nothing to do with these important parts of their lives, it is likely to amount to nothing more than a magic formula for getting into heaven. And if money is totally removed from salvation, the way in which it is handled is likely to be no different than the approach taken by people who are completely without religious values.

The clergy who are struggling most seriously with questions of money are often concerned, above all, with getting people to see it in relation to the rest of their lives, especially their values. It is necessary, these clergy are finding, to start at that point because of the prevailing tendency in our culture to compartmentalize money from our values. Two-thirds (68 percent) of the working public, in fact, agree that money is one thing; morals and values are completely separate. And church members are just as likely as nonmembers to take this view. Thus, clergy feel compelled to challenge the conventional view. "I try to say let's be candid about one of the realities of our lives," explained the pastor of a large Presbyterian church in Chicago. He said the basic point he tries to communicate is that "money is simply an extension of who you are. It's what you generate from the work of your hands and the sweat of your brow."

In arguing for a more integrated or holistic view of money, clergy nevertheless find themselves having to talk about everything at once and thus being able to say very little about money that is clear or distinct. And, sensing the difficulties they face in talking about money, they sometimes turn to other, more familiar topics. A carefully crafted sermon on the theme of money, for instance, turns from an exposition of the biblical passage to some practical implications. Expecting to hear some thoughts about money, one hears instead, "The lesson has applications far beyond financial matters. It applies to the investment of our thought processes, our energy, our time, our talents, our friendships, everything."

Paradoxically, trying to get people to focus on other things than money also has the effect of diminishing the importance of actually taking about money. "Money has tremendous symbolic value for us," asserted an Episcopal priest. "It symbolizes acquisition. It symbolizes power. It symbolizes status, and those are the sort of goals, the goods, that our society is organized around." He was thus aware of the connections between money and other values, unlike some of the clergy who insisted that money was really "just a piece of paper." Yet for this priest, money stood for the *wrong* values, and so he preferred not to think about it at all. "Speaking as a Christian person," he confessed, "I really have no interest in those things."

Another pastor found that he had modified his views of money over the years. Having been influenced by the twelve-step movement, he used to tell people that money was an addiction and that the only way to recover from this addiction was to give one's money away. That advice, of course, generally fell on deaf ears. Lately, his view has been that "money is just the exchange of energy between people and has no value in itself." This view is consistent with his belief that money is one of the lesser values in life. But an "exchange of energy" is about as easy to preach on as molecular motion. "I'm convinced money isn't any more than that," he asserted. But he admitted, "I don't know what that means for the individual."

Clergy also risk having their messages taken the wrong way because of the examples they use to make holistic arguments more concrete. Typically, their examples focus on giving to the church. Having heard that their money is an extension of who they are, parishioners are then told that the best reflection of their spiritual values is to give freely to the church. "The basic things we talked about in this church," said the pastor of an evangelical Protestant church, "is that all income and all resources are God's. They're given to us to sustain our needs, but they are basically resources to fund his kingdom." As he talked, it became clear that funding "his kingdom" meant supporting the church. But if money is really part of the larger picture, parishioners know there should be other ways in which it demonstrates their spirituality. Sacrificing to send one's children to college may be one way, or keeping up the value of one's home. But such examples are less likely to be mentioned. Church members may, therefore, hear messages about money but still come away feeling that little has been said about the broader implications of their faith for their finances.

Ambiguity, I should note, also creeps into the clergy's admonitions about money because clergy are used to speaking in formulaic language—drawing phrases and examples from scripture—whereas a growing share of the laity, especially younger people, lack the biblical knowledge to make sense of these admonitions. A conversation with a pastor who asserted that the Bible is very clear ("like black and white") in what it says about money illustrates this problem. Asked to explain what he meant, he asserted, "Money is the ultimate idolatry." Which means? "Idolatry is the very nature of sin. It is putting our confidence and intention and value on something that's not real." So money isn't real? "It has the appearance of reality, but 'heaven and earth will pass away, but my word will not pass away.' Ecclesiastes talks about this. That's what I mean. Jesus talked about it." He knew what he meant. When we talked with some of his parishioners, a few of them could repeat the same phrases. But when we listened to them discuss their lives at a Bible study group, it was clear that money was still very real to them.

## NO OFFENSE

The remaining reason why laity do not think very much or very deeply about the implications of faith for their money is that what they hear in church simply assures them that all is well rather than stirring them to think in new ways. It is not surprising that this message is what they hear in many middle-class churches. The middle class may be in a precarious economic position, having to work harder and harder to pay its bills, but it has just enough money, and it prides itself on the comforts that it feels it deserves, so any hint of preaching *against* money is dangerous indeed.

In fact, just the opposite message prevails in some churches. They view God essentially as the candyman, a sugar daddy who is there to promote health, happiness, and personal success on the part of the believer. God's abundant blessings, in this view, include all the material amenities to which the middle class may aspire. At Grace Church, the Midwestern megachurch we considered in chapter 2, for example, the pastor looked out one morning at his 2,000-member audience, seated comfortably in the new auditorium, and announced flatly, "God wants to prosper you. Some of you are living under a spirit of poverty, and you are proclaiming to others that you're under that poverty as if it's a badge of virtue. It is not. God wants to prosper you." He instructed his audience to say with him, "God wants to prosper me."[6]

An old-fashioned "gospel of wealth" that encourages believers to become rich is of course no longer fashionable in most middle-class churches (we have become too sophisticated to swallow such teaching). The gospel of wealth has been replaced by a newer, more subtle message that says get as much as you can, but don't think bad thoughts in the process. What thoughts? Greedy thoughts, for one. It is okay to want all the money you can get just as long as you aren't too greedy. Thus, 83 percent of church members agree that "being greedy is a sin against God." Yet only 14 percent say they were ever taught (by anyone) that wanting a lot of money is wrong.

Some clergy, of course, speak out boldly against the desire for riches, arguing that God loves the poor better than the rich, or at least cautioning their middle-class listeners that they would have more time to spend with their families and more energy to cultivate their spirituality if they spent less time pursuing more and more money. But it is much more common for clergy to supply their congregants with huge loopholes to crawl through on their way to the celestial city. One of these loopholes allows middle-class congregants to have all the wealth they can get as long as they do not place their *ultimate trust* in money. The pastor of a large, wealthy congregation in an upper-income community explained to us that "the scripture warns against those who desire to be rich." Interested in what he took this to mean, given his location, we listened intently as he explained, "That is, the desire to think of security only in terms of finances. The rich fool who had a great harvest and said, 'Boy, you've got it made.' Just build bigger barns and say to your soul, 'Take it easy. You've got it made the rest of your life,' and God called him a fool because he thought security lay in what he owned." In other words, the problem is not spending all one's time building bigger barns but only thinking that life after death can be purchased.

Perhaps without intending to, clergy also give legitimacy to middle-class ways of *making* money. Applauding methods of business is one example. Although businesspeople sometimes complain that clergy are hostile to their way of life, it is just as common to find pastors speaking positively about business methods.[7] Indeed, the pastors of large churches with multimillion-dollar budgets function much like businesspeople themselves, so it is not surprising to hear them praising the ways of the marketplace. Yet, in doing so, their arguments sometimes take strange turns. Listen to what the pastor of a large nondenominational church said in preaching about the steward described in Luke 16 who went around collecting his master's debts by cutting special deals: "You can always find someone who's willing to scheme and scrimp and save and sacrifice and lose sleep and give up friends and even his family for the sake of success." This comment sounds like a criticism. But it isn't. The pastor went on to exhort his congregation to be just as energetic in doing church work! "I think Jesus is saying," he concluded, "what would happen if those who know Christ were just as enterprising and as clever as this businessman?"

## SPEAKING UP

Having reasons to be silent, feeling ambivalent, and being reluctant to offend anyone, the simplest course is for the clergy to say even less about money than they do now. In many of our conversations, clergy also admitted that they had tried to say something about money but had quickly become frustrated. "It doesn't seem to me that we're making a whole lot of headway in changing anything," one man in his fifties confided. "I have tried to preach on it, and it makes a dent with some people, but for most people it just doesn't compute. It just doesn't compute." Other than his annual stewardship sermon, he has largely quit talking about money. Most clergy, however, feel that, if anything, they should say *more* about the relationship between faith and finances. Despite all the cultural forces impeding frank discussions of money, clergy know that personal finances are a necessary part of life and thus a concern to which the churches should minister.

A few clergy have even found that talking about money isn't actually as awkward as they thought it would be. If they like to preach sermons linked closely to scriptural texts, they can compose whole sermons on money just by stringing together Old Testament verses that talk about it or by explicating Jesus' many sayings about money. Others found it easy to talk about money by speaking of their own worries and mistakes.[8] "Here's some advice," joked one pastor, "I'm not using it." Humor, in fact, proved to be one of the best icebreakers of all. "Money causes great difficulties," quipped the pastor at a Baptist church in Texas. "I met a lady the other day who said, 'I didn't want to marry my husband for his money, but that's the only way I could figure out how to get it.'"

"My favorite story," the same pastor went on, "is about a lady who was just, for lack of a better word, a snob. And she turned to her husband as their new house was completed and said, 'Honey, if it weren't for my money, this house wouldn't be here.' And then, as the new furniture arrived, she said, 'Honey, if it weren't for my money, this furniture wouldn't be here.' And then the entertainment center arrived with the VCR and the stereo system. And she said, 'Honey, if it weren't for my money, this stereo system wouldn't be here.' And the man looked up and said, 'Honey, if it wasn't for your money, I wouldn't be here!'"

All of the pastors we talked to who had found it possible to preach about money did so, above all, because they took the subject seriously. They did not treat it as a concern unworthy of truly spiritual people or as a side issue compared with the real work of the church. They recognized that money matters to virtually everyone and that sound teaching about personal finances is part of the church's responsibility. "Sometimes we get super spiritual about things," one pastor told his congregation. "We say money can't buy happiness, and that's absolutely right. But happiness can't buy groceries. And so we have to have a balance because money, we have to have it to survive in this world."

What, then, *are* some of the things clergy are saying about money? The messages vary, of course, depending on the particular issues with which congregations are struggling and how the clergy feel compelled to minister to them. That there *is* something to say, however, is clear from the few examples we found of clergy who did make a pointed effort to speak to financial issues.

First, there are lessons in financial responsibility. Middle-class parishioners perhaps do not need to be reminded of their financial burdens. Yet with credit-card debt soaring, thousands of families filing for bankruptcy each year, and the advertising industry promoting a feeding frenzy of impulse purchases, encouragement to be prudent, to invest, and to keep track of one's money may well be valuable. Even if the stern deity of the Puritans is no longer popular, clergy still have a powerful tradition at their disposal for teaching such lessons. "God's going to come and examine the books, and he's going to expose the faithfulness or lack of it of his people in the use of those material possessions he has entrusted to them," admonished one pastor. "That's a sobering thought," he continued. "It's more nerve-racking than an IRS audit when the God of the universe looks at our financial records!"

Financial responsibility can be integrated with religious teachings in other ways as well. "Moderation of personal desires" was the phrase several priests used to say what they thought needed to be taught about money. Like sexual temptations or overeating, they observed, money robs us of our full potential if we let our desires control us. One priest, for example, said he talks a lot with the young people in his parish about the need to stay in school and to study rather than quitting or taking after-school jobs just to buy all the things they want. "So-and-so has a Buick, okay? I've got to have a Buick," they tell him. "No," he responds, "you can get along with something less. About $5,000 less." At another church, the pastor told us the main problem he senses is that people in his congregation just don't think carefully enough about their money. They don't maintain budgets or record their expenses. So they come to him complaining that they don't have enough money to go out to eat and then tell him a week later about the $700 television they've bought. The solution, he feels, is to approach money the way he tries to get them to study the Bible—rationally, reflectively, and systematically.

Second, the churches can teach lessons in generosity. Parishioners can be cautioned against using all their money for themselves rather than giving some of it to the needy or simply being more generous with their time rather than devoting themselves only to getting and spending. If pastors lack the authority to make such appeals themselves, they can frame them in the words of others. Consider the following anecdote in one of the sermons we heard. "I read a little story the other day about a man who was going through the agony of a divorce. He came to his pastor and talked to him about the pain that he was experiencing, and he said, 'You know, pastor, I think I've discovered why our marriage failed. I was going through all the canceled checks for the last two or three years the other day, trying to straighten out the financial affairs, and it struck me as I went through them one at a time how most of them were indications of things spent on ourselves, our indulgences, and so little of it was spent on other people.'"

The pitfall that clergy sometimes fall into in teaching lessons about generosity is encouraging it by offering *selfish* and even materialistic reasons. Following is an example. "If we are willing to give to others, God will continually refill that supply, and we will end up with more than we started out with. I think we often make the mistake of saying the rich can afford to be generous; the poor cannot be. Maybe that's why some of us are poor, is because we have withheld what God wants us to share." The same speaker drove home the point by observing that "the generous man will be prosperous, and he who waters will himself be watered. Very clear." Clergy are often careful to point out that God's return on our giving may not take monetary form and that we should be generous whether we receive anything in return or not. Yet it is easy for a materialistic message to be communicated, especially when pastors talk about people scooping their money to God and God scooping it back, but just using a bigger shovel.

Talking about generosity is sometimes difficult, clergy say, because church people already think they are generous just because they give money or time to the church. Some of the pastors we talked to made it a special point, therefore, to challenge this assumption. "Some Christians are just stingy," a pastor pointed out to his congregation. "Ever notice that? These guys who go to a nice restaurant and leave a gospel tract and a nickel. That's just not a good witness, folks. That's being stingy, and God won't bless that."

Third, the churches can challenge the implicit gospel of wealth that still prevails in middle-class culture. Although we might not admit it, many of us believe that people who have money are better than those who do not have it. We may not consider them any happier or any closer to God, but we respect them more and pay more attention to what they have to say. We do it when we listen to millionaires and movie stars on television talk shows. We do the same thing, perhaps, when we assume that the posh church with the new auditorium is preaching the gospel more effectively than the run-down church in an older section of town. The way in which some clergy challenge the gospel of wealth is simply to tackle it head on. "They believed that wealth was an evidence of the blessing of God," said one pastor, inviting his middle-class listeners to identify with Jesus' critics. "Poverty was an evidence that a person must have offended God." So, he explained, people dismissed Jesus and his followers because they didn't have money. But the people were clearly mistaken in this view, the sermon went on to point out. Indeed, one point always to keep in mind, the pastor cautioned, "is that material blessings are no indication of God's attitude toward a person."[9]

Fourth, the churches can play a pastoral function in relation to members' concerns about money. A priest we talked to in California strongly urged fellow clergy to include discussions of money in the pastoral counseling they do with couples planning to be married. "Think of all the times money arises as a family issue," he said. "And help people recognize that they have to talk about money without ignoring the habits and personalities involved." At an evangelical church in Pennsylvania, an all-day seminar on finances for single women provided another example of the pastoral function. Noting the heavy emotional burden that finances create, the leader began by emphasizing that "God is the source of all of our financial resources" and asserted that "if we can really believe that, it takes away a lot of the emotional strain." She then devoted her attention to practical ways of dealing with financial concerns, offering suggestions about budgeting, keeping records of major purchases, working out disagreements with friends or relatives concerning money, avoiding impulse buying, learning to do comparison shopping, waiting for sales, locating secondhand items, making safe investments, and avoiding high interest payments. The speaker also gave each participant a packet of resource materials, including free pamphlets, tax guides, lists of books, and phone numbers. The seminar could well have taken place at a community center and have been conducted without any reference to religion. Yet by sponsoring it, the church demonstrated its recognition of the importance of finances and the relevance of faith to these issues.[10]

Finally, the churches can be a place where more personal, practical, ongoing discussions of money take place. Small groups are an especially valuable way of promoting such discussions. "People want to be known, people want to be cared about, they want to relate" was how one pastor described the reason for having small groups in his church. People join small groups in order to make friends, to study the Bible and pray together, or just to escape the children for an hour. Once they become acquainted, they are more likely to break the taboo of silence surrounding their concerns about money. In one church, for instance, members of a small men's group that prayed together every week over a period of several years began to talk openly about how they were spending their money and whether their purchases were consistent with their religious values. At a women's Bible study group in another church, the members prayed every week for a member who was on the verge of declaring family bankruptcy. She wasn't sure afterward which was the greater miracle: avoiding bankruptcy or experiencing such love from her friends.

Even in small groups, finances are one of the hardest issues for churchgoers to discuss candidly. Members may pray for a family without an income or give thanks when someone receives a promotion. They probably find it easier to discuss sick relatives, the latest antics of their three-year-old, or how the new organ sounded at church than to study systematically what the Bible teaches about money. But small groups can be guided by their leaders, even behind the scenes, and clergy often stimulate small-group discussions, perhaps more than they realize, by the sermons they preach.

## THE CONSEQUENCES

A few sermons and small-group discussions about finances are not going to challenge middle-class church members to lead their lives in fundamentally different ways. People are still going to take their cues from the advertising industry, and they will find that many of their financial decisions are already being made for them—by the Internal Revenue Service (IRS), for example. They may, as one pastor complained, "go out and live on Monday pretty much the same way they did on Friday." But the churches *can* make a difference.

Consider the following from our survey (here, limiting our attention to church members who attend services regularly so that we are not in danger of simply comparing more active and less active members in general).[11] Among those who had heard a sermon about personal finances in the past year, approximately a third said they had also thought a great deal in the past year about what the Bible teaches concerning money and about the relationship between religious values and their personal finances. In comparison, fewer than a fifth of those who had not heard a sermon about personal finances had thought this much about these issues.[12] Thinking about these issues, in turn, is associated with some other differences. For instance, 92 percent of those who had thought a great deal about the relationship between religious values and their finances agreed that the Bible contains valuable teachings about money, compared with only 39 percent among those who had thought hardly at all about this relationship. Among the former, nine out of ten had thanked God for some financial blessing in the past year, compared with only half of the latter. And among those who thought a lot about faith and finances, more than half thought materialism is an extremely serious problem in our society, compared with fewer than a quarter of those who had not thought about the faith-finances connection.[13]

Not all the news is this good—again pointing to the ambivalence and ambiguity that people are apparently confronted with even when they do hear about finances in church. Having heard a sermon on personal finances and having thought a lot about the implications of religious values for one's finances had no statistical effect on the following: attaching high value to making a lot of money, saying that rich people are happier than other people, having been taught that it is wrong to want a lot of money, wanting an expensive house or car or other nice possessions, or keeping a family budget.

One area in which sermons on personal finances do make a difference, though, is in the likelihood of parishioners coming to their pastors to talk about financial concerns. Although most church members (even those who attend regularly) do not seek out their pastors on such topics, the percentage is considerably higher among those who have heard a sermon on finances: 10 percent rather than 2 percent. Apparently it helps to know that the pastor is interested in such issues. If the churches can make a difference in the ways in which people think about their money and handle their personal finances, there is something to be gained by the churches as well. Certainly, the churches may benefit financially (as we consider in the next chapter). But in a larger sense, the churches will also have proven themselves relevant to the real concerns that animate their middle-class members in everyday life. Parishioners will be more likely to remain interested.

Failure to address the overwhelming concerns that the public faces in dealing with finances is thus a contributing factor to the present crisis in America's churches. Sensing that religion has nothing to say about its financial concerns, the public may experience momentary enthusiasm about spirituality but then lose interest when spirituality seems to be only a transient feeling or become frustrated when others remain indifferent. "They'll come to me and they'll be real excited," said one of the pastors we interviewed. "They'll want to sit down and talk about this wonderful thing that's happening in their life. But then they get frustrated. Their friends aren't interested. They just don't see the value."

# nine

# THE GOSPEL OF GIVING

When Jacob Brodsky was growing up, the church was his life. His parents, his brother and sister, his grandparents, and his seventeen aunts and uncles all belonged to the same parish on the south side of Chicago. He remembers not being allowed to eat or even drink water after midnight on Saturdays until he took communion on Sunday morning. Nobody ate meat on Friday, and if you weren't a good Catholic, you couldn't be buried in the cemetery.

Now, at age fifty-five, Jacob Brodsky says he has no respect for the church. "All the rules are different," he complains. "Everything's changed." The old Polish customs that used to be so much a part of the church are gone. There is no sense of community. Jacob says he has pulled more and more into his own family. He works hard as an automobile mechanic to support his wife and two teenaged sons. He is sending the boys to Catholic school because he thinks they get a better education there. But he says, "You can read the Bible, but it's not going to help any. There's no miracles out there as far as I can see. You've just got to work for it."

What irritates Jacob most about the church is that it always seems to be after his money. He gives regularly, putting a $20 bill in the envelope with his number on it each week. "At the end of the year, if they haven't gotten the full amount, you get a letter," he explains. "They send you a letter that says we think you're $129 short, and then you've got to prove you're not. If you don't pay, they raise the kids' tuition. It's extortion."

Jacob figures he'll keep on giving about $1,000 a year to the church. He doesn't mind giving something because he thinks some good comes from it. But he says he'll make his other donations to United Way instead. The clergy's attitude toward money just rubs him the wrong way. Like the time he found out that somebody who hadn't been to church in years got buried in the parish cemetery. "Oh yeah," somebody told him, "his family just paid off the priests and he got in." Or like the time he went on a retreat with his priest. "He had more booze in his room than I've ever seen in a tavern. Maybe he needs it. But it was pretty disheartening to see." Jacob isn't going to quit giving entirely. But he isn't going to increase his giving either.

Earlene Rogers, age twenty-five, was raised in a Southern Baptist church in North Carolina. Her parents, she thinks, were deeply influenced by the 60s, became more liberal, and reacted against the strict religious values of their Baptist and Presbyterian parents. They did, however, remain active Southern Baptists and took Earlene and her sister to church in their suburban neighborhood every Sunday. Earlene wasn't quite sure what the church believed about Jesus or God but says it taught her that the essence of Christianity is helping others.

Earlene is now a social worker. So is her husband. They live in an apartment in a large city in another part of the country. They go to church just about every Sunday but attend different ones because they have not yet found one they feel comfortable with. Earlene says spirituality is an important part of her life. She still holds the religious beliefs she was taught as a child but thinks she needs to develop these beliefs and become more certain that they are really hers.

She and her husband give money to churches and other organizations depending on how they happen to feel at the moment. She does not see broader connections between her faith and her finances. When she was little, she used to pray, asking God to give her a new bicycle, but she realizes this view was childish. She is amused by some of her fundamentalist friends who still seem to hold that view. "A friend of my husband's is very into spirituality," she reports. "And he's getting ready to quit his job and wait for Jesus to find him a new one. And a friend of mine has relatives that act in a similar way. When they find a beach house, they say that Jesus found the beach house. And she said to me, 'Now listen, Jesus doesn't have time to be finding your friend a job because he's looking for a beach house for my in-laws!'" Earlene says that her own spirituality focuses on bigger and more mysterious things such as love, birth, and death. "Money," she says, "has nothing spiritual connected to it."

Yet, perhaps curiously, Earlene's spirituality does encourage her to be a generous, giving person. She thinks of stewardship as "helping people, like helping the poor, or volunteering your time to do work, or somehow offering your services to other people." She thinks of her job as a social worker in this light. And she gives money regularly to Habitat for Humanity. There, she feels, the money is going directly to helping other people. She is less interested in giving to the church and to other large charitable organizations because it isn't clear to her how the money is being used.

Scott Simpson, thirty-six, is a lawyer in Minnesota. His father taught at Moody Bible Institute in Chicago. His mother stayed home and raised the children. They were faithful members of the Swedish Baptist church, sent Scott to its youth group every Sunday during high school, and were pleased when he decided to attend an evangelical college. He still describes himself as an evangelical Christian, attends a theologically conservative Presbyterian church every Sunday, and gives generously of both his time and money to the church. He says his view of giving is quite different from his parents' view, however. They were strict; believed in living simply; and, although they never had much money, gave a tenth of it to the church. Scott, in contrast, says, "I believe God gave us the capability to have fun and enjoyment and to revel a bit, and to see places and to experience them, and to see the arts and to appreciate them, and to just enjoy all facets of life. And who knows, maybe I'm subscribing more to Renaissance theory than a Christian theory, but I am different in that I do believe life is there to be lived. If I were expressing it from a Christian perspective, I'd say that God's given us the ability to appreciate things like art or music and different places and different peoples, and dance and whatever, and it's there to be taken and to be enjoyed."

Scott says his attitudes were shaped mainly by attending a Christian college. There he began to have a "more expansive" view of the world. He learned there were things to enjoy and to appreciate. His basic religious beliefs didn't change, but he became less sure that they were true for everyone. He says that participating in sports also helped him to think of life as something to be enjoyed. His father encouraged him to be involved in sports as a way of disciplining himself. Scott found it more a way to have pleasure. He denies that he is a hedonist or a materialist, contrasting himself with his mother-in-law, whom he considers someone who shops too much (a "shopaholic"). But he thinks the "perfect middle way" is to get all the enjoyment out of life that God intends for us.

Comparing his religious giving with that of his parents, Scott says he doesn't give as much "percentage-wise" and is "not as rigorous" in his views about supporting the church. Still, he feels comfortable giving what he does because he knows it amounts to more in percentage terms than most people give. Scott counts his time as a contribution as well. He spends one evening each week attending a Bible study group, another evening serving on a committee at the church, and often watches the children on Saturdays while his wife does church work. He also says his job is part of his ministry. He chose his career, he says, because there are too few dedicated Christians in the legal profession. Asked directly how his faith influences his finances, though, he admits, "It's mostly made me feel guilty for not living more simply and giving more of my money away." Reflecting, he adds, "It's funny, I sort of view prayer and consulting the Bible as just incongruous with financial decisions. I just keep those two worlds separate."

These examples illustrate the range of opinions among American churchgoers about giving money to support the church and other charitable causes. Jacob Brodsky gives reluctantly. Earlene Rogers gives irregularly and mostly to humanitarian organizations. Scott Simpson gives generously to the church but feels guilty and still keeps his faith and his finances in different boxes. In all three cases, giving is a reflection of the person's religious values, and their level of giving is at or above the national standard. Yet their comments also reveal what the churches are up against in trying to raise money and elevate current levels of giving. Parishioners harbor misgivings about the ways in which clergy raise money and the ways in which they use it. Parishioners are attracted to other organizations that seem to make better use of their contributions. And even if church members feel guilty about not giving more, they believe that God wants them to enjoy life rather than sacrificing their own desires, and they feel they are already doing quite a lot, just by virtue of their work and the time they may be donating to the churches.

It would be misleading to suggest that American churchgoers are totally repulsed by the subject of church finances because it is by no means the case. In my national survey, nearly three-quarters of all church members (72 percent) agreed with the statement "I should give God a percentage of the money I earn," and the same number agreed that "churches use the money they get wisely and responsibly." Yet other responses in the same survey indicate that church giving is not entirely a happy subject. Clergy would, for instance, argue that one of the reasons for attending church is to give some of one's money back to God. Yet only a third (36 percent) of church members say that "the opportunity to give back some of the money God has given you" is very important to them when they attend religious services. Another third (34 percent) of church members say that "churches are too eager to get your time and money," and nearly the same number (30 percent) say "it annoys me when churches ask me to give money."[1]

How are the churches responding to these perspectives among their middle-class parishioners? Are the clergy speaking in old-fashioned platitudes that fall on deaf ears? Are the clergy accommodating their appeals to make middle class members feel good about themselves? How much personal frustration, pain, and anguish are the clergy experiencing in trying to raise money? And what are some of the strategies that clergy are finding most effective?

. . .

## FRUSTRATION

In answering these questions, we must begin by acknowledging that fund-raising is a source of considerable frustration to many clergy. They find it difficult to appeal for money. They would rather preach on almost any other subject. They feel awkward when they do engage in fund-raising. And they worry that they are not as effective as they should be in bringing in the needed support.

This awkwardness is nothing new. One scholar who has studied the history of church finances argues that clergy had to start making special appeals for money toward the end of the nineteenth century, just when Victorian sensibilities made it especially troublesome to speak about money. "Late Victorian sensitivities," he writes, "made the issue of money very difficult to discuss. The clergy, in particular, were deeply embarrassed by the topic's worldliness and by the vulnerability they felt being dependent on the giving of other people."[2]

These sensitivities are still with us. With rising costs and tighter budgets, clergy find themselves especially troubled by the sense that they must pay more and more attention to soliciting donations. "It eats me inside every Monday when I get a report on the offering," explained one pastor. His church was not in bad financial shape. But he felt increasing pressure to be more effective in soliciting funds because every cost line in his budget was rising, yet he believed that people in his congregation didn't have the ability to give any more. "I just don't like doing it," admitted another pastor. "It's disturbing to people, and I feel like a beggar." Another confessed, "My heart just isn't in it. I do it, but it's hard."[3]

Pastors often admit it is difficult to talk about church finances because of the general sensitivity in our society about speaking openly and frankly about money. They also find themselves in the middle of contradictory or conflicting views held by parishioners. The third who come to church to give some of their money to God probably don't mind hearing about giving, while the third who are annoyed by appeals for money clearly do mind. Or, as the survey also reveals, 60 percent of church members say they would like the churches to emphasize giving money to religious programs *more*, while 40 percent say the churches should emphasize this issue *less*.[4] One pastor, in fact, registered precisely this tension when we asked him how often he preaches about giving: "Well, some of my members think I don't talk about it often enough," he lamented, "and others say I talk about it too much."[5] But there are other—perhaps more important—sources of frustration as well.

One of the clearest reasons why clergy feel frustrated is that it does take more money to operate churches, even without expanding programs, than ever before. Clergy blame themselves if giving falters or does not cover their expenses. Hard times make it more difficult to discuss what is already a sensitive topic. Clergy know they must talk about giving but worry that parishioners will be repulsed if they seem too interested in money. Clergy also express frustration because they believe that levels of giving reflect the public's attitude toward the church. Pastors acknowledge that giving may decrease because of problems in the wider economy. But they also hold themselves responsible. "The first thing people do if they're not pleased with what's happening in the church," observed one of the priests we interviewed, "is cut off their funds. They figure that's the only thing that will make a difference; cut off their water."

A related source of frustration is the sense that things are changing so that, somehow, the old methods of raising money no longer work. The pastor of a Presbyterian church with a Japanese American membership mentioned, for example, that the older members thought of the church as family and just supported it each year without being asked but that younger and newer members didn't have the same sense of responsibility. At a nearby Catholic church, the priest told us that people used to give a little every week when they came to mass, but now that most people no longer attend mass regularly he is searching for other ways to solicit donations. Several of the African American pastors we interviewed also expressed concern that their middle-class members are giving less or less regularly, apparently because they feel less dependent on the church to help them during personal emergencies. A Lutheran pastor admitted he's frustrated because his members no longer know each other and thus do not hold each other accountable for supporting the church. He feels he has to do more of the work of raising money all by himself.

Another reason for feeling frustrated is that clergy perceive themselves—rightly, as it happens—to be engaged in ever more serious competition for scarce contributions. Their members, they fear, are like Earlene Rogers: willing to give but spreading their money around rather than directing all their contributions to the church. Among church members nationally, this pattern is in fact fairly typical, judging at least from attitudes. For example, 48 percent of church members agree that "I'd rather give money to a needy family than to a church" and 55 percent *disagree* with the statement that "giving money to churches is more important than giving it to other organizations."[6] Certainly within the American public at large, this competition is increasingly evident. While giving to religious organizations still constitutes *half* (51 percent) of all charitable giving in the United States, this percentage has fallen slightly in recent years, and some trend studies of average household donations suggest that contributions to causes such as environment, health, and youth organizations have risen, while donations to religious organizations have remained static.[7]

Many of the clergy we talked to expressed particular concern about competition from television ministries. Research studies indicate that most people who give money to television ministries give as much or more to their local churches than people who do not donate to television ministries.[8] Clergy, however, *perceive* their members to be giving money to television ministries that *might have been given* to the local church—a proposition that is difficult to substantiate but is nevertheless a source of frustration. As one pastor commented, "I know we are being hurt by Pat Robertson's 700 Club because I was in a home the other day and saw a 700 Club Bible there."

Some of the clergy we talked to also registered a sense of inadequacy in the face of new fund-raising mechanisms being used by television preachers and by other charitable organizations. Within their own congregations, they find it hard to get acquainted with people and to earn their trust, partly because people move in and out of communities so often but also because churches are now larger and clergy are busier than ever before. In comparison, as one pastor observed, "Reverend So-and-So on television is a daily guest in their homes. They feel like they know him better than they know me." Clergy also sense how difficult it is, as a small, local organization with limited funds, to compete with national organizations with seemingly unlimited budgets for marketing studies and slick advertising. They might feel better were they aware that studies of charitable giving show that people are more inclined to give to small, local organizations than to large, national ones. Yet again, it is their perception that matters most.

The increased competition that clergy are now experiencing is a special feature of the middle-class church; not that all Americans aren't bombarded with appeals, but middle-class Americans are especially subject to such requests because of the organizational networks that are part of middle-class life. "There are probably ten different ways graduates from the university are hit for money," noted the pastor of a church located not far from a large state university. "This wouldn't have been the case maybe thirty years ago," he said. "The hospital here tries to raise money. The town built a $26 million performing arts center in 1982 almost entirely by subscription. I go over to the symphony, and I see thirty people there from this parish, and they are regular contributors. Their names appear on the giving list. So they're giving, and they're giving bigger and bigger amounts of money. I find I get solicitations from every school I ever attended, and from the Humane Society. Boy, it's endless."

Pastors also find themselves in the awkward position of feeling frustrated because they consider it *legitimate* to give to other causes. As one pastor admitted, "God wants people to take what they have and give it to other people. I'm not looking at it in a selfish sense of giving it to the church. God wants us to take what we have and give it to others. Give it to other people. It doesn't matter where." His frustration is about having to make special appeals for *church* giving when he really believes that other outlets may be just as good. This is one of the reasons why he makes fund-raising appeals as seldom as possible.

For many clergy, fund-raising is also a source of frustration because it seems to compromise what they want the church to be. They recognize that it takes money to keep church programs in business, but they want to avoid letting the church become a business. That is, it bothers them to make special financial appeals or to raise the money needed to expand programs and to build larger buildings, especially if they feel at all that they are making people uncomfortable or playing on their emotions. They do not want the church to use Madison Avenue techniques or to fall into the syndrome of thinking that a bigger budget necessarily means the church is doing God's work better. They want membership in the congregation to be based on love and acceptance rather than ability to pay. The pastor of a Nazarene church in Kansas put it well when he said, "I fear that the dominant message is not 'just as I am without one plea' but 'just you and your checkbook are welcome here.' I think that sends a contradictory message."[9]

## PASSING THE BUCK

Clergy find that a good way of avoiding this frustration is to let somebody else make the appeal for money. Occasionally professional fund-raisers are brought in; or missionaries are asked to testify on behalf of the church; or the youth pastor, choir director, or Christian education minister are asked to make special appeals. More commonly, lay members are used. The head of the finance committee makes a presentation detailing the needs of the church. Individual members are asked to give short speeches to the congregation explaining why they give. Or members are asked to phone each other to solicit annual pledges. One pastor put it bluntly: "I prefer that if we're going to appeal for money to get somebody else to do it. I was in a church in another situation where I saw that the pastor ended up being the bad guy because he ended up legitimately appealing for money. There was nothing wrong with that in my mind, but he became the bad guy. They saw him as being a money grubber and going after money. I'd rather be broke than to have that opinion of me."

Letting the laity do it has the advantage of letting clergy remain in the wings, much as college professors do, for example, when staff from the development office are sent out to raise money on their behalf. Laity can feel more involved and take more responsibility for the health of their own congregation. Special expertise can be mobilized (perhaps the finance chair is a banker or marketing specialist). And laity may find it more convincing to hear fellow members tell why they *do* give than to hear clergy explaining why they *should* give.

But clergy remain visibly and vocally involved in the fund-raising process whether they enlist the help of others or not. Clergy know what the financial needs of the congregation are. Parishioners look to the clergy to provide leadership. Clergy provide the primary frameworks for understanding giving in spiritual terms. And while laity may speak about giving in ways that reflect cultural assumptions more than sound theological principles, clergy have the training and the responsibility to represent the best counsel that biblical tradition has to offer. "The buck stops at my desk," was how one pastor explained it. "I'm the one. I'm the leader."

It is difficult to demonstrate scientifically that clergy actually make a difference when they preach about finances and giving. Nevertheless, it is worth considering the fact that in our survey—looking only at church members who attend services at least once a week—we found that giving was substantially higher among those who had heard a sermon about stewardship within the past year than among those who had not heard a sermon on this topic. Specifically, the average amount given in the past year among those who had heard a stewardship sermon was $1,588, compared with only $668 among those who had not heard a stewardship sermon. There is the possibility, of course, that this difference is due to something else; for example, being active in Sunday school classes or fellowship groups. When we looked just at regular churchgoers who were active in Sunday school classes or fellowship groups, however, we found that those who had heard a stewardship sermon were still substantially more generous in their giving than those who had not heard a stewardship sermon.[10]

But if such evidence suggests the value of preaching about finances and giving, other evidence suggests just as strongly the importance of *what* views are communicated. Simply devoting more emphasis to fund-raising, for instance, has costs as well as benefits. When asked what would make them more likely to give money to their church, only 7 percent of church members in our survey said they would be more likely to contribute if their pastor placed more emphasis on giving money, whereas 30 percent said they would probably be *less likely* to give.

If we look at active churchgoers who have heard a stewardship sermon in the past year, we also see that the way in which parishioners *understand* giving makes a considerable difference to their actual level of giving. Those who understand the importance of giving some of their money to God as part of the worship experience, for example, give about twice as much as those who do not understand this idea.[11] Those who believe it is important to give a *percentage* of their income to God give about $1,000 more per year than those who do not believe this.[12] And there is about the same difference between those who consider giving to the church more important than giving to other organizations and those who see no difference between the church and other organizations.[13] These differences are only illustrative, but they suggest that clergy can talk about giving and still be relatively ineffective unless they communicate clearly and convincingly the reasons why people should give. Thus, we need to examine what clergy are saying about giving and how they are saying it. Doing so helps us to understand better why the churches are experiencing financial difficulties and how the clergy may be able to address these difficulties more effectively.

## DEFLECTION

Because fund-raising is a difficult task, many clergy in fact do it halfheartedly. I do not mean that they fail to ask for money at all but that they do so in such an oblique way that parishioners can easily dismiss their appeals or miss hearing them at all. The sermon is intended to focus on monetary giving but winds up dealing mostly with faith or prayer or consists mainly of stories that divert attention away from the central argument. Deflection is the opposite of the tactic we considered in the last chapter that diminishes general teachings about faith and finances by focusing only on giving. Here, the problem is that teachings about giving are deflected by making them so general that people can go away thinking they have fulfilled their Christian responsibilities without giving any money at all.[14]

At one of the churches we visited, there was a large banner on one wall of the sanctuary that read, "Stewardship is key." Aha, we thought, here is a church that is in the midst of a fund-raising drive. When we asked the pastor about the banner, though, we learned that it had nothing to do with money. "No," he explained, "we're trying to get people to realize that how they live their life is stewardship." That, of course, is a worthy aim. But it may deflect members from focusing on financial giving if stewardship is defined so broadly.

By trying to set appeals for money in a larger context, the appeal itself is deflected onto other issues—vote, do your best, be thrifty, express yourself—these matters are all so important that money is greatly diminished compared to the importance it probably has in people's lives. The money you give, one sermon concluded, is really just "symbolic of our total offering of ourselves in service and devotion to God." But if it is only a token, only a symbol, then surely the dollar amount given is not important.

In addition to talking in broad generalities, using *churchspeak* is one of the best ways to deflect arguments about giving so that nobody knows what they mean.

Churchspeak is the special language that clergy know well but that is seldom heard outside the church. It consists of heavily stylized language, generally of biblical origin, that people would seldom use in ordinary speech. Words such as *shepherd, Lord, sanctification, covet, trespasses,* and *kingdom* or phrases such as *lamb's book, washed in the blood,* and *lifted up* are examples. These words and phrases have rich meaning for people who may have been reared in deeply religious homes or who have spent long hours studying the Bible. For most Americans, though, churchspeak has been severed from the deep practices and communities that make it meaningful. It has become cant, the familiar singsong of the morning homily that puts one to sleep.

The term *first fruits* is an element of churchspeak that figures prominently in discussions of giving. Many of the clergy we talked to said they encourage parishioners to give of their "first fruits." We asked them what they meant. Many of them said it was like harvesting a field of wheat; you take the first bushel of grain, not the last, and give it to God. Others quoted biblical examples of giving the first calves that are born each season to be used as burnt sacrifices for God. One recited the frequently used sermon illustration of a man whose cow gave birth to twin calves, one of which died a few weeks later, upon which the man announced to his wife, "It's sad; God's calf just died." Some of the pastors explained that giving of one's "first fruits" means giving intentionally, consciously, or cheerfully.

It is little wonder that church people can fail to be inspired by the language of first fruits. The imagery is romantic but quite remote from a society that now has too few farmers to be counted separately in the United States Census. The concept *can* be interpreted to mean writing a check to the church at the beginning of each month rather than at the end. But if taxes and five other kinds of withholding have already been taken, this is hardly first fruits. If the idea is giving *intentionally,* then virtually anything, other than accidentally losing one's wallet in the vestibule, would count. And if it means giving *cheerfully,* the best advice is to give whenever you're having a good day.

This form of deflection has become especially problematic because most people no longer have a clear, articulate sense of the *church.* They believe it is possible to be a good Christian without going to church. They believe they should figure out their own spirituality without being very much influenced by what the church says. They take issue with the church, asserting their own authority to decide what is true over the church's ability to decree truth. And they are firmly committed to the idea that God works in mysterious ways throughout all of life rather than just through the clergy or the church. Thus, when the clergy tell people that they should give as a "sign" of their commitment to God or to assist in God's work, parishioners know implicitly that an important question remains unanswered. Give, yes. But why give to the church? Why not give at the office, to a homeless

THE GOSPEL OF GIVING 169

person on the street, or by supporting the Sierra Club's efforts to maintain the sanctity of God's creation?

I doubt that clergy fully realize what a leap they make when they assume that people automatically associate church or clergy with God's work. Among church members nationally, for instance, fewer than half agree that "the clergy are doing God's work more than any of the rest of us are."[15] Clergy themselves, schooled in ideas about the priesthood of all believers, might also disagree with this statement. Yet they talk as if their own work and that of the church were synonymous with God's work. Asked why he thought people should give money to the church, for example, a well-educated senior pastor of a large upper-middle-class Presbyterian church replied, "I think people should give money to the Lord's work because they're believers and they want to support the Lord's work." It did not occur to him to defend the idea that "the Lord's work" and "the church" were the same thing.

The extreme emphasis on personal salvation that characterizes many American—especially evangelical Protestant—churches adds to this kind of deflection in two ways. First, people are encouraged to "get their heart right with God" above all else and thus to make other activities, even giving, secondary; indeed, they are taught to assume that once they have their heart right with God, everything else will follow naturally. Second, the emphasis on personal salvation takes attention away from institutions and the activities or resources needed to keep institutions running.

We gained a clear example of how this emphasis on personal salvation can deflect attention away from giving at one of the small independent evangelical churches we studied. There, the pastor told us that it isn't "his business" how people spend their money and that he has given up trying to change their attitudes. He didn't mean that he had become a libertarian. Not by any means. But he was convinced that he should focus on personal salvation and that any emphasis on institutional activities was counterproductive. "Nobody changes until they change their relationship to God," he explained. "It's not going to happen by us teaching anybody nothing. One, they're not going to listen to us. Two, it's not until a person finds out that he's accountable to God and has a relationship with God that God will begin to deal with his heart." To clarify what he meant, he referred to the efforts of some evangelical Protestants to change society by becoming involved in conservative politics. "I think it's a joke when you talk about the Moral Majority and the evangelical right wing and that type of thing. I think we're just wasting our time to try and change the society through politics, because we're not doing anything different by forcing people to do something they don't want to do and it's going against what we even believe. We don't want people to do things because they're forced to do it."

Applying this argument to giving, he observed, "If we want people, really, to deal with the issue of money and how they address money and that type of thing, it's not going to change until *they* change their attitude towards God. You can't talk to them about money. You can't talk to them about what they're doing or how they're doing it. I wouldn't bother."

One other way of deflecting attention from financial giving, I should emphasize, is by talking about stewardship. As we saw in chapter 7, stewardship is often discussed in all-encompassing terms that provide listeners with an easy way to escape thinking about money. For instance, if stewardship means saying thank you to God for a beautiful day and not cutting down sacred trees, then church members may wonder why they should give money especially to the church. One pastor was particularly candid about this. Asked why church giving was declining, he murmured, "Probably because of people like me who don't like to talk about money." Then, defending himself, he said, "I don't like to discuss money, but I don't mind talking about stewardship."

## CIVILITY

Besides deflecting attention from financial giving to other ways of giving, clergy also diminish their appeals by offering audiences countless excuses for not giving more or not giving at all. Sermons and prayers may include appeals for money, but because the pastor does not want to come on too strong, he or she includes qualifying phrases that *soften* the appeal (a word that many pastors used). They tell people they don't have to give at all, or should give only if they want to, or can give just by being thankful and living a good life. As one pastor explained, "I usually will say, 'We realize that a lot of you are already giving all that you can give.' Even when I'm praying for the offering, I usually will end it, 'Lord, bless this congregation, those who will give and those who cannot.' It's strictly a voluntary basis. I never know who's going to give and how much. I just make the appeal known and let the Lord convict that person or family to give."

The most extreme way of being civil about money, of course, is not to talk about it at all. Few clergy can get away without making financial appeals once in a while. But some clergy did tell us they seldom make explicit appeals. And the reason is that they wish to accommodate parishioners' concerns. A Catholic priest in California, for instance, explained that he asks for money as infrequently as possible because of the perception that "priests are talking about money all the time." He noted that he personally did not depend directly on the level of giving in his parish.

"A priest gets the same salary no matter where. If I was working in a ghetto over here in the next parish, I would get as much of a salary as I get here, which is a wealthier parish. But people, when you talk about money they think that well, all he wants is money, and I don't want any money except what the parish needs to keep it operating." An Assemblies of God pastor made a similar observation. He also tries to avoid asking for money because of "the negative image of the clergy that 'All they ever talk about is money.'" One of the Asian American pastors we interviewed said he keeps quiet about money too. "People complain," he said, "that you can get *in* the church free, but you can't get *out* without paying!"[16]

A more common form of civility is the radical privatism that is so evident in other aspects of American religion. Faith, we tell ourselves, is strictly a personal matter: Nobody can tell us what to believe; we should decide for ourselves; and, having decided, we should keep it to ourselves. This way, nobody has the right to judge our beliefs; in fact, they don't even know what they are. And we certainly do not have the right to go around judging others' beliefs. Thus, we avoid embarrassment and interpersonal conflict.

In matters of giving, privatism appears when the idea that a person must *want* to give is extended to suggest that whatever a person wants to give is the appropriate amount. People hear, in effect, that their giving is such a private matter that it pretty much depends on how they feel. An example comes from Cornerstone Bible Church. Having heard that his predecessors had trouble raising money in the congregation, Pastor Higgins decided to be more "laid back" about giving. "I don't want you to give money here if you don't want to," he said. "Don't. Don't do it! You do it because you want to do it. You do it because it comes from the heart." Referring to the previous pastor, he elaborated, "They had guys in here beating them over the head: 'You need to give, you need to give, you need to give, you better give, you better give, you better give, you know God's going to get you, God's going to get you,' and then I came along and said, 'Don't worry about it.' God's not interested in getting you. You need to do what's right between you and God, and you know what that is, and I know what's right between me and God. I don't know what's right between you and God, but I know what's right between me and God."

At a church like Cornerstone, giving may be encouraged, despite privatism of this kind, because the congregation is small, because Pastor Higgins finds other ways in which to tell members how much to give, and because he lets them know how much he *thinks* they should give. He claimed, at least, that giving has not gone down because of his way of making appeals. He did admit, however, that some members started giving less.

• • •

# TITHING

Clergy's discomfort in asking for money is particularly evident when they interpret the biblical principle of tithing.[17] "I believe that the principle of giving in scripture is the principle of tithing," asserted a Baptist minister. But, he went on to say, "God's not so concerned what we do. It's really our heart." Asked what he meant, he said, "Our giving, in terms of money, should be based on what God has laid on our own heart to do. The Bible tells us that God loves a cheerful giver." In other words, it's not how much you give but your attitude about giving.

Pastors have learned that strict definitions of tithing can seem like what they call *legalism*, so they are reluctant to tell people that they should give a certain amount. In the theology of the Protestant Reformation, especially that of Martin Luther, legalism meant following certain rules about good works in the expectation that this behavior would result in salvation rather than having faith in God's grace as a way of attaining salvation. Contemporary interpretations, however, extend this idea to mean that *any* emphasis on what is right or wrong or on what people should or should not do should be avoided. Applied to tithing, the concern about legalism can thus result in avoiding the whole topic—sometimes by arguing that it is an "Old Testament" doctrine that Christians do not need to take seriously—or by shifting the attention from behavior to attitudes.[18]

Even in churches where tithing is emphasized, clergy are sometimes reluctant to put bite in the topic by talking about average incomes or by suggesting specific amounts to be given based on assumptions about incomes. Older clergy and laity remembered when churches took this approach. But now clergy are reluctant to challenge the pervasive sense that family incomes are strictly private. "One way of doing stewardship drives," noted a Lutheran pastor, "is to look at the incomes of people or try to determine the incomes of people and then approach them personally and say, 'Well now, we have a pretty good idea you're making this amount. We think based on that if you were to tithe, you could give x amount.'" He added, "Our stewardship board strongly resists that kind of an approach. They just see our people as being very sensitive to that. They'd be very offended if we tried to use that approach here."

This concern about privacy means that *social pressure* cannot be used as effectively as it may have been in the past. The Lutheran pastor I just quoted said it had once been customary in his congregation to publish the amount each family had given to the church at the end of each quarter. This practice had created a lot of bitterness, he said. The current practice, like that in most churches, is to ask members to fill out a pledge card—stating what amount they expect to give during the coming year—that only the finance secretary sees. The advantage is that people feel less pressured. The disadvantage, he said, is that about half his members choose not to fill out a card at all. Another disadvantage is that members who do make pledges may feel no need to think about their reasons for giving or not giving. They would feel this need more acutely if someone else knew the amount they contributed. For example, the pastor at one church—where members are aware that he knows how much they give—observed that people sometimes come to him and explain why they can't give more than they do. At another church, the finance secretary said it helped to have members call on each other during the annual pledge drive. That way, even if specific dollars were not discussed, members sometimes felt it necessary to come up with more thoughtful reasons for their level of giving.

Tithing, like stewardship more generally, is also weakened as a mechanism for soliciting church finances because clergy themselves are increasingly reluctant to say that the entire tithe must go to the church. A Catholic priest who told us he emphasizes tithing, for example, said he explicitly encourages his parishioners to give 5 percent of their money to the church and 5 percent to other causes. The pastor of a Pentecostal church numbering several thousand members in Atlanta was less direct but implied a similar logic. "I believe in tithing, and I think it's fair. If a person makes a dollar, they give God ten cents. And I don't think it's just to support the church. I think it's because it makes the person feel they're a part of the earth. Sort of like paying interest on this place. God's put us here and developing us into responsible individuals. I guess it's like saying, 'Hey, I'm here and I breathe this air, and I produce vegetables out of this earth, and now I'm coming back to pay my dues.'"

Paying one's dues is the way Earlene Rogers and a lot of other people who do volunteer work and give money to charitable organizations other than the church talk about their motivation. If all of creation has been given to us, and if we have benefited from other people, then it makes sense to pay one's dues in a broader way than just to the church. The church may talk about stewardship, but it is not the banker that collects interest on God's creation.

## NEED-BASED APPEALS

Finding it hard simply to raise money in general, clergy are turning increasingly to need-based appeals, asking for contributions to pay for special projects or to cover emergencies such as fixing the roof or purchasing a new organ. These appeals work, judging from what clergy say about them. But we also need to consider how these appeals are altering the meaning of giving.

Most of the clergy we talked to said it was easiest to raise money for a need "that people can visualize," as one pastor put it. In one California church, the pastor said his members had responded generously when he asked for money to help families whose homes had been destroyed by one of the recurring fires during the dry season. In another church, contributions suddenly peaked when the pastor announced that $100,000 was due next month on the mortgage. Other pastors spoke of being able to raise money because rain was leaking in on people's heads on Sunday mornings or because the furnace quit working.

Need-based appeals can also focus on the overall package of needs rather than a specific item. Faced with a recession in his community and needing to raise half a million dollars for the next operating year, the pastor at one of the churches we studied asked his finance chairman to speak to the congregation one Sunday in December, after which he said, "This is the need and if you'd like to respond to it, that's okay." Later, he explained to us that he didn't think it was legitimate to tell any stories specifically designed to get people to give. In fact, he told the congregation, "We are not going to use any kind of gimmick. This is the need. If you want to give to it, that's fine. If not, we'll make other choices later about what the consequences of that are." The offering that morning totalled $48,000, leading the pastor to believe that he had done the right thing.

A Presbyterian pastor, preaching a stewardship sermon, provided another example of need-based appeals. She explained to her congregation that they should think about giving in the following context. Remember first that when a church calls a pastor, it enters into an implicit agreement stating in effect that "because we think it is so important that you minister with us, and not have to be distracted by concerns of how you will support yourself, we—this congregation—agree to support you." The assumption, she noted, is that the pastor will do things for the kingdom of God. So the next legitimate question to ask is, "What is this all really doing for the kingdom of God?" Quickly passing over "worshiping and praising on Sunday," she answered by pointing out her own activities—"I do much visitation and pastoral care"—and then focused on the activities from which people in the church benefit, such as classes in Christian doctrine, parents' classes to help them communicate better with their children, committees responsible for putting on the Sunday service, and other education and fellowship opportunities. Why should people pay? "Your money makes these things possible." There is nothing here about biblical principles of giving, only an argument concerned with meeting needs. The logic is similar to the fee-for-service arrangements that characterize professional relationships in other spheres.

One would think need-based appeals would be particularly effective if they focused on meeting desperate human needs, such as helping orphans, the homeless, or victims of fires and floods. Pastors did mention such needs. Yet many pastors acknowledged—sometimes critically—that their members seemed to respond most readily to an appeal for money to build something. A new wing on the church was not only something they could visualize but also something they could take pride in, just as they might a new house or a new car. Some pastors expressed regret that it was less easy to solicit donations to cover the rising costs of health insurance for staff, let alone to operate counseling programs or to support the national ministries of their denominations.

Need-based appeals are a reflection of the culture in which we live. Most Americans no longer lead a hand-to-mouth existence, but we do live from one trip to the automatic cash machine to the next. Few of us keep family budgets; instead, we know that certain items—taxes, Social Security, retirement, insurance—are simply taken out automatically, and the rest is a matter of paying our bills and meeting emergencies. By raising money sporadically for this need this month and another need next month, the churches reinforce this way of handling money rather than giving their members a different example to follow. They continue to talk about "first fruits giving," telling parishioners they should plan ahead and give regularly when they receive their paychecks. Yet, in reality, they say to parishioners, "Sorry, another need just came up; dig in your pockets and see if you can give some more."

Need-based appeals are thus problematic because they reinforce short-sighted, purchase-and-spend orientations toward money rather than challenging these orientations with broader, theologically grounded arguments about the relationships among giving, stewardship, and godly living. One of the sermons we examined explicitly challenged the legitimacy of need-based appeals for this reason. "There's a combination of motives [for giving]," the pastor observed, "none of which are the urgencies of some financial need. As a matter of fact, if we were in a crisis financially, that wouldn't be the time to talk to you about giving."

Another difficulty that need-based appeals raise is increasing conflict *within* congregations about which needs to emphasize. Part of the problem is that many churches have grown larger and added programs to the point that each department of the church functions almost like an autonomous unit. Several pastors, for example, observed that they themselves did not appeal for money often but that there were fund-raisers going on almost constantly because all of the various departments were appealing for money. This sort of competition also makes it difficult for churches to cover basic operating expenses such as salaries and utilities. In several churches, for instance, the basic budget had been cut because parishioners had given generously to special appeals needed to meet mortgage payments. The finance chair at one church explained that it was "always tricky" to get people to give "on top of" their regular giving rather than shifting donations from one place to another. At another church, the pastor complained that members were increasingly willing to give when something "jerked their emotions" but then gave less to regular offerings.

For example, he noted that a hundred members had recently signed up to support orphans in Central America after a missionary came and presented an emotional appeal but that other programs in the church were being cut back.

The other problem with need-based appeals is that needs are always relative. One person's need is a luxury to someone else. Pastor Higgins at Cornerstone Bible Church offered this analysis: "What we have here in terms of a building and property and everything in all the churches today, you don't see that in scripture. You don't see that concept. All those early churches were in someone's home. All of them were for a couple of centuries. Now, all of a sudden, somebody got the idea of building a place, which to me is okay, but I'll tell you what has happened is that giving has become, instead of meeting the needs of people, it's become meeting the needs of a building or a property." He thinks this focus is okay to a point because buildings also serve people. But his comment underscores the fact that people must come to some agreement about what a legitimate need is. The pastor may have one view, loyal members another view, and marginal members still a different one.

While some pastors fret that the needs of today's churches may be extravagant, it is more common for clergy to recognize that need-based appeals are self-limiting when they are tied too closely with a logic of meeting emergencies or covering only short-term necessities. An Episcopal priest, for instance, said this mentality was one of the problems in his denomination. "Episcopalians only give as much money as is needed," he observed. "They look at the situation and they evaluate whether the church needs more money to function. They only give enough to survive and sustain. They do not give enough to grow and expand and improve. So if you say to them, 'We need to change the entrance, because people have to have that to get in,' they'll give $100,000. If you say to them, 'If you'd give another $100,000, we would be able to reach out and minister widely and increase our numbers,' they say, 'I don't want that.' It's a survival mentality, and that has its bad side."

Many of these problems cannot be remedied apart from efforts to include broader understandings of giving along with appeals focusing specifically on needs.[19] It does help, though, for churches to provide as much information as possible about their ministries, the costs of these ministries, and how contributions are allocated. It does not inspire confidence when clergy refuse to give even crude estimates of their budgets. It inspires greater confidence when churches make honest efforts to present their needs and opportunities.

The pastor of a church with several thousand members made this point forcefully. "A lot of people in a big church like this don't even know how much you're doing, like in public housing or for the indigent, or for the AIDS community, which we're very much involved in. We have a medical group here of some 200 people who work with the homeless. We go in and find the people and examine them. We do a lot of medical fairs. And a lot of our people who come may not see that, so we have to do videos and give information. The more they know, the more informed they are, the more they want to share."

## REDEFINING THE MOTIVE

The other way in which clergy are adapting their message in order to raise money also has worrisome consequences; that is, appealing for money by emphasizing self-interested motives for giving,[20] such as getting a lot of money in return. No pastor, of course, would say that this should be the *primary* motive for giving.[21] But this message is what audiences are likely to hear, especially when pastors tantalize their listeners by telling them that God promises cash rewards.

On the sprawling campus of an independent evangelical church near Philadelphia, an audience—not of hillbillies or polyester-suited rednecks but of upper-middle-class professionals and executives—listened approvingly as their pastor introduced today's sermon on giving. "Suppose I were to say to you that I know of an investment opportunity which guarantees a return of 10,000 percent. Would you be interested? Of course you would, if you believed me. I'd probably have to move out of the way for fear of being trampled as you came to be first in line." He continued, "Well, I do know of such an investment tip, and I got it from the most infallible source there is, the Lord Jesus Christ himself." As the sermon progressed, we realized increasingly that the pastor was not merely trying to get our attention in order to talk about something else. He stated clearly that he was talking about money. And he quickly disabused us of the idea that there is anything unchristian about wanting or having a lot of money. Chiding his listeners for even thinking that Jesus thought of money as "filthy stuff" to be gotten rid of, he observed that the Bible is just as interested in what we get back from our giving as it is in what we give.

What do we get back? According to this pastor, the basic biblical doctrine is that "it is more profitable to give than to receive." He admitted that he was altering the familiar statement that it is more *blessed* to give than to receive. But he wanted us to know that the blessing we receive is not just a good feeling. "The blessing [Jesus] promises is a real tangible return in this life." Money. Houses. Leisure time. Friends. These are the rewards we can expect.

Sermons are marvelous rhetorical devices. The audience sits quietly. Yet the speaker includes their silent voices, expressing their unexpressed doubts in the sermon itself. Isn't it selfish to think about giving this way? The pastor challenged this concern directly. "I realize there are some of you who are sitting there saying, that's not a very worthy motive for giving, is it? I mean, I thought Christianity was more altruistic than that. I'm supposed to give because I want something? Well, that's exactly what Jesus said. It's not wrong to give and expect to get a return." And why would Jesus have appealed to our selfishness in this way? "He understood human nature, didn't he? And he knew that sometimes we're not as absolutely pure in our motivation as we like to think we are. And so he encouraged us to say to ourselves that one of the good reasons for giving is that we can expect God's blessing in return."

If we believe sermons such as this, we come away affirmed in our selfishness and in our desire for money rather than challenged to live differently. We also have a good reason to give money to the church. "Doesn't it seem reasonable," the sermon concluded, "to say that when you're faithful in giving generously, that the Lord's going to see to it that your income becomes a more generous income?"

To be sure, some middle-class church members may not be impelled to give in hopes of gaining wealth or even happiness because they already enjoy the comforts of life. But efforts to turn these comforts into a reason for giving also raise diffi-culties. The essence of this appeal is that Americans should give generously because they have been blessed generously. The basic notion is biblical, but the specific ways in which it is interpreted are likely to fall on deaf ears. Consider the way one pastor framed it: "How affluent we are. How blessed we are. We need to consider that in our giving. We have the privilege of not having to worry the way many peo-ple do." Yet the fact is that most Americans do worry about paying their bills and about not having enough money. It is thus unlikely that we will give because we feel too blessed to have any financial worries.

Or consider the argument that our "very affluent lifestyle puts a greater burden on us to think about using our resources for God's purposes." Here the emphasis rests less on thankfulness and more on responsibility. The principle is that much will be required of those to whom much has been given. But few Americans believe they are not already behaving responsibly. Is it not especially responsible, parish-ioners may ask, to pay high taxes to provide for the common good and for strong military defenses in an uncertain world, and is it not being more responsible to work longer hours to pay for one's children's education than to give extra dollars to the church? Having resources is a motive for being responsible, in short, but not necessarily a reason to give money to the church. That additional piece of the argu-ment needs to be made.

But American religion is, of course, quite diverse, and one of the ways in which it is served by this diversity is by having critics within its own midst. A few of the pastors we talked to recognized how easy it is for churches to accommodate their arguments to the prevailing culture. Some of the pastors in old-line denominations were especially vocal in making this criticism. Their sense of having been around for a few centuries and having weathered a few storms in the past gave them confidence that it was better for the church to stay true to its principles, even though times might be hard, than to compromise.

Rector Stuart Morgan at Saint Andrew's Episcopal Church is one example. Using himself as an illustration, he told how he tried to get closer to his teenaged son at one point by trying to imitate his interests and habits, only to realize before long that his son needed an adult in his life more than another teenager. He thinks the same is true of society and the church. "The church needs to sit tight and let the materialistic Americans of this world grow up to faith and grow up to higher spiritual values. We don't need to change. We just need to let people change. The church is where it ought to be. It's where it always was. It's like every parent throughout history. They don't need to change and become snotty-nosed adolescents to identify with their kids, and wear silly leotards, and tie their hair up in funny ways, and paint their faces purple. They just need to be adults, and the kids will come along if they see that adult life. I think our society will grow up to a better Christianity in years to come. In some respects, I view some of the very raving fundamentalist and immature churches in our society as good boot camp for a real mature faith. I think they have a real place. We have a number of people here who have come to this church after an adolescent time. I'm talking about some of the little bootleg congregations that form and have an identity in a local community. They aren't tied to anything, and they're just silly little Christian groups who kind of pray for better salaries and sexy lives and healthy kids. There's more to life than that, and they grow up and eventually realize it, and they become mainline Christians with a broader picture."

As self-justifying as this comment is, it nevertheless points to the fact that America's churches are stronger collectively than they are individually. If no church is perfect, they at least share different imperfections. And pointing the finger, if done without malice, can be a way of realizing more clearly what these imperfections are.

## ADVICE FROM THE PULPIT

Although the churches' financial health depends on members' willingness to contribute, clergy must be wary of trying simply to make their members happy. It is difficult to compare fund-raising appeals because many other factors go into the financial success of particular churches. Nevertheless, some of the clergy we spoke to offered comments that seem to reckon with the larger problems we have considered in this and in previous chapters. For this reason, their advice is particularly worthy of consideration.

The place to begin, many of the pastors we talked to insisted, is by recognizing that fund-raising is a *means* for accomplishing goals but should not be a goal itself. "I don't want them to give more of their money, of their material goods," was the way one pastor put it. "I want them to walk and develop a relationship with God. That's my priority." Another pastor said, "I'm concerned that we don't serve a building but that we serve the Lord, and the building may be a means to that end. We're grateful for this facility. But if our whole reason for being is to support this building, that's not a good reason for being."

In emphasizing that giving is a means, some pastors also make a special point of arguing that it is a means to becoming a *better person*, not just a way to accomplish the goals of the church. "What works best," noted the pastor of one of the largest churches we studied, "is not allowing people to feel like you're coming at them just for their money, but that they're a better person if they know how to give." This emphasis can, of course, feed the self-interested orientation that dominates American culture. But clergy stress that giving has special value because it makes us better people, paradoxically, by encouraging us to be *less selfish*. Giving away some of the money to which we are attached and that we would otherwise use for selfish purposes, they argue, frees people to be more themselves, to find a larger sense of personal identity in other things, and to be more like God.

Rector Stuart Morgan at Saint Andrew's Episcopal Church summarized his way of appealing for money this way. "It's essential for our health and well-being to share what we have," he tells his congregation. "We need not be identified and tied to our material things, including our money. It's a reflection of us, but it's not us. It is godly to give." He is also careful to point out that our well-being may increase, but not our finances. "You're certainly poorer if you tithe," he said. "I could do a lot with the $6,000 a year that I could go spend on other things. You're not richer. I don't say to people, 'If you give money, you'll get more.' I think if you give money you have less of *money*, but you have something more of something else." He specifically distances himself from preachers who make appeals in terms of financial promises. "Some people will say to you, 'But I gave $10,000 to the church, and the next year I became a millionaire.' It's likely if they'd have given zero to the church they would have been a millionaire the next year anyhow, because I don't think God runs around rewarding tithers by making them millionaires. If he does, why doesn't he do it for me? I think that's a manipulation of God, and I would never say to people, 'Give because then you will get rich yourself.' I know that's a message from some people. 'You think money's evil, give it to me. God will make you rich.' No, he won't. God doesn't do that."

Whether an appeal that promises greater well-being will net more for the church than one promising parishioners that God will make them rich is not clear. An important side benefit, though, may be that clergy themselves feel better talking about money. At Saint Andrew's, for instance, Rector Morgan said he actually enjoys making appeals to his congregation for money. The reason, he explained, is that "I know that the more you give, the more you receive in blessing of knowing how rich you are, knowing how blessed you are, knowing it's God's and it's not important anyhow. I like doing it to people because I think the more they can learn it the more at peace their life will be." Almost as a footnote, he added, "Oh, it's also good to get it in so we can afford to run the place, but I think that's secondary."

If giving is to be encouraged by promising the givers a greater sense of well-being, the churches must also be prepared to serve as the vehicle for cultivating that sense of well-being. It will not come about magically or simply as part of the person's interior ruminations but as part of a community in which support and encouragement are present. Charity must begin at home, as the saying goes, not by caring only for needs within the church but by realizing that church members will give more generously and enable the church to serve others if they receive enough from it to be motivated.

The so-called program church, supplying a wide range of ministries to young people, couples, children, and other special-interest groups, is testimony to the fact that clergy already recognize the value of ministering to their own. Still, there is so much more to be done, especially in helping members deal with such important issues as their concerns about work and money. "I think programs that respond to people's real and expressed needs, programs that are supportive," was the answer a United Church of Christ pastor gave when asked what would help increase the level of giving at this church. He then added an important observation: "This conversation prompts me to realize that we may have missed lots of folks who could have used some help along the way in relationship to business concerns, for instance. We just don't do much, and yet this is such a *big* part of people's lives. Wow! We've not done anything."

In focusing on specific needs and programs, it is also important that churches keep their emphasis on the distinctive spiritual teachings and activities that make them the church rather than becoming just another club, place to play softball, or seminar on stock options. A Presbyterian pastor expressed this point nicely when he observed, "People who are having their needs met, people who have a sense of the presence of God, people who are brought into the presence of the majesty of Christ, people who are relieved of a sense of guilt because of the forgiveness and grace of Christ, people who are taught to pray and for whom prayer is a reality, people who have come to an appreciation of the Bible as the Word of God, they give."

As counteradvice to the view that giving is best motivated by appealing to people's selfish interests, it is also well to keep in mind that religious truth often runs against the grain of popular cultural assumptions. Indeed, the currently neglected doctrine of repentance suggests that godly living implies turning away from these assumptions, and in the case of giving, this turning away may involve notions such as sacrifice or obligation that have fallen into popular disfavor.[22]

It is worth considering what one pastor said in framing his remarks about giving one Sunday morning. "Everything about God's ways are backwards to man's," he asserted. "Somehow we have the idea that God's the one that's out of step, but if you'll go back to the beginning, there was a time we were in step, and then we turned around and went the other direction. Repent means to reverse your direction, to reverse your mentality, to turn around and come the other way. And it's in the area of the practicals, the material details of life, that we find the greatest difficulty of really corresponding to the Lord's way." He used the idea of worship to illustrate his point. "We may well rise in an understanding of the wisdom, for example, of worship. Worship is not inherent in our nature. Maybe some attitude toward a supreme being may latently be there and be awakened by different emotions and then by the preaching of the Gospel, but we do not inherently worship the Lord with all of our heart." By the same token, giving to the church may not be easy to reconcile with middle-class lifestyles. Giving is a practice, a form of "spiritual discipline," as some pastors put it. It requires effort and must be based on commitment.[23]

If learning how to give—and then giving—is hard work, it is also a matter of grace. It happens, the church has always held, because of divine empowerment that facilitates and enriches the experience of giving. One pastor expressed this idea especially well. "We have such a tendency to isolate the material matters of giving from true spirituality. We don't see giving as a grace," he observed. "It is a duty. It is a financial obligation. It is something that maybe we say, 'All right, I will do it because I believe that the principle of the tithe is there, and it's something that ought to be done.' But in terms of realizing it as a loveliness of grace that grows and flows through you, we're not inclined to think that way. And the longing of the Lord is to teach us all to abound. To show us how much he can flow through you."[24]

The other piece of advice that stands out is one pastor's insistence that *love* must be the primary motive for giving. "To me the heart of Christianity is the motivation," he said. "And the motivation to serve God, to live for God, is not the law, but it's God's grace. It's God's love for us. That should be our motive." Other techniques could be used to raise money, he suggested, but they would not be right, even if they brought in huge sums, unless they emphasized the right reason. "Our message," he asserted, "flies in the face of human nature. We're really called to respond out of love, knowing that we're in a world that doesn't respond naturally out of love." Apparently he was right. Most church people would undoubtedly agree with his argument, but he was the only one of the clergy who emphasized love in talking about giving.

## THE FISCAL DILEMMA

The dilemma the churches find themselves in is real. On the one hand, rising costs and deepening social needs put pressure on the churches to raise more money in order to do more (or to avoid doing less). Clergy are faced with the necessity of asking their parishioners to give more frequently, more regularly, or more generously. And clergy are having to focus on finances more and more simply because donations have not been rising as fast as personal incomes or church expenditures. On the other hand, the church has no reason to exist if it simply perpetuates the emphasis on money, materialism, and commercialism that prevails in the culture at large. Clergy are thus reluctant to put too much emphasis on fund-raising, and they stress the importance of saying things that may need to be said, even if contributions fall as a result. "The churches need to say more strongly that life is not about consuming but about serving and caring and loving," was how one pastor put it. "That would really be bucking the societal trend." Yet he also noted, "We're unwilling to buck the trend. As churches, we're more comfortable just going with the flow."

Life is full of dilemmas like this. The churches can choose one horn of the dilemma or the other: focusing so much on raising money that they become part of the materialism of our age, or bucking the trend so vehemently that they lose the resources needed to continue. The expedient course always lies in the middle. Rather than raising money by selling personal prosperity and happiness, the churches can encourage giving as an alternative to materialism and consumerism. They can do so, however, only by demonstrating that the gifts received are being used for higher purposes. In the process, some of what is said will inevitably be unpopular. But the very reason why institutions such as the church exist is to insulate their members from having to jump through hoops defined by other people's standards of popularity. Therefore, clergy and church members alike must think harder about what it means to be the church and why the church should be supported.

Based on our conversations with clergy, I would be reluctant to say that clergy who preach more often or more boldly about giving necessarily have larger or more prosperous churches than those who don't.[25] It is evident, however, that some clergy have thought about financial giving more deeply than others and are more comfortable talking about it. These pastors uniformly emphasize that money is integral to the rest of life. It reflects who we are and what we value. If we are to worship God, this worship must include our finances. If we are to be generous people, we must also be generous with our money.

# ten

# GIVING TO THE POOR

If it were in Mexico City or Soweto, it would be calleda shantytown. Here in a prosperous Midwestern city that prides itself on commerce, insurance, and being one of the pharmaceutical capitals of the world, it is known simply (when anyone thinks about it at all) as a low-income area. In livable space, the house amounts to no more than 700 square feet, a tiny, one-story clapboard structure with walls so thin the cold arctic air that comes sweeping across the plains blows right through. But at least it's a house. Conley, a ninth grader, sleeps in a small room with a mattress on the floor, a couple of posters on the wall, and some plastic milk cartons stuffed with books. There is no other furniture. He lives here with his mother, father, and sister. Next door is an identical dwelling occupied by a frail woman in her late seventies. Next door to that is a vacant lot where Conley and his neighbor have vegetables growing. Trucks rumble by on the expressway. The rest of the neighborhood consists of boarded-up buildings, vacant lots, and four-story project dwellings put up during Lyndon Johnson's Great Society period.

Conley grew up in one of these dwellings. But when he was twelve and his sister was ten, his father and mother both lost their jobs. The utility company turned off their electricity, and they were forced to move out. They had no place to go. All they could do was store what few belongings they had at his aunt's apartment and declare themselves homeless. Fortunately, the African Methodist church they had been attending operated a shelter for the homeless, and the church provided refuge for Conley and his family. He and his father were given a little cubicle. His mother and sister shared a comparable one. There was one bathroom in the building, a shower, and a kind of soup kitchen for people in the shelter as well as those who came in from the street. Conley was afraid of all the strange people and spent as much time as he could in his cubicle. Helping others became his way of saving himself.

After a few weeks, Conley realized he had time on his hands. He was still attending school, of course, but had long hours in the evenings and on weekends with nothing to do. So he started tutoring. One day he was wandering around the church building and noticed that the classrooms there were empty and unused. There were children of all ages in the shelter. When he had lived in the projects, he had sometimes played school in the park. Why not do it again? he thought. The woman who ran the shelter said she didn't mind. He went to his principal and got some materials the school was going to throw away. As soon as he found a community agency willing to bring over a few desks, he was in business. All that winter, for nine months while he was homeless, Conley ran his school, every afternoon and evening and all day Saturday. The kids would come, or their parents would send them, about twenty in all, and he would help them with their homework, or teach them to read, or just give them papers to work on.

The ceiling leaked, and some of the kids didn't want to be there. But Conley discovered quickly how rewarding it was to help. In fact, he vividly remembers one of his first pupils. "It was when I first started living there, I met a four-year-old girl named Sarah. She was the youngest student I ever had. She couldn't read or write, and within three days she could read small books like *Cat in the Hat* and *Green Eggs and Ham*. She read a couple of read-along books that I had on tape. I taped my voice, reading a book and taping it. She read along with it." He remembers how good that made him feel. "It was touching to me because I had done something for someone. It was just spectacular for me. I had a great feeling about it."

Conley goes so far as to say that he had a lot of fun with his tutoring. But it would be dishonest to suggest that it was all roses. He missed his home. He missed the friends he had known where he lived before. On one occasion he persuaded one of the deacons at the church to drive a van over every day and pick up some of these children so he could tutor them. But that project lasted only a few days. He also found that it was painful when his pupils moved on, which they did frequently as they were shunted from shelter to shelter. Of little Sarah, for example, he says, "She was always real shy, but when it came to art, she really came alive. See that picnic table out there. Me and her painted it together. I was really upset when she left. Just when you got used to someone, they'd move out. I saw her a couple of weeks later at the train station with her mom. They'd been moved to a different shelter."

Two years have passed since Conley and his family moved out of the shelter themselves and started getting back on their feet. But he still goes back every day to do his tutoring. The few books he has, stuffed into his plastic milk cartons, are his lending library. Children in the neighborhood come to his window to check them out. He seems old for his years. At fifteen, he has already experienced more trouble than many people would want to in a lifetime. When asked why he still does volunteer work, he muses for a moment and says, "Like they always say, you do something for somebody else, you always get something back." He pauses, though, as if somehow that saying has become trite. Then he adds, "But I really don't think much about that now. It was just something in me that always wanted to help someone else, because people have always helped me during my lifetime. So I thought that it was time to give something back."

## MINISTERING TO THE POOR

This is the kind of story that shows what churches can do to help the poor. It is a true story. Conley Wellman got back on his feet because the church was there. It provided shelter and food when he needed it. And it opened his eyes to ways in which he could help others. Conley did not start tutoring other children because of deep theological principles. The day he went wandering through the empty church is symbolic. He was bored, looking for something to do, and realized the opportunity that lay before him as he inspected the empty classrooms. But he *was* there. In fact, he had always been there. All his life, he had attended church regularly. He went on Sunday mornings but also on Sunday evenings, to youth group or drill team on Wednesday evenings, and often to church dinners or fellowships on Monday evenings. His view of God, while not sophisticated, was quite tangible. God was very much like the "elderlies" at his church. Nice. Interested in people doing their best and doing what's right. A spirit, Conley says, "who wants people to love each other and care for each other."

Conley Wellman is still poor. His parents have found new jobs but are still struggling to make ends meet. Most of the people at Conley's church are poor. They have few resources to share. Middle-class churches are vastly better off financially. They also teach that God wants us to love and care for each other, but now that these churches are also experiencing tight budgets, their role in ministering to the poor is in danger.

Yet the *needs* are more clearly in evidence than ever before. Since 1970, the number of persons living below the poverty line in the United States has increased by approximately eight million. This figure includes approximately one of every five children. Among African Americans, it includes nearly one of every two children.[1] Studies of overall income distribution in the United States also suggest that the poor have become poorer during the past two decades—the proportion of total income received by the lowest quintile, for instance, declined by 16 percent between 1970 and 1990.[2] Other problems, such as homelessness and AIDS, have also grown enormously. During the same period, however, public assistance programs have generally been reduced, leaving more to be done by private agencies, including churches. During the 1980s, for example, government funding for vocational rehabilitation was reduced by 50 percent, child nutrition funding was cut by more than two-thirds, and food stamp programs were cut by nearly three-fourths.

In order to understand the full implications of the present crisis in the churches, we must consider the ways in which middle-class churches have been helping the poor, how these efforts are now being curtailed or how they are falling short of meeting community needs, and what some churches are hoping will be effective in motivating their members to keep these ministries vibrant.

Throughout their history, the churches have played an active role in helping the poor. In the New Testament church, apostolic teachings quickly encouraged the formation of deacons' funds to assist the needy within congregations and to send financial help to other congregations facing severe financial difficulties. Over the centuries, these efforts gradually expanded to include the founding of almshouses, hospitals, and community relief programs. During the Middle Ages, the church literally stockpiled grain to be doled out to indigent parishioners in times of emergency.[3] After the Protestant Reformation, congregations worked closely with city magistrates to make relief available but also to determine who should be eligible for such support.[4] Our own history has included many similar efforts. Benevolent associations were founded to channel aid from established churches to less prosperous sections of the population. Temperance societies tried to instill middle-class virtues of sobriety and personal discipline in poorer communities. Deacons' funds continued to make personal assistance available to faithful but poor members of the churches themselves.[5]

At the end of the twentieth century, the churches have adapted to very different means of assisting the poor than those that were common at the end of the previous century. Government welfare programs, housing subsidies, unemployment and job-training programs, disability and old-age insurance, and a huge number of secular charitable organizations are all part of the contemporary picture. These are the agencies to which we look to help the needy. In my survey of working Americans (in which 89 percent said "the condition of the poor" is a serious social problem), for instance, favored solutions for helping the needy included government policies to stimulate economic growth, social services, and businesses taking a more active role in such help.[6] A national survey concerned with giving and volunteering showed that 84 percent of the public agrees with the view that "to bring relief to needy people requires, first and foremost, changes in social and economic policies."[7] Another survey, concerned with the public's attitudes toward homelessness, revealed that 63 percent of Americans think the government is not doing enough to solve the problem and that approximately two-thirds of the public would like local, state, and federal agencies to do more.[8] Yet the churches have also borne part of the burden of caring for the poor, and there is widespread sentiment that the churches should continue to be actively involved. In my survey, for instance, 50 percent of church members said it would do a lot to help the needy "if more people took an active role in their churches," and 55 percent said it would help a lot "if more people gave a few hours a week to doing volunteer work." In the study of attitudes toward the homeless, 56 percent of the public said religious institutions should be doing more.

Providing assistance to their own members who are in need is probably the most common way that churches minister to the poor. Like Conley Wellman's church, they make a special effort to care for members who have fallen on hard times. In San Xavier's parish, for instance, members of an organization called the Legion of Mary—a group of about thirty people—routinely visit the elderly and those who cannot leave their homes, many of whom are poor. The parish also provides free tuition for families who cannot afford to send their children to Catholic schools. At Redeemer Baptist, the deacons take up a special offering once a month for the pastor to use when members call asking for emergency help to tide them over until their next check or because they are out of work. Another African American church routinely sends $25 checks to each of its senior citizens for Christmas. One of the recipients explained that she was down to her last dollar and couldn't have paid her bills without this "check from heaven." Overall, even among church members who have been employed during the past year, one in twenty say they have received some kind of financial assistance from their church.[9]

Middle-class churches generally need to reach outside their own memberships in order to help the truly disadvantaged who live in other communities and in other parts of the world. A majority of the churches we studied maintained a special fund for this purpose. Typically, a substantial part of this fund was set aside for emergency requests that came directly from individuals living in the area.

"I can show you a file of literally hundreds of people that we've given money to for food or for utilities, and people that we've put up in hotels or motels because they come in and have no place to sleep," remarked the pastor of a Korean church. Only the day before, the pastor had bought a bus ticket for a man who was stranded on his way to another city. Another man had stopped by the previous day, and the pastor had taken him to the church kitchen and fed him.[10]

Churches typically have other resources besides money that can be used effectively in dealing with emergency needs. At Cornerstone Bible Church, Pastor Higgins received a call one Saturday night at 11:30 P.M. from a woman whose son-in-law had just turned her out on the street. Pastor Higgins arranged a motel room for her that night and found a family she could stay with for the next several weeks.

Rather than wait for the random stranger to come to them, most churches in middle-class neighborhoods have also devised ways to reach more systematically into areas where the poor are concentrated. An Episcopal church in suburban Chicago, for example, rents a storefront in a low-income section of the city where volunteers from the church can dispense emergency food and clothing. A suburban church in Philadelphia helps the poor in Georgia by purchasing handicrafts from them in bulk and selling them in a store at the church. And a church in California pays the salary of an African American pastor whose home in the inner city doubles as an outlet for toys, clothing, and tutoring.

One of the advantages of larger churches is that they are able to operate special ministries for the poor. At a large church in downtown Chicago, for instance, a social service center with its own staff provides a shelter for seventy-five homeless men, runs a soup kitchen for these and other homeless people, delivers meals to people in several other locations, and tutors 350 children who live in public housing projects. The church also spends $30,000 every summer running a two-week program for inner-city children, has a minority scholarship program, and sends its youth group out periodically to renovate low-income houses.

Churches also help the poor in other areas by participating in larger networks and alliances. Some observers believe the growth of denominationalism in American religion during the nineteenth century was promoted by the desire to channel resources from local churches to other churches or kinds of ministries in which broader needs could be met. Denominational structures still provide a conduit for channeling resources to the needy in other areas.[11] Increasingly, these structures are being augmented (or replaced) by ad hoc alliances within local metropolitan areas. An individual church in a middle-class neighborhood adopts a "sister church" in a low-income area. Or several middle-class churches, perhaps from different denominations, join forces to support a homeless shelter or an inner-city youth center.

A small Baptist church in New Jersey has developed a partnership with a mission church on Coney Island and helps it minister to the homeless in that area. "They don't have any place to live; they just live under the boardwalk and this church offers soup kitchens for them and showers and they have clothing distributions," the pastor explained. "So we are constantly sending vanloads of clothing and food." The pastor of another Baptist church described a Thanksgiving program to feed the homeless that involved cooperation among several churches in his city. He thought the project had worked but also observed that cooperative ventures are sometimes hampered by the fact that each congregation has different traditions and wants to do things its own way. In another area, five churches rotate opening their basements to the homeless. "It avoids burnout," explained one of the pastors. "You don't feel like you're having to be there all the time."

It is worth emphasizing that churches are part of what sociologists call the institutional environment.[12] They participate in organizational networks, working organization-to-organization to identify and meet needs in their communities rather than ministering to the poor only on an individual basis. Small churches with few resources of their own may withdraw into themselves as a way of protecting these resources, but increasingly churches are working together with government agencies and with secular organizations in order to address the complex problems facing the poor and other disadvantaged groups.

An example is a Presbyterian church in Texas that has "adopted" a school in a nearby section of town that is predominantly populated by African Americans with low incomes. The pastor and the principal meet periodically, and members of the church have helped with projects such as painting the school and donating equipment. In the same community, the mayor organized a "think tank" that meets regularly to talk about community needs and how to address them. The pastor of the Presbyterian church is a member of this think tank. He said it benefits his congregation to know about the larger issues facing the community. Some of his members have also become directly involved. For instance: "Here's a housing development that is in such bad condition that people can no longer live in it. So we mobilized volunteers to go down and put a new roof on, Sheetrock, paint, and did a whole project of several hundred units so poor people could live there again." Or for another example: "A problem with street gangs surfaced, and there's now a program called the Street Academy where people actually take some young people off the streets and teach them to get them through school and get them back into the schooling system."

Another example of the way in which churches are adapting to the institutional environment in which they are embedded is an information and referral system called Love, Inc. Developed by a large nondenominational church in Pennsylvania, Love, Inc., is a clearinghouse that all churches in the area can tap into by telephone. It includes information on social ministries of all the various churches, as well as resources available from county and city social service agencies and other nonprofit agencies, so needy families who come to particular churches for help can be assisted in the fullest possible way.

Although monetary donations are an important part of churches' ministries to the poor, clergy and lay leaders emphasize the value of personal involvement as well. The reason is that assistance with a personal touch is assumed to be more effective—to both the recipient and the caregiver. For example, the pastor of one church talked about a "block partnership" program that tried to link his suburban church members with people in the inner city. "We identify a block in the inner city," he explained, "and we send one or two families that meet with those people, will not give them money, but give them expertise in how to work through the system, whether it is the welfare system or whatever. The main thing is to try to help people get away from dependence."

Another pastor offered an eloquent summary of how personal interaction with the poor can change the attitudes of middle-class people. "People who get first-hand acquaintance with people in need," he observed, "begin to understand the structural origins of poverty and homelessness. They also begin to overcome some of their own stereotypes and caricatures of people, and they begin to see that these are real human beings who somewhere or another just aren't as lucky as the rest of us." At another church, the pastor organized a special service so that volunteers who had recently spent a week working with Native Americans in Oklahoma could share what they had learned with the rest of the congregation. "It was just an over-whelming worship experience," he recalled. "These twenty-five people were just going on about how their lives had been changed and about their feeling of mutu-ality with people who are quite different, in very different situations, certainly very different economic realities, and yet a sense that we were in something bigger together."

This emphasis on personal involvement encourages churches to participate selectively in the larger institutional environment of caregiving. Although many churches contribute money to larger organizations or provide volunteers who sit on the boards of these organizations, churches favor smaller and more localized pro-grams that bring members into direct contact with the needy and that provide members with a sense of ownership and responsibility. A Presbyterian church in Philadelphia serves as an example. Its members participate in a variety of citywide programs but take special pride in having purchased and renovated housing for five homeless families. Members of the church have continued to take special interest in these families, for instance, tutoring some of the children and in one case pro-viding child care and financial assistance to help a single mother finish schooling as a medical technician.

Overall, two things stand out about the ways in which churches have been min-istering to the poor in recent years. One is that the specific kinds of ministry, while legitimated in broad religious language about caring, are an *adaptation* to the cur-rent system of government, community, and private nonprofit provision for public welfare that has developed during the latter half of the twentieth century. Churches do not provide massive monetary relief, health care, or housing to the poor.

Churches avoid the doctrine of entitlements that undergirds public assistance programs. But churches meet short-term emergency needs among their own members, contribute to the needs of other people who may be working to keep their own churches alive, and provide volunteer assistance that may be lacking from other agencies. Churches have also adapted to the geographic configurations of poverty by channeling assistance out of middle-class neighborhoods to churches, civic organizations, and individuals in low-income areas and in other countries. The other point is that the churches—by adapting in these ways—have, in fact, been able to contribute meaningfully to helping the poor, despite the growth of other programs. Helping poor people negotiate the welfare system is a prime example. The monetary assistance is there, but people may still need help figuring out how to get it. Churches have been able to play a useful role. Working with schools, government agencies, and international relief organizations is also an example. Cooperation with these organizations enables churches to contribute by identifying special needs that are not being filled in other ways.[13]

## THE SHORTFALL IN CHURCH PROGRAMS

The pressures that have emerged in middle-class churches have, however, begun to make it harder for these churches to minister as effectively to the needy as clergy would like. Because optimism prevails and because clergy want to put a good face on their activities, they generally emphasize what *is* being done rather than what is *not* being accomplished. Nevertheless, it is clear that the middle-class squeeze is being felt by those who are already most in need.

We saw in chapter 2 how Father Martinez struggles at San Xavier's parish in Texas to set aside enough time and money to minister to the needs of the poor families in his church and to the large number of poor immigrants who live in the area. He says he never has enough time or money to meet the needs even of those who come directly to him asking for assistance. He is thankful to have a person on his staff who oversees the social ministries of the parish. She sees about twenty needy people every day. But this year her budget has been cut by $25,000. The parish, Father Martinez says, is also hampered by inadequate facilities. He would like to organize a clothing and furniture drive but has no space.

At an Asian American church in California, the pastor boasted about his congregation maintaining a discretionary fund for the poor and having donated approximately $25,000 worth of old clothes to an inner-city mission in the past year. But he also admitted that he has been unable to increase programs for the poor to more than 3 percent of the church's overall budget. He says his members feel themselves under increasing economic pressures and want whatever they give to stay within the church itself. "When you look at the need out there," he mused, "we're doing a pitiful amount."

The church I mentioned that has initiated Love, Inc., is relatively well funded and has enjoyed an overall increase in its budget in the past few years. However, the pastor said designated giving has focused on new buildings and programs for the church's own members to the point that Love, Inc., is running a deficit and is having to scale back operations. Giving to the deacon's fund, he said, is also declining: "We're battling to have enough in that fund to help families. There are more needs than we could meet right now."

At first glance, the average church may appear to be a bustle of activity on behalf of the poor—taking up special offerings to send to Ethiopia and Appalachia, sending out food baskets on Thanksgiving, and collecting toothbrushes for people in nursing homes. But clergy, listening to their members' overriding concerns about their own finances and finding it hard to mount more active social ministries, admit that this activity is often more show than substance. "Although we are constantly doing little things here and there," the pastor of a church in New Jersey confessed, "I don't think our efforts could be considered more than token. We just don't really have that overriding focus; we just have lots of little focuses and we make lots of little offerings and gifts. We can write up long lists of things we do, and what we're talking about is only a few hundred dollars and a few people."

Cornerstone Bible Church and Saint Andrew's Episcopal Church both exemplify the pressures churches are facing in ministering to the poor. At Cornerstone, Pastor Higgins wishes he could do more but said he just doesn't have a sizable enough membership. The few people he has need to devote their time and energy to building up the congregation itself. Saint Andrew's is much larger, yet its $200,000 annual budget includes only $8,000 for the Social Aids and Concerns program. "There's always other uses for the money," Rector Morgan complained. "Everybody has other agendas."

Other pastors also perceive a trade-off between their members' own needs and their ability to mount programs for the poor. Some pastors, in fact, have found ways to legitimate not asking for more. One of the priests we interviewed, for instance, said it was his policy to encourage parishioners to give 5 percent of their income to the church and 5 percent to the poor. The latter, he explained, could include the time and money they spend helping elderly parents or the cost of sending their children to Catholic schools. At an evangelical Protestant church, the pastor argued that about half the church's overall budget benefited the poor but included in that figure the 40 percent devoted to the support of missionaries.

Most clergy want their churches to be actively engaged in helping the poor. Yet, faced with tight resources, pastors are looking harder at the kinds of people and programs they support. Many pastors told us they would give food or clothing to needy individuals but not money. They worried that money would be wasted but also admitted they simply didn't have any to spare. Other pastors said they supported sister churches or mission programs in their own communities, but were less willing to send money or volunteers to other areas. "The poor will always be with you," said one pastor, quoting Jesus. "When you try to go out someplace beyond your community," he observed, "you start to stretch yourself pretty thin. I think if every church took care of their own backyard, everything would be all right."

Even such common programs as deacons' funds and soup kitchens are being trimmed back or eliminated at some churches. The problem is not that they are unable to raise a few hundred dollars to support these programs. But pastors and lay leaders are feeling "burned" by the fact that recipients keep coming back and by the fact that handouts seem to have such a small impact on the larger problems. Sensing that housing programs, job training, and relocation may be the solution but not finding an inexpensive way to participate in these programs, churches are dropping out of the helping business entirely.

Some churches, of course, are still making a highly visible effort to help the poor. In fact, these churches are sometimes featured so much in the media that the shortfall in ministering to the poor is hidden from public view. But even these churches are experiencing economic pressures that make it hard for them to do as much as they would like. A church in Philadelphia that gives top priority to its social ministry, for instance, recently mortgaged its building in order to carry on its programs. A church in Chicago with a long-standing goal of devoting 50 percent of its income to social ministries has been unable in recent years to keep this figure above 30 percent. The pastor of another socially oriented church said he is having to defend this emphasis much more actively to his congregation because his members are less secure financially and therefore less willing to take risks with the church's resources.[14]

Cuts in staff are another way in which ministries to the poor are being curtailed. "At one point we had a full-time minister who was directing that work," explained the pastor of a relatively wealthy church in talking about his social ministries department. "It was much more effective under him than it is right now under a woman who is more of a secretary-level person. She doesn't go into the ghetto. She is more a responder to people who are there and call her. And so at this point I think our program is a little bit on the down side."

In other cases, staff cuts were not a problem only because needed staff had never been hired. With the growing professionalization of caring activities, churches have been struggling to keep up. Social workers, family therapists, and nurses—to name a few—are needed to care for the disadvantaged, not just untrained volunteers who

can cook a meal or give away an old coat. Some churches have tried to provide professional services by opening counseling centers or by hiring parish nurses. Of the
churches we studied, however, only several of the larger ones were able to support
these kinds of ministries. Other clergy expressed interest but admitted they did not
have the resources. Indeed, it was sometimes difficult for them to do anything at
all. "To be honest with you," said the pastor of a midsized Episcopal church when
asked about social ministries, "there's just one of me, and I haven't gotten around to
that yet."

As the needs mount in their communities, clergy are also becoming increasingly
aware that new programs are needed that cannot possibly be funded under present
conditions. A priest told us, for example, that he was shocked one day when the
bishop told him his parish was doing more for the needy than any other parish in
the diocese. "We're hardly doing anything," he said. "I'd like to have somebody full
time to organize social ministries. I wish we could afford to do that, put someone
on full time and get this whole thing rolling. I'd like to build a home for battered
wives, a halfway house for kids, a nursing home, low-cost housing for the elderly
poor."

In the final analysis, churches are now at the point where even those that have
been most active in helping the needy are beginning to wonder if they can continue
at existing levels. Clergy recognize that it is easy to operate social programs when
times are good. None of the tough choices have to be faced. The new wing can still
be built. The choir can still purchase new music. Belt-tightening makes the choice
to help others harder. "We haven't had to make a choice between heating the place
and feeding people," admitted the pastor of one of the more affluent churches we
studied. "I don't know what would happen," he said. "We'd probably act like most
churches. We'd heat the place."

## MOTIVATING THE MIDDLE CLASS

The only clear way to improve the churches' efforts to minister to the needy is by
motivating middle-class church members to give more generously of their time and
money. A large proportion of members, in fact, say it is important to help the
needy. In my survey of working men and women, for instance, 87 percent of those
who were church members said it was very important or absolutely essential to help
people in need. Church members also regard helping the needy as one of the legitimate tasks of the church. In the survey, 81 percent of church members said they
would like the churches to put more emphasis on providing job training, housing,

and other services to the poor. So it is simply a matter of the churches finding more effective ways to motivate their members to become directly involved.

But motivating people is never easy. Despite the fact that many people give lip service to the idea of helping the needy, they also attach high value to having nice things themselves, making a lot of money, being successful, and enjoying themselves. Clergy give high praise to the members of their congregations who *are* involved in helping the poor, but one of the frustrations most clergy share is that more of their members are not involved. "The frustration," explained a priest in a relatively well-educated suburban parish, "is when we want to do something about the poor and only a very small number of people come and listen." Their only concern, he said, is "me, my family, my immediate need." Not far away, the rector of an Episcopal church offered a similar observation. "We have poor neighborhoods all around us," he said, "but none of the congregations in this area are doing anything. I think it's just too threatening to people."

Middle-class parishioners may not be concerned simply with themselves, but they hold individualistic assumptions about hard work and self-reliance that sometimes make it difficult for them to respond generously to the poor. The same priest, for instance, said many of his members believe the poor should pull themselves up by their own bootstraps. "I remember one day becoming livid," he recounted. "I was out at the end of the sidewalk shaking people's hands after mass, and someone said to me, 'Let them help themselves.' This is a man who came up from zilch, nothing, and is now high, high up. It's kind of like Kirk Douglas in his living room saying that he is glad he was poor at one time. I felt like saying, 'Wait a minute. Didn't something get lost? How about reaching back now? You climbed in the boat, how about pulling someone else out?'"[15]

Sensing that their members *could* be doing a lot more, clergy are experimenting with ways of trying to increase their parishioners' motivation to help the poor. Yet when we look at what the churches are actually doing and what the clergy think should be done, we find that the very mechanisms that are being used have mixed consequences. They work but have built-in limitations.

Many clergy believe their members are eager to assist the needy but hold back simply because they are not presented with opportunities to do so. Their solution to the problem of motivation is thus to start more programs. One pastor, for instance, remarked that the greatest challenge he faces in ministering to the poor is "identifying specific needs where people can help and don't feel like they're just throwing money down a rat hole or throwing their energies away." Another pastor suggested that the way to proceed was to start one program, get people excited by it, then use that energy to launch another program, and so on.

Programs are attractive in contemporary church settings because church growth studies and surveys of members' opinions indicate that people like this approach.

They attend—or at least they attend this church instead of that one—because of the youth group or because the church has an active program for helping the homeless. Clergy who think of themselves more as executives or administrators than as teachers or public speakers also favor programs. Launching new programs lets them use their organizational talents rather than having to motivate people in other ways. "It's not going to happen as a result of anything I say," said one pastor about getting people more involved, "it's going to happen as a result of the momentum from our programs."

But starting more programs is self-limiting for at least three reasons. First, it generally takes staff time, volunteer time, and money to run these programs, and with tight resources churches are finding it impossible simply to start new programs in hopes of enlisting larger donations of time and money. Second, churches that start new programs often discover that they are simply duplicating the programs already in place at other churches or through secular nonprofit associations; more programs may thus compete with each other for smaller pieces of the overall share of volunteer time and money available in any given community. And third, new programs may enlist the help of a few new volunteers, but the assumption that people have free time that they don't know what to do with is mistaken. Indeed, most programs of social ministry look like pyramids, with a few congregants providing most of the volunteer work and most of the rest doing little or nothing.

The problem with trying to motivate people to help the poor simply by asking them to become involved in programs is evident in studies of volunteers. In one national study, active church members were asked about various reasons for giving and volunteering. Then these people were asked if they had actually done anything in the past year to help the homeless. People who said they gave or volunteered because someone asked them to or because they had free time were no more likely to have helped the homeless than people who said these reasons were unimportant. In contrast, people who gave intrinsic reasons for volunteering—such as recognizing the importance of helping others or feeling compassion—were significantly more likely to have helped the homeless than people who did not give these reasons.[16]

Starting more programs, I should note, is also something that many pastors are not eager to do. They recognize some of the limitations I have just mentioned. They also worry about generating complaints from parishioners who already feel guilty for not doing more. The priest who said it was okay to count sending one's children to Catholic school as part of giving to the poor, for instance, said his parish's program for assisting the poor—consisting mainly of collecting food baskets a couple of times a year—works pretty well. The reason he thinks so is that nobody complains. He said he want to avoid a "backlash" where people start asking, "Why are we supporting that?" God looks at the whole world, he explained, so anything that is positive, no matter how small, is okay.

The stress on programs is often shaped by another prevailing middle-class value: the idea that one's activities should be *results oriented*.[17] This value is reinforced by the churches' emphasis on responsibility. To be responsible at work means not only showing up but working to get the job done. And to be responsible with one's money means not only using it cautiously but also earning a high rate of interest on one's investments or gaining a lot of personal satisfaction from one's purchases. By the same token, helping the poor should be done in a way that assists them to climb out of poverty and to lead more productive lives.[18] This attitude can scarcely be faulted. But it does limit the kinds of programs middle-class churches are willing to support.

One such limitation is the tendency to focus on programs that have immediate payoffs. Rather than treating the sick person who is going to enter a long period of convalescence—and certainly not the sick person who is going to die anyway—assistance is devoted to the person who will make a dramatic recovery and be up and around in a few days. A vivid illustration of this emphasis is embedded in the remarks of a Presbyterian pastor who heads a large congregation of upper-middle-class parishioners. Asked what his church does to help the *poor*, he alluded in passing to some contributions to an inner-city ministry but then talked animatedly about 200 Asian immigrants whom the church was helping to learn English. It was not clear from his remarks whether these immigrants were especially poor. What he did emphasize—with some pride—was that most of the Asians had become "self-supporting."

Another way in which results-oriented programs shape the churches' definition of helping the poor is by focusing attention on the *particular results* achieved in isolated cases. This limitation is almost the mirror image of the one I just mentioned. That one encourages churches to run programs that help large numbers of people to be self-supporting, whereas this one encourages churches to take a blind view of how successful the larger program is as long as *one person* is dramatically helped. The stereotypical example would be the single convert a missionary brings home (or the story told about a single convert) after decades of toil by dozens of missionaries: The one success story proves that the entire enterprise was worthwhile.

In talking to clergy and parishioners alike, we found that it was quite common to focus on the single convert rather than paying attention to how effective or ineffective whole programs might be. "We have an indigent black man who lives in the vicinity, and we have a cadre of men who stop and see him on a regular basis," observed the pastor of an evangelical church when asked about his church's efforts to help the poor. "They transport him where he needs to go. They bring him to church when he is able to come to church, and we subsidize him monthly from the deacon's fund." He cited this as evidence that his church's efforts were "working beautifully." Another pastor talked about several specific individuals who had been helped by his church. When he paused to reflect on the larger issue of poverty, though, he said it would be nice if the churches could somehow work on long-term solutions, such as finding ways to redistribute food more effectively so that nobody went hungry.

It is true that people may work harder if they think they are moving mountains than if they feel their efforts are in vain. We found, for instance, that church people who have helped the homeless in the past year are somewhat more likely than those who have done nothing to believe that social problems such as poverty and homelessness can be completely solved by volunteers. Yet this attitude is widely shared even among people who are doing nothing to help the poor.[19] In talking with volunteers and clergy who had worked with the homeless over long periods, moreover, we found that most had experienced frustrations and knew that success stories were often quite rare.[20] Thus, focusing only on these instances of success in hope of motivating volunteers is likely to have mixed results.

Clergy are also fond of relating stories about the one or two people in their congregations who exemplify caring for the poor. At a church in Michigan, the pastor told a moving story, for instance, about a man in his congregation who is confined to a wheelchair but "goes down into the inner city and finds the vagrants under bridges, in back of stores, in the garbage, and he sits with them and talks about Christ to them. And he says, 'They can't beat me up because I'm in a wheelchair, they don't want to hurt me.'" As touching as such cases are, they may deflect attention from how well the church as a whole is ministering to the poor.

Everyone relies on *frames* for thinking and talking. We block out certain thoughts in order to have others (enjoying our birthday cake by not thinking about our upcoming surgery). The way to avoid thinking only in certain frames is to put ourselves in circumstances that force us to think in others. Middle-class congregants can be highly insular, thinking about the inner-city mission once a year when the director comes and tells a heart-warming story about an individual who was helped. Keeping the larger picture in mind is important as well. "We've fed a lot of people and given a lot of clothing," observed the pastor of a Baptist church. "We've been successful in what we've done. But we're a long ways from stamping out the problem of hunger in our city or in our state. So when you judge it against that, we haven't done very well at all." Recognizing the larger problems encourages him to do more. Yet even this frame—defining giving in terms of solving a problem—is limited.[21]

It is understandable, of course, for churches to want results. Having a choice between a program that produced results and one that didn't, the former would be the obvious favorite. Yet results are not entirely what giving is about. "I don't want to measure things that way," one pastor responded when he was asked how well his various programs for helping the poor worked. "The main thing," he cautioned, "is to be faithful."

The churches' doctrine of love stresses caring for people *unconditionally*, not in order to change them. If the motivation for helping the poor is to turn them into productive middle-class Christians, then efforts to assist the poor are likely to flag if these results are not achieved. "It's all just a one-way street. We help them and never get anything back. They promise to repay us, but they never do." These were the complaints, one pastor told us, that he heard repeatedly from his members. Even the members who were directly involved in helping poor people in his community began to lose their motivation. "They were feeling burned," he said.

This pastor took action to correct the situation. "I talked with some of the elders in the church about it," he reported. "And we all have the same feeling. We decided we would rather be guilty of being too naive about helping people than to not help them at all." Speaking about his own views, he added, "I think it's wrong to be stingy and not help somebody that God wants to help." Research among church members supports this orientation. Those who believe simply that it is a *moral duty* to help people in need are nearly three times more likely to be involved in helping the poor than those who do not believe so.[22]

In addition to starting new programs, many clergy believe that middle-class parishioners can be motivated to pay more attention to the needs of others only by becoming *better Christians*. This view emphasizes that the underlying problem is spiritual rather than purely financial or programmatic, and that the church's primary task is to assist people in developing their spirituality. As people become more Christlike, they will thus try to emulate Christ by helping the needy.

This view generally includes some recognition of the fact that American culture at the end of the twentieth century is riddled with selfishness and with the pursuit of material interests. It does not assume that people are simply eager to help others and would do so if they could only find an appropriate way. It highlights the potential opposition of the spiritual to the material. Yet this view is also self-limiting.

Focusing on spirituality can be a way of avoiding responsibility for those parts of human behavior that are thereby assumed to be nonspiritual and therefore secondary. This problem is evident in the fact that church members who emphasize spirituality are no more likely to have helped the poor than those who consider spirituality less important.[23] It is also evident in the ways in which some clergy talk about spirituality. Listen to how one pastor explained why his church was not doing more to help the poor. "Our emphasis is spiritual, not social. Our number one priority in this church is to reach people for Christ, to make sure that they understand the claims of Christ, to give them an opportunity to enter into a relationship with Christ. Now see, we believe that by doing that that's going to affect every other aspect of their life. And so we approach it from that direction." His concern was with personal salvation. He believed that having a relationship with Christ had implications for "every other aspect" of life. He had not thought much, however, about the connections between spirituality and work or money. Thus, when asked specifically how he might be able to motivate his congregation to become more involved in helping the poor, he thought for a long time and said, "I don't know."[24]

The pastor of an Assemblies of God church in Oregon said he and his congregation had also focused on spirituality at the expense of social ministries but were beginning to think differently about the two. "We had a dichotomy of our spiritual mission and our social mission," he said. "We were interested in the eternal welfare of people instead of the reality of life." That view frustrated his church's efforts to be of genuine assistance to the poor. His present view is different: "I don't think it's an either/or; I think it's both."

At a large Pentecostal church in Atlanta, the head pastor provided one of the clearest reasons for linking the spiritual and the social as closely as possible. "We believe, number one, that the gospel has to do with a personal commitment to salvation," he asserted. "We don't back away from that. We believe there's a personal experience that one has. But then if that isn't turned into social action, you've really not had a meaningful experience, because the first thing you do is you look out beyond yourself and say, 'Now, what can I do?'"

If one tendency in the churches is, as it were, to emphasize spirituality too much, the opposite tendency is also evident. Asked how they would motivate people to become more involved in helping the poor, some pastors feel compelled primarily to combat the assumptions of middle-class culture on its own terms. That is, they talk about the real reasons why people are poor and the *social* benefits to be derived from helping the poor. For example, stating that the arguments he would make are "classic," the pastor at a suburban Methodist church that was relatively uninvolved in efforts to help the poor said he would try to show "that there are reasons why people are poor—root causes that need to be understood—and that it's not laziness necessarily." He said he would also want to show that "in helping the poor we are in fact helping the society. That a certain amount of money invested here will help us all down the road."

In cases like this, the prevailing frame for talking about poverty is one that may have wide appeal outside the churches—at least if middle-class prejudices toward the poor can be overcome. The churches can thus be part of the larger public discourse about how to alleviate poverty. Yet those who are convinced by this language may find no special reason in it to contribute through the churches. They could just as well help the poor by volunteering directly at the homeless shelter rather than making an interim stop at the church. Moreover, the fact that there may be some truth to these stereotypes—for example, that people are partly responsible for their own problems—means that rebutting them may have only modest consequences for actually getting church members involved in helping the poor.[25]

The other way in which clergy are trying to motivate church members to be more concerned about the poor is by emphasizing what the caregivers will *receive* from their efforts. This emphasis is similar to the arguments we considered in the last chapter about the joy of giving. It too is rooted in an inability to find other language within the traditions of the church itself for talking about the relationship between spirituality and broader economic concerns. The pastor I just quoted, for example, responded to additional probing by discussing the pros and cons of various types of involvement. He said it would be a bad idea to ask people to give money to soup kitchens or homeless shelters because they would do so "out of a sense of duty." He said it would be better to ask people to help paint a window or repair someone's roof. That way, "they would get something out of it."

Helping the poor for purely selfish reasons may not be ineffective. Most volunteers do experience good feelings from their efforts. And therapeutic language has become so common in our culture that pastors resort to it often in trying to exhort parishioners to lead godly lives.[26] What better way, then, to help people? Doing good for others enhances our self-esteem, which frees us to be of service. The logic is simple, yet there is little evidence to support it. Except for extreme cases of personal malfunction, people with lower levels of self-esteem are just as likely to help the needy as people with higher levels of self-esteem.[27] And, as a motivator for helping, good feelings rank relatively low.[28]

Selfish reasons are also self-limiting. They fail to emphasize the importance of giving as a value in itself. They fail to consider that middle-class people have many other ways of "getting something" for themselves—whether it be shopping or helping their own families. These arguments also fail to consider the genuine costs involved in helping others. People who are already strapped for time and experiencing too much stress are not likely to relish the thought of spending their one free evening repairing someone else's roof.[29]

## CHARITY BEGINS AT HOME

We come, then, to the ironic possibility that the best way for the churches to stimulate greater efforts on behalf of the poor is to do a better job of ministering to their own middle-class parishioners. That is, church members' own needs must be taken into account, especially as they are being asked to serve others. Appeals for volunteer time must take into account the time pressures that people already experience in attempting to balance work and family commitments. And programs devoted to helping the poor must be connected to the ways in which middle-class people understand their own money and their own lifestyles.

I do not suggest that all the needs of middle-class churchgoers must be met before they can help others. But people who are overwhelmed with the pressures and anxieties of their jobs, who are neck-deep in credit-card debt, or who scarcely have time to run their own children to the doctor are unlikely candidates to serve others. In fact, active church members who work long hours, are dissatisfied with their work, and value making a lot of money are significantly less likely to be involved in service activities such as helping the poor, the sick, or the elderly than members who work fewer hours, are happy with their jobs, and place less emphasis on money.[30] Churches that provide support groups, pastoral counseling, and lessons in setting priorities for their own members are making a start toward freeing people to assist the wider community.[31]

Giving may be more blessed than receiving, but most people learn the joy of giving by first receiving. As children, we are largely the recipients of love, learning that it feels good to have people care for us. We do not automatically make the connection between that form of selfish love and extending our own concern to others. Such learning is usefully modeled by seeing people in our churches, schools, and neighborhoods caring for each other and by being given opportunities to help others in small ways. But the incentive to help others is generally heightened by the fact that we already know what it is like to experience love. Like Conley Wellman, we are motivated to "give back" because of what we have already received.

To say that charity begins at home can mean that it ends there as well. But the clergy we spoke to who had thought most deeply about their ministries to the poor insisted that charity at home necessitates taking a new look at standard middle-class lifestyles and expectations. "When you've got millionaires, and fancy homes, and people traveling right in the same vicinity of folk who don't even have a house to live in—sooner or later you're headed for a major conflict between the haves and the have-nots," argued one pastor. "We need to rethink our priorities and start to focus more on human worth and equal opportunities." Other pastors talked about the need to reexamine how much we eat and how we spend our money as part of our ministry to the poor.

Are their arguments valid? Members' views would suggest so. In my survey, church members who attended services regularly were substantially more likely to have thought a great deal about their responsibility to the poor if they had also thought more about the relationship between faith, work, and money in their own life. Those who had been taught that wanting a lot of money was wrong were also more likely to have thought a lot about their responsibility to the poor. And those who had reflected on this reponsibility were, in turn, more likely to consider it morally wrong to have a lot of nice things when others are in need and to agree that God cares how they use their money.[32] Other research shows that church members who believe in giving back to their communities and who think people with resources have a special obligation to help those lacking resources are particularly likely to become directly involved in helping the needy.[33]

If these broader perceptions of the relationships between faith and one's own financial circumstances influence how much people think about their responsibility to the poor, the latter—concern for the poor—also redounds to the financial health of the church. At least, those who are more concerned about the poor are more generous in their financial support of the church. For instance, among church members who attend services weekly, those who have thought a great deal about their responsibility to the poor in the past year gave an average of 3.3 percent of their income to religious organizations, compared to an average of 2.3 percent among those who have thought about this responsibility a fair amount or a little, and only 2.0 percent among those who have thought about it hardly at all. Actual involvement in helping the poor is associated similarly with financial giving: Among those who have done volunteer work in the past year to help the poor and the needy, the average contribution to religious organizations amounted to 3.4 percent of income, compared with only 2.3 percent among nonvolunteers.

The possibility that greater interest on the part of churches in helping the poor would stimulate financial giving is also suggested by the fact that 65 percent of church members say they would give more generously if the church were doing more to help the needy. Some confirmation for this possibility is suggested by the fact that active church members who think the churches are *not* doing enough to help the needy are already contributing at somewhat higher levels than those who are complacent about what the churches are doing. And those who think the churches should be doing more, rather than less, to provide housing and job training for the poor are also already giving at higher levels. We cannot, of course, sort out exactly what causes what with data like these, but it does appear that more generous financial support of the church and wanting the churches to do more for the poor go hand in hand.[34]

Charity begins at home in another sense too. The church that best demonstrates caring is one that draws its boundaries loosely. If only white-collar professionals feel comfortable attending, their caring—even at its best—is likely to focus on a narrow range of concerns. They can simply block out the needs of others, a problem that many pastors find difficult to overcome. Talking about these frustrations, a pastor in Texas put it well when he observed, "The biggest frustration is just communicating to our people that there are all kinds of people out there who are going hungry, who don't have clothes to wear, and who don't have places to live." His members, he said, "go to work, drive the same road every day, come to church, go out to eat, and go to the mall. They don't see the need. 'Out of sight, out of mind.' You need something there to keep that in the forefront all the time."

If the church opens its doors to a more diverse group of people, some of the concerns of middle-class life begin to pale in comparison with others. The pastor of a church in Chicago that tried hard to diversify its membership admitted it was not always easy. "Churches, by their very nature," he said, "find their economic median and hang on to it." But the advantages of remaining open and of challenging the unstated norms that define acceptability in terms of appearances, manners, and economics, he said, were considerable. "When the CEO of a large company sits in the same pew as a guy who is homeless, there's something redemptive going on."

And redemption can occur even more effectively if the CEO is not simply sitting beside the homeless person but spending time helping that person. "The problem in my congregation," complained one pastor, "is that they think *they* are the poor." He thought the best way to disabuse people of that idea was to expose them to the truly poor. If helping the poor has a therapeutic effect, that is, making middle-class people realize that their own concerns about money are not so great after all, then perhaps this result too can be a way of ministering to the middle class. Indeed, the emphasis then shifts from simply helping the poor to learning from them as well—from giving in a patronizing way to discovering something fundamental about the common ground of all humanity.[35] A Baptist pastor said it best: "Finding Christ in the broken places, the marginalized places, is part of working out our *own* salvation."

# eleven

# WORKING FOR SOCIAL JUSTICE

*The thing about social justice, it seems to me, is that we have a lot more rhetoric than anything else. I could mouth on about social justice and all, but when you ask me what are we doing, I have to examine my heart and say probably not much.*
**Assemblies of God pastor, Oregon**

I have argued that the churches are experiencing difficulties keeping themselves solvent and helping the needy because they fail to communicate clearly the implications of faith for the ways in which their members work, value money, spend their money, and think about material possessions. One important way in which the churches might focus on these implications is speaking out more forthrightly about social justice. In the past, religious leaders have often found precedents within their own traditions and in the Bible itself for doing this. They preached critically against social practices that exploited the poor, gave unfair advantages to the rich, and discriminated against oppressed and disadvantaged minority groups. The churches were in the forefront of efforts to protect the rights of all citizens, ensure equality of opportunity, and reduce the systemic evils associated with huge disparities of wealth and power.

Virtually all clergy, as we have seen, are committed to doing something to help the poor. Many of them also recognize that helping the poor requires working to change social structures that contribute to the problem in the first place—putting up a fence at the top of the cliff to keep people from falling over rather than standing at the bottom with bandages, as one pastor put it. Such clergy regard social justice as a legitimate part of their ministry. Yet, in comparison with their role in speaking on behalf of social justice throughout most of our nation's history, the churches seem to have fallen silent on this topic. Compared with their involvement in concerns about civil rights, discrimination, poverty, and social welfare during the 1960s and 1970s, the churches of the 1980s and 1990s seem to have lost interest in these issues or have become ineffective in addressing them.[1]

Why? To be sure, working for social justice has never been easy. Many people outside the churches have thrown up their hands as well, asking whether it doesn't make more sense to tend one's own garden than try to understand the tangled thickets of the welfare state. Within the churches, social justice issues often generated more controversy than anything else. Parishioners objected when they saw clergy on picket lines and asked if this kind of activism was what the churches should really be doing.[2] One reason why the churches have fallen silent, therefore, may be that they have grown weary. People remember that social activism didn't work or stirred up trouble, so they oppose it.

But the problem cannot be understood simply in terms of members' resistance. Many church members supported the clergy's efforts to work for social justice during the 1960s and 1970s and stayed active in the churches because it was a way of contributing positively to the common good. Many church members still say they are interested in social justice.[3] Activating them, however, has proven more difficult. Even those who are most directly involved in helping the sick or the poor say they have little understanding of what it might mean to work for social justice.[4]

Clergy chalk up the problem to parishioners' indifference. Most people, a number of clergy point out, live in narrow worlds defined by their own interests and needs. If they have any time left over, they spend it "loving their neighbors," as one pastor remarked, and feel they have done their duty. An hour at the soup kitchen absolves them of the responsibility to think about larger questions of inequality and injustice.

This sort of indifference may be especially prominent among the white middle class. Black, Asian, and Hispanic pastors told us their members were sensitized to problems of injustice from personal experiences with discrimination. At San Xavier's, for instance, Father Martinez said that many of his parishioners have come recently from Central America and know firsthand about human rights violations and injustice. White Anglos in working-class settings talked about personal awareness of inequality and exploitation as well. Some of the pastors we spoke to who had grown up poor were also keenly aware of the importance of social justice because of their own experiences. A Nazarene pastor in Kansas, for example, said he had seen his factory-worker parents having to pay too much for things because they didn't have the opportunity to make good investments or learn about tax loopholes. He knew what it was like to be discriminated against in subtle ways by the other children at school, his teachers, and even the clergy because he didn't dress quite right; hadn't learned to play tennis and golf; and hadn't been taught to hold his head high, look people in the eye, smile condescendingly, and pretend to be a leader.

Among those who have known no other existence than middle-class life, it is much harder to understand at a deep personal level why social justice is an important issue. Several of the pastors we talked to admitted that they had not appreciated its importance until they began spending time among the poor or had become acquainted with the homeless, immigrants, or minority people who were victims of discrimination. These pastors admitted it was easy for middle-class church members to be indifferent. One pastor put it this way: "If you polled them and asked if they thought there should be social justice, they would say, 'By all means.' If you asked them, 'What does that mean to you?' they would say, 'Nothing.'"[5]

In addition to the broader disillusionment that many people feel about social reform, then, the churches may also be suffering from members' indifference. Longer tenure in the middle class means less interest in the plight of others.[6] And having to struggle harder to maintain their place in the middle class may mean less time and energy to devote to larger issues.

Still, the trouble—as with the other topics we have considered—is that clergy themselves are frequently unable to provide strong and effective leadership in working for social justice. They too may be preoccupied with other things. More importantly, however, their ways of thinking and talking about social justice are part of the problem. Many say explicitly that they are uninterested in such matters or regard them as low-priority issues. Others consider social justice important but understand it in ways that divert energy from doing anything particular about it. The few who have thought longest and hardest about it are often frustrated to the point that they feel like voices crying in the wilderness.[7]

## THE VOICE OF OPPOSITION

At Cornerstone Bible Church, Pastor Higgins said he would never use the term *social justice* or give much emphasis to working for social justice. He typifies the opinion of a large minority of the clergy. They oppose the church becoming involved in issues of social justice for three reasons: These issues fall within a category that they consider political, they are not good investments of energy, and the churches have a better way of dealing with them anyway. Injustices do exist, and they are evil. And churches should tend to the immediate needs of those who suffer. But the prevailing reasons for not championing social justice itself are clear.

The first reason for opposing efforts to promote social justice is that they are categorized as political activities.[8] Pastor Higgins, for instance, said that social justice is "a political agenda-type thing." And that is a problem, he explained, because there is a difference between the "social agenda," as he called it, and "a biblical agenda." At a Lutheran church in Oregon, the pastor made a similar observation. When asked why his congregation was not involved in social justice activity, he explained, "It has to do with the political dimensions of justice. I think groups that talk about social justice have a stronger political agenda than many of our people want to get involved with."

Categorizing social justice as a political activity means that it is more appropriately dealt with by other organizations than the church. Activities concerned with social justice do, of course, have to do with politics insofar as they focus on legislation to ensure equal rights, for example, or the use of government initiatives to pay for welfare programs or to encourage employers to treat employees more fairly. Churches that work for social justice often find their members signing petitions or sending representatives to town meetings or participating in public hearings. But pastors who oppose social justice because it is political do so because politics itself has worrisome connotations.[9] It connotes conflict, self-interest, the use of force, and an obsession with particular issues, all of which may seem to run against the grain of churchly behavior. A woman who pastors an independent church in Kansas put it this way: "You get into forceful things, forceful stands, making issues out of things. I believe we don't have to make issues out of things. We just teach truth and change people's lives that way."[10]

The second reason for opposing efforts to promote social justice is that such efforts are ineffective. Pastor Higgins said he would never lead his congregation to focus on social justice because "the true solution to our social ills is *not* focusing on temporal needs." In his opinion, poor people who are fed will still experience problems the next day because they have not met their "real need" for a relationship with God. "I know Christ," he said, "and I know these things will all be resolved. The scripture isn't lying to us. God will deal with it. He's going to make it all right."

The woman in Kansas also thinks working for social justice is likely to be ineffective. Her church sends individual members to a nearby housing project to help families there and to invite them to church. She doesn't think there is any way to make life better for everyone in the project or to reduce the likelihood of their being there in the first place. "If we can get four or five individuals who will respond," she said, "we're glad about it."

This emphasis on helping a few individuals rather than working to change larger social patterns is quite common[11] and has often been described by experts on the subject as a reflection of the underlying individualism of American culture.[12] It is, and yet not quite in the way we might think. The pastor in Kansas provides some insight into the underlying logic. She thinks that social reforms will be ineffective because many poor people are lazy and just prefer not to take responsibility for themselves. According to social critics, this concept is one of the ways in which American individualism encourages us to blame the victims for their own problems. If we think they are at fault, we excuse ourselves from having to do anything to help them.

But this pastor *is* directly involved in trying to help the poor. How does she reconcile these efforts with her view that the poor are just taking advantage of those who try to help them? She said there is a Christian or biblical view of the poor that is consistent with both viewing the poor as part of the problem and trying to help them. "In the Bible," she explained, "it just refers to the poor. It doesn't say the poor who are trying. It doesn't say the poor who are not taking advantage of you. It just says the poor. And if that's who we are to give to, then we're just to give to the poor. We're not to put restrictions on it, because God doesn't. And the Bible says, 'It's the goodness of God that brings man to repentance.' And sometimes just being good to them is something that God uses in their life in the long run."[13]

What we might call *Christian individualism*, therefore, differs from secular individualism because the biblical mandate is to help the poor even if they don't work hard. But Christian individualism seems, in this example at least, to encourage charity to individuals rather than large-scale social reforms.[14] It does not exactly say that helping the poor should exclude social reforms, but it does imply that token efforts are sufficient. They fulfill the Christian's responsibility to do something. And with the personal touch present, the chance also exists to talk about one's faith.

The other reason for turning away from social justice is because the churches have a better solution. Pastor Higgins explained, "I'm not worried about justice, not in my life, because I believe in the grace of God and I've accepted His gift of grace." God's grace allows Pastor Higgins to feel that he is "just as good as anyone else" even though others have more money or power. So he is not especially concerned about his rights and whether or not he is being treated equally. He applies the same logic to other people. They should not worry, either, because God promises to take care of them if they are believers. Quoting one of the Psalms, he stated that "the children of God that follow after his ways and do what he wants us to do" will have their "physical and material" needs met. He added, "In Matthew 6:33 it says, 'Seek ye first the kingdom of God and his righteousness and all these things shall be added unto you.'" He was referring to food and clothing and shelter will be added unto you then. If we go after food, clothing, and shelter, that's all we'll get, but if we go after God's righteousness, he'll give us all the blessings that come with that on that side plus the food, and the shelter, and the clothing."

The preferred option for the churches is to focus first on spiritual needs on the assumption that other things, such as physical needs, will be taken care of in due course. Pastor Higgins said he believes that the "real need" is people's relationship with God, not their material need. "It's not that we don't want to meet that need. The Bible tells us that we should meet the need, but that's still not the priority. It's like the old saying, 'You give a man a fish and he eats for a day; you teach him to fish and he eats for a lifetime.' The same principle applies to the spiritual walk, spiritual relationship to God, and life in general." If the church only focuses on people's physical needs, he said, it will have accomplished nothing other than extending "their misery another day or another week."

Because the spiritual solution is long term—the kingdom of God being slow in arriving, either apocalyptically or through individual conversions—the churches must do something to alleviate suffering in the short term. They must look out for church members who are in need, help those who come looking for assistance, and perhaps run some small programs in the community. In providing such aid, church members must be mindful of other opportunities created by these programs, especially opportunities to make converts.

Pastor Higgins said there is a poor community just down the road from his church. "It's pretty hard to drive by and not see what the problems are there," he admitted. "They are very poor and have physical and material needs that should be met." He said, as we saw in chapter 10, that he would like to have the resources to do more for these people. He told a story about visiting a large, nationally known megachurch near Chicago and seeing people bringing so many bags of food and old clothing that the church hardly had room for it. He envies churches like that. All he can do is hand out a few meals and encourage his members to go down the street and help the poor.

The separation between the so-called temporal and spiritual realms is key to understanding what kind of emphasis this orientation actually places on helping the poor. Pastor Higgins believes it is important to be genuinely concerned about the temporal needs of the poor and to be sincere in one's efforts to meet these needs. Yet, because he believes the spiritual realm is different from—and superior to—the temporal realm, he also worries about placing too much emphasis on meeting these needs. "The real goal in giving food to these people is to give us the opportunity..." He trailed off, but it is clear from the context that he meant the opportunity to address people's need for a relationship with God. "We don't force ourselves on anybody," he said. "If they don't want to hear what we have to say, that's okay. We give people all the room and the space in the world they need. We want to honestly, genuinely be concerned about their welfare. They have what we call felt needs. Their felt need is that they need food. Now, that's not a real need. We know that, but we call it a felt need because they feel it. Their real need is a relationship to God, because if they have a right relationship with God, God's going to take care of them."

It would be mistaken to conclude that Pastor Higgins is a hardhearted Christian who cares only about people's souls. As he tries to articulate the connection between real needs and felt needs, though, he clearly runs into difficulty. He has the soul in one category and the body in another. Thus, the obvious solution is to build a bridge between the two, showing his followers how they can minister better to people's souls by providing for their physical needs, or teaching converts more clearly how having a relationship with God will take care of their hunger. But his language is weak at this critical juncture. When asked specifically how he bridges the gap between giving people food and giving them a real relationship with God, he admitted, "I don't know that we do the bridging." He added, "I don't stress that. We don't even address it. If it happens, that's great, but if it doesn't, that doesn't matter either."

The solution to the problem created by separating the spiritual from the temporal is to overcome the distinction itself. As Pastor Higgins continued to struggle to find the right words, he hit on this solution himself. Rather than focusing on the recipient and trying to separate physical needs from spiritual needs, the giver focuses inward and attempts to express unconditional love. Pastor Higgins put it this way: "If we really are genuinely concerned about these people, then we are not going to go in with an ulterior motive. We don't want it to come across as having an ulterior motive. If we honestly do care about them, we'll give them the food whether they agree or think the way we think or not. That's unconditional love. Unconditional love says I don't care what you believe or what you think about me or whether you believe the same things about God that I believe; that doesn't matter, I'm still going to do what's right to you and for you. That's unconditional, but if we can encourage them our way, that's great. That's just an added benefit."

In a sense, though, the argument that church members should love others unconditionally comes around full circle to the problems I have already mentioned. Love unconditionally, yes. But how? Do what? Pastor Higgins finds himself admitting that working for social reform might be one way to express love. But he says there are social agencies for such work. He is not opposed to their efforts. He just isn't interested in supporting them because their work still seems to him to focus only on physical needs. The church is a better agency because it understands real needs and has a concept of unconditional love. Yet, in reality, this idea means one-on-one contact with the poor because in that way, the helper can be motivated by "genuine concern" and the recipient can be encouraged to believe "our way."

## FAINTHEARTED SUPPORT

Rather than opposing efforts to promote social justice, a more common orientation among clergy is to support the idea but to define it in such a way that it fits easily into the normal programs and activities of the church.[15] Members can sign a petition once in a while or listen to a sermon about individual rights but do not have to rethink their values or reevaluate their lifestyle. At Saint Andrew's Episcopal Church, Rector Morgan said he likes the term *social justice* and thinks it is important for the church to talk about it. Asked why, he explained, "I feel strongly that our biblical faith, both from the Judaic side and the Christian side, demands that we act with justice, which translates into love and care for those who are disenfranchised. Not judgment. We're not called to judge the poor. We're called to love them and care for them in the system."

The choice of words here is interesting because they reflect the ambiguities that many pastors feel in talking about social justice. On the one hand, words such as *disenfranchised* and *system* suggest that social justice concerns social institutions, such as law, government, or the economy. On the other hand, a phrase such as *love and care* is likely to connote direct efforts to meet the needs of individuals. A priest in Oregon expressed similar ambiguity. He defined social justice in terms of rights ("to life, liberty, and the pursuit of happiness") and said he favors the church's emphasis on institutions, legal action, workers' movements, and other organized efforts to bring about social justice. He fears, however, that most of the people in his parish think of social justice only as "trying to help people who are down and out." As he talked, it became clearer why this attitude might exist. He said he tries to preach about social justice, hoping to get across the "principle," but he "leaves the application to them" to figure out. He also tries not to offend. For instance, he thinks there is too much greed and materialism in our society and argues that a strong emphasis on social justice would run against the interests of business. But for a prayer he was preparing for the city council the day we spoke to him, he said he was going to focus on "the rights and dignity of the individual." He explained, "I'm wording it in such a way that I'm not going to offend them in any way."

Inadvertently, clergy who believe it is important for the churches to work on behalf of social justice also undercut this concern by bringing in some of the assumptions about giving to the poor that we considered in chapter 10. One is that programs must produce tangible effects to be worthwhile. The other is that effects are more tangible if they touch the emotions by affecting individual lives. Rector Morgan illustrated how both of these assumptions might lead one of his listeners to conclude that, well, social justice may be important, but it sure isn't interesting enough to get my time. He observed straightforwardly that working for social justice is not emotionally appealing. "What makes sense is that the rich get richer and the poor get poorer, that the powerful have more power, and that's an emotional thing. People who grab for power feel more sense out of getting more and more power. They don't feel it's great to give away their power." So we have to go against our emotions to be interested in social justice.

We also have to face the fact that social justice is hard to accomplish. Rector Morgan said, "I always remember the War on Poverty. Lyndon Johnson. We were going to stamp out poverty in the United States. There not only is poverty now, it's far more widespread today than it was in the 60s. So a person is tempted to say, 'Oh, forget it. We're losing ground. Let's just build a big wall around our place, huge bars on the windows, and forget it.' Some days it's discouraging and I feel it's a losing battle. I see abused kids and I think, oh, this is awful. People living in cars. We're not gaining ground."

These remarks are intended to encourage people to work for social justice because of "the biblical mandate to do it" rather than doing such work because it feels good or produces results. Yet the emphasis is so much on the barriers one faces in working for social justice that the listener is likely to focus on other ways of caring for the poor. Indeed, Rector Morgan said his congregation probably thinks of social justice in that way. "I think at this point it's like a 'we're caring for the poor,' charitable thing. I don't think it's moved to the point of saying we ought to go and confront the daylights out of our government. I think we need to move to that point. We need to go to our state governments and our national government." Noting his church's concern with the homeless, he added, "We're so busy rearranging the deck chairs on the Titanic that we haven't gone upstream to see who's throwing these people in!"

Finding ways to motivate people to do *something* without encouraging them to be content doing only a little is perhaps the hardest task for churches that have moderate levels of interest in social justice. Early in the twentieth century, churches became actively involved in social reform, buttressed by the conviction that the world would gradually get better and better if only people of goodwill tried hard. This assumption is still evident in some churches. For instance, Rector Morgan said that one must take the "long perspective" in order to see that small acts of kindness here and there add up. "I don't think the next twenty years will be particularly different than the past, but over a number of years more and more women will get elected to Congress, more and more compassionate people will be part of the government, I believe. They will have come from situations, they will have seen their children not going from the postwar wealth to suburbs in California to great and better jobs. They'll have seen more and more of their children and grandchildren lost in drugs; lost in idle, meaningless lives; lost in unemployment, broken marriages, poor health care. I think they will then come back to work to change it. And we, like Europeans, after we've had another fifty or 100 years of culture under us will respond more clearly."

But if this kind of social progressivism is needed to buttress involvement in social justice efforts, one of the reasons these efforts are often halfhearted is that progressivist assumptions are hard to sustain. Few clergy, in fact, talk as Rector Morgan does about the U.S. populace becoming more compassionate "like Europeans." Said one, "I doubt that we are evolving into a better and better community." His church had no programs in the area of social justice. He thought it should be doing something, just to combat evil. But he could not bring himself to focus on social justice in hopes that the world would become a better place.

More common than social progressivism is the view that any sense of hope for the future must be rooted in Christian theology itself. Clergy talk about hope as the central message of their traditions. But they also find it hard to describe this hope in a way that is more than a psychological crutch. They often do not want to entertain ideas of miraculous intervention in social affairs. So they encourage believers to think positively, even if they aren't accomplishing much.

Clergy have also adopted some of the "good-society" rhetoric that has long been part of the American democratic tradition and that has reemerged in recent years, especially in the communitarian movement.[16] While denying the idea that society can become progressively better, good-society proponents argue that vigilance is needed just to maintain the status quo. They point to apathy, crime, and other social ills as evidence that people must work harder for the common good. Included in this work must be activities promoting greater equality and fairness. "When there are major problems within a society, then eventually it destroys that society," observed an African American pastor. "So to work for social justice, to work for that which is right for everybody, improves the quality of life in that society. And so I think it's necessary to have social justice in order to have a good society." In this view, the churches can work for good, just as individuals within the church can. Yet some of the clergy we talked to found that this rhetoric did little to motivate their members. People were too selfish, or they thought it was best to let professionals and other specially trained persons do the work to combat social ills.

Still another reason why many churches pay lip service to social justice but do relatively little to promote it is that, unlike the opponents of church involvement in social justice, their leaders have few reasons to offer for the churches being *different* from other organizations. The logic here is that churches are simply doing their small part, throwing pebbles into the stream of history. They have no special insight, no corner on the concept of social justice. When asked what the churches have that other agencies don't, for example, Rector Morgan said the churches are more efficient. What he meant is that churches do not have to pay taxes; can rely on the volunteer efforts of dedicated members; and call on people who may not lie, cheat, or steal from the public. That, of course, may be a weak argument, especially for the unchurched or marginal members who know very well that churches are subject to corruption just like other organizations.

Underlying this problem—not being able to identify strong reasons why the church should be involved in social justice—is the more general problem of the absence of distinct theological arguments about the special connections between biblical faith and social justice. A priest in California expressed a common view of social justice, for instance, when he defined it as "the rights that people have, natural rights, human rights. The right to work, the right to have a job, the right to a decent existence, the right not to be enslaved in any way." These were words included in his tradition but not characteristic of it. Thus, when he was asked what people in his parish did on behalf of social justice, he said, "Nothing." Asked why not, he responded, "People just cannot be involved in all sorts of different things. After all, you have to give people time to work and be involved in the human side of life, too."

## VOICES CRYING IN THE WILDERNESS

A few churches specialize so actively in working for social justice that this work becomes their main reason for existence. Their pastors have thought long and hard about social justice, can speak eloquently about what it means and why the churches should be involved, and are at the forefront of programs within the churches and in the wider community to promote social justice. These clergy are not halfhearted in their commitment, and they do not try to make social justice palatable by turning it into something else.

But they do valorize social justice. They make it a kind of heroic activity that ordinary mortals can scarcely understand or appreciate. Their churches are dedicated almost entirely to activities focusing on political advocacy and achieving social reform. Working for social justice becomes the root principle of living spiritually and virtuously. Only the most dedicated need apply.

"To be faithful to the Bible, we *have* to talk about social justice," argued the pastor of an American Baptist congregation that has become known in its community as a social activist church. "It's a dominant theme throughout the Old and New Testaments." He feels that God has a grand design or "vision" for the world that involves "justice and peace and wholeness." Thus, "for the church to say that they're not concerned about social justice would be to say that we don't really care about what God is up to."

To put this understanding of social justice into practice, his church is organized around ten central activities, all of which aim to promote justice in one way or another. These include ministries to and for the homeless (including political advocacy with the city), a program to help indigenous peoples market handmade products, a consciousness-raising program that takes delegations from the church to various Third World countries, a residence to house visiting leaders from Third World countries, a program focusing on environmental concerns, a peacemaking group, a task force to provide sanctuary and political asylum for refugees, a committee that specializes in advocacy on behalf of resistance groups in Central America, a support and advocacy group for people with AIDS, and a women's resource center.

People can attend a church like this and not be involved in social justice activities. But they probably would not feel comfortable. "I think concern for issues of peace and justice is pretty widely shared here," the pastor said. "You couldn't be very comfortable here if you weren't." The church has also gained a reputation in the wider community for specializing in peace and justice issues. Indeed, some of the other pastors we spoke to said it was hard for them to do very much because members interested in social justice left to go to this church.

Members not only become involved in social justice issues; they are also encouraged to make this involvement a life-encompassing commitment. Many of the members are engaged full time in religious work and are employed by religious organizations. Others also make heavy commitments to the church. One of the members we talked to, for instance, said she has spent at least twenty hours a week for the past five years organizing visits for resistance leaders from Central America and raising money for a resistance group there; she has also made several visits to Central America herself. The pastor said the church is distinctive, compared to other organizations, because it offers "a holistic solution to the human dilemma." He explained that this solution focuses on "building community" and that it requires people to "make a strong investment."

The reason churches like this feel they are voices crying in the wilderness is twofold. In asking for strong commitment from their members, they recognize that few will be willing to comply. They liken themselves to Old Testament prophets, speaking truth but not making themselves very popular—"courageous, go-against-the-grain" kinds of people, as one person put it. The other reason they feel like lonely voices is that the wider society is, in their view, a negative, inhuman place, much like a wilderness. This pastor, for example, described the United States as "one of the most patronizing, imperialistic kinds of setting in the world."

Churches like this are making a clear statement on behalf of social justice. Their

presence in the community serves as a reminder that some people, at least, are serious about peace and justice. By concentrating so heavily on peace and justice, these
churches also produce tangible results. Real dollars are sent to resistance groups in
Third World countries. The city council has second thoughts about running the
homeless off the streets. Young people are inspired to become social workers and
political activists. This is the kind of dedication it may take to jar middle-class
institutions out of their complacency. Yet it is also clear that such churches are rare.
Not many people are willing to make the commitment they require.

## THE CHURCHES' LIMITED ROLE

Opposing, redefining, and valorizing social justice are all ways in which middle-
class churches have adapted to the relatively comfortable place they occupy in mid
dle America. These orientations permit them to say—and even do—something on
behalf of those lower on the economic scale. But not very much. Nothing risky.
And nothing likely to be very effective, either, in bringing about social justice or in
altering the larger society. Even at the church that focuses so much on social justice, the pastor mused that "it's a very safe congregation." He observed, "We still
haven't taken the risks that we need to take. We're beginning to move in faithful
directions, but it hasn't taken as deep a root and effect as it needs to take."

Opposing efforts to bring about social justice is a good way to keep a church's
mission focused on churchly (i.e., spiritual) things and thus to prevent the church's
resources from being dissipated. A church such as Cornerstone has few resources to
spend. Its pastor's time is limited, and its members' donations go mostly to cover
operating expenses. Pastor Higgins's opposition to working for social justice is
rooted in but not determined by his theological understandings. Other pastors with
conservative, evangelical orientations and with a strong emphasis on personal spirituality found it possible to be interested in social justice.[17]

Redefining social justice permits church members who want to dabble in a little
of everything to find a place to do it within the church. Although many of the pastors we talked to felt frustrated because their congregations were not more active,
they could at least take pride in the one lawyer in their church who had written a
brief on behalf of an indigent client or in the fact that in some small way a portion
of the offerings went to support a denominational bureau that was lobbying against
discrimination.

Valorizing social justice encourages bold—even zealous—commitment, but on
the part of only a few, who can take special pride in the fact that they are indeed

among the few. They attend social justice-oriented churches because their special talents and interests are appreciated. Their good deeds may be the envy of other pastors and church members in the wider community. These deeds are valuable, both for what they accomplish and for what they symbolize, yet it is hard for ordinary people to relate to these heroic efforts.

These ways of dealing with social justice, it would appear, work pretty well for the churches. Middle-class congregants can boast that they are not bigots and can attend their churches without having to change their own lifestyles. How then do these orientations toward social justice contribute to the present crisis that the churches are facing? By rendering the churches irrelevant to the ways in which important questions of justice are dealt with in our society. Church people sometimes wonder why the government seems capable of dictating more and more of their lives. They get upset when the government tells them they cannot pray in school, but they forget that they have already asked the government to handle everything else. Preachers lament the fact that lawyers are everywhere and that U.S. society has become litigious. They forget that the churches are party to the problem by having nothing to say about social justice.

"The church is not respected as it used to be," was the way one pastor summarized the problem. Mentioning prohibition against prayer or religious symbols in public places, he lamented the fact that "the church has lost its clout." But he also disagreed that the solution was to focus all the church's energy on freedom-of-religion lawsuits. Instead, he thought the churches needed to regain the attention and respect of public officials.

In a medium-sized city in Connecticut, approximately twenty churches are experimenting with a way of regaining their power. Faced with rising crime, racial conflict, and a growing disparity between the rich and the poor in their city, these churches have formed an alliance of their own pastors and representatives from secular agencies and are training forty volunteers from each church to participate in city and statewide planning efforts, to monitor public housing, and to make sure that legal counsel is provided to people of all income groups. The goal is to work for equal rights and in turn to improve the quality of life for all members of the community. "The churches have to do something," explained one of the leaders. "The churches have the value system that works in this world, but for some reason the churches don't seem to be able to do anything except what I call show-and-tell to effect any real change. They just don't." He said the churches' loss of power has been a source of deep personal frustration. "If you did a power analysis of this country, you're going to find the churches down on the bottom. They're way below the unions. They'd be down on the bottom of the rung. Churches are just becoming a place where we can go and feel good on Sunday and have diversions. I don't understand it. I don't see any power. If one looked at the endowment portfolio of the churches that are in the United States of America and added up what that endowment portfolio summed to, the money that they could put on the table if they dumped out their coffers, you've got enough to change economic ills and social justice, but you don't see that."

This pastor hopes the coalition in his community can serve as a model for other communities. The main need, he feels, is new leadership. "We need to identify those with talent, minds, and gifts to solve the problems we have in this country. I see a dearth of leadership in this nation, and that's because the leadership is coming out of the powerful and the rich, rather than a search for the poor, humble child who really has the mind and the heart to solve our problems and to lead us out of this chaos."

## RAISING CONSCIOUSNESS

Middle-class churches ultimately may be too deeply embedded in the dominant social order to challenge it very much. Apart from the few churches that valorize the quest for justice, we found that the ones most interested in social justice were actually marginal to mainstream middle-class life in some way. For instance, the pastor of a Japanese church said his members were actively concerned about social justice because of their families' relocation experiences during World War II. They were working not only for reparations for themselves but also for the rights of new immigrants who were not being treated fairly under California law. For another example, the pastor of an African Methodist Episcopal church said his members had faced enough discrimination that they were doing a lot to challenge current legal structures and work for racial equality.

But for most middle-class people, social justice is likely to be difficult to understand intuitively. As one pastor explained, the members of his church were "too individualistic" and "too success oriented" to understand why some people were not benefiting from the American system. Working for social justice can fail to inspire deep commitment from church members for all the reasons I have suggested. Yet the churches do serve, on occasion, as enclaves in which a passion for social justice is stirred up.[18]

How does this stirring up happen? It is seldom because someone read a book or heard a sermon or served in an administrative capacity. Rather, a passion for social justice springs from becoming involved in a set of social practices that exposes one both to needs and to potential solutions and that does so in such an encompassing way that a personal response is required. Some of the clergy with whom we spoke offered poignant examples from their own experience.

Rector Morgan said he had initially become interested in social justice during the Vietnam War. Reading about the war and seeing pictures of it on television made him aware of how much the government can control individual lives and of how possible it is for the government to be wrong. It was not until he went to seminary and became personally and professionally involved in the Episcopal church, however, that questions of injustice forced him to respond. The occasion was the controversy over ordination of women in his denomination. He considered it wrong for women to be denied this possibility. In protest, he refused to be ordained himself. A year later, the church reversed its stance, and Rector Morgan was glad to be able to be employed. Meanwhile, though, he said "it drove my bishop crazy because he'd spent all this money educating me and I wouldn't take a job." That experience steeled his resolve to work for gender equality within his congregation.

At a racially integrated church in Atlanta, the pastor—a man in his sixties—told how he had been appointed by the governor in the early 1960s to a commission established to demonstrate the validity of separate-but-equal schools. "I saw the hurt of the indigent black community and also the sharecropping farmers of south Georgia, that many of them were not given the justice or the opportunity they ought to have," he recalled. That experience prompted him to join the Atlanta Christian Council and to become active in the civil rights movement. As he built his own congregation, he tried to speak against social injustice. The result, he said, was the shaping of his public identity. "I felt rejection from my peers because they were conservative evangelicals and didn't want to get involved in such things." Thirty years later, he finds himself still putting social justice near the top of his congregation's priorities.

For Father Martinez, the decisive event occurred just before he came to San Xavier's. He was working directly with immigrants and saw how much they had suffered. "They told me their stories, how they came across, how they suffered coming across. This one man, I still remember. God, he came across, and I literally had to go to the apartment to pick him up because he was so skinny. I picked him up to take him to the doctor because he stood five days walking from the border to here. And do you know what he ate on the way over here? All he could find to eat was dog biscuits. How much they suffer, trying to find a better life for themselves and a better opportunity for themselves." Father Martinez said he still feels a special concern for people who are struggling for basic human dignity. He believes that capitalism and socialism are both "oppressive human systems" that degrade people. "So the church," he said, "can be a critical voice for those who are suffering."

These pastors could point to specific experiences that had prompted them to think about social justice. Those events gave them something concrete to talk about when they described their interest in social justice. It was evident from their comments, however, that the specific event was less important than the social context in which it occurred. These pastors were engaged in practices, such as attending seminary or preaching or doing community work, that kept the reality of inequality and injustice before their eyes.[19] Even their more immediate experiences were significant because they were part of a community that reinforced those experiences and interpreted their meaning.

For instance, looking back on a formative experience he had as a teenager working for three weeks on a Navajo reservation with a group of fellow Episcopalians, one pastor captured the *social* dimension of this experience nicely when he remarked, "It affected me viscerally to see the needs up close and personal. And to do that in a community of faith. Every day began with eucharist and every evening closed with prayer. It was a communal experience. We prayed together, played together, worked together, and fought together."

As they have tried to preach about social justice, these pastors have tried to replicate the same process in their congregations. They talk often about the biblical mandate to be concerned about mercy and justice and about the implications of this mandate for the ways in which American social institutions function. They also try to draw some of their parishioners into activities and organizations where they will be reminded during the week that human institutions are inevitably flawed and need constant correction.

The church, both as a community of words and as a community of deeds, becomes a place where life is experienced differently than in ordinary middle-class routines. Contrasting the church to a business lunch or a golf game, for instance, one pastor talked about it as a place where people can come to reflect about the larger character of life, including the course of our society and its effects on the poor and the disadvantaged. "The normal patterns are shattered," he suggested, "and the usual cycle is interrupted." At a deep level, he believes, people know they need that kind of interruption. "You don't need to go to church to baptize all your prejudices."

It is the logic of these teachings and activities that especially stands out. Rather than emphasizing the logic of payoffs—either tangible results or good feelings— and focusing only on individual relationships that may be best at warming the heart, these clergy emphasize *responsibility*. Working for social justice, they argue, is something that people should do in obedience to God, as part of God's created order, and in rhythm with the inevitable cycles of decay and renewal of all systems. Even if one's efforts are ineffective, the task is to stay committed and work for what is right. After all, "Jesus didn't make much of a stir either," observed one pastor. "The church is not called to do what the church does based on how viable it is and how great an impact it will make," he added. "Social justice is part of the expression of the Gospel in the world. We're not charged with trying to figure out is it worthwhile because this is all the good it's going to do. You do it. Isaiah essentially as a prophet felt he was a failure. He read his whole ministry as a failure. But he did not say, 'You know, the long term doesn't look good in this field, so I'm going to back out.'"

Replying to a question about the effectiveness of working for social justice, a United Church of Christ pastor probably expressed the idea of responsibility most clearly. "Working for social justice has *never* been very effective. But it's something we continue to do. Its legitimacy doesn't lie in its effectiveness. It is just something that we continue to raise. I don't think you can change systems by preaching at them, but you keep trying to raise consciousness, keep trying to be sensitive to issues that need political attention. In the long view of history, there is a truth that causes the collapse of systems and the renewal of societies too. There is some sort of providential activity working things out, not always in spite of us but sometimes through us."

Getting such ideas across is difficult given the prevailing emphasis in American culture on success. Talking about social justice can be one of those activities that seem destined to fail because they focus too much on the needs of others and do not minister enough to the concerns of the middle class itself. Yet there may be lessons about social justice that can be beneficial even for the middle class. One may be that middle-class comforts are systematically related to the discomforts of people elsewhere: for example, the misery of sweatshop workers in East Asia whose subsistence wages make it possible for middle-class Americans to clothe themselves inexpensively.

Another lesson for the middle class may be that godly programs and divine truths are not always the ones that succeed. "I had a man sitting here just the other day," said a pastor. "He was crying because he'd lost his job. All he'd ever heard was that God would bless him. He felt like God had abandoned him." This pastor continued, "The lesson of social justice is that there is still hope, even when we fail. God is not the God of capitalism. God is God."

# twelve

# STRATEGIES FOR SURVIVAL

Is the church going to be a vital part of American society in the future? We asked this question of the clergy we interviewed. To a person, they said yes. But many also expressed concern about the future. They worried that the church would have a diminishing influence on society. They also wondered if certain strategies would prove more effective than others.

It is troubling, however, to hear how clergy talk about the future of the church. Those who say it will remain strong in the future base their arguments on the logic of necessity: Because people *need* spirituality, they argue, the churches will remain strong.[1] They fail to recognize that growing numbers of people are looking outside the churches for spiritual guidance. Other pastors base their optimism on theological grounds, paying little attention to social conditions. They argue that the church will prosper because God has promised it would. Those who are less optimistic generally focus more on changing circumstances. But some conditions receive attention at the expense of others. Most clergy, for instance, argue that the breakdown of community is hurting the church. They do not seem to recognize that the breakdown of community is in turn connected with the ways in which economic conditions are changing. Or clergy decry the arrival of new immigrants who are not Christians and wonder if the churches will be able to convert them. What most clergy fail to recognize are the ways in which current economic conditions in the churches themselves will have an impact on the future.[2]

Clearly, the churches are having to face new realities. Contributions are declining relative to parishioners' incomes. Family budgets are already stretched, and most families cannot count on their incomes rising as rapidly as they did a decade or two ago. With hard work and clever marketing, some churches can raise millions for new buildings and large ministries. But all churches are having to deal with higher fixed costs. Insurance, health benefits, and maintenance costs have all been rising steadily. Churches will be lucky if they can maintain staff and programs at their present size. The day is gone when churches can also build hospitals, nursing homes, retirement communities, and colleges. More and more people are dependent on churches for emergency meals, shelter, and counseling. But many churches are devoting meager sums to these efforts, and many needs are going unmet. Churches still enlist the help of large numbers of unpaid volunteers to teach classes, mow the lawn, visit the sick, and paint the belfry. But many parishioners are already working harder than ever before and have little energy left over for other commitments.

Times of austerity force all organizations to reconsider their priorities. Businesses that are floundering cut back by firing employees, making other employees work harder and produce more, closing operations that are losing money, and selling off units that may be peripheral to the company's main activities. Churches can ill afford to follow the same strategies. To be sure, they can fire the choir master who produces pretty music but who does little to cultivate Christian virtue as a person. Or they can let senior pastors go and replace them with novices who come cheaper. But churches without choirs or without experienced clergy are likely to lose a share of their members' interest and support. Pastors can also decide to focus on "the basics" and let everything else go. For instance, they can preach and encourage people to pray and attend church and leave it at that. To separate spirituality from the rest of life, however, runs against the very nature of spirituality.

Faced with hard times, the churches must resolve to do more rather than less. They must not retreat from the hard issues that middle-class Americans are facing in their work and in thinking about their money and material possessions. Nor can the churches focus entirely on giving. Parishioners may be kindhearted, wanting to help the needy and willing to donate time and money to their churches. But their giving will not increase if clergy do nothing but ask more often and more urgently. The churches must be more active in ministering to the *economic* concerns of middle-class parishioners themselves, helping them to understand their work as ministry, to cope with stress and burnout, to keep their priorities straight with respect to money, and to manage their resources with greater care.

One of the Nazarene pastors we interviewed offered a compelling statement about where the churches are going wrong. He said he had been rethinking his ministry during the past year since having surgery that brought him close to death. He concluded that the clergy talk about giving in a way that simply makes people angry. Members listen but go away saying, "Well, all the church is really up to, the church's hidden agenda is they want more money. They are not interested in my well-being; they just want more money." He said the church has also "bought into the very value system that it's trying to critique." For instance, "a pastor can't sit in a lake house or a mountain retreat that he owns while his kids are attending Harvard and do much critiquing about undue gain and exploitation of wealth."

Churches can take a lesson from their experience in relating faith to politics in recent years. Worried that faith was becoming increasingly marginalized in public life, religious leaders have organized movements around every issue from school prayer to nuclear arms, from abortion to gay rights, and they have encouraged church members to vote, sign petitions, participate in rallies, and send money to religious lobbying groups. These activities have enjoyed considerable success at least in terms of mobilizing more church people to vote and attracting media attention to the work of religious groups. Parishioners became agitated enough to send money or to vote in particular ways because they were convinced that *moral* issues were at stake. They opposed government policies or they opposed particular candidates because they believed it was "immoral" to—fill in the blank—tell schoolchildren they couldn't pray out loud during class, permit gays and lesbians to join the armed forces, send Patriot missiles to Europe, or spend tax monies to support artists whose work seemed sacrilegious.

The people who became most agitated about these issues were probably well intentioned. Most of the people who followed these leaders probably felt deeply about the issues that were being discussed. The truth of the matter, however, is that few of these issues made any difference to the ways in which most church members actually lived their lives. They were *symbolic*, rather than behavioral (except in the case of the few individuals who made genuine sacrifices for the movements that emerged around these issues). People could devote a few minutes on a given Tuesday in November to vote Republican rather than Democratic—or vice versa—and then go about their daily business the same way whether the Republican or the Democrat won. They could send in a petition about school prayer, knowing that their own children would pray—or not pray—every evening before they went to bed anyway. They could wax eloquent about abortion, knowing that they would never have one, or about gays in the military, neither being one nor knowing any. Ultimately, these issues were easy to become incensed about because they made no difference to the ways in which most middle-class church members lived their lives.[3]

How we work and how we spend our money are much more dangerous matters to consider. Were we to think very deeply about these issues, we might actually have to change the way we live. One part of us acknowledges that these are *moral* issues too, just like the political issues that bother us. We believe it is immoral to be greedy. We say it is immoral to live high on the hog when others are starving. We even say that discrimination and exploitation in the workplace are immoral or that it is immoral to spend so much time working that we neglect our marriages and our children. But another part of us has been trained to consider these matters simply as "preferences." Because they fall into the economic compartment of our lives, we tell ourselves that we have the right to make whatever choices we want. As long as we don't blatantly lie, cheat, or steal, it makes no difference how we work or what we buy.

Little wonder, then, that the churches have found it hard to say anything meaningful about the economic lives of ordinary Americans. Most of us would rather keep our faith separate from our résumés or our checkbooks. If we go to church, we want to hear sweet sermons on the blessings of life, not something that will make us squirm in our seats. We want to be reassured that all will be well as long as we believe in God and give token amounts to the work of the church. Like the man who complained, "Preacher, now you're meddling," we would think it wrong for the clergy to say very much about our finances and our time.

Virtually all of the clergy we talked with agreed in principle, however, that their ministries should pay special attention to economic matters. Arguing that these matters lie at the very core of our lives, one pastor explained their importance this way: "We have to make money, we spend money, and that is very much a part of who we are. And the way we spend our money is really the way we spend ourselves." At Cornerstone Bible Church, Pastor Higgins made virtually the same point: "Money is really who we are in one sense. When you go and you work and you labor and you do what you do for a living, when it's all said and done, what do you get for it? You get a paycheck. That represents you." Focusing less on preaching and more on the marriage counseling that he does, Rector Morgan at Saint Andrew's spoke even more forcefully about the importance of addressing economic concerns. "People are being barraged by advertisements that lie to them from one end to the other," he observed. "Buy this car and it'll never break down. Every car will break down. Buy this house and you'll have happiness. Probably it's the reason you won't have happiness if you can't afford it. Take this job and you'll be a totally complete person, when in fact most jobs demean us in some respect by the time we're done with them in our lifetime, including church jobs. I think the church needs to stand there and give an alternate view to all that. Maybe the church is the only one in society that will say that—other than some very few radical organizations in our world."

Despite saying that economic concerns fall within the orbit of faith, few clergy address more than a small fraction of these concerns, and they do so in such general ways or with such specific reference to church programs that parishioners are unlikely to be challenged by what they say. Except for a few seminars sponsored by churches (and led by laymen and laywomen), the clergy we talked to had virtually nothing to say about which kinds of career values should be most important, how a believer might go about making the right decision in buying a new home or a new car, or how to teach children to put money and material goods in proper perspective.

Although it has not occurred to many clergy that they should be saying more about these issues, a few recognize the problem and argue that it is the clergy's responsibility to do more. Realizing that people are reluctant to have anything influence their work or their purchases besides dollars-and-cents considerations, these clergy say it is the churches' role to preach more effectively. One of the priests we talked to, for instance, said the problem was that the clergy were not keeping economic issues "in the forefront of congregational life." He said the clergy need to become both more pastoral and more prophetic in dealing with these issues. A United Church of Christ pastor went further. Accusing the church of being "chicken" and of being "too concerned about its own butt," he argued that the church is doing little more than making sin comfortable. "Sin has a way of dulling our senses," he explained, "and the church is interested in keeping its patrons coming and giving their money rather than calling them to holiness, calling them to reality, calling them to the fact that we worship a crucified God and not some superhero, and that there's a cost to discipleship, there's a cost to grace."

The clergy's silence on these issues is symptomatic of the more general problem that has befallen religious discourse in our time. Clergy are reluctant to say much about anything for fear of offending or for fear of appearing stupid. The first fear encourages them to tell personal anecdotes and to cultivate the idea that anything is acceptable as long as somebody feels good about it, or has prayed, or is sincere. The second fear encourages clergy to show off their knowledge of esoteric Bible verses (in fundamentalist churches) or of esoteric theological interpretations (in liberal churches) rather than saying anything that might connect to the daily concerns of real people. People come away from such sermons as they might from a lecture on molecular biology—uplifted for having been exposed to something that makes no difference.[4]

We know, of course, that Americans are intensely individualistic and that we are, for the most part, an educated and informed society. Thus the clergy can sit back, feeling that their congregants already know what is right or wrong and that people are capable of making their own decisions. Especially on matters of economic "preference," clergy can say, well, think about it, pray about it, do whatever you feel

God wants you to do. Clergy can convince themselves that people are pretty responsible and that the choice, after all, is up to each individual. Clergy can thus refrain from saying anything specific on matters of work and money.

The grand delusion is that we then make these decisions purely in a vacuum. We do not pray and in the privacy of our hearts decide whether to go into one line of work or another or whether to purchase a new entertainment center. We listen to the advice of our friends, talk to headhunters and vocational counselors, and watch about twenty commercials in any given hour of television viewing. We're getting our cues from somewhere; just not from the churches.

Clergy do have strong opinions on economic issues. They lament the materialism of our society and the pressures to work harder and to spend more. They worry that young people are being corrupted by false or misleading values of the marketplace. They acknowledge that poor people are often victims of institutional arrangements, and they know that wealth and generosity do not go hand in hand. Most clergy realize that there is theological support for these opinions. Still, they find it hard to say anything that might seem to criticize the ways their parishioners are living.

The list of excuses that clergy give when confronted directly with the contradiction between their principles and their practice in talking about money is as long and as varied as the religious section of any metropolitan telephone book. Some argue that work and money, while important, are not really as important as God, so the church should talk about God rather than work and money. Some report that they have tried to speak about economic issues but found that their attempts caused conflict in the congregation, so they backed off. Some are quiet because they disagree with statements on economic justice, put out by their denominations, that they consider socialist. Many worry that they don't know enough about economics or finances to say anything intelligent. Many don't want to seem to be begging for donations.

What would happen if the clergy spoke more boldly about the ways in which middle-class Americans work and spend their money? A horrible backlash? No change? Or more dedication to the churches' programs? We can only speculate. This experiment has not been tried. It has, of course, been tried on a small scale— in one or another local church. And in some cases, people responded positively. What would happen on a larger scale can only be guessed. Lifestyles are difficult to change, especially once jobs have been taken and financial commitments have been made. More active interest in spirituality is probably hard to generate as well: Many people say they would like to be more spiritual, but few seem willing to spend time doing so.

It is the case, however, that people who think more deeply and more often about the connections between their faith and their finances also support their churches more generously than other people. It is also the case that contributions are higher among people who have listened to stewardship sermons, who consider the idea of stewardship meaningful, who relate their faith to their work, who believe the Bible contains valuable teachings about work and money, and who consult their pastors about their problems at work or with finances. Many church members say they are tired of hearing the clergy beg for money and would give no more if the clergy begged harder. But most church members do want their church to be more supportive to working families, to speak against materialism, and to draw practical applications for their lives. The opportunity is thus present for churches to minister to the economic concerns of their parishioners and to enlist more support for church programs at the same time.

Whatever the churches may do generally to minister to their congregations, it is clear that particular congregations are likely to adopt different strategies depending on their locations, the needs of their members, and the resources available to them. Let me turn, then, to some of the alternatives that specific congregations might pursue and consider the strengths and weaknesses of these alternatives.

## AUTHENTICATING THE FAITH

One strategy is for the church to abandon the middle class, as it were, by focusing less on the pressures that most Americans are facing and instead "authenticating" itself "among the broken people of society," as one pastor put it, by following Jesus' example and living among the poorest of the poor. In the extreme version of this approach, churches would sell their property in the suburbs and focus all their efforts on inner-city, rural, and other low-income areas. Less extreme interpretations would favor some significant shift of resources. In this view, the problem is that the churches have focused on middle America, where there are no serious needs. The solution is to concentrate on underclass America, where the needs are readily evident.

This option is worth taking seriously, especially in light of the fact that so few churches are making any significant commitment of resources to the underclass at all. Some of these churches can focus their energies on the truly needy because endowments, rather than middle-class supporters, cover their financial needs. Others can rely on staff provided by denominational resources or other churches. The people who participate in these ministries often find themselves so challenged and rewarded that their commitment increases. At a minimum, middle-class churches could do more to authenticate themselves by focusing more of their resources on ministries to the needy. Donations would probably do more than cover the cost. And volunteers would probably find that their own priorities were being influenced.

The problem with shifting primary attention to the underclass is that the churches' financial base clearly lies within the middle class, and their longevity depends on maintaining this base. That maintenance requires clergy to focus on charitable appeals, stewardship, and forging other links between faith and economic matters. For sheer survival, the churches' main strategy must focus on the majority of their members.

Apart from survival, however, the churches must also recognize the desperate needs that exist among the middle class itself. Clergy cannot assume that people are living spiritual lives just because they have three color television sets, or that they have no need for pastoral counseling because they work in professional and management positions. Parishioners suffering from severe burnout in their work will simply find the church less relevant to their total way of life if the clergy—and fellow church members—have nothing to offer for this special moment of need.

Need, in fact, is the issue. Churches have always recognized the value of being there when people died or when they lay languishing in hospitals. The needs of middle class members now include the serious problems that arise in their economic lives as well. Parishioners need help figuring out what line of work to enter next, getting back on their feet after losing their job, finding time to be a responsible employee as well as a working parent, and knowing how to spend their money. Such needs do not have to be fully resolved before the churches can help the hungry and the homeless. But focusing only on the hungry and the homeless is not likely to keep the churches in business.

## GOOD THINGS IN SMALL PACKAGES

A more promising strategy for the churches is to initiate small groups in which members discuss work, personal finances, and stewardship, among other topics, and hold each other accountable in these areas. The advantages of small groups are considerable: They cost relatively little to operate, especially if they meet in homes or in unused classrooms in churches; leadership is generally drawn from the laity and from members who have already benefited from participation in groups; study guides and other materials can be obtained readily and inexpensively in almost any subject on which groups wish to focus; small groups provide intimate and informal interaction that can be the basis for sharing concerns about work, money, or other personal issues; and these groups can focus on practical applications of faith to the concerns of everyday life.

A number of the pastors we interviewed spoke enthusiastically about the uses of small groups. Pastor Higgins was just starting a small-group program at Cornerstone. Even though his church was small, he felt groups were necessary in order to acquaint newcomers with each other. Rector Morgan said about 150 of his 300 regular attenders were currently involved in small groups, most following a model that had been used successfully in Catholic churches. Redeemer Baptist has five missionary groups and eighteen Bible study groups that meet on Wednesday evenings. The one Pastor Hill leads has grown to about 100 people, but he insists it is still "small." Grace Church sponsors a number of small Bible study groups, including several for working women and one for men. Another pastor described small groups as "the mainstay of our ministry." He credited them with moving his church away from tradition and more toward the "real concerns" of his members.

Small groups are already widely in use in many churches. Approximately 40 percent of the total adult population in the United States is currently a member of some small group that meets regularly and provides caring and support for those who participate in it. These groups are enormously diverse, including self-help and support groups of all kinds, book discussion clubs, sports groups, hobby groups, civic organizations, and musical groups. But 60 percent of the people who are currently involved in a small group participate in one that is formally sponsored by a church. And these groups consist mainly of small, informal Sunday school classes; Bible study and prayer fellowships; and a few other groups such as choirs, church committees, or Alcoholics Anonymous meetings sponsored by churches. Most of the members of these church-related groups participate regularly, usually meeting every week or every other week for more than an hour. Most members continue to participate in the same group for at least several years, and a majority of members claim that their group has had a significant positive impact on their faith. They especially appreciate the sharing that takes place in their groups, the opportunity to pray, and the love that develops among group members.[5]

Small groups are thus a resource that churches can rely on to help them weather hard times. There is already a considerable base of small-group activity on which to build. Pastors sometimes express frustration about elevating overall participation in small groups to a high proportion of the total congregation. But small groups can be expanded in many churches without much additional effort, and other churches can focus on improving the quality and content of groups already in existence. At present, members of small groups do contribute more than nonmembers to the financial support of their churches. Members also are more likely to volunteer for other church activities, and many say their level of involvement in the church has increased as a result of being in their group. If pastors are too busy or feel themselves ill equipped to address the economic concerns of their members, then small groups can be a way in which responsibility for these concerns is turned over to the laity.[6]

The limitations of small groups, though, must also be recognized. Among church members currently in small groups, relatively few say they discuss economic concerns or provide financial assistance to each other. Despite the fact that sharing includes such intimate topics as health problems, marital relations, child rearing, and personal anxieties, group members are generally reluctant to disclose details of their salaries or expenditures to each other, and they use these groups, like church services, as escapes from work rather than places to raise penetrating questions about the direction of their careers or the challenges facing them in their work. More importantly, small groups develop informal norms of tolerance and acceptance. These norms encourage members to affirm whatever each member happens to say or believe rather than delving into controversial or challenging issues. Group members thus develop the feeling that their lives are already okay rather than being encouraged to examine their priorities. Small groups also suffer from a lack of theological rigor. Few groups systematically study the Bible in its entirety or focus on the accumulated theological wisdom of the church. Group members are more likely to focus on pragmatic, personal opinions that may, again, be self-congratulatory rather than challenging.[7]

For these reasons, clergy and other religious leaders must guide small groups in order to challenge members to relate their faith more closely to economic concerns. Such guidance has to be light-handed, or members' sense of ownership and responsibility for their groups will diminish. But clergy can participate in the planning of small-group programs to ensure appropriate training, selection of topics, and integration with other activities of the church. Several of the churches we studied, for instance, used structured small-group programs set up by their denominations to expose members to a balanced understanding of biblical concepts over a two-year period. Several other churches provided small groups oriented toward discussing the pastor's sermons and applying biblical ideas to their lives. If pastors preached more often about work, money, stewardship, and related topics, such groups could provide a way of enhancing understanding of these issues.

## THE MEGACHURCH OF TOMORROW

At the congregational level, the development of larger churches with membership numbering in the 2,000 to 10,000 range is another likely strategy for the future.

The main attraction of large congregations is that they can provide many more specialized programs than smaller churches can. Grace Church, with its layers of assistant pastors and program directors, its school, youth groups, and jail ministry, is an
example. People who might otherwise lose interest in the church can be drawn in
because there is a music program that makes use of their special talents, or an
opportunity to gain experience as a teacher, or a singles club that sponsors exciting
ski trips. Because they offer so many different programs, megachurches can also
become places at which some members spend almost all of their time. One can serve
on committees three nights a week, go skating at the church rink another evening,
spend Saturday afternoon at the church theater with the children watching Christian movies, and stay that evening for a potluck supper or dinner dance. Spending
large amounts of time at the church is no guarantee that people will integrate their
faith more completely with their work life or with the way they think about their
money; they may, however, meet other people from work or find themselves talking about personal issues with fellow members of the church bowling team.

Megachurches appear to be increasing both in numbers of congregations and
more broadly in influence within American religion. As many as one church member in five already attends a congregation of more than 1,000 people, although
many of these congregations would not qualify as megachurches in the strict sense
of the word. Megachurches attract attention by the sheer visibility of their physical
plant (as in the case of Grace Church). They have the resources to advertise or to
provide programs for the wider community, such as concerts and athletic events.
And they sometimes provide staging grounds for political rallies or ways of exer-
cising influence in denominational politics.[8]

Although some churches like Grace Church (as we saw in chapter 3) evoke
charitable contributions no higher than the national level as a proportion of family
income, megachurches as a whole appear to do a reasonably good job of soliciting
donations. In my survey, for instance, Protestants who attended churches of more
than 1,000 members gave 3.7 percent of their family income to the church, compared with an average donation among all Protestants of only 2.0 percent. (Among
Catholics there were no differences, but size of parish is less likely to be a valid
indicator of the megachurch phenomenon among Catholics than among Protestants.) The reason for this higher level of giving is probably a combination of
church programs, effective preaching, and the location and lifestyle of members; it
does not appear to depend on denomination or the theological orientation of the
church.

Counterbalancing the above-average giving at megachurches, however, is the
fact that these congregations also have higher costs than most smaller churches.
This difference exists largely because megachurches are explicitly trying to do new
things and to impress their communities by showing that religion can be just as

upbeat and clever as any other new organization in town. Thus, instead of buying an existing church that has fallen into disrepair, megachurches spend tens of millions constructing new complexes in new areas. The advantage is that people in these new areas are attracted. The disadvantage is that congregants must give generously just to pay off the mortgage. In addition, megachurches require not only the front-line clergy who preach and who work directly with parishioners and volunteers but also several layers of administrators, coordinators, and planners.

Another potential limitation of megachurches is that their theology—more so than in most of the other churches we studied—emphasizes a gospel of good feelings, self-interest, and pragmatism. This emphasis is evident in sermons that tell parishioners to give because it will make them happy or rich, in teachings that associate the calling with feeling good about oneself, and in implicit messages that equate church growth with biblical truth and prosperity with right living. One reason for this emphasis is that megachurches are often prospering themselves. Their programs and auditoriums are bigger than those of any other church in town; their pastors' salaries are high; and their members may be commuting from new, upper-middle-class housing developments. Under such conditions, it is easy for a kind of triumphalism to overtake the congregation's outlook toward Christianity. Megachurches may also be tempted to adopt this outlook because their roots in ecclesiastical tradition are intentionally shallow. They do not aspire to the humility of Teresa of Avila, the dedication of John of the Cross, or the scholarship of John Calvin; instead, they present themselves as the church for people who are fed up with church. Having no other compass than their own sense of what the Bible means and what works, they are easily guided by the pragmatism and individualism of American culture itself.

It remains unclear whether megachurches are increasing the overall vitality of American religion or whether they are simply taking energy away from older and smaller churches. Our conversations with clergy produced predictable disagreement on this issue. Pastors at megachurches insisted that they were drawing members and dollars from people who would not be involved with other churches anyway. Pastors of neighboring churches pointed to specific families who had left their congregations for greener pastures and livelier chorales. It is clear that overall attendance at churches has not risen in the nation at large during the past two decades, and overall membership has actually declined. Since these decades are the period in which most megachurches have emerged, they are at best keeping religious commitment constant rather than increasing its numerical strength. This constancy, of course, is no small achievement. As members become disgruntled with established churches and as a new generation of young families returns to the churches, megachurches may be offering them an attractive alternative.

Because of their size, their present resources, and their perception of themselves as the wave of the future, megachurches are also most likely to change the way in which churches support themselves financially in the years ahead. Fees for professional services are already a significant component of many megachurch budgets. Rather than relying on voluntary contributions to support a general budget, megachurches charge fees for specific programs, thus requiring those who benefit from these programs to cover their costs. Tuition for the schools that churches such as Grace Church operate is one example. Other examples include per-session fees to consult with therapists employed by the church's counseling center; tickets to attend concerts given by the church choir or the monthly church dinner; and fees for workshops, retreats, continuing education seminars, camping trips, and singing lessons. Such fees have the advantage of linking program costs more directly with demand. Programs that do not attract paying participants fail. The disadvantage is that marketplace logic replaces the language of stewardship. A sense of participation in a community and of corporate responsibility for the entire congregation may also be lost. An added disadvantage is that programs needed by people who cannot afford them are likely to be neglected.[9]

Megachurches may also find themselves tempted to use creative financial strategies, especially if they start running into economic difficulties. These strategies may follow the lead taken by secular nonprofit organizations in recent years. Repertory theaters, for instance, list the names of their most generous donors in playbills, provide special lounges and refreshments for these donors during intermission, and solicit advertisements in playbills from local businesses. Churches have, of course, taken all of these measures in limited ways already—inscribing names on pews and stained-glass windows, giving special recognition to the most generous few, and including business advertisements in church leaflets. The next step may be to follow the example of other organizations that trade their ability to attract audiences for donations from corporate sponsors. Like the Brand X bowl game or the Brand Y half-time report, the next step may be the Pepsi Nativity Pageant or the Chevrolet Church of Our Savior. Parishioners would probably adapt easily to these innovations, paying no more attention to the Pizza Hut sign in the vestibule than to the names of Rockefeller, Trump, and Wu inscribed on the bookplates in their hymnals. At one of the megachurches we studied, the pastor, in fact, seemed quite unself-conscious about the fact that his education building was named after one of the nation's wealthiest men—who, incidentally, had also been charged with misconduct by the Securities and Exchange Commission.

Such strategies, however, run the risk of further secularizing American religion.[10] Although churches have encouraged people to compartmentalize their faith and their finances, they have at least helped parishioners to keep the two separate rather than allowing the logic of American capitalism to blatantly penetrate sacred space. Rather than pastors implicitly condoning the materialism of the middle class, the churches of tomorrow would explicitly show religion and wealth as cozy bedfellows. The churches might be able to pay for larger buildings, but they would become less distinguishable from any other place of commerce and entertainment.

## SALVAGING THE PROGRAM CHURCH

Though megachurches may continue to increase in size and number, they will not replace the smaller churches of 200 to 500 members that are the norm at present. Most Americans attend the churches they do because these churches are familiar to them. They probably have not attended the same church all their lives, and they will likely shift to another at some point, but there is a high level of inertia that keeps them where they are. They have friends there; they know the pastor; the liturgy is familiar. Even if they switch, they will not all be attracted to the new megachurch in town. They may attend an occasional concert there or visit once in a while out of curiosity, but they would no more give up the smaller church nearby than they would shop exclusively at Wal-Mart rather than the local deli. The so-called program church will still be the most convenient place to find music, Sunday school, youth, visitation, and community outreach programs.

In one respect, though, the medium-sized church is in the worst financial position of all because its members give proportionally less than do members of larger or smaller churches. Among Protestants, for instance, people who attend churches with 200 to 300 members give the lowest amount as a proportion of total income (1.4 percent); those in churches of 100 to 200 members or in churches of 300 to 500 members also give at lower than average levels (1.8 percent); while those in churches of 500 to 1,000 members give at about an average level (2.2 percent) but still less than the average in churches of fewer than 100 members (2.3 percent) or more than 1,000 members (3.7 percent). Still, medium-sized churches often have members who do not attend and who make no demands on clergy time or on church facilities but who give a few hundred dollars a year. Very small churches, such as Cornerstone Bible, may have very loyal members but so few that it is difficult to cover expenses.

The most significant weakness of the program church is that it is a hybrid form of social organization, bred by historical circumstances that may now be working to undermine its effectiveness. The program church came into existence around the start of the twentieth century, largely in response to the growth of urban populations and the increasing demand from the middle class for leisure-time activities that would involve the entire family. Churches that traditionally offered only the Sunday morning and evening worship service, a few Sunday school classes, and midweek prayer meeting now sponsored couples clubs, scouting activities, women's guilds, semiprofessional choirs, and countless other activities. At the time, churches held a monopoly over many such activities. They at least competed on even ground with salons, bridge clubs, coffee klatches, and Masonic lodges. But now—in addition to the declining availability of leisure time itself—churches must compete with television, theater complexes that offer more than a dozen movies any evening of the week, professional athletic teams that attract as many as 50,000 spectators to a typical event, and growing numbers of community organizations and professional associations.

For the program church to survive, it will have to focus special attention on developing a distinct identity for itself.[11] Some medium-sized churches have little choice in this matter. Their identity is already defined, for example, by virtue of being the only Methodist church in the county or by being the Lutheran church located nearest to a local retirement community. A growing number of program churches will also be identified with new immigrant communities, serving Korean, Haitian, Salvadoran, Slovenian, and other ethnic groups. For these churches, work and money may be important issues indeed. Other program churches will develop their niche in the religious market more intentionally—through an exceptional choir program, the best scout troop in town, or the funniest sermons. Program churches that can challenge their members to think more constructively about their work or to play an active role in ministries to the homeless may have a special role to fill—particularly if other churches are neglecting these issues.

From a theological perspective, the program church is thus likely to be associated with the best of times and with the worst of times in the years ahead. At its best, the program church is well positioned to challenge the middle class to lead unconventional lives of dedication, service, and sacrifice—to present an alternative view, as Rector Morgan observed. The program church is small enough to foster community among its members, to enlist volunteer help, and to give its clergy a prominent voice within the congregation but not so small that it must worry constantly about keeping its doors open at all. The program church, like some of the ones that we studied, can create a distinct niche for itself as a place where people are especially challenged to work for social justice, to become involved in serving the needy, or to give sacrificially to missions and evangelism projects. At its worst, the program church will be the typical garden-variety congregation of middle-class members who attend from habit, who go to enhance their image in the community and to meet new clients and customers, and who seldom hear anything that challenges them to live differently from their neighbors.

Although one scenario is preferable from a theological standpoint to the other, both kinds of program churches will continue to play a prominent role in American religion. However, they will probably decline in number and importance in comparison to the larger and more visible megachurches with which they must compete. And hard times will force them to think harder about which programs to maintain, which staff to hire or fire, and which building projects to undertake. The program church will, as one pastor mused, have to learn how to subtract.[12] Because of their numerical prevalence, these churches, nevertheless, are the ones in which lessons about stewardship, the role of faith in the workplace, and the link between biblical teachings and money will have the greatest impact. Thus, the clergy who hold positions in these medium-sized churches bear a special responsibility to focus more attention on these important concerns.

## TOUGH BUSINESS

Regardless of size, middle-class churches need to confront the difficult questions of how much to follow the course of least resistance and how much to push parishioners toward a deeper faith. Flabby times encourage flabby lives. It is little wonder that the churches have been soft in recent decades.[13] They peddle good feelings and easy-to-digest spirituality. Little is said about social responsibility—or discipline or repentance. The message is the same thing people are used to seeing on television. Speed-reading through inspirational booklets is like surfing through the cable channels. Each topic is separate. There is no coherence. Deep faith is a verse here and a verse there. Spirituality is for occasional moments of grace, not for an integrated life.

Yet parishioners and clergy need to pay heed to what their own traditions say about the need to apply their faith to all realms of life. Father Martinez at San Xavier's expressed the essential idea particularly well. "We're Christians every day of our lives. I'm not just a Christian at church. I'm a Christian at work and at play and wherever I go." He said the church must, for this reason, not become "an outside force." It needs to be "inside the economic and the social realities of our lives," not part of a divided reality.

All things considered, the middle-class church probably needs to be half its present size and twice its present strength. Those who keep their names on church rolls for no good reason might just as well disaffiliate. Those who attend church because they leave feeling more spiritual will increasingly find that they can achieve the same feeling by meditating at home, participating in a religious retreat, or listening to Mozart. Smaller churches or fewer churches could still minister powerfully to the need for support and guidance that some of their members experience.

One thing certain to make the church half as large and twice as strong would be clergy taking a harder look at the gospel of wealth. Implying that ordinary people will become rich if they give generously—and that rich people are dandy because they give generously—has been a favorite theme of American clergy. They admire the wealthy businessman in their congregation who coughs up the cash for a new program. They want him to know how much he is appreciated, and they certainly don't want to alienate him. The lifeblood of their ministries depends on the rich. As one pastor acknowledged in a personal conversation, if the top eight families (out of 1,000) quit giving, his church would go bankrupt. Clergy, therefore, are reluctant to say anything negative about wealth or greed or overconsumption or exploitation.

Most clergy, as we have seen, deal with wealth strictly as a matter of individual morality. It is great to make a lot of money, they argue, as long as one does not cheat to do it. They argue that money making is a talent, like being able to play the piano, and one should just use that talent to the fullest. What they avoid are the tough issues that surround the culture of wealth in our society. For instance, clergy seldom deal with the question of young people choosing careers in the hope of making a lot of money rather than to serve God or to help other people. Clergy are equally silent about wealthy athletes and movie stars who provide misleading role models for young people. Little is said about the ethics of making huge sums of money selling things that the public does not need or that may require social programs to clean up after them. Thus, the owner of a liquor store or a gambling casino is embraced just as warmly as a social worker or a teacher (more so, if he gives more). Nor is there any preaching about corporations that pay top executives a thousand times more than average workers or about brokers who use church connections to build up client lists.[14]

Tough-minded churches also need to be aware of the *institutional* realities that govern contemporary life. Middle-class parishioners may not be able to work fewer than fifty hours a week because their employers insist on such effort. Their employers, in turn, may think the only way to compete effectively is by squeezing more hours of work from their employees without paying them any more. But employers may not have considered other factors—such as burnout and employee turnover—or other options—such as part-time and contract work. Churches that simply tell individual members to work less and enjoy themselves more (at church dances) are unlikely to have much of an impact on such circumstances. Churches that work with local business councils to consider institutional alternatives are likely to make more of a difference.

The list of such issues is huge. The problem of juggling work and family commitments, for example, can only be addressed partially by churches counseling people to take their families more seriously. Family-leave policies that legally require employers not to discriminate against parents who must take time off from work for neonatal care, for example, can make more of a difference. Yet churches have largely neglected speaking about such policies. Day care for aging parents is another example. One of the churches we studied worked with community agencies and other congregations to provide meals, parish nurse visits, and hospice care for elderly residents. Most churches have done little to address the institutional ways in which such care might be provided.

Churches can do only so much to address such institutional issues because clergy time and finances are limited. However, one reason time and finances are limited is that clergy fail to communicate to parishioners what is already being done—and what could be done. Some clergy themselves do not know exactly what is happening because these activities are delegated to a junior staff member whom they seldom see. Other clergy consider it sufficient to print an announcement once in a while in the church bulletin rather than talking about concrete programs in the morning sermon.

Many of the clergy we talked to seemed still to be fighting the battle over the so-called social gospel that emerged at the start of the twentieth century. They saw a conflict between a personal gospel concerned with salvation and a social gospel concerned with institutional reform—or at least they worried that parishioners might see such conflict. One pastor, for example, decided to preach a sermon on social justice in the workplace but wound up devoting most of his time to explaining why his remarks should not be regarded as a retreat to the social gospel. Yet those who did speak easily about institutional issues saw simply that a personal gospel is little more than amusement—"something to help us laugh and have a good time," as one remarked—if it does not deal with the social realities among which we live.

The New Testament teachings to which the contemporary church still looks for legitimacy never suggested that things would be easy. The twelve disciples would probably be amazed to see the sprawling megachurches that now represent themselves as the Kingdom of God. The Old Testament prophets certainly would be. Somewhere along the way, the churches decided that bigger was better. Their star rose as they discovered how to make everyone feel at home. They are likely to continue this strategy in the future. Faced with the opportunity of constructing new buildings, they will say to themselves, "If we build it, they will come." Perhaps. But the churches also have an obligation to challenge those who come to lead better lives than they would otherwise. That is the toughest business of all.

# METHODOLOGY

The research on which this book is based consisted of bringing together three kinds of primary information: quantitative data from surveys, textual data from sermons and other religious documents, and qualitative data from churches. The quantitative data I have relied on most extensively is from my survey of the U.S. labor force. Conducted for me by the Gallup Organization among a representative national sample of approximately 2,000 men and women who were employed full or part time in 1992, this survey was particularly valuable because it included many questions about work, money, and attitudes toward material possessions as well as specific questions about religious commitment and the relationships between faith and economic attitudes and behavior. A copy of the questions is included in my book *God and Mammon in America*, which presents the main findings and an interpretation of social conditions that influence the relationships among faith, work, and money. In this book, I have further analyzed these data to examine more specifically the ways in which church experiences influence these relationships and to compare responses among church members with the views of clergy. I have also drawn selectively from several other national surveys, including ones conducted by Independent Sector, Inc., in Washington, D.C., in recent years on patterns of giving and volunteering and two that I designed, one on altruism and one on small groups. These surveys contain some useful information on values, giving patterns, and religious commitment.

Textual information comes mainly from more than 200 sermons on stewardship, work, money, and related issues. At each of the churches we studied, we asked the pastor if he or she kept copies of sermons and, if so, whether we could obtain some of them. In most cases, pastors did keep copies and were willing to make them available to us. In a majority of cases, we went through files of sermons for the past several years, scanning more than 100 sermons at each church, and selected one or more that dealt with the issues under consideration. In other cases, pastors selected sermons themselves and gave them or mailed them to us. We also visited about 20 churches where the pastor was not available for an interview but where we were able to pick up additional sermons. In this manner, we obtained about 70 sermons on cassette tape, which we then transcribed, and about twice that number that were already transcribed. To supplement this information, we also went through religious periodicals, commentaries, and books to find sermons or articles on stewardship and related topics. Our aim was not to conduct a quantitative content analysis of these texts but to read them and understand them in terms of major themes, arguments, and examples.

The most important source of information is the qualitative data we collected in churches and from clergy. Knowing that we did not have the resources to conduct a sample survey of clergy or to do intensive ethnographic work in a large number of churches, we decided to follow a purposive sampling design in which we tried to maximize diversity among congregations in order to heighten the possibility of being able to generalize and to reduce the chances of representing only certain kinds of churches. We collected information at 60 churches in all, chosen to include a wide variety of congregations in terms of size, denomination, location, and racial or ethnic composition.

Twenty-one churches had an average attendance of 200 or less, another 21 had an average attendance of more than 200 but less than 1,000, and the remaining 18 had an average attendance of 1,000 or more. Within each category there was also wide variation in size. For example, the small churches ranged from 70 to 200; the middle-sized churches from 250 to 900; and the large churches from 1,100 to 8,000.

Within budget constraints, regional diversity was maximized by selecting churches in each of the four main geographic areas of the continental United States. Twenty-four churches were located in the East, 14 in the South, 13 in the Midwest, and 8 in the West. Churches were selected so that some of each size were represented in each of the four regions. In all, churches were selected in 14 different states.

All churches were composed primarily of middle-class members, but within a broad definition of *middle class* an attempt was also made to include a range of socioeconomic groupings. Taking into account as much evidence as possible about each church, it appeared that 6 were probably best classified as upper middle class, 42 as middle middle class, 10 as lower middle class, and 2 as too mixed to be classified under a single designation. Approximately half of the churches (34) were located in suburbs of large metropolitan areas, 11 were located in small towns or rural areas, and 15 were located in urban zones.

Twenty-one denominations were represented plus 5 independent churches. For larger and more established denominations, an attempt was made to secure some variety within each denomination, while smaller denominations were generally represented by 1 or 2 churches. Thus, there were 8 Roman Catholic churches, 8 Presbyterian churches, 7 Methodist churches, 6 Episcopal churches, and 5 Southern Baptist churches. An attempt was also made, especially for smaller denominations, to select churches in the region in which the denomination was most clearly identified; for example, United Church of Christ churches were chosen in New England, Missouri-Synod Lutherans in the Midwest, Mennonites in Pennsylvania, Reformed churches in Michigan and New Jersey, Nazarenes in the Midwest, and so on.

An attempt was also made to include a range of racial and ethnic diversity. Five of the churches were composed primarily of African Americans, 4 about equally of blacks and whites, 3 of Hispanics, and 2 of Asian-Americans.

The churches also varied markedly in age: 4 were founded before 1800; 7 between 1800 and 1859; 13 between 1860 and 1899; 18 between 1900 and 1959; and 18 in or after 1960. Only 3 of the churches were less than twenty years old, and the youngest had been in existence nine years. Thus, in dealing with financial problems of churches, the study is not biased toward new churches that may not yet be financially solvent. On the other hand, a sufficient number of the churches have been in existence less than thirty years and are still growing that the study does not exclude younger or more dynamic institutions either. When trends over the past five years were compared, 39 were growing at least modestly in membership, while 21 were either stagnant or declining.

Theologically, 32 of the pastors described the dominant orientation of their church as conservative, 14 as moderate, 7 as liberal, and 7 as mixed. There is thus a wide range of theological views represented. If, as some have argued, conservative churches are financially healthier than nonconservative churches, then there is no reason to think the churches represented in the study are any less healthy than the national norm. In comparison with other studies, parishioners are about equally divided among conservatives, moderates, and liberals, but congregations tend to be described by informants as conservative in much greater proportions (Bible study and prayer groups also tend to be described this way). Two potential sources of bias in such descriptions are that liberal and moderate pastors sometimes describe their congregations as conservative because they feel the average parishioner is conservative in relation to the clergy's orientations; and conservative or moderate pastors sometimes describe their congregations as conservative because the term is more acceptable both to their congregants and to denominational leaders.

We also tried to avoid bias in choosing particular churches by identifying them in varying ways. We identified a majority of the churches by obtaining lists of all churches in a given geographic region and making phone calls to determine which churches fit our sampling criteria and whether or not clergy were willing to be interviewed. We also asked our interviewees if there were other churches in their area that might be interesting to visit, and if so, why. We also phoned or visited regional denominational headquarters in some cases to gain information about size, social-class composition, and other congregational characteristics.

Personal interviews were conducted at each of the 60 churches by a trained research associate with professional interviewing experience. In addition to the interview, information was obtained from each church by asking for annual membership and financial reports, copies of stewardship or pledge campaign materials, brochures for new members, leaflets for the weekly service, announcements, copies of congregational histories, and any other information that might be readily available. The buildings were toured, and photographs of the church, pastor, and neighborhood were taken.

The interviews were conducted with the pastor of the church, and in the case of multiple pastors, with the head pastor whenever possible, and in other cases with an ordained pastor knowledgeable of both the congregation and church finances. Each interview lasted between two and three hours. We sought to include questions that allowed the respondent to speak from several vantage points: specifically, as preacher, asking for sermonettes or sermon outlines and for summaries of recent sermons preached on various topics; as pastor or counselor, asking what the respondent tells people in the congregation who come for advice on selected issues; as administrator, asking about programs, budgets, staff, and financial needs; as informant, asking about the lifestyles, beliefs, and attitudes of parishioners; and as person, asking about beliefs, background, and training. Each interview was tape recorded with the permission of the respondent, and all tapes were transcribed. By agreement with the respondents, we have kept their personal identities and the identities of their churches confidential.

In addition to the clergy interviews, we also obtained qualitative information in three other ways. First, a year after our initial interviews, we contacted half of the clergy again, either in person or by phone, and interviewed them again, focusing especially on changes that might have taken place in their churches, how economic conditions were affecting their churches, and what they had been focusing on since our previous interview. Second, to see if we were systematically missing anything important by interviewing clergy, we conducted interviews with lay leaders, such as parish presidents and heads of deacon boards, in 20 of the churches. These interviews went over some of the same topics as the clergy interviews. And third, we drew on approximately 100 in-depth interviews with laity (some of whom were in the same churches as the clergy we interviewed); these interviews formed the basis for my previous book but also included additional information on the same topics that we were asking clergy.

Personal and church names used in the text are pseudonyms; locations and other identifying characteristics are intentionally framed in general terms, but none of the information reported about congregational characteristics has been deliberately falsified. Verbatim quotes taken from interviews have been edited only for grammar and clarity. Each interview followed a semistructured format. A standard set of questions was asked each respondent, but probes and follow-up questions varied, depending on the responses given. A copy of the standard questions follows.

## INTERVIEW GUIDE

First, I need to get some basic information about you and your church....

1. Your position here is (what)?

2. And you have been here how long?

3. How many other clergy are on staff here?
   *If any others: What are their positions?*

4. About how many members does the church have?

5. How many people, would you say, attend the Sunday worship service(s) in an average week?

6. And, just for the record, this church belongs to which communion or denomination?
   *If unclear: Which denomination is that?*

7. When did this particular church come into existence?

8. Is its membership currently growing, declining, or staying about the same?
   *Probe to see how much growth or decline there has been in, say, the past ten years.*

9. How would you describe the congregation in terms of age and family style at this point?

> *If "diverse," probe: Would there be more older people, or more middle-aged people, or more people with small children, or what?*

10. How would you describe the congregation theologically?

> *Probe: Are most people fairly conservative or fairly liberal?*

11. How would you describe the congregation's political views?

> *Probe: What would be some political perspectives that would be pretty widely shared in the congregation (e.g., on nuclear arms, or abortion)?*

12. And how would you describe the congregation economically?

> *Probe: What are the main sorts of occupations?*
> *Probe: Do many of the women work at jobs outside the home?*
> *If so: What sorts of jobs?*
> *Probe: What would you guess the average family income in your church to be?*
> *(If unable to say, is the average family fairly well off, just making it, struggling—or how would you describe it?)*

13. What sorts of economic concerns do you see among the people in your church?

> *(For each one mentioned, ask: Could you give me an example of that?)*
> *Any other economic concerns?*

14. Do people in your church seem to be very interested in relating their faith to the economic part of their lives?

> *If yes: How do people try to relate the two?*
> *If no: Why do you think that is?*
> *If "it varies": Could you give me an example of how people do try to relate the two? How about an example of people who don't relate the two?*

15. What sorts of connections do you want people to make between their faith and the economic part of their lives?

> *If necessary: Could you explain what you mean? Or: Could you give me an example that would show what you mean?*
> *Any other connections you want people to make?*

16. What kinds of difficulties have you found in trying to get people to relate their economic lives to their faith?

> *Could you give me an example of that?*
> *Any other difficulties?*

Let's focus for a few minutes on the issue of work....

17. At one time, the doctrine of "the calling" was a common way to get into this issue. How would you describe your understanding of "the calling"?

    *Probes: So are you saying...*

    *(Unless already clear): Is "the calling" something you feel is important to empha-size, or not? Why or why not?*

18. (Unless covered in Q. 17): Do you feel, as some people say, that it is "God's will" for someone to choose a particular vocation rather than a different one?

    *(If necessary): Tell me why you think this.*

19. If someone came to you for advice about whether to take a certain job, what sorts of things would you say to them?

    *Anything else?*

20. Do you have much of a sense overall of the actual work your congregants do, or not?

    *Why is that?*

21. What sorts of problems or concerns do people in your church bring up about their work?

    *Any others? Can you give me a specific example?*

22. What sorts of things do you do to deal with these problems and concerns?

    *Can you give me a specific example?*

    *How well did this work, do you think?*

23. In what ways would you like to see people in your church relating their faith more directly to their work lives?

    *If necessary: Could you explain what you mean?*

    *Any other ways?*

24. What kinds of support does the church provide for working people? For example, day care, groups for working women, men's support groups, classes that discuss work issues, etc.?

    *Probe: Anything else? For each one, ask: Tell me about this; what exactly does it do?*

25. Does your church have any ministries that are actually in the workplace?

    *For example, a Bible study held at a corporation?*

    *Anything else?*

26. (Perhaps already mentioned) Do you find yourself dealing much with people experiencing "burnout" in their careers?

*If yes: What have you done to try to help? (give examples)*
*If yes: Why do you think people are getting burned out in their careers? (give an example)*

27. Do you deal much with people who have been laid off from their jobs?
*If yes: Could you give me an example that would show how you tried to help someone who had been laid off?*

28. What kinds of family problems do you see that are connected to the work people are doing? For example, marital problems because both spouses are too busy, or neglected children, or alcoholism?
*Probe: Just to be more specific, could you tell about some particular case—what the problem was, how the church got involved, what kind of help was given?*
*(If necessary): So, was this problem connected to the work they were doing?*
*Any other problems (child abuse, alcoholism, etc.)? (ask for examples)*

29. Have you been doing anything recently with the topic of "business ethics" or "professional ethics"?
*If yes: What have you done? What were the main points you tried to get across?*

30. Do you find it hard to get people to do church work because they are so busy with their jobs?
*If no: Why not?*
*If yes: How do you deal with this? Do you try to encourage people to get more involved, or do you mostly back off?*
*Do you think everyone should give some time to the church, or is it okay if they just serve God through their work?*
*Do you think people in your church regard their own work as more important, the church's work as more important, or is there any difference?*
*Which of the two in your own view is more important?*

Next, I have a few questions about stewardship. . . .

31. What does *stewardship* mean—could you give me a little sermonette on it? Or: Could you elaborate on that?
*Probe: So how would you apply that understanding in the world today?*

32. (Unless already covered) In relation to the environment, then, what would the idea of stewardship have to say?

33. How does it apply to the use of someone's individual talents, let's say, if someone has a musical gift?

34. What are the limits to applying this concept? Should we be Puritans who

work all the time trying to cultivate our talents, or can we say, "Enough is enough"?

35. What about somebody whose talent is making huge amounts of money? Is it stewardship for that person to make as much money as possible? Again, what are the limits?

36. (Unless already clear) What would be an example of "bad" stewardship? That is, somebody who was not a good steward?

Let me turn next to some questions about money. . . .

37. Do people in your church talk openly about their money concerns, or are they reluctant to talk about it?
> *Why do you think they (do or don't)?*
> *When they talk about it, what issues come up?*

38. Have you ever preached or taught a class about money?
> *If no, why not? Anything that comes close?*
> *If yes, what were the main points you tried to bring out?*
> *Anything else?*

39. If somebody came to you who was having trouble knowing whether they were being wise with their money, what kinds of advice would you give?
> *Any other advice?*
> *Would you feel comfortable giving them advice?*
> *Would you suggest they talk to anyone else?*

40. Some people feel too much emphasis is placed on money in our society. Do you feel this way, or not?
> *Why do you (don't you) feel this way?*
> *If too much: What can the churches do to change this? Anything else?*

41. How often do you appeal to people to give money to the church?
> *What things do you say? Anything else?*
> *What sorts of appeals do you think work best?*
> *Why, in your view, do these appeals work best?*
> *Do you like appealing for money, or not? Why or why not?*

42. (Unless already covered) So, why do you think people should give money to the church?
> *If necessary: Could you elaborate?*

43. As you know, giving in many churches has been declining, at least relative to people's incomes. Why do you think this is?

*If necessary: Just in your own opinion, are the churches doing something wrong, or what's the problem?*

44. In your own congregation, what do you think it would take to get people to give substantially more than they are now?

*If respondent can't answer, try this: What sort of program do you think would have the greatest success in getting people to give more?*

45. Is the financial condition of your church something you think about very much, or not?

*If yes: What are some of the specific issues you are concerned about? What are you doing to address these issues?*

*If no: Why isn't this something you think about?*

46. Do you hold yourself responsible when offerings decline?

*Why is that?*

47. Do you think your church has been hurt by competition from other groups who try to get people to give money?

*If no: Why hasn't it been hurt?*

*If yes: What groups have hurt it?*

*If yes: Why do you think your church has been hurt?*

Then, I have some questions about the poor and social justice. . . .

48. What sorts of things do people in your church do to try to help the poor?

*Note: Especially through the church itself, but also as individuals.*

*Can you give me some specific examples?*

*How well do you think these programs work?*

*Can you point to some people who have been helped in tangible ways? How were they helped?*

*How were your own people—the helpers—affected by doing this?*

*Any other things the church does to help the poor?*

49. What have been some of the main frustrations in trying to get the church to do more for the poor?

*Did anything really work well?*

*Did you try anything that didn't work so well?*

50. Among all the various things your church is involved in, how much of a priority is given to helping the poor?

*Are you comfortable with this level of priority? Why?*

51. If you were going to challenge your congregation to be more involved with helping the poor, what would you emphasize?

> *Probe: What do you think would motivate them most?*

52. What about social justice? Is that a term you would use?

> *Why or why not?*
> *What do you understand social justice to mean?*
> *If necessary: Could you elaborate a bit?*

53. Do you think people in your church understand the concept of social justice very well, or not?

> *Why do they (don't they) understand it?*
> *What do you think their understanding of it is?*

54. Was there ever a particular event, or experience in your life, that caused you to become especially interested in social justice?

> *If yes: What was it? How did it affect you?*

55. Is your congregation involved in anything that is specifically concerned with social justice?

> *If not, why not?*
> *If yes, what? Tell me about it. Anything else?*

56. Some people say our economic system is so powerful that working for social justice isn't likely to be very effective. What do you think?

> *What difference can working for social justice make?*
> *What can the churches do that other agencies can't do?*
> *Do you think the problem will ever be solved?*

Finally, now that we've talked about a lot of specific things, I want to return to a few general issues....

57. Speaking for yourself now, what do you think the Christian faith has to teach us about our economic lives? If you had to sum it up in four or five sentences, what would you say?

> *Anything else?*

58. Are economic matters, in your view, an important part of what the church should be dealing with, or not such an important part?

> *Why or why not?*

59. What do you think keeps the church from dealing with economic issues more effectively?

> *Anything else?*

60.  As you look toward the future, do you think the church (in general) is going to remain a powerful factor in our society, or do you think its impact will be reduced?

*Why? What do you think will make the difference?*

And then just for bookkeeping purposes . . .

61.  You are how old now?

62.  Where did you get your college and seminary training?

63.  And you are (male, female), and this is (town), and the date is . . .

64.  We covered a lot of territory; did anything I asked (or didn't ask) spark anything else you wanted to mention?

# NOTES

INTRODUCTION

1. Many of these changes are discussed in my book *The Restructuring of American Religion: Society and Faith Since World War II* (Princeton: Princeton University Press, 1988).

2. Statistics on the changing incomes and economic circumstances of the American population are summarized in Lawrence Mishel and David M. Frankel, *The State of Working America, 1990–91* (New York: M. E. Sharpe, 1991).

3. See chapter 3 for evidence of the middle-class character of America's churches.

4. The Methodology section at the end of the book describes our research in greater detail.

CHAPTER 1

1. For overviews of the history and contemporary state of the churches in America, see Mark A. Noll, *A History of Christianity in the United States and Canada* (Grand Rapids, Mich.: Eerdmans, 1993); Sydney E. Ahlstrom, *A Religious History of the American People* (New Haven: Yale University Press, 1972); Jay P. Dolan, ed., *The American Catholic Parish: A History from 1850 to the Present*, 2 vols (Mahwah, N.J.: Paulist Press, 1987); Barry A. Kosmin and Seymour P. Lachman, *One Nation Under God: Religion in Contemporary American Society* (New York: Harmony Books, 1993); C. Eric Lincoln

and Lawrence H. Mamiya, *The Black Church in the African American Experience* (Durham: Duke University Press, 1990); Mark A. Noll, Nathan O. Hatch, George M. Marsden, David F. Wells, and John D. Woodbridge, eds., *Eerdmans' Handbook to Christianity in America* (Grand Rapids, Mich.: Eerdmans, 1983); and Wuthnow, *The Restructuring of American Religion: Society and Faith Since World War II.*

2. Although the differences between American and European religious conditions have long been discussed, there is a recent literature that focuses especially on voluntarism and competition as sources of vitality in American religion; see Roger Finke and Rodney Stark, *The Churching of America, 1776–1990: Winners and Losers in Our Religious Economy* (New Brunswick, N.J.: Rutgers University Press, 1992); and R. Stephen Warner, "Work in Progress Toward a New Paradigm for the Sociological Study of Religion in the United States," *American Journal of Sociology* 98 (1993):1044–1093.

3. On the effects of religious competition, see Kevin J. Christiano, *Religious Diversity and Social Change: American Cities, 1890–1906* (Cambridge: Cambridge University Press, 1987); and on church and state comparisons, see David Martin, *A General Theory of Secularization* (New York: Harper & Row, 1976).

4. The history of some of these contributions is discussed in Robert Wuthnow and Virginia A. Hodgkinson, eds., *Faith and Philanthropy in America* (San Francisco: Jossey-Bass, 1990).

5. The extent to which religious commitment in the United States outstrips that in other industrialized societies has been estimated mainly from opinion polls. Gallup Organization figures, for instance, show that average weekly attendance is 42 percent of the adult population in the United States, compared with 24 percent in Western Europe; other indicators such as religious membership; belief in God; and belief in heaven, hell, and life after death suggest similar differences; see "Religious Belief and Practice in Western Europe Below Levels Found in America," *Emerging Trends* 14 (December 1992):1. C. Kirk Hadaway, Penny Long Marler, and Mark Chaves, "What the Polls Don't Show: A Closer Look at U.S. Church Attendance," *American Sociological Review* 58 (1993):741–752, challenge the Gallup figures, suggesting that counts in churches indicate weekly attendance rates closer to 28 percent. They argue that the United States may not be that different from Western Europe, although it is unclear whether the European poll figures might also be inflated. The Hadaway, Marler, and Chaves study does not show, of course, whether church attendance has been declining in recent years. Their work is, however, compatible with the argument of this book in that it casts some doubt on the assumption that the churches are as strong as often suggested.

6. Michael Gannon, "Clashing with the Pope," *New York Times Book Review*, February 6, 1994, 37.

7. Figures reported in David Briggs, "Passing the Plate," *Intelligencer/Record*, December 17, 1993, C5.

8. U.S. Bureau of the Census, *Statistical Abstract of the United States: 1992*, 112th ed. (Washington, D.C.: U.S. Government Printing Office, 1992), p. 431.

9. Virginia A. Hodgkinson and Murray Weitzman, *Giving and Volunteering in the United States, 1992* (Washington, D.C.: Independent Sector, Inc., 1992), p. 54.

10. Quoted in Gustav Niebuhr, "Churchgoers Are Putting Smaller Portion of Their Incomes into Collection Plates," *Wall Street Journal*, July 31, 1992, B1.

11. Daniel Conway, *The Reluctant Steward: A Report and Commentary on the Stew-*

*ardship and Development Study* (Indianapolis: Christian Theological Seminary, 1992), pp. 17–18.

12. Ibid., p. 5.

13. Virginia A. Hodgkinson, Murray Weitzman, and Arthur D. Kirsch, *From Belief to Commitment: The Activities and Finances of Religious Congregations in the United States* (Washington, D.C.: Independent Sector, Inc., 1988), report some financial information for a sample of churches nationwide; research currently in progress by Nancy Ammerman, Peter Berger, Carl Dudley, C. Kirk Hadaway, R. Stephen Warner, and others promises to yield a much clearer sense of congregational finances in the next few years.

14. This proportion is comparable to the *one-third* of Presbyterian presbyteries that have reported per-member decreases in giving in recent years; *Comparative Statistics, 1992* (Louisville: Presbyterian Church, U.S.A., 1993), p. 5.

15. From my 1992 survey of the U.S. labor force; see Wuthnow, *God and Mammon in America* (New York: Free Press, 1994) for further detail on the survey.

16. From my 1992 survey of the U.S. labor force (ibid.). The mean amount given in the past year to religious organizations of all kinds among church members was $898.

17. Hodgkinson and Weitzman, *Giving and Volunteering*, consider the relationship between recession and charitable contributions in some detail.

## Chapter 2

1. The term *megachurch* generally refers to congregations with memberships of more than 1,000 but also is used more accurately to describe newer churches, many of them nondenominational, that are explicitly aiming to be large rather than older established churches that simply happened to become large.

2. Research examining patterns of religious switching in national samples of the U.S. population between 1973 and 1990 shows that liberal denominations, such as Episcopalians and Presbyterians, continued to experience net losses of members during this more recent period as well; see David Briggs, "Secular Lifestyle Stiff Competition in Church Membership Battlefield," *Intelligencer/Record*, January 28, 1994, A6; and C. Kirk Hadaway and Penny Long Marler, "All in the Family: Religious Mobility in America," *Review of Religious Research* 35 (1993):98–110.

3. Japanese companies purchase raw lumber, process it on ships (floating lumber mills) a few miles off the coast, and ship it back for sale in the United States Some of the logging industry has also shifted to the American South, where environmentalist groups have not bec 1 as well organized.

4. Morgan's comments are worth noting in full: "There's a paradigm, a model of life that's found, I think, in Carl Jung. It's been a long time since I've read it, but it relates life to the equivalent to the ascent of a mountain and the descent of a mountain. And he says that maturity is, in the first half of your life, just always to stay in synch with where you are chronologically. And so the first half of your life you are doing material things. You are progressing forward. Get an education, get the basis to make a living, get the basis to buy a house with a one-car garage, then a two-car garage, get a raise in pay, move on up the ladder. And that hits the peak of life at middle age, and there's always this goal up at the top of the mountain of material success. And then Jung says religiosity comes when you cross over the peak of that mountain and start down the other side. And there's a goal there, too, but it's the valley of the shadow of doubt.

You're going to earn less money, but you don't care. Peace, deep peace, comes in your life, even if you're not praying for a new car. In fact, you no longer pray for more babies. You couldn't have any and wouldn't want them anyhow, and you're just praying that maybe the ones you've got stay alive and turn thirty-five with grace. I think what happens in a lot of Episcopal churches, I think it looks more solidly at the second half of life and addresses the eternal life issue and has not paid much attention to the issues of the first half of life—money, joblessness."

5. Michael J. Mandel and Christopher Farrell, "The Immigrants," *Business Week*, July 13, 1992, 114–122.

6. William J. Wilson, *The Declining Significance of Race: Blacks and Changing American Institutions* (Chicago: University of Chicago Press, 1980); and William J. Wilson, *The Truly Disadvantaged: The Inner City, the Underclass and Public Policy* (Chicago: University of Chicago Press, 1987).

7. C. Eric Lincoln, "Black Methodists and Middle Class Mentality," in James Gadsden, ed., *Experiences, Struggles and Hopes of the Black Church* (Nashville: Tidings, 1975), pp. 58–68.

8. Harold Dean Trulear, "The Black Middle-Class Church and the Quest for Community," *The Drew Gateway* 61 (Fall 1991):44–59.

9. Lincoln and Mamiya, *The Black Church in the African American Experience*; Evelyn Brooks Higginbotham, *Righteous Discontent* (Cambridge, Mass.: Harvard University Press, 1993).

CHAPTER 3

1. Figures reported in the text are from my survey of the U.S. labor force (see the Methodology section at the end of this book); they pertain to church members who are employed full or part time. Other surveys that include those who are not presently employed show that slightly larger proportions of church members live on low incomes but do not alter the overall conclusion.

2. My analysis of a national survey conducted in 1988 by the Gallup Organization for Independent Sector, Inc.

3. David Kusnet, *Speaking American* (New York: Thunder's Mouth Press, 1992), p. 152.

4. John Kenneth Galbraith, *The Culture of Contentment* (New York: Houghton Mifflin, 1992).

5. Barbara Ehrenreich, *Fear of Falling: The Inner Life of the Middle Class* (New York: Harper, 1989). According to a 1992 Gallup Poll, "Six in ten Americans (61 percent) say they are dissatisfied with the next generation's opportunity to live better than their parents. A similar proportion (58 percent) are unhappy with a poor person's opportunity to get ahead in this country by working hard." Larry Hugick, " Recession Shakes Faith in the American Dream," *The Gallup Poll* 56 (February 2, 1992):1.

6. Bruce Nussbaum, "Downward Mobility," *Business Week*, March 23, 1992, 56–64; Nussbaum's interviews included some with laity at one of the churches we studied. See also Brian O'Reilly, "Preparing for Leaner Times," *Fortune*, January 27, 1992, 40–63.

7. Juliet B. Schor, *The Overworked American* (New York: Basic Books, 1991).

8. Exact proportions are 66 percent and 16 percent, respectively. These and other figures reported in this chapter, unless otherwise indicated, are from my survey of the U.S. labor force.

9. These findings are similar to those of several other surveys; see for example John P. Robinson, "Your Money or Your Time," *American Demographics* 13 (November 1991):22–26; and the New York Business Group on Health, *Study of Working Women and Stress* (Princeton: The Gallup Organization, 1991).

10. Comparing people who attend religious services at least once a week on average and those who attend less but who go at least once a year, the percentages, respectively, for the following areas are: scoring at the low end of the scale on work satisfaction, 27 and 30; say they sometimes feel burned out with their work, 41 and 47; say they have experienced serious burnout in the past year, 26 and 24; say they often go shopping to relieve stress, 14 and 10; and say they go shopping often or sometimes to relieve stress, 44 and 43.

11. The respective percentages who say that the following motivate them a great deal are: trying to fulfill your own potential, 68 and 66; knowing you've helped someone, 70 and 66; being paid more money, 44 and 51; and praise from your boss, 46 and 41.

12. The respective percentages who say that wishing they had more money describes them very or fairly well are 79 and 85, and who say the same about worrying about their finances, 48 and 54.

13. The percentages, respectively, who say having a beautiful home, a new car, and other nice things is very or fairly important to them are 74 and 79.

14. Myron Magnet, "The Money Society," *Fortune*, July 6, 1987, 26–31.

15. For the two groups, respectively, the percentages who say each of the following is a serious or extremely serious problem are: the condition of the poor, 92 and 94; problems in our schools, 91 and 93; and political corruption, 89 and 91. The two groups are also indistinguishable in terms of the proportions that say the breakdown of community, moral corruption, the breakdown of families, and corruption in business are serious problems.

## CHAPTER 4

1. Perhaps curiously, pastors sometimes encourage parishioners to hope for immediate rewards and then find their members experiencing frustration when these rewards are delayed; at Grace Church, for instance, Pastor Fisher observed, "When they are trusting God in very difficult times, and they don't see immediate responses, there's waiting, and there's patience, and there's a continual seeking after God's provision without immediate response. So that's a struggle. It's a struggle for any person to grow in faith and to be stretched that way. And to see people that prosper, who perhaps are not spiritual, as the Psalms say, the Psalmist cries out 'Lord, why the wicked prosper.' And to see people who may not be faithful to God prospering when they are faithful, and they're not in this immediate circumstance. So that's one of the biggest areas of concern."

2. At San Xavier's, Father Martinez encourages his parishioners explicitly to assimilate to the American values of self-reliance and self-realization: "I always tell them, and

I probably tell them this at all the masses, not to lose hope, not to lose hope in themselves. Because once they lose hope in themselves and their giftedness and who they are, they are going to lose everything. They lose hope in themselves, hope in God, and hope in who they are, just because they don't speak any English or just because they don't speak Spanish even well, or write it, or whatever, you lose hope in yourself and in God. I always tell them you'd lose everything. You're never going to amount to anything because you're going to close yourself off from everything. And I tell them that constantly. I always tell them I want you to learn more, and more, and more, and educate yourselves more. Even if you don't have a great-paying job, but educate yourselves even more."

3.  Several members of the clergy referred explicitly to Wesley's dictum; for instance, one summarized his own views this way: "John Wesley put it well. Nobody's ever said it better than John Wesley, the Anglican revivalist: 'Make all you can, save all you can, give all you can.'"

4.  Quantitative evidence on clergy attitudes toward economic issues is sparse, but see James Davison Hunter and James E. Hawdon, "Religious Elites in Advanced Capitalism: The Dialectic of Power and Marginality," in Wade Clark Roof, ed., *World Order and Religion* (Albany: State University of New York Press, 1991), pp. 39–65; and James Davison Hunter and John Steadman Rice, "Unlikely Alliances: The Changing Contours of American Religious Faith," in Alan Wolfe, ed., *America at Century's End* (Berkeley: University of California Press, 1991), pp. 318–339.

5.  I do not mean to imply that many pastors are critical of the American system of free enterprise. When they talk about problems in society, they are much more likely to blame government than the private sector. Pastor Hill at Redeemer Baptist Church provided one example: "The reason we're suffering in the way that we are is that they've taken prayer out of the schools, they've taken religion and our faith away from our government. It used to be 'In God We Trust,' now we trust in each other and they're saying no. Because of the attitude that America has take—there was a time that America was feared by all countries, but the minute we turned our back on God, now all countries grasp America by the throat and shake her. A country without a God is a country that has no future."

6.  We observed some tendency, however, for pastors to argue that people who really believed in God would also have their economic troubles resolved. At Cornerstone, for instance, Pastor Higgins gave the following example: "I counseled with a couple last week. They're very concerned about their economic situation because their job was going to be terminated and they didn't know what they were going to do, didn't know where they were going to go, didn't know what's going to happen. The job itself carried a lot of stress with it and everything. I just said well, one, I reassured them that first, God was going to meet their needs because of the promises of God's word, what it said about meeting their needs and just take them back to Scripture and share with them those things that will build their confidence in those areas. And I said, 'We need to take it to God and let God deal with it.' Well, this was like a Wednesday. On Friday, out of the clear blue, another employer that she used to work for called her up and said 'We're looking for somebody, would you come back and work for us?' That type of thing, when that happens, and it was better pay, better job, less stress, all the things that she was concerned about all of a sudden were gone."

CHAPTER 5

1. A compelling personal account of this problem is found in William E. Diehl, *The Monday Connection: A Spirituality of Competence, Affirmation, and Support in the Workplace* (San Francisco: Harper San Francisco, 1990). Chapter 3 of my book *God and Mammon in America* considers the relationships between faith and work in the American labor force in some detail. Other useful evidence is presented in Stephen Hart and David Krueger, "Faith and Work: Challenges for Congregations," *Christian Century*, July 15–22, 1992, 683–685.

2. For this reason some theologians have called for a thoroughgoing effort to rethink the meaning of work from a faith perspective; one of the more effective of such attempts is Miroslav Volf, *Work in the Spirit: Toward a Theology of Work* (New York: Oxford University Press, 1991).

3. There is no lack of devotional guides seeking to relate faith and work, including some that draw on personal anecdotes as well as theological and historical insights; see John A. Bernbaum and Simon M. Steer, *Why Work? Careers and Employment in Biblical Perspective* (Grand Rapids, Mich.: Baker Book House, 1986); William Droel and Gregory F. Augustine Pierce, *Confident and Competent: A Challenge for the Lay Church* (Notre Dame: Ave Maria Press, 1987); Lee Hardy, *The Fabric of This World: Inquiries into Calling, Career Choice and the Design of Human Work* (Grand Rapids, Mich.: Eerdmans, 1990); John C. Haughey, *Converting Nine to Five: A Spirituality of Daily Work* (New York: Crossroad, 1989); Paul G. Johnson, *Grace: God's Work Ethic* (Valley Forge, Penn.: Judson Press, 1985); William Mahedy and Christopher Carstens, *Starting on Monday: Christian Living in the Workplace* (New York: Ballantine Books, 1987); John C. Raines and Donna C. Day-Lower, *Modern Work and Human Meaning* (Philadelphia: Westminster Press, 1986); and Graham Tucker, *The Faith-Work Connection: A Practical Application of Christian Values in the Marketplace* (Toronto, Canada: Anglican Book Centre, 1987).

4. Examining the previously cited books and others written especially from an evangelical perspective, Marsha Witten finds an overwhelming emphasis on work as a fulfillment of God's plan for the world; see Witten, "'Where Your Treasure Is': Popular Evangelical Views of Work, Money, and Materialism," in Robert Wuthnow, ed., *Rethinking Materialism*, (Grand Rapids, Mich.: Eerdmans, 1995), ch. 5.

5. For further discussion of these attitudes among church members and in the general population, see my book *God and Mammon in America*, ch. 3.

6. On the possible decline of the work ethic and its roots in changing religious teachings, see Larry Blackwood, "Social Change and Commitment to the Work Ethic," in Robert Withnow, ed., *The Religious Dimension: New Directions in Quantitative Research* (New York: Academic Press, 1979), pp. 241–256; Daniel Yankelovich, *New Rules* (New York: Random House, 1981); James Davison Hunter, *Evangelicalism: The Coming Generation* (Chicago: University of Chicago Press, 1987), ch. 3; and Ronald Inglehart, *Culture Shift* (Princeton: Princeton University Press, 1990).

CHAPTER 6

1. As one pastor explained, "The church usually gets involved because one of the two partners in the marriage comes to us and says, 'Look, it's falling apart.' Well, why

is it falling apart? And then you begin to explore, and sometimes one of the reasons is he's never around, he's always working, he's a workaholic, or whatever. And sometimes alcohol's part of that scene."

2. A Presbyterian pastor offered a similar analysis: "I think a lot of jobs are becoming more demanding, not less. I can remember when I began my ministry one of the threats supposedly was that we were all going to have more time on our hands than we knew what to do with. Machines were going to take over. Well, I think it's not only that the jobs are more demanding, but companies are getting leaner and meaner and it's produce brother or sister. It's produce more. What have you done for me lately kind of thing. I think some of it is self-imposed. I mean, people are running scared, so they're trying to really work harder and improve their mettle and worth to the company. But I think the workplace itself has become much, much more demanding."

3. The following remark, made by the rector of an affluent Episcopal church, is especially revealing: "One of the things that's alarming, whether or not it has anything to do with work or not, I have no idea, one of the things we're seeing a lot more of is violence at home, abuse. Now, whether that's just because there's more freedom about coming out with that stuff, whether it's actually happening more, I don't know. There's a tremendous amount of heavy drinking and alcoholism. [Q: You mean violence in the home?] Domestic violence, yeah."

4. Robert S. Weiss, *Staying the Course: The Emotional and Social Lives of Men Who Do Well at Work* (New York: Fawcett, 1990); and Arlie Hochschild, *Second Shift* (New York: Viking, 1990), provide instructive interviews with men and women about the mix of family life and work commitments.

5. For an example concerning work, see Diane Fassel, *Working Ourselves to Death: The High Cost of Workaholism and the Rewards of Recovery* (San Francisco: Harper San Francisco, 1990): Although most Americans would like to work less, relatively few say they are working themselves to death; see my book *God and Mammon in America*, ch. 3.

6. The assumption that work is meaningless seems to go along with pastors' view that the workplace is alien territory. A quotation from one sermon illustrates this point clearly: "Our society has cut work off entirely from God. It values it, it measures it, it motivates it, leaving God out, omitting God entirely. And as a result, all too often work becomes repetitive, meaningless, just plain unpleasant. You got to get through it, over the hump of Wednesday, down to Thursday and finally Friday, so you can enjoy the weekend."

7. Another pastor remarked, "People around here tend to be very private, so it's not likely that we're going have a lot of people coming when there might still be an opportunity to work on the thing and say, 'Look, I think I'm in trouble.' It's usually we find out, well, so-and-so has split or so-and-so, some kid, was found taking drugs, and then we look at what's going on the family situation and see that. One of the things that we do is to try especially to support younger families with a ministry here that's specifically directed toward them. And the associate pastor who does that tries specifically to talk with the people who he sees headed in that direction of workaholism and neglect of their families and tries to get them to see that."

8. A Presbyterian pastor expressed this thought when he remarked, "I would have quit preaching a long time ago except I believe that God takes the seed of the word and puts it in the heart, and sometimes it sprouts right away and sometimes it's a long time bearing fruit."

9. In my 1992 survey of the U.S. labor force, 52 percent of weekly church attenders said they had "heard a sermon that inspired them to work harder" in the past year, and 68 percent agreed that "people who work hard are more pleasing to God than people who are lazy."

10. Among weekly church attenders in my labor force survey, 56 percent said it is very important to them when they go to church to experience "feeling comforted," while 43 percent said the same about "hearing sermons that inspire you to work harder."

## Chapter 7

1. This pastor, a Unitarian, expressed his reservations about stewardship this way: "*Stewardship*, first of all, wouldn't be a word that I would be really comfortable using, partly because it would have a negative connotation for a lot of the people in my congregation who've come out of the more traditional denominations, whether it's from the Catholic or from the Protestant tradition. So what I'd probably talk about more than stewardship is a word that's gotten a lot of play within our own Unitarian circles in recent years...the idea of *covenant*. The covenant community, or the covenanting community."

2. Another illustration of the emphasis on responsibility comes from a sermon at a Lutheran church: "Any one of us who works for somebody else, anyone who works in a place needs to realize that we are stewards of the things that have been given to us, and so we are spiritually the stewards of whatever God has given to us. Beware of covetousness because stewardship says that it belongs to God, and we have a responsibility of what God has given to us to do with what we can do."

3. Pastor Higgins at Cornerstone Bible Church illustrated the view that environmental concerns are important but perhaps overplayed in light of the assumption held by conservative churches that the present world will pass away and be replaced by a heavenly kingdom: "Definitely God has given us this place to live, and we are very, very responsible for its condition, very responsible. I certainly don't see it as being *the* great priority because I do believe, according to the word of God, that one day this planet, as we know it, will not exist. It will be a different place, so that's not the great priority, but we are stewards of it."

4. One of the other examples dealt with a supermarket setting: "There was an ad some years ago for the Albertson markets in the Los Angeles area. It was on television. It was a great ad which expressed exactly what a steward was. The ad showed a grocer in his typical grocer apron, you know what they're like, standing by his beautiful vegetables and fruit, by his produce department. And he said, 'This is Joe Albertson's market. But the produce department is mine.' He was a steward. That was his responsibility. It all belonged to Albertson, but he had to do a good job with what he had the responsibility for in that business."

5. "It might be that the Lord is going to use that individual in music, if he's playing in an orchestra where maybe he's on the road with people and he's the only Christian and maybe he can witness."

6. A candid example of how stewardship becomes largely a matter of struggling with one's own feelings about things is provided by one of the women pastors we interviewed: "I really personally am struggling with that [stewardship] right now. Because a

really good friend of mine, her husband is an investment banker on Wall Street. And I know the kind of money they have, I know the kind of cars they drive, and I have a hard time reconciling that with—because I think part of Christianity is simple living. I don't know. I don't know him at all. I only know her. But I feel like I would not really have a lot to talk about with him. To me I guess the main reason, this is more personal, but to me it's like money is, it's kind of like I do my ministry and then the fact that I get paid keeps food on the table. So if someone whose main goal is to rake in money, it's just very difficult for me to understand, putting all their gifts and talents into that, into making themselves rich is hard for me to understand. I mean, I guess a lot of it depends on what they do with their money. You know, like, 'cause my husband's often said, 'Boy, I wish I could win the million-dollar lottery, because then I would open up a center for homeless people.' But this guy, for all I know, he makes his money just to get his family rich. I have a hard time with that. I don't know if that answers the question."

7. Robert W. Lynn, "Faith and Money: The Need for a New Understanding of Stewardship," in Daniel Conway, ed., *The Reluctant Steward* (Indianapolis: Christian Theological Seminary, 1992), pp. 29–32.

8. Few clergy seemed to recognize that stewardship might mean doing something to challenge workplace norms. One who did, an Assemblies of God pastor, remarked, "There should be a morality that invades the workplace not because I'm out there as a clergyman protesting or even proclaiming, but it's the leaven and the salt and the light penetrating because people are distinctively different because of their focus of faith. I think that that should drastically affect the workplace."

## CHAPTER 8

1. The number of books and articles that have attempted to relate issues of faith and money in recent years is relatively small but includes a range of arguments and perspectives; among others, see Randy Alcorn, *Money, Possessions and Eternity* (Wheaton, Ill.: Tyndale House, 1989); Larry Burkett, *Using Your Money Wisely: Biblical Principles Under Scrutiny* (Chicago: Moody Press, 1985); Jacques Ellul, *Money and Power* (Downers Grove, Ill.: Inter-Varsity Press, 1984); Walter L. Owensby, *Economics for Prophets: A Primer on Concepts, Realities, and Values in Our Economic System* (Grand Rapids, Mich.: Eerdmans, 1988); and Ronald J. Sider, *Rich Christians in an Age of Hunger*, rev. ed. (Downers Grove, Ill.: Inter-Varsity Press, 1984); see also the selected papal teachings included in David J. O'Brien and Thomas A. Shannon, eds., *Catholic Social Thought: The Documentary Heritage* (Maryknoll, N.Y.: Orbis Books, 1992); for a brief introduction to some historical arguments, see "Contented Stewards Enjoy God's Gifts" [no author listed], *Discipleship Journal* 25 (January 1, 1985); and on wealth, see Thomas Schmidt, "The Hard Sayings of Jesus," *Christianity Today* 33 (May 12, 1989):28–30; and Wayne A. Grudem, "Investing in What Lasts," *Christianity Today* 33 (May 12, 1989):31–34. Another resource is Ministry of Money, an organization that provides seminars on the relationship between personal finances and faith; its article "Guidelines for Writing Your Money Autobiography," ed. Dale A. Stitt, can be obtained from Ministry of Money, 2 Professional Drive #220, Gaithersburg, MD 20879.

2. Several of the clergy we interviewed suggested that Jesus probably said more about money than virtually any other topic.

3. These figures pertain to church members who are currently working full or part time; from my 1992 survey of the U.S. labor force; see my book *God and Mammon in America* for further details on the survey.

4. Michèle Lamont, *Money, Morals, and Manners: The Culture of the French and the American Upper-Middle Class* (Chicago: University of Chicago Press, 1992), esp. ch. 3.

5. Wuthnow, *God and Mammon in America*, esp. ch. 5.

6. He was not speaking metaphorically, as another quote from his sermon (among others) demonstrates: "Go to Proverbs 13:21, 'Evil pursueth sinners, but to the righteous good shall be repaid. A good man leaveth an inheritance to his children's children and the wealth of the wicked,' is what, 'laid up for the righteous.' That's you, saints. The wicked right now may seem to prosper for a season, but they're laying up wealth for the saints of God. I want to tell you something. We may hit a recession in this country and there's all kinds of forecasts, all kinds of gloom and doom. But I want to tell you something, God's people will be prospered. God's people will be held in his hand and lifted up. So the wealth of the wicked is being laid up for his saints. That's you and me!"

7. A typical example of an "antibusiness" orientation is the following: "If you watch television and the media, you see people that have gone high up in business, and so often it's about get the money. The organizations that exist, companies that exist, where they focus on making money for the stockholders, with disregard for the people who are really making that money for them. It's unjust, it's immoral." Yet the priest who made this statement was by no means hostile to the businesspeople in his parish.

8. As one pastor said in a sermon about finances, "I want to first give us some principles of how to be miserable and broke. We've got to approach it from the negative first, you understand? And then I'm going to give you some principles for the abundant living that God had in mind for us. So first of all, principles for how to be miserable and broke. I know them well."

9. This point was emphasized fairly commonly in sermons on money; for example, another pastor remarked, "Jesus Christ, who had everything, who owned all the cattle on a thousand hills, came to be born where cows eat. He who was rich became poor for us. And so if we start to think about that, sometimes we can give up some of our pleasures that we think become so important."

10. The speaker wove together practical suggestions from secular sources with principles from the Bible that reinforced the importance of paying attention to these practical suggestions. For example, her remarks about saving money included the following: "In Proverbs, this matter is spoken of, in chapter 6. The problem of saving: 'Go to the ant o sluggard. Observe her ways and be wise, which having no chief, officer or ruler, prepares her food in the summer and gathers her provisions in the harvest. How long will you lie down, o sluggard, when will you arise from your sleep? A little sleep, a little slumber, a little folding of hands to rest and your poverty will come in like a vagabond and your needs like an armed man.' Not very subtle. It is painful, it does take work."

11. The figures in the text are based on an analysis of those in the U.S. labor force survey who were currently church members and attended every week on average (approximately one-third of the total sample).

12. The exact figures were: 34 percent of those who had heard a sermon had thought a great deal about what the Bible teaches about money, and 36 percent had thought this much about the connection between religious values and their finances;

among those who had not heard such a sermon, the figures, respectively, were 19 percent and 18 percent. More of those who had heard a sermon than those who had not heard a sermon had also thought "a fair amount" about these issues.

13. Percentages among those who had thought a great deal, a fair amount, a little, or hardly any about the relationship between religious values and personal finances, respectively, who said each of the following were: agree that the Bible contains valuable teachings about money, 92, 84, 72, 39; thanked God for a financial blessing, 91, 83, 71, 56; and said materialism is an extremely serious problem, 56, 32, 25, 23.

CHAPTER 9

1. Figures reported in the text are from my 1992 survey of the U.S. labor force. The percentages pertain to the responses of 1,232 persons (out of a total of 2,013) in the survey who said they were currently members of a church.

2. Lynn, "Faith and Money," p. 29.

3. Clergy frustration in this area is also evident in published advice to pastors and laity about church finances and giving; see, for example, Jerry Hayner, "The Uneasy Marriage of Money and Ministry," *Leadership* 8 (Winter 1987):12–21; Joseph M. Stowell, "Putting It on the Line: Teaching People to Give," *Leadership* 8 (Winter 1987):22–29; and Stanley Allaby, Ed Hales, Roy Jacobsen, and Manzer Wright, "Financial Facts of Pastoral Life," *Leadership* 8 (Winter 1987):130–139.

4. The exact wording of this question was, "Would you like to see churches and synagogues emphasize each of the following a lot more, somewhat more, somewhat less, or a lot less?" The responses reported in the text were to the statement "encourage people to give more time and money to religious programs."

5. Another pastor started his sermon on stewardship with a similar observation: "Two people came out of the last worship service and spoke to an usher. Probably many people spoke to the usher, but two things he repeated to me. He said the response to last hour was quite diverse. I said, 'Well, try me out, what'd they say?' He said, 'One person said you didn't hit it nearly hard enough. The other person came out and said you hit it way too hard.' Over the years, I think there's probably been two criticisms of me in this area that have been most prevalent. And that is, I speak too much about money and giving to the church. And on the other hand, I speak too little about our financial obligations; I don't hit it hard enough."

6. Results from my survey of the U.S. labor force.

7. See especially Hodgkinson and Weitzman, *Giving and Volunteering in the United States: Findings from a National Survey, 1992 Edition* (Washington, D.C.: Independant Sector, 1992), pp. 36–37.

8. The most extensive examination of the relationship between church giving and giving to television ministries, based on national survey data, is George Gerbner, Larry Gross, Stewart Hoover, Michael Morgan, Nancy Signorielli, Harry E. Cotugno, and Robert Wuthnow, *Religion and Television* (Philadelphia: The Annenberg School of Communications, University of Pennsylvania, 1984).

9. A Presbyterian pastor said he does not like to appeal for money because "I think it takes the focus off of what we are here for. I was watching a religious television program, which I don't watch very often, but the man spent an awful lot of time begging for money. And I thought, man, you know, that turns me off, and I suspect that that's

an offense to anybody that you have to spend all your time begging for money. If your ministry is the Lord's ministry, if you're really doing the Lord's work, he'll prompt people to give."

10. Among those who had participated in Sunday school classes, average giving was $2,150 among those who had heard a stewardship sermon, compared with $1,045 among those who had not heard a stewardship sermon. A difference, incidentally, was also evident among persons who had not attended Sunday school classes ($985 compared with $510). Among persons who had participated in small fellowship groups or Bible study groups, the respective figures were $1,927 and $919. And among persons not in small groups, the figures were $1,125 and $567.

11. Among church members who attend church every week and who have heard a stewardship sermon in the past year (a total of 410 people in our survey), those who said it was very important to them to have the opportunity to give back some of their money to God when they attend religious services gave an average of $2,071 in the past year, compared with $879 among those who said it was fairly important and only $658 among those who said it was not very important.

12. For those who agree that they should give a percentage of their money to God, the average level of annual giving was $1,654, compared with $613 among those who disagreed.

13. The figures were $1,966 and $945, respectively.

14. W. A. Poovey, who states that "no subject causes more trouble in the church than money," also notes in passing that clergy "have found a number of ways to mute or dilute all talk about money"; see *How to Talk to Christians About Money* (Minneapolis: Augsburg Publishing House, 1982), pp. 9–10.

15. Forty-five percent of working Americans who were church members said this was a true statement; 50 percent said it was false (from my survey of the U.S. labor force).

16. Sensitivity to public opinion was quite common among our respondents. Another pastor accounted for his hesitancy to engage in fund-raising this way: "It is a sensitive issue. I know that people consider it a private issue. I'm also, myself, personally sensitive to what I see in the mass media, religious groups and churches that make constant appeals for money and become associated with Christianity as something that's just another way to make money, that religion is out for money. And the complaint that some people have, 'All the church talks about is money.' I don't want people to understand the church that way, that what we're interested in is their pocketbook."

17. On tithing, the brief summary of principles in Albert C. Winn, "Tithing Is More Than the Number Ten," in Nordan C. Murphy, ed., *Teaching and Preaching Stewardship: An Anthology* (New York: National Council of the Churches of Christ in the U.S.A., 1985), pp. 82–86, is a useful introduction.

18. The following statement illustrates the concern about legalism in the area of church finances: "If I wanted to really get legalistic and make people feel real guilty, I could probably raise a lot more money, but I don't think that's what I'm about. Personally, I couldn't do that, and I don't believe that's what the church is about."

19. A sermon we examined did a good job of putting need-based appeals in perspective by pointing out that needs are not the best reason to give: "Needs. It would be very easy for us to convince you of our ministry, and to go right down the line, I have a

list here in front of me. I am not going to yield to the temptation to tell you the needs of this church and where we are all over the world and how much we have to have come in to meet the needs all over the world. You say, well, why don't we reduce our giving around the world? Reduce it, then we can make it easily. Because it wouldn't be fair to you, and it wouldn't be fair to our obligation to the world. We stretch so that all of us— stretch in our program so that all of us will stretch in our benevolence. But it's not the needs that constitute the reason for giving. We could have beaucoup needs and it still wouldn't mean that that's why you are to give."

20. On self-interest and church finances, see David L. McKenna, "Financing the Great Commission," *Christianity Today* 31 (May 15, 1987):26–31.

21. Actually, a few of the ones we studied did.

22. For a similar argument, see Eugene B. Habecker, "Biblical Guidelines for Asking and Giving," *Christianity Today* 31 (May 15, 1987):32–34.

23. The pastor of a Korean church also emphasized the need to go against the grain: "We've been afraid, a lot of churches, a lot of pastors have been afraid to teach their people that stewardship is a part of being a Christian, and they're afraid they're going to offend somebody. I learned a long time ago that if I'm afraid of offending somebody, I'll not be a good pastor."

24. In another sermon grace was emphasized this way: "Now, why do we give? I think it can be summarized by the word *grace*. God has given me everything."

25. In my survey, there *is* some evidence that giving is more generous in large congregations than in small congregations, at least among Protestants. Average annual giving by size of congregation for Protestants who are church members and who attend services at least once a week is as follows: $1,100 in congregations with fewer than 100 members; $1,273 in congregations of 100 to 199 members; $1,118 in congregations of 200 to 299 members; $1,409 in congregations of 300 to 499 members; $1,479 in congregations of 500 to 999 members; and $2,976 in congregations of 1,000 or more members. Among Catholics, giving peaks in midsized parishes (the respective figures are $275, $300, $423, $929, $588, and $546). It is possible, of course, that members of large Protestant congregations give more simply because they have higher incomes than members of smaller congregations. Controlling for income, however, only partially alters the results. In families with above-average incomes, members of large congregations give about twice as much as members of small congregations. Among families with lower incomes, giving is the same in large and in small congregations. Chances are, these differences have less to do with appeals from the clergy than with the availability of programs or with broader religious orientations (members of large Protestant congregations are only slightly more likely to say they have heard stewardship sermons in the past year, for instance, than members of smaller congregations). These results must also be considered tentative because they are based on approximately 330 cases out of the total sample.

CHAPTER 10

1. U.S. Bureau of the Census, *Statistical Abstract of the United States: 1992*, (Washington, D.C.: Government Printing Office, 1992), p. 456. The figures reported in the text are from the 1990 census.

2. Timothy T. Clydesdale, *Money, Faith, and Divided America: A Study of How Religious and Economic Differences Influence Attitudes Toward Race Relations, Poverty, Work, and Family* (Princeton University, Ph.D. dissertation, 1994), chapter 1.

3. On this era, see Michel Mollat, *The Poor in the Middle Ages: An Essay in Social History* (New Haven: Yale University Press, 1978).

4. Examples are given in Harold Grimm, "Luther's Contribution to Sixteenth-Century Organization of Poor Relief," *Archiv für Reformationsgeschichte* 61 (1970):222–223; Robert M. Kingdon, "Social Welfare in Calvin's Geneva," *American Historical Review* 76 (1971):50–69; and Natalie Zemon Davis, "Poor Relief, Humanism, and Heresy: The Case of Lyon," *Studies in Medieval and Renaissance History* 5 (1968):217–275.

5. Overviews of the role of benevolent associations and other religious mechanisms for addressing social needs can be found in Robert H. Bremner, *American Philanthropy*, 2nd. ed. (Chicago: University of Chicago Press, 1988); and Wuthnow and Hodgkinson, eds., *Faith and Philanthropy in America*.(San Francisco: Jossey-Bass, 1990).

6. In the national survey of working men and women that I conducted for my book *God and Mammon in America*, 46 percent said it would help a lot (as a way of helping the needy) to have "policies to promote faster economic growth," 24 percent said "spending more money on government social welfare services" would help a lot, and 59 percent said "getting businesses to take a more responsible role in their communities" would help a lot.

7. Hodgkinson and Weitzman, *Giving and Volunteering in the United States*, p. 228.

8. Mark Clements, "What Americans Say About the Homeless," *Parade*, January 9, 1994, 4–5; the survey, conducted among a nationally representative sample of 2,503 adults, showed that 67 percent would like local government to do more for the homeless, 63 percent would like state government to do more, and 64 percent would like the federal government to do more.

9. From my survey of the U.S. labor force.

10. The pastor of a Mennonite church in a smaller city also talked about how common it was for people to come to him seeking emergency assistance: "It's amazing how many people stop here and want a handout. They mainly want cash, and we will not give cash to anybody. But we'll say, 'If you need food, we'll help you.' And I refer them to the guy from our church who takes care of that. I refer them to him, and he does an excellent job of just relating to them and caring for them."

11. For instance, the pastor of an African Methodist Episcopal church emphasized that "we give quite a bit of money to our denomination. Our denomination has a huge missions program, and we send a lot of money to Africa. When they had the hurricane that destroyed a lot of the houses down in the Caribbean, we sent a lot of money to that through our denomination's missions program."

12. Walter W. Powell and Paul J. DiMaggio, eds., *The New Institutionalism in Organizational Analysis* (Chicago: University of Chicago Press, 1991).

13. A revealing example of churches working with other agencies to identify unmet neets came from a pastor in Philadelphia who discovered through a partnership arrangement with a church in El Salvador that a government retraining program had recently helped sixty women learn how to be seamstresses, but all sixty remained unemployed because no job placement assistance had been provided. Through its donations and volunteers, the church in Philadelphia was able to help overcome this problem.

14. This concern was echoed by a number of pastors; one, for instance, remarked, "Because of their financial instability, their first priority, first, always, forever, is to survive. So they're very ingrown that way. Helping the poor's a very low priority. Their first priority is surviving. And as long as their first priority is to survive, they're always going to stay ingrown. And that's a real concern of mine."

15. A similar sentiment among his members was mentioned by another pastor: "There's still the idea that if these people would get out and work, they wouldn't be poor. It doesn't matter that there aren't many jobs or that jobs are minimum wage, if they would get out and work. And it's a disgusting sight for people, it's a disgusting thought for people, if people don't work but just want a handout." Nationally, according to the previously cited survey of attitudes toward the homeless, public opinion is about evenly divided—54 percent say the homeless are *not* responsible for their situation, while 46 percent say they *are* responsible or are unsure.

16. These conclusions are drawn from my own analysis of a national survey conducted in 1992 by the Gallup Organization for Independent Sector, Inc. Of the 929 people in the survey who were church members and who attended religious services at least once a week, 41 percent had done something in the past year to help the homeless or people on the street. Among those who said that being asked by someone they knew was a major reason for volunteering, 43 percent had helped the homeless. Among those who said this was a minor reason for volunteering, 43 percent had helped, and among those who said this was not a reason at all, 34 percent had helped (the last response was relatively infrequent, causing the overall statistical relationship to be insignificant). Among those who gave these responses to a statement about having free time as a reason for volunteering, the respective percentages were 45, 44, and 42. In contrast, the percentages, respectively, for varying degrees of importance attached to feeling compassion were 46, 37, and 22, and to the importance of helping (with four response categories), 43, 41, 21, and 9.

17. Said one pastor, "I think the hardest thing for people to do is to become excited about giving if you never see the connection between the beneficiary and the one who gives it, where you actually feel that you've really benefited somebody. You just kind of throw money into a pool, and you're never quite sure what happens. People are more results oriented."

18. Although the churches we studied generally supported homeless shelters and soup kitchens, some of the pastors we interviewed expressed reservations about these programs because they did not produce long-term results. As one remarked, "A lot of these people, they're professional soup-kitchen people. It's a way of life. They get up in the morning, they do nothing, they go and they know which soup kitchen has the best breakfast. And they go there and they have a nice breakfast and then they loaf for the rest of the day. And then lunchtime, they know what soup kitchen has a nice lunch and they go there and they eat lunch. And then when it's time for dinner, they know who has the best dinners. And they do this day in and day out. What are the soup kitchens doing to make these people productive people in society?"

19. In the Gallup/Independent Sector survey mentioned previously, 71 percent of all church members who attend services weekly agreed that "if we all volunteer time and effort, social problems like poverty and homelessness can be overcome." Among those who had worked directly with the homeless in the past year, 78 percent agreed. Yet only 24 percent agreed strongly.

20. Examples are presented in my book *Acts of Compassion* (Princeton: Princeton University Press, 1991). This statement is also based on interviews with teenage volunteers such as Conley Wellman.

21. The pastor in Michigan who told the story about the man in the wheelchair also offered his own criticisms of the insularity of his congregation: "There is a clanism here that you will not find in big cities. A clanism which says, 'We've been in this church a hundred years, our families are all in this church, we're in this church, and we've grown together. We've got our little groups together. We will be oblivious to the rest of the world, simply because we're very content and we're very happy here.' That I've tried to break, and I've just sensed that inch by inch there is a little bit of breakthrough there, where people begin to say, 'Hey, let's try to help them, help other people a little bit more.'"

22. My analysis of the Gallup/Independent Sector data shows that 47 percent of active church members who strongly agree that "I feel a moral duty to help people who suffer" have worked directly with the homeless in the past year, compared with 39 percent who somewhat agree, 31 percent who somewhat disagree, and 17 percent who strongly disagree.

23. Among church members who attend services every week (in the Gallup/Independent Sector survey), 44 percent of those who say "making a strong commitment to your religion or spiritual life" is absolutely essential have helped the homeless in the past year, compared with 38 percent of those who say such a commitment is very important, 37 percent of those who say it is somewhat important, and 42 percent of those who say it is not very important (the differences are not statistically significant). When spirituality is linked with a concept of service, however, the results are different. For instance, 46 percent of those who say that "religious concerns" are a major motivation for them to be involved in volunteering have helped the homeless, compared with 41 percent who say it is a minor motivation, and only 24 percent of those who say it is not a motivation.

24. The emphasis on spirituality sometimes appears to short-circuit thinking about what may actually be needed to motivate even well-intentioned Christians to help the poor. A pastor who said he was uncomfortable with the low level of involvement at his church in social ministries illustrated this possibility when he remarked, "I'm not comfortable with it, but I recognize people are people. And if you can constantly give them the emphasis on the Lordship of Christ and we are out to reach the lost, they get that in their mind, they're going to start thinking that way, and then they do it."

25. In my analysis of active church members in the Gallup/Independent Sector survey, I found that 54 percent of those who strongly agreed that "most people with serious problems brought their problems on themselves" had helped the homeless in the past year, compared with 41 percent who somewhat agreed, 33 percent who somewhat disagreed, and 31 percent who strongly disagreed. The causal ordering here may run in both directions: As some of our clergy mentioned, direct exposure to the homeless makes volunteers realize that some of the problems are self-inflicted, and believing so may be conducive to thinking that one-on-one volunteering can make some positive difference.

26. Marsha Witten, *All Is Forgiven: The Secular Message in American Protestantism* (Princeton: Princeton University Press, 1993).

27. Among regular churchgoers in my study of the labor force, 32 percent of those

who said they had been bothered a lot by "not feeling good about yourself" had been involved in social service activities such as helping the poor, the sick, or the elderly in the past year, as had 35 percent who had been bothered a little by such a feeling, and 32 percent who had not been bothered.

28. See the evidence on this from two national surveys in my book *Acts of Compassion*.

29. The expectation of enjoyment appears to be a positive inducement to volunteering, but instrumental reasons probably are not. In the Gallup/Independent Sector survey (active church members only), 45 percent of those who said they do volunteer work because they enjoy it had helped the homeless, compared to 32 percent who said this was not a very important reason why they volunteered; in contrast, there were no significant differences among those who attached greater or lesser importance to volunteering so that others would help them if they needed it.

30. In my survey of the labor force, 33 percent of church members who attend services every week say they have been involved in social service activities such as helping the poor, the sick, or the elderly in the past year. This figure rises to 38 percent among those who work fewer than forty hours a week and falls to 28 percent among those who work more; it falls to 27 percent among those who are very dissatisfied with their work and rises to 46 percent among those with the highest levels of job satisfaction; and it sinks to 20 percent among those who say making a lot of money is absolutely essential to them and rises to 46 percent among those who say money is not very important.

31. Although focusing first on the congregation's needs can mean focusing *only* on those needs, some of the clergy we interviewed were keenly aware of the importance of striking a balance. One pastor said it especially well: "You can't help the poor if you're not doing other things, if you don't take care of your own family, if you don't take care of your own health. So if we're not here as a congregation, you know, we could take everything that we own, we could go sell it all and give it to the poor one time. Or do we give to the poor a lot more if we're doing it over a period of time?" In my survey, I found that 50 percent of parishioners who talked often with their pastors about work-related stress were involved in social service activities, compared with 35 percent of those who rarely did so, and only 29 percent of those who never did.

32. The results reported in the text are based on the 598 persons in my survey of the U.S. labor force who were currently church members and who attended religious services at least once a week. The percentages who said they had thought a great deal about their responsibility to the poor within the past year among those who had thought different amounts about the relationship between their faith and their work were, respectively: a great deal, 62; a fair amount, 24; a little, 16; hardly any, 12: Among those who had thought varying amounts about the relationship between religious values and their personal finances, the percentages who had thought a great deal about their responsibility to the poor were: a great deal, 63; a fair amount, 27; a little, 26; hardly any, 9. Among those who had ever been taught that wanting a lot of money was wrong, 43 percent had thought a great deal about their responsibility to the poor, compared with 30 percent among those who had not been so taught. Among those who had thought varying amounts about their responsibility to the poor in the past year, the percentages who said it is morally wrong to have nice things when others are starving were: a great deal, 35; a fair amount, 30; a little, 22; hardly any, 22: The percentages who dis-

agreed that God does not care how they use their money were: a great deal, 86; a fair amount, 83; a little, 80; hardly any, 56.

33. Some of the strongest differences in the Gallup/Independent Sector survey were between church members who said that "giving back to society some of the benefits it gave you" was a major reason for volunteering and those who said this was not a reason for volunteering (48 and 27 percent, respectively, had helped the homeless in the past year); and there were comparable differences (47 and 23 percent) for these responses to "feeling that those who have more should help those who have less."

34. Among church members who attend services at least weekly, those who say the churches do a good job of helping the needy give 2.6 percent of their income to religious organizations on average, compared with 3.4 percent among those who say this statement is false. Among those who want the churches to do more to provide job training, housing, and other services to the poor, the average contribution is 3.1 percent of income, compared with 2.7 percent among those who want the churches to do so somewhat less, and 2.3 percent who want the churches to devote a lot less attention to helping the poor. Those who say it is morally wrong to have a lot of nice things while others are starving are also more likely to give at higher levels (3.2 percent of income compared with 2.6 percent among those who disagree).

35. Some clergy recognize, of course, that the redemptive process involved in caregiving may also strengthen parishioners' commitment to the church. For example, the pastor of an evangelical church explained, "The main reason why some people are still with us is because they went there to go do something for these other people, but instead they found friends. They found that it brought out something better in themselves to be doing that."

## CHAPTER 11

1. On the extent of clergy activism in the 1960s, see especially Harold E. Quinley, *The Prophetic Clergy: Social Activism Among Protestant Ministers* (New York: Wiley, 1974).

2. Some of this controversy was documented nicely in Jeffrey K. Hadden, *The Gathering Storm in the Churches* (Garden City, N.Y.: Doubleday, 1969). Some evidence on Catholics' attitudes toward clergy activism is presented in Andrew M. Greeley, *The American Catholic: A Social Portrait* (New York: Basic Books, 1977).

3. In my survey of the U.S. labor force, 31 percent of church members said they would be more likely to give money to their church if it spoke out more on social justice. This was a small proportion compared with the 65 percent who said they would give more if their church did a better job of helping the needy. Still, only

10. percent said they would give *less* if their churches spoke out more on social justice.

4. In my research among volunteers, I found that many expressed difficulty in understanding what social justice was all about; see *Acts of Compassion*, ch. 9.

5. The pastor of an educated, upper-middle-class congregation offered a similar observation: "I think that if you sat down and talked with most people and explained to them what this means, I think they would agree. But I'm not sure that if you just said, 'Do you believe in social justice?' that they'd even know how to answer that."

6. A pastor who had served in churches in rural Mississippi and in a declining sec-

tion of Los Angeles pointed out that middle-class flight out of poorer neighborhoods is also part of the problem because it leaves fewer resources in those areas: "The greatest problem in our society, anywhere in the world, is that you don't have the people at the need level living there with the intention of being there. Because education and success lift you out. And then what we do is develop programs to replace our presence."

7. For an extended examination of understandings of social justice among church members, see Stephen Hart, *What Does the Lord Require? How American Christians Think About Economic Justice* (New York: Oxford University Press, 1992).

8. On compartmentalization, see also ibid., ch. 3.

9. What people dislike about politics is examined in some detail in Robert N. Bellah, Richard Madsen, William M. Sullivan, Ann Swidler, and Steven M. Tipton, *Habits of the Heart: Individualism and Commitment in American Life* (Berkeley: University of California Press, 1985), ch. 8.

10. Several pastors also opposed working for social justice on the grounds that politics, as a secular area (in which "people are working apart from God," as one pastor put it), is too filled with corruption for church people to become involved with it.

11. The pastor of a Presbyterian church illustrated the perception that individualism is one of the main reasons why the churches have not been more interested in social justice: "Christianity in America has been highly individualistic, privatistic, concerned mostly with me and God and not so much with me and my neighbor and even much less with God and society. So we're kind of reaping what we've sown. I think that there are many of us who have been trying to work at that, but as I look at it today, I think we are still largely individualistic."

12. This literature is summarized conveniently in Ann Shola Orloff, *The Politics of Pensions: A Comparative Analysis of Britain, Canada, and the United States, 1880–1940* (Madison: University of Wisconsin Press, 1993).

13. She elaborated: "When we first started giving, both my husband's and my concept was, How many jobs have you looked for? How long has it been since you went to your first job? Oh well, you haven't looked? Well, then we'll just pray that God gives you a job. And it was all very trite, very cut and dried, very easy. But then God began to give us a compassion for those people, and there was something that changed in the inside of us. It was different. It was easier to give and not have an expectation. It was easier to give and not care if we were being ripped off. I guess a lot of it goes back to the big picture. What ultimately happens in their life, not what do *you* see happens in their life, but what ultimately does God use to change people's lives."

14. In the general public, the relationships among attitudes toward the poor, support for various kinds of social reform, and different kinds of individualism have been examined in Richard A. Apostle, Charles Y. Glock, Thomas Piazza, and Marijean Suelzle, *The Anatomy of Racial Attitudes* (Berkeley: University of California Press, 1983), and in my book *The Consciousness Reformation* (Berkeley: University of California Press, 1976).

15. Pastors themselves were quite aware that it is easier to give lip service to social justice than to spell out precisely what it means or what should be done to further it. Terms such as *social justice* or the run-on word *peaceandjustice* are sometimes masks that make it harder to see what is actually at issue. The pastor of a Presbyterian church, for instance, said he prefers not to talk about social justice for this reason: "I think it has become a buzzword that maybe has lost its meaning, and it's much better

to talk about the specific problems of unfairness in our legal system that make it hard for some people to find legal help, or to talk about the injustice of laws that promote prejudice."

16. Robert N. Bellah, Richard Madsen, William M. Sullivan, Ann Swidler, and Steven M. Tipton, *The Good Society* (New York: Knopf, 1991); Amitai Etzioni, *The Spirit of Community* (New York: Crown, 1993).

17. In a survey of congregations, 43 percent of congregational representatives reported that their church was engaged in some kind of "civil rights and social justice" activity; this proportion was higher in congregations identifying their theological orientation as "liberal" (65 percent), but a sizable minority of "conservative" (38 percent) and "very conservative" (30 percent) congregations also reported some involvement; Virginia A. Hodgkinson, Murray S. Weitzman, and Arthur D. Kirsch, *From Belief to Commitment: The Activities and Finances of Religious Congregations in the United States* (Washington, D.C.: Independent Sector, 1988), p. 24. In my survey of the U.S. labor force, church members who said they would give *less* if their church spoke out more on social justice were somewhat more likely to identify themselves as religious conservatives than church members who said they would give more (62 percent and 48 percent, respectively, chose one of the three conservative options on a six-point scale ranging from conservative to liberal). Consistent with my argument about smaller churches needing to conserve resources, those who said they would give less if their church spoke out more on social justice were more likely to be members of small churches than were those who said they would give more (36 percent and 20 percent, respectively, were from churches with fewer than 200 members).

18. The pastor of a downtown church in Chicago offered a fitting comment on the role of the church in combating suburban isolationism: "There's an isolationist dynamic that lives and breathes in every suburban area in the country. That's why you're there. You're there for better schools, which means better funding in white schools. You're there because of safety. You don't want to hassle with street problems. You're there because of dirt, noise, blah, blah, blah. Those are all economic, racial issues. The church, I think, has a very important role to play to make sure the people in the suburbs know that they live in a different kind of world."

19. My use of the term *practices* follows that of Jeffrey Stout, *Ethics After Babel: The Languages of Morals and Their Discontents* (Boston: Beacon, 1988), pp. 266–292.

CHAPTER 12

1. An example of this kind of argument came from a pastor who asserted that the church would definitely remain strong and become stronger in the future. When asked why, she explained, "The reason I think it will continue to be powerful is because as there are more and more problems, people need to go someplace to find answers, and I believe the only place we really can find the answers we need in our life is with God and a relationship with him."

2. A Polish priest who *did* attempt to connect economic issues with the future of the church illustrated some of the confusion that arises when clergy reflect on the contradictory expectations that society holds of the church: "I think that people are going to look to the church to take more of a leadership role in some of the things that we've talked about today, in the social justice areas. I think they're going to look to the church

to stay out of economics, but they're going to look to us for more leadership in social justice. How we divide the two is difficult because I think they go hand in hand. And how people divide them, I'm not sure either."

3. On symbolic politics, see James Davison Hunter, *Culture Wars* (New York: Basic Books, 1991); James Davison Hunter, *Before the Shooting Begins* (New York: Free Press, 1994); and Robert Wuthnow, *Christianity in the Twenty-First Century* (New York: Oxford University Press, 1993), ch. 12.

4. A Methodist pastor emphasized the clergy's tendency to talk theology because, he suggested, they do not understand economics: "The theologians of the church don't think economics is important and think theology is more important. They're saying the spiritual is more important than the temporal, and they make the stupid, antithetical-to-God distinction between the sacred and the secular, which doesn't exist in the mind of God, I believe, and shouldn't exist in our minds but does, and we always give the secular short shrift. The spiritual is always more important than the secular. And therefore, our people, they live and breathe that atmosphere. That's an unquestioned assumption of the church, and therefore it must be right, and therefore economics can't be very important. And my livelihood therefore is an economic matter, and therefore of no concern to the church."

5. The conclusions about small groups summarized in the text are from my book *Sharing the Journey: Support Groups and America's New Quest for Community* (New York: Free Press, 1994); see also my edited volume, *Small Groups and Spirituality* (Grand Rapids, Mich.: Eerdmans, 1994).

6. The effects of small-group participation on giving and volunteering and its relationship with other faith/work/money orientations are dealt with throughout my book *God and Mammon in America*.

7. Jody A. Davie, *Women of Faith: Communication of Belief in the Protestant Mainline* (Philadelphia: University of Pennsylvania Press, 1995), has shown in her research on women's Bible study groups that even the deepest personal religious experiences and insights are sometimes not shared in these groups.

8. On the role of large congregations and their clergy in denominational politics, see Nancy T. Ammerman, *Baptist Battles* (New Brunswick, N.J.: Rutgers University Press, 1991).

9. I have also discussed fee-for-service arrangements in *Producing the Sacred: An Essay on Public Religion* (Urbana: University of Illinois Press, 1994).

10. I use the term *secularization* advisedly. Many discussions of secularization focus on institutional differentiation and would thus not regard the mixing of commercial advertising and religion as an indicator of secularization. I regard such blurring of boundaries as problematic for the churches because of the penetration of sacred space by the norms of another dominant institution.

11. I understand this quest for a distinct identity to be the concern that underlies recent emphasis on congregational "images." See especially Carl S. Dudley and Sally A. Johnson, *Energizing the Congregation: Images That Shape Your Church's Ministry* (Louisville: Westminster/John Knox Press, 1993).

12. "I have an axiom of churches, and that is that they know how to add, but they don't know how to subtract. And so you're okay as long as you keep adding things, because people have the discretion of going or not going, but those who run them have to keep adding and running. But that's where the rub comes in for us, because we're

really looking at a whole different way of doing ministry, which I think is much over-due."

13. A few of the pastors we talked to thought harder times for the churches would actually bring about a revival. A pastor in Virginia, for instance, thought there might be another reformation of the churches; otherwise, he predicted, "History tells me that people get fat and happy and then the churches decline."

14. Corroborating evidence is presented in another study that focused on members of affluent churches; its authors write, "Affluent churches and their members are much more oriented toward nurturing faith than toward promoting justice in their communities, their nation, or their world. Although fairly heavily invested in nurturing the faith of members, affluent churches typically invest little capital and little time to helping the poor and reforming injustice. Their members, though cognitively concerned about the poor and hungry, tend to contribute little money or material goods, and particularly little time to social ministry programs." Alan K. Mock, James D. Davison, and C. Lincoln Johnson, "Threading the Needle: Faith and Works in Affluent Churches," in Carl S. Dudley, Jackson W. Carroll, and James P. Wind, eds., *Carriers of Faith: Lessons from Congregational Studies*, (Louisville: Westminster/John Knox Press, 1991), p. 100. See also Bruce C. Birch and Larry L. Rasmussen, *The Predicament of Progress* (Philadelphia: Westminster, 1978).

# SELECTED BIBLIOGRAPHY

Ahlstrom, Sydney E. *A Religious History of the American People*. New Haven: Yale University Press, 1972.

Alcorn, Randy. *Money, Possessions and Eternity*. Wheaton, Ill.: Tyndale House, 1989.

Allaby, Stanley, Ed Hales, Roy Jacobsen, and Manzer Wright. "Financial Facts of Pastoral Life." *Leadership* 8 (Winter 1987):130–139.

Ammerman, Nancy T. *Baptist Battles*. New Brunswick, N.J.: Rutgers University Press, 1991.

———. *Bible Believers*. New Brunswick, N.J.: Rutgers University Press, 1987.

Apostle, Richard A., Charles Y. Glock, Thomas Piazza, and Marijean Suelzle. *The Anatomy of Racial Attitudes*. Berkeley: University of California Press, 1983.

Bakhtin, M. M. *The Dialogic Imagination*, trans. by Caryl Emerson and Michael Holquist. Austin: University of Texas Press, 1981.

Balmer, Randall. *Mine Eyes Have Seen the Glory: A Journey into the Evangelical Subculture in America*, rev. ed. New York: Oxford University Press, 1993.

Beckford, James A. *Religion and Advanced Industrial Society*. London: Unwin Hyman, 1989.

Bellah, Robert N. *Beyond Belief: Essays on Religion in a Post-Traditional World*. New York: Harper & Row, 1970.

Bellah, Robert N., Richard Madsen, William M. Sullivan, Ann Swidler, and Steven M. Tipton. *Habits of the Heart: Individualism and Commitment in American Life*. Berkeley: University of California Press, 1985.

————. *The Good Society.* New York: Knopf, 1991.

Berger, Peter L. *Facing Up to Modernity: Excursions in Society, Politics, and Religion.* New York: Basic Books, 1977.

————. *The Sacred Canopy: Elements of a Sociological Theory of Religion.* Garden City, N.Y.: Doubleday, 1967.

Berger, Peter L., and Thomas Luckmann. *The Social Construction of Reality: A Treatise in the Sociology of Knowledge.* Garden City, N.Y.: Doubleday, 1966.

Bernbaum, John A., and Simon M. Steer. *Why Work? Careers and Employment in Biblical Perspective.* Grand Rapids, Mich.: Baker Book House, 1986.

Birch, Bruce C., and Larry L. Rasmussen. *The Predicament of Progress.* Philadelphia: Westminster, 1978.

Blackwood, Larry. "Social Change and Commitment to the Work Ethic." In Robert Wuthnow, ed., *The Religious Dimension: New Directions in Quantitative Research,* pp. 241–256. New York: Academic Press, 1979.

Bourdieu, Pierre. *Language and Symbolic Power.* Cambridge, Mass.: Harvard University Press, 1991.

Bremner, Robert H. *American Philanthropy,* 2nd ed. Chicago: University of Chicago Press, 1988.

Briggs, David. "Passing the Plate." *Intelligencer/Record,* December 17, 1993, C5.

————. "Secular Lifestyle Stiff Competition in Church Membership Battlefield." *Intelligencer/Record,* January 28, 1994, A6.

Burkett, Larry. *Using Your Money Wisely: Biblical Principles Under Scrutiny.* Chicago: Moody Press, 1985.

Christiano, Kevin J. *Religious Diversity and Social Change: American Cities, 1890–1906.* Cambridge: Cambridge University Press, 1987.

Clements, Mark. "What Americans Say About the Homeless." *Parade,* January 9, 1994, 4–5.

Clydesdale, Timothy T. *Money, Faith, and Divided America: A Study of How Religious and Economic Differences Influence Attitudes Toward Race Relations, Poverty, Work, and Family.* Princeton University, Ph.D. dissertation, 1994.

Conway, Daniel. *The Reluctant Steward: A Report and Commentary on the Stewardship and Development Study.* Indianapolis: Christian Theological Seminary, 1992.

Cuddihy, John Murray. *No Offense: Civil Religion and Protestant Taste.* New York: Seabury, 1978.

Davie, Jody A. *Women of Faith: Communication of Belief in the Protestant Mainline.* Philadelphia: University of Pennsylvania Press, 1995.

Davis, Natalie Zemon. "Poor Relief, Humanism, and Heresy: The Case of Lyon." *Studies in Medieval and Renaissance History* 5 (1968):217–275.

Diehl, William E. *The Monday Connection: A Spirituality of Competence, Affirmation, and Support in the Workplace.* San Francisco: Harper San Francisco, 1990.

Dolan, Jay P., ed. *The American Catholic Parish: A History from 1850 to the Present.* 2 vols. Mahwah, N.J.: Paulist Press, 1987.

Droel, William, and Gregory F. Augustine Pierce. *Confident and Competent: A Challenge for the Lay Church.* Notre Dame: Ave Maria Press, 1987.

Dudley, Carl S., Jackson W. Carroll, and James P. Wind, eds. *Carriers of Faith: Lessons from Congregational Studies.* Louisville: Westminster/John Knox Press, 1991.

Dudley, Carl S., and Sally A. Johnson. *Energizing the Congregation: Images That Shape Your Church's Ministry.* Louisville: Westminster/John Knox Press, 1993.

Durkheim, Emile. *The Elementary Forms of the Religious Life.* New York: Free Press, 1965; originally published 1915.

Ehrenreich, Barbara. *Fear of Falling: The Inner Life of the Middle Class.* New York: Harper, 1989.

Eliasoph, Nina. "Political Culture and the Presentation of a Political Self: A Study of the Public Sphere in the Spirit of Erving Goffman." *Theory and Society* 19 (1990):465–494.

Ellul, Jacques. *Money and Power.* Downers Grove, Ill.: Inter-Varsity Press, 1984.

Etzioni, Amitai. *The Spirit of Community.* New York: Crown, 1993.

Finke, Roger, and Laurence R. Iannaccone. "Supply-Side Explanations for Religious Change." *Annals of the American Academy of Political and Social Sciences* 527 (1993):27–39.

Finke, Roger, and Rodney Stark. *The Churching of America, 1776–1990: Winners and Losers in Our Religious Economy.* New Brunswick, N.J.: Rutgers University Press, 1992.

———. "Religious Economies and Sacred Canopies: Religious Mobilization in American Cities, 1906." *American Sociological Review* 53 (1988):41–49.

Fischer, Claude S. "Ambivalent Communities: How Americans Understand Their Localities." In Alan Wolfe, ed., *America at Century's End*, pp. 79–91. Berkeley and Los Angeles: University of California Press, 1991.

Foucault, Michel. *The Archaeology of Knowledge.* New York: Harper & Row, 1973.

Galbraith, John Kenneth. *The Culture of Contentment.* New York: Houghton Mifflin, 1992.

Gannon, Michael. "Clashing with the Pope." *New York Times Book Review*, February 6, 1994, 37.

Gans, Herbert J. *Middle American Individualism: Political Participation and Liberal Democracy.* New York: Oxford University Press, 1988.

Geertz, Clifford. *The Interpretation of Cultures.* New York: Harper & Row, 1973.

Gerbner, George, Larry Gross, Stewart Hoover, Michael Morgan, Nancy Signorielli, Harry E. Cotugno, and Robert Wuthnow. *Religion and Television.* Philadelphia: The Annenberg School of Communications, University of Pennsylvania, 1984.

Giddens, Anthony. *Modernity and Self-Identity: Self and Society in the Late Modern Age.* Stanford: Stanford University Press, 1991.

Glock, Charles Y., and Rodney Stark. *Religion and Society in Tension.* Chicago: Rand McNally, 1965.

Greeley, Andrew M. *The American Catholic: A Social Portrait.* New York: Basic Books, 1977.

———. *Religion: A Secular Theory.* New York: Free Press, 1982.

Grimm, Harold. "Luther's Contribution to Sixteenth-Century Organization of Poor Relief." *Archiv für Reformationsgeschichte* 61 (1970):222–223.

Grudem, Wayne A. "Investing in What Lasts." *Christianity Today* 33 (May 12, 1989):31–34.

Habecker, Eugene B. "Biblical Guidelines for Asking and Giving." *Christianity Today* 31 (May 15, 1987):32–34.

Hadaway, C. Kirk, and Penny Long Marler. "All in the Family: Religious Mobility in America." *Review of Religious Research* 35 (1993):98–110.

Hadaway, C. Kirk, Penny Long Marler, and Mark Chaves. "What the Polls Don't Show: A Closer Look at U.S. Church Attendance." *American Sociological Review* 58 (1993):741–752.

Hadaway, C. Kirk, Stuart A. Wright, and Francis M. Dubose. *Home Cell Groups and House Churches.* Nashville: Broadman, 1987.

Hadden, Jeffrey K. *The Gathering Storm in the Churches.* Garden City, N.Y.: Doubleday, 1969.

Hardy, Lee. *The Fabric of This World: Inquiries into Calling, Career Choice and the Design of Human Work.* Grand Rapids, Mich.: Eerdmans, 1990.

Hart, Stephen. *What Does the Lord Require? How American Christians Think About Economic Justice.* New York: Oxford University Press, 1992.

Hatch, Nathan O. *The Democratization of American Christianity.* New Haven: Yale University Press, 1989.

Haughey, John C. *Converting Nine to Five: A Spirituality of Daily Work.* New York: Crossroad, 1989.

Hayner, Jerry. "The Uneasy Marriage of Money and Ministry." *Leadership* 8 (Winter 1987):12–21.

Higginbotham, Evelyn Brooks. *Righteous Discontent.* Cambridge, Mass.: Harvard University Press, 1993.

Hodgkinson, Virginia A., and Murray Weitzman. *Giving and Volunteering in the United States: Findings From a National Survey, 1992 Edition.* Washington, D.C.: Independent Sector, Inc., 1992.

Hodgkinson, Virginia A., Murray Weitzman, and Arthur D. Kirsch. *From Belief to Commitment: The Activities and Finances of Religious Congregations in the United States.* Washington, D.C.: Independent Sector, Inc., 1988.

Hopewell, James F. *Congregation: Stories and Structures,* ed. by Barbara G. Wheeler. Philadelphia: Fortress Press, 1987.

Hummon, David. *Commonplaces: Community Ideology and Identity in American Culture.* Albany: State University of New York Press, 1990.

Hunter, James Davison. *Before the Shooting Begins.* New York: Free Press, 1994.

———. *Culture Wars.* New York: Basic Books, 1991.

———. *Evangelicalism: The Coming Generation.* Chicago: University of Chicago Press, 1987.

Hunter, James Davison, and James E. Hawdon. "Religious Elites in Advanced Capitalism: The Dialectic of Power and Marginality." In Wade Clark Roof, ed., *World Order and Religion,* pp. 39–65. Albany: State University of New York Press, 1991.

Hunter, James Davison, and John Steadman Rice. "Unlikely Alliances: The Changing Contours of American Religious Faith." In Alan Wolfe, ed., *America at Century's End,* pp. 318–339. Berkeley: University of California Press, 1991.

Inglehart, Ronald. *Culture Shift.* Princeton: Princeton University Press, 1990.

Johnson, Paul G. *Grace: God's Work Ethic.* Valley Forge, Penn.: Judson Press, 1985.

Kellstedt, Lyman, and Corwin Smidt. "Measuring Fundamentalism: An Analysis of Different Operational Strategies." *Journal for the Scientific Study of Religion* 30 (1991):259–278.

Kingdon, Robert M. "Social Welfare in Calvin's Geneva." *American Historical Review* 76 (1971):50–69.

Kosmin, Barry A., and Seymour P. Lachman. *One Nation Under God: Religion in Contemporary American Society.* New York: Harmony Books, 1993.

Kusnet, David. *Speaking American.* New York: Thunder's Mouth Press, 1992.

Lamont, Michele. *Money, Morals, and Manners: The Culture of the French and the American Upper-Middle Class.* Chicago: University of Chicago Press, 1992.

Leinberger, Paul, and Bruce Tucker. *The New Individualists: The Generation After the Organization Man.* New York: HarperCollins, 1991.

Lincoln, C. Eric. "Black Methodists and Middle Class Mentality." In James Gadsden, ed., *Experiences, Struggles and Hopes of the Black Church*, pp. 58–68. Nashville: Tidings, 1975.

Lincoln, C. Eric, and Lawrence H. Mamiya. *The Black Church in the African American Experience.* Durham: Duke University Press, 1990.

Luckmann, Thomas. *The Invisible Religion: The Transformation of Symbols in Industrial Society.* New York: Macmillan, 1967.

Lynn, Robert W. "Faith and Money: The Need for a New Understanding of Stewardship." In Daniel Conway, ed., *The Reluctant Steward*, pp. 29–32. Indianapolis: Christian Theological Seminary, 1992.

MacIntyre, Alasdair. *After Virtue: A Study in Moral Theory*, 2nd. ed. Notre Dame: University of Notre Dame Press, 1984.

Magnet, Myron. "The Money Society." *Fortune*, July 6, 1987, 26–31.

Mahedy, William, and Christopher Carstens. *Starting on Monday: Christian Living in the Workplace.* New York: Ballantine Books, 1987.

Mandel, Michael, and Christopher Farrell. "The Immigrants." *Business Week*, July 13, 1992, 114–122.

Martin, David. *A General Theory of Secularization.* New York: Harper & Row, 1976.

McKenna, David L. "Financing the Great Commission." *Christianity Today* 31 (May 15, 1987):26–31.

Mishel, Lawrence, and David M. Frankel. *The State of Working America, 1990–91.* New York: M. E. Sharpe, 1991.

Mollat, Michel. *The Poor in the Middle Ages: An Essay in Social History.* New Haven: Yale University Press, 1978.

Niebuhr, Gustav. "Churchgoers Are Putting Smaller Portion of Their Incomes into Collection Plates." *Wall Street Journal*, July 31, 1992, B1.

Noll, Mark A. *A History of Christianity in the United States and Canada.* Grand Rapids, Mich.: Eerdmans, 1993.

Noll, Mark A., Nathan O. Hatch, George M. Marsden, David F. Wells, and John D. Woodbridge, eds., *Eerdmans' Handbook to Christianity in America.* Grand Rapids, Mich.: Eerdmans, 1983.

Norris, Kathleen. *Dakota: A Spiritual Geography.* New York: Ticknor and Fields, 1993.

O'Brien, David J., and Thomas A. Shannon, eds. *Catholic Social Thought: The Documentary Heritage.* Maryknoll, N.Y.: Orbis Books, 1992.

Orloff, Ann Shola. *The Politics of Pensions: A Comparative Analysis of Britain, Canada, and the United States, 1880–1940.* Madison: University of Wisconsin Press, 1993.

Owensby, Walter L. *Economics for Prophets: A Primer on Concepts, Realities, and Values in Our Economic System.* Grand Rapids, Mich.: Eerdmans, 1988.

Poloma, Margaret. *The Charismatic Movement: Is There a New Pentecost?* Boston: Twayne, 1982.

Poovey, W. A. *How to Talk to Christians About Money.* Minneapolis: Augsburg Publishing House, 1982.

Powell, Walter W., and Paul J. DiMaggio, eds. *The New Institutionalism in Organizational Analysis.* Chicago: University of Chicago Press, 1991.

Prelinger, Catherine M., ed. *Episcopal Women: Gender, Spirituality and Commitment in an American Mainline Denomination.* New York: Oxford University Press, 1992.

Quinley, Harold E. *The Prophetic Clergy: Social Activism Among Protestant Ministers.* New York: Wiley, 1974.

Raines, John C., and Donna C. Day-Lower. *Modern Work and Human Meaning.* Philadelphia: Westminster Press, 1986.

Reynolds, Charles H., and Ralph V. Norman, eds. *Community in America: The Challenge of Habits of the Heart.* Berkeley and Los Angeles: University of California Press, 1988.

Rice, John Steadman. *A Disease of One's Own: Psychotherapy, Addiction, and the Emergence of "Co-Dependency."* Princeton: Princeton University Press, 1993.

Riesman, David, Nathan Glazer, and Reuel Denney. *The Lonely Crowd: A Study of the Changing American Character.* New Haven: Yale University Press, 1950.

Robinson, John P. "Your Money or Your Time." *American Demographics* 13 (November 1991):22–26.

Roof, Wade Clark. *A Generation of Seekers: The Spiritual Journeys of the Baby Boom Generation.* San Francisco: Harper San Francisco, 1993.

Schmidt, Thomas. "The Hard Sayings of Jesus." *Christianity Today* 33 (May 12, 1989):28–30.

Schor, Juliet B. *The Overworked American.* New York: Basic Books, 1991.

Sider, Ronald J. *Rich Christians in an Age of Hunger*, rev. ed. Downers Grove, Ill.: InterVarsity Press, 1984.

Stout, Jeffrey. *Ethics After Babel: The Languages of Morals and Their Discontents.* Boston: Beacon, 1988.

Stowell, Joseph M. "Putting It on the Line: Teaching People to Give." *Leadership* 8 (Winter 1987):22–29.

Tannen, Deborah. *You Just Don't Understand: Women and Men in Conversation.* New York: Ballantine Books, 1990.

Trulear, Harold Dean. "The Black Middle-Class Church and the Quest for Community." *The Drew Gateway* 61 (Fall 1991):44–59.

Tucker, Graham. *The Faith-Work Connection: A Practical Application of Christian Values in the Marketplace.* Toronto, Canada: Anglican Book Centre, 1987.

U.S. Bureau of the Census. *Statistical Abstract of the United States: 1992*, 112th ed. Washington, D.C.: U.S. Government Printing Office, 1992.

Volf, Miroslav. *Work in the Spirit: Toward a Theology of Work.* New York: Oxford University Press, 1991.

Walker, Alice. "In Search of Our Mothers' Gardens." In Patricia Bell-Scott, ed., *Double Stitch: Black Women Write about Mothers and Daughters*, pp. 196–205. New York: Harper, 1991.

Warner, R. Stephen. "Work in Progress Toward a New Paradigm for the Sociological

Study of Religion in the United States." *American Journal of Sociology* 98 (1993):1044–1093.

Wilson, William J. *The Declining Significance of Race: Blacks and Changing American Institutions.* Chicago: University of Chicago Press, 1980.

———. *The Truly Disadvantaged: The Inner City, the Underclass and Public Policy.* Chicago: University of Chicago Press, 1987.

Winn, Albert C. "Tithing Is More Than the Number Ten." In Nordan C. Murphy, ed., *Teaching and Preaching Stewardship: An Anthology*, pp. 82–86. New York: National Council of the Churches of Christ in the U.S.A., 1985.

Witten, Marsha G. *All Is Forgiven: The Secular Message in American Protestantism.* Princeton: Princeton University Press, 1993.

———. "The Restriction of Meaning in Religious Discourse: Centripetal Devices in a Fundamentalist Christian Sermon." In Robert Wuthnow, ed., *Vocabularies of Public Life*, pp. 19–38. New York: Routledge, 1992.

———. "'Where Your Treasure Is': Popular Evangelical Views of Work, Money, and Materialism." In Robert Wuthnow, ed., *Rethinking Materialism*, ch. 5. Grand Rapids, Mich.: Eerdmans, 1995.

Wuthnow, Robert. *The Consciousness Reformation.* Berkeley: University of California Press, 1976.

———. *God and Mammon in America.* New York: Free Press, 1994.

———. *The Restructuring of American Religion: Society and Faith Since World War II.* Princeton: Princeton University Press, 1988.

———. *Acts of Compassion.* Princeton: Princeton University Press, 1991.

———. *Producing the Sacred: An Essay on Public Religion.* Urbana: University of Illinois Press, 1994.

———. *Sharing the Journey: Support Groups and America's New Quest for Community.* New York: Free Press, 1994.

———, ed. *Small Groups and Spirituality.* Grand Rapids, Mich.: Eerdmans, 1994.

Wuthnow, Robert, and Virginia A. Hodgkinson, eds. *Faith and Philanthropy in America.* San Francisco: Jossey-Bass, 1990.

Yankelovich, Daniel. *New Rules.* New York: Random House, 1981.

Zelizer, Viviana A. *The Social Meaning of Money.* New York: Basic Books, 1994.

# INDEX